Rutgers Meets Japan

Ceres
RUTGERS
STUDIES
IN HISTORY

Ceres: Rutgers Studies in History

Lucia McMahon and Christopher T. Fisher, Series Editors

New Jersey holds a unique place in the American story. One of the thirteen colonies in British North America and the original states of the United States, New Jersey plays a central, yet underappreciated, place in America's economic, political, and social development. New Jersey's axial position as the nation's financial, intellectual, and political corridor has become something of a signature, evident in quips about the Turnpike and punchlines that end with its many exits. Yet, New Jersey is more than a crossroad or an interstitial "elsewhere." Far from being ancillary to the nation, New Jersey is an axis around which America's story has turned, and within its borders gather a rich collection of ideas, innovations, people, and politics. The region's historical development makes it a microcosm of the challenges and possibilities of the nation, and it also reflects the complexities of the modern, cosmopolitan world. Yet, far too little of the literature recognizes New Jersey's significance to the national story, and despite promising scholarship done at the local level, New Jersey history often remains hidden in plain sight.

Ceres books represent new, rigorously peer-reviewed scholarship on New Jersey and the surrounding region. Named for the Roman goddess of prosperity portrayed on the New Jersey State Seal, Ceres provides a platform for cultivating and disseminating the next generation of scholarship. It features the work of both established historians and a new generation of scholars across disciplines. Ceres aims to be field-shaping, providing a home for the newest and best empirical, archival, and theoretical work on the region's past. We are also dedicated to fostering diverse and inclusive scholarship and hope to feature works addressing issues of social justice and activism.

For a complete list of titles in the series, please see the last page of the book.

Rutgers Meets Japan

A Trans-Pacific Network of the Late Nineteenth Century

EDITED BY HARUKO WAKABAYASHI
AND FERNANDA PERRONE

Rutgers University Press
New Brunswick, Camden, and Newark, New Jersey
London and Oxford

Rutgers University Press is a department of Rutgers, The State University of New Jersey, one of the leading public research universities in the nation. By publishing worldwide, it furthers the University's mission of dedication to excellence in teaching, scholarship, research, and clinical care.

978-1-9788-3911-3 (cloth)
978-1-9788-3910-6 (paper)
978-1-9788-3912-0 (epub)

Cataloging-in-publication data is available from the Library of Congress.

LCCN 2025017751

A British Cataloging-in-Publication record for this book is available from the British Library.

∞ The paper used in this publication meets the requirements of the American National Standard for Information Sciences—Permanence of Paper for Printed Library Materials, ANSI Z39.48-1992.

rutgersuniversitypress.org

Contents

Note on Japanese Names and Terms

Romanization

Throughout this volume, Japanese words, names, titles, and place names are spelled using the modified Hepburn system. Macrons are used to indicate long vowels, except for commonly used words that appear in standard English dictionaries, such as shogun, daimyo, Kyoto, and Tokyo.

Proper Names

Japanese names are given in Japanese order: surname first and then given name, except in citations for English-language works, where the author's name appears in the Western order.

Dates

Dates have been converted into the Gregorian calendar; however, they may appear in the Japanese calendar when citing original sources, in which dates and months will be referred to by number (e.g., "the twentieth day of the first month") instead of by the Gregorian months and dates (e.g., "January 20").

Aliases

Many Japanese students, particularly those who left Japan illegally without official permission from the shogunate, used false names while studying abroad. Below is a list of aliases used by the first Japanese students who studied at Rutgers College and Grammar School.

Original Name	Alias
Yokoi Saheita	Ise Satarō
Yokoi Daihei	Numagawa Saburō
Yagi Yasohachi	Kusakabe Tarō
Hatakeyama Yoshinari	Sugiura Kōzō
Ichiki Kanjūrō	Matsumura Junzō
Yoshida Kiyonari	Nagai Iosuke
Iwakura Tomosada	Asahi
Iwakura Tomotsune	Tats(u)

Rutgers Meets Japan

Introduction

In 1867, Kusakabe Tarō (1845–1870), a young samurai from Fukui, Japan, matriculated at Rutgers College in New Brunswick, New Jersey, as one of its first international students and one of the early students in the new science curriculum. He was a top student, inducted into the Phi Beta Kappa Society, the New Jersey chapter of which had just been established at Rutgers a year before. Unfortunately, he died of tuberculosis in April 1870, only weeks before commencement. In the same year as Kusakabe's death, his friend and tutor, William Elliot Griffis (1843–1928), Rutgers class of 1869, left for Japan to teach English and science, first in Kusakabe's home province of Fukui and then in Tokyo. He stayed in Japan for three and a half years, and upon his return to the United States he published *The Mikado's Empire*, which became an authoritative book on Japanese history, culture, and society at the time. As one of the early *oyatoi gaikokujin*, or "foreign employees" (*oyatoi* or *yatoi* in short), Griffis became the leading interpreter of Japan before World War I and spent his life writing and lecturing about Japan and Asia.

Kusakabe and Griffis are fondly remembered today in New Brunswick and Fukui as symbols of friendship between the United States and Japan.[1] However, the two were only a small piece of the vast network that bridged Rutgers and Japan in the late nineteenth century. The Reformed Church in America (RCA) sent missionaries to Japan soon after the Treaty of Amity and Commerce between the United States and Japan was signed in 1858.[2] These missionaries were instrumental in sending Japanese students to the United States, the first of whom found their way to Rutgers College, which had only recently become independent of the RCA. By the late 1860s and 1870s, Rutgers and its preparatory grammar school had attracted dozens of Japanese *ryūgakusei*, or "overseas students," transforming New Brunswick into a hub of Japanese nationals who formed a network that extended to the major cities of New York, Philadelphia, and Boston, and from there to the smaller towns of New England. This network intertwined with a wider web of Protestant ministers, educators, and missionaries—both men and women—that encompassed Rutgers College and the neighboring New Brunswick Theological Seminary. It further stretched to Dutch Reformed parishes throughout the Eastern Seaboard and westward as far as the Dutch enclave of Holland, Michigan. The Rutgers alumni, in return, went to Japan as missionaries, teachers, and advisors to the new Meiji government, and through their connections with the Japanese students, they quickly found themselves encompassed into a network of reform-minded leaders of the time. This book examines the role and impact of this early Rutgers-Japan network, particularly in the exchange of culture and knowledge.

The Rutgers-Japan transnational network is noteworthy in many ways. Some of the first Japanese students sent to Rutgers were sons, nephews, and associates of prominent leaders of the emerging modern state. Rutgers therefore found a connection to the most influential figures of the new Japan, and its students, alumni, and professors took part in key historical moments of modern Japanese history. In particular, the Rutgers network played a pivotal role in the reform and modernization of education in Japan. A number of leading universities proudly claim their historical connections to Rutgers: Some were founded by missionaries of the Reformed Church who had graduated from Rutgers, and others with the support of Rutgers alumni (both Japanese and American) or David Murray (1830–1905), a former Rutgers professor who served the Japanese government as the superintendent of educational affairs from 1873 to 1878.[3] The partnership that was formed through this network led to a deeper and wider appreciation of each other, as documented in the William Elliot Griffis Collection (hereafter the Griffis Collection) at Special Collections and University Archives, Rutgers University Libraries. Throughout his life, Griffis accumulated countless letters, manuscripts, and Japanese artifacts that his family donated to Rutgers after his death. The Griffis Collection and the Archives of the Reformed Church in America at the New Brunswick Theological Seminary's Sage Library are major resources used by contributors to this book.

The connection between Rutgers and Japan first received attention from historians in the 1960s, with the launch of the Griffis Collection at Rutgers University, through the efforts of Ardath W. Burks. In 1967, Burks organized a three-day international conference, "Rutgers-Japan Conference: A Centennial Celebration of Cultural Exchange," held at Rutgers University, New Brunswick, as part of the two hundredth anniversary of the university's founding. The outcome of the conference, attended by both American and Japanese expert scholars in the field, was published in 1985 as *The Modernizers: Overseas Students, Foreign Employees, and Meiji Japan*, edited by Burks and later published in Japanese by Umetani Noboru.[4] The second conference, held in 1987, took place in Fukui and focused specifically on the *oyatoi*, the outcome of which was *Za*

Yatoi, a volume in Japanese edited by Shimada Tadashi, Umetani, and others, published in English in 1990 by Edward R. Beauchamp and Akira Iriye as *Foreign Employees in Nineteenth-Century Japan*. The volume includes chapters on two former Rutgers students who taught in Japan: William E. Griffis and Edward W. Clark.[5] In the late 1970s and 1980s, with the surge of the Japanese "economic miracle," several books and dissertations, in both English and Japanese, explored the role of the overseas Japanese students and the foreign workers invited to Japan in the early years of Japan's modernization, and several of those noted the critical role of Rutgers.[6] Since then, however, few works have been published that fully engage this material.

In recent years, the emergence of new interpretative frameworks focusing on global history, transnationalism, network theory, and cultural encounter have sparked new interest in this early international connection.[7] The subject of Western impacts on Japan's modernization in the late nineteenth century has become an important topic, especially as Japan commemorated the 150th anniversary of the Meiji Restoration in 2018.[8] There has also been a rising interest in local history as many of the universities and churches in Japan that were founded in the 1870s celebrate their sesquicentennials (the ban on Christianity was officially lifted in Japan in 1873). However, while studies in these fields have, in one way or another, touched upon the importance of Rutgers alumni and the missionaries of the Reformed Church in the early U.S.-Japan encounters, most have focused primarily on an individual or an organization, and thus far none have been able to draw a full picture of their impacts.[9] This coedited volume brings together scholars of diverse interests and nationalities to unravel this complex web of human connections that linked Rutgers and Japan in the local and global contexts. Their research delves deeply into archival sources in both English and Japanese. The authors have explored untranslated diaries and letters, some of which have never before been available to Japanese and/or Western audiences. While each chapter focuses on specific individuals, together the chapters reveal the unforeseen and often lasting connections that were forged *among* those individuals, and the unexpected consequences of the human interactions and cultural exchanges that took place across the Pacific.

Rutgers Meets Japan is divided into five parts: part I, "The Bakumatsu Network and the First Japanese Students"; part II, "The Japanese Students in New Brunswick and Beyond"; part III, "The American Teachers in Japan: Griffis, Wyckoff, and Clark"; part IV, "The Rutgers-Japan Network in Action: The Iwakura Mission and Educational Reform in Japan"; and part V, "Reformed Church Missionaries and Early Christian Education." The book concludes with an epilogue, "Griffis's Legacies: Rutgers and Fukui."

Part I focuses on several transitional figures of the Bakumatsu period who laid the foundations of the Rutgers-Japan network. In chapter 1, James M. Hommes views the Bakumatsu and early Meiji periods through the lens of Guido F. Verbeck (1830–1898), one of the first Protestant missionaries to the newly opened mission field of Japan. Arriving in 1859 when Christianity was proscribed, he made his greatest impact as an educator, teaching in two schools in Nagasaki and then later in Tokyo. Verbeck became a lynchpin of the Rutgers-Japan network through the samurai students he taught and whom he recommended for study abroad, often at Rutgers. This chapter assesses Verbeck's impact as a teacher, missionary, and advisor to the new Meiji government.

In chapter 2, Haruko Wakabayashi, with Fuji Takagi, continues the theme of tracing the roots of the Rutgers-Japan network to the Bakumatsu period. The chapter focuses on two significant figures of the period: Matsudaira Shungaku (1828–1890), the daimyo of Fukui in the province of Echizen; and his advisor, the famed Confucian philosopher Yokoi Shōnan (1809–1869). It also examines the roles played by Shungaku and Shōnan during the final years of the Tokugawa regime, the network through which they exercised their influence, and their vision of the new Japan that led to the sending of the first Japanese students to New Brunswick: Yokoi Saheita and Daihei, nephews of Shōnan, attended Rutgers Grammar School, while Kusakabe Tarō from Fukui matriculated at Rutgers College.

In chapter 3, Noriko Ochiai and Yukako Otori explore the role of Katsu Kaishū (1823–1899) in the lives of Rutgers' Japanese students. Katsu, a Tokugawa naval officer remembered today as "the father of the modern Japanese navy," is known best for having negotiated a peaceful transition of power from the shogun to the emperor. His relationships with the younger generation, however, have not been explored until now. In 1868, he sent his teenage son, Koroku (1852–1892), to New Brunswick accompanied by his disciples, Takaki Saburō (1841–1909) and Tomita Tetsunosuke (1835–1916), as Koroku's guardians. In 1871, Koroku became one of the first Japanese students at the U.S. Naval Academy, and his guardians both gained diplomatic posts in the United States, which enabled them to support Japanese *ryūgakusei* from near and far.

Part II explores the experience of Japanese students in New Brunswick and beyond. In chapter 4, Satoshi Shiozaki places these students in the context of Japanese students in the northeastern United States during the late nineteenth century. He compares the experience of Japanese students in New Brunswick with that in Boston and Monson (Massachusetts) and Brooklyn, New York. Although the largest concentration of Japanese students in the early 1870s was in New Brunswick, Shiozaki demonstrates that Boston likewise served as a hub. Japanese students on the East coast frequently corresponded and visited each other, laying the foundation for a network that continued to thrive into the twentieth century.

In chapter 5, Fernanda Perrone digs deeper into the experience of the Japanese students at Rutgers. She gives background on the evolution of Rutgers College, placing it in the context of the history of education and the development of New Brunswick. At the time that the first Japanese students arrived, Rutgers was expanding and developing, as shown by the establishment of the Rutgers

Scientific School in 1864. In addition to academics, a lively student culture developed, including fraternities, clubs, athletics, and elaborate student pranks, in which the Japanese students participated to various degrees.

In chapter 6, the final chapter of part II, Haruko Wakabayashi reveals the little-known history of the Japanese students who studied with Rev. Edward Tanjore Corwin (1834–1914), pastor of the Hillsborough Reformed Church at Millstone, in the late 1860s and 1870s. The diaries of two of those students, Orita Hikoichi (1849–1920) and Kanda Naibu (1857–1923), vividly portray their lives in the parsonage and the warm relationship they developed with Corwin, his wife, and his children, having been welcomed into the church and its community. The diaries also reveal that these students were not isolated in this country parish: A branch rail line that ran from New Brunswick to Millstone gave them easy access to New Brunswick, and the Japanese students from New Brunswick frequently came to visit, allowing them to participate in the Rutgers-Japan network.

Part III considers the other side of the network: the Rutgers graduates who worked in Japan. With the opening of Japan to the West, many Americans and Europeans found an opportunity to work in Japan as teachers and government advisors. Among the first of such *oyatoi* were the former Rutgers students William Elliot Griffis (class of 1869), Edward Warren Clark (class of 1869), and Martin Wyckoff (class of 1872). Chapters 7 and 8 focus on these three Rutgers graduates who taught in Japan and examine their early years in Japan as teachers in local schools. In chapter 7, Fernanda Perrone examines Griffis's experiences in the provincial city of Fukui. In 1870, Griffis was invited by Matsudaira Shungaku, through Guido F. Verbeck, to teach in Fukui, where he witnessed the dismantling of feudalism in 1871. Perrone also discusses Martin Wyckoff (1850–1911), who took over Griffis's position after Griffis left for Tokyo. Wyckoff later taught in Niigata, returned to the United States in 1877 to complete his graduate work, and then went back to Japan in 1881, this time as a missionary.

Griffis's close friend, Edward Warren Clark (1849–1907), discussed in chapter 8 by A. Hamish Ion, taught Western Studies in English and French between 1871 and 1873 in Shizuoka, the ancestral home of the Tokugawa shoguns. This was where the last shogun, Yoshinobu, retired following the Meiji Restoration and to where many of his former retainers, among whom was Katsu Kaishū, followed him. Clark's appointment in Shizuoka was facilitated by Griffis and Katsu, and in his two years there, he had an outsize influence through the teaching of English and Christianity in the region, laying the foundation of the Shizuoka Christian band. Ion further demonstrates Clark's impact on Japan's intellectual community at the time, as seen through the friendship Clark formed with Nakamura Masanao (1832–1891), one of the leading progressive thinkers of Meiji, who was busy translating John Stuart Mill's *On Liberty*.

In chapter 9, the final chapter of part III, we come back to William Elliot Griffis as Joseph M. Henning focuses on Griffis the writer. Griffis began sending newspaper articles back to the United States soon after his arrival in Japan, so he was already known as something of an expert on Japan before the publication of *The Mikado's Empire* in 1876. Henning traces Griffis's later career, showing through his writings how his time in Fukui remained a touchstone of his identity as a "Japan hand." As Henning demonstrates, Griffis both benefited from and contributed to his alma mater's trans-Pacific network. The Griffis Collection at Rutgers University reveals how Griffis's eleven months in Fukui and the Rutgers-Japan network that he maintained throughout his life had a profound influence on his life and subsequent career.

Part IV demonstrates the Rutgers-Japan network in action. More specifically, it focuses on the Iwakura Mission, a diplomatic mission to the United States and Europe dispatched in 1871 by the new Meiji government headed by Iwakura Tomomi (1825–1883), whose two sons were attending Rutgers Grammar School. The chapters in this section examine various ways in which the Rutgers-Japan network was involved in the Mission and helped shape the foundation of Japan's modern education as envisioned by the Mission. In chapter 10, John E. Van Sant explores the experience and influence of a group of students who were secretly sent by the Satsuma domain (present-day Kagoshima) in 1865 to study at University College London. In 1867, six of them journeyed to the United States to join the Brotherhood of the New Life, a quasi-Christian and utopian colony in Brocton, New York. Among them was Mori Arinori (1847–1889), who left for Japan in the spring of 1868 and returned to the United States in 1872 as chargé d'affaires of the United States to prepare for the Iwakura Mission's arrival. Seeking better educational opportunities, Hatakeyama Yoshinari (1842–1876), Matsumura Junzō (1842–1919), and Yoshida Kiyonari (1845–1891) also left the colony shortly after and found their way to Rutgers College. Although none of these students graduated from Rutgers, upon returning to Japan they all rose to leadership positions in the Meiji government, making significant contributions in foreign affairs, finance, education, and the military.

Hatakeyama Yoshinari's role in the field of education is further emphasized by Haruko Wakabayashi in her chapter 11 on the Iwakura Mission. The chapter demonstrates that although Rutgers was not part of the official itinerary of the Iwakura Mission, the Rutgers network was indispensable in its planning and implementation. Verbeck's "Brief Sketch," which outlined his vision of a mission to observe and learn from the West that he shared with his former student, Ōkuma Shigenobu, is known to have inspired the Iwakura Mission. Meanwhile, Hatakeyama, who served as secretary of the Mission, was a leading member of the commission for overseas students, which determined rules and regulations for Japanese students studying abroad. He was also instrumental in the Mission's selection of his mentor, Rutgers professor David Murray (1830–1905), to serve as superintendent of the Ministry of Education in Japan.

The career and influence of David Murray are analyzed by Benjamin Duke and Fernanda Perrone in chapter 12. In his years at the ministry, from 1873 to 1878, Murray played an important role in laying the foundation for modern education in Japan. His influence encompassed women's education, teacher training, and the curriculum at the University of Tokyo, Japan's premier institution of higher education. Most importantly, Murray's conviction that education in Japan should be governed by the central authority of the Ministry of Education became a key component of the Education Law of 1880. Today he is remembered in Japan as the "father of modern education."

Part V turns to a final component of the Rutgers-Japan network: the influence of Reformed Church missionaries in Meiji Japan. In chapter 13, Koji Nakajima focuses on James H. Ballagh (1832–1920), class of 1857, the first Rutgers graduate in Japan and a longtime missionary, church planter, and educator in Yokohama. After his arrival in 1861, Ballagh made important contributions to the early development of Christianity and the Christian Church in Japan. He baptized the first Japanese Protestant, and as he founded the first Protestant church in Japan, the Kaigan Church in Yokohama, he believed in creating cross-denominational Protestant churches and passing on church leadership to native Christians. He was not only an evangelist; he was a Bible translator and an educator, teaching at Yokohama Academy and the Senshi School, and later served on the boards of Meiji Gakuin and the Ferris Girls School.

James Ballagh was one of several Rutgers graduates who was connected with Meiji Gakuin University, which is the subject of chapter 14, by Naoto Tsuji. Meiji Gakuin is known as the oldest Protestant school in Japan, dating its founding to 1863 when Presbyterian missionaries Clara and James C. Hepburn started an English academy in their home in Yokohama. However, its origins lay in multiple institutions—the early schools started by the non-Presbyterian missionaries that grew into the Tokyo Union College, the Tokyo Union Theological Seminary, and the Eiwa Preparatory School—which merged to form an interdenominational school. Tsuji traces the significant contributions made by thirteen missionaries who graduated from Rutgers College and New Brunswick Theological Seminary in the early development of Meiji Gakuin.

As a men's college, Rutgers did not produce female graduates who could teach in Japan, but it did produce male advocates for women's education. William Elliot Griffis was one. His older sister Margaret joined him in Japan in 1872, where she taught at a short-lived girls' school, the Kanritsu Tokyo Jo Gakkō.[10] In chapter 15, Rui Kohiyama focuses on Eugene S. Booth (1850–1931), a graduate of both Rutgers College and the New Brunswick Theological Seminary and a longtime principal of Ferris Seminary, an all-girls school in Yokohama, and Kimura Kumaji (1845–1927), a graduate of Hope College and New Brunswick Theological Seminary. In the first part of her chapter, Kohiyama analyzes Booth's objectives at Ferris Seminary and how they differed from Japanese ideas of traditional womanhood and gender relations. In the second part, she explores the influence of Kimura, who founded Meiji Jo Gakkō in 1885 as an alternative to Ferris and later established another school, the Gakushū-sha, in the village of Komoro outside of Tokyo. By focusing on women's schools started by Japanese

Christians, Kohiyama traces the process of indigenization and infiltration of what was begun by Reformed Church missionaries into wider Japanese society by the beginning of the twentieth century.

In the epilogue, Ryuhei Hosoya places special emphasis on William Elliot Griffis as a key figure in the Rutgers-Japan network, both past and present. He points to Griffis's claim to have found the "truth"—a common humanity among different cultures—during his one-year sojourn in Fukui. This "spiritual awakening" made him an advocate for Japan through his many books, articles, and lectures, and throughout his life, he kept his connections with the network in Japan. Although his legacy, which connected Fukui and Japan in general to the United States, lapsed during World War II, there was a revival of cultural exchange and academic engagement among Rutgers (including the New Brunswick community), Fukui, and Japan in general beginning in the 1960s. This led to the forming of an academic partnership between Rutgers University and the University of Fukui in 1981. Furthermore, New Brunswick and Fukui have been actively engaged in cultural exchanges as sister cities since 1982, and New Jersey and Fukui Prefecture have been sister states/prefectures since 1990. The legacies of Griffis and the Rutgers-Japan network were reaffirmed in 2020 when Fukui and Rutgers celebrated 150 years of friendship amid the COVID-19 pandemic.[11]

The trans-Pacific network illustrated in this volume spanned not only across national boundaries but also across class, gender, and professions. The Japanese members of the network were samurai, of both high and low ranks, of Tokugawa and anti-Tokugawa factions. Their American counterparts, on the other hand, were missionaries, pastors, teachers, students, and merchants who were predominantly from the middle class. The most active members discussed in this volume are inevitably men, for Rutgers was an all-male institution at the time; however, there were some notable female participants: Mary Kidder, the RCA missionary who went to Japan as a single woman and founded the Ferris Seminary; William Griffis's sister Margaret and many of the missionaries' wives, who made significant contributions to girls' education in Japan; Tsuda Umeko and the female Japanese students who came to the United States with the Iwakura Mission; and, we should not forget, the women who looked after the Japanese students in America—that is, the landladies of the boarding houses in New Brunswick and the wives of the professors and pastors. The network also connected the cultural, political, and economic centers—Tokyo, Yokohama, Nagasaki, Washington, DC, New York, Boston, and New Brunswick—to peripheral locales, such as Fukui, Kumamoto, Satsuma, Shizuoka, Millstone, and Monson, forming a conduit through which information, knowledge, and friendships flowed and spread in unexpected directions.

The impact of the network on Japan's modernization was certainly immeasurable, but it did not simply go in one direction. While it provided the Japanese with knowledge of the West, the Japanese were selective in adopting Western institutions, science, and technology to their own needs. The direction of influence also went the other way: The Japanese in Japan and overseas influenced the Westerners with whom they came in contact in the ways they perceived the world, and through their contact with writers like William E. Griffis, they shaped the way Japan was understood by the West. The network was an unintended consequence of the shared interests of the Japanese leaders, who sought to build a modern nation, and the American missionaries, whose primary goal was to proselytize. However, in unimaginable ways, it transformed the lives of countless individuals, who then became agents of change in their respective communities. These pioneers laid the foundation of relations between the United States and Japan.

Notes

1 The two are remembered in New Brunswick and Fukui in various ways: Kusakabe's grave stands among those of other Japanese students at the Willow Grove Cemetery in New Brunswick, where a memorial service is held every year by Buddhist priests and the members of the New Brunswick and Japanese communities in the area. At the "Griffis Museum" in Fukui—a reconstruction of Griffis's American-style home—a Christmas event has been held each year since 2022 in remembrance of a Christmas party that Griffis held for his students and friends in 1871. Rutgers University and the University of Fukui have been academic partners since 1981, and New Brunswick and Fukui City have been sister cities since 1982. On October 16, 2023, Governor Phil Murphy of New Jersey signed a memorandum of understanding with Fukui Prefecture, reaffirming a "proud partnership the people of New Jersey have shared with Fukui." The agreement, which promotes cooperation in education, culture, and economy, states that its roots lay in the friendship between Kusakabe and Griffis. (For more on the legacies of the two, see the epilogue to this volume.)

2 The Treaty of Amity and Commerce signed between the United States and Japan was the first of the unequal commercial treaties between Japan and the Western powers that imposed restrictions on Japanese sovereignty.

3 To name a few: the University of Tokyo, Tokyo University of Foreign Studies, Meiji Gakuin University, Ferris University, and Senshū University.

4 Ardath W. Burks, *The Modernizers: Overseas Students, Foreign Employees, and Meiji Japan* (Boulder, CO: Westview Press, 1985); Ardath W. Burks and Noboru Umetani, eds., *Kindaika no suishinshatachi: Ryūgakusei, oyatoi gaikokujin to Meiji* (Kyoto: Shibunkaku Shuppan, 1990). On works in Japanese on foreign employees in Meiji Japan, also see Shigehisa Tokutarō, *Oyatoi gaikokujin: Kyōiku, shūkyō* (Tokyo: Kajima Kenkyūjo Shuppankai, 1968) and UNESCO Higashi Ajia Bunka Kenkyū Sentā, ed., *Shiryō oyatoi gaikokujin* (Tokyo: Shōgakkan, 1975).

5 Shimada Tadashi et al., *Za yatoi: Oyatoi gaikokujin no sōgōteki kenkyū* (Kyoto: Shibunkaku, 1987); Edward R. Beauchamp and Akira Iriye, eds., *Foreign Employees in Nineteenth-Century Japan* (Boulder, CO: Westview Press, 1990).

6 See, for example, Edward Beauchamp, *An American Teacher in Early Meiji Japan* (Honolulu: University Press of Hawaii, 1976); H. J. Jones, *Live Machines: Hired Foreigners and Meiji Japan* (Vancouver: University of British Columbia Press, 1980); James Thomas Conte, "Overseas Study in the Meiji Period: Japanese Students in America, 1867–1902" (PhD diss., Princeton University, 1977); and Marilyn Bandera,

"A Case Study in Educational Motivation: *Ryugakusei* and Rutgers College" (MA thesis, University of Hawaii, 1970). Japanese sources include Ishizuki Minoru, *Kindai Nihon no Kaigai-ryūgaku shi* (Kyoto: Minerva Shobō, 1972); Inuzuka Takaaki, *Satsumahan Eikoku ryūgakusei* (Chūkō Shinsho, 1974); Kanai Madoka, *Tomī to iuna no Nihonjin* (Tokyo: Bun'ichi Sōgō Shuppan, 1979); and Yamashita Eiichi, *Gurifisu to Fukui* (Fukui: Fukuiken Kyōdoshi Kondankai, 1979).

7 See, for example, Michael Auslin, *Pacific Cosmopolitans: A Cultural History of U.S.-Japan Relations* (Cambridge, MA: Harvard University Press, 2011); Joseph M. Henning, *Outposts of Civilization: Race, Religion, and the Formative Years of American-Japanese Relations* (New York: New York University Press, 2000); Fernanda Perrone, "Invisible Network: Japanese Students at Rutgers During the Early Meiji Period," *Kindai Nihon kenkyu* 34 (2017): 448–468; and Fernanda Perrone, "The Rutgers Network in Meiji Japan," *Rikkyo American Studies* 39 (2017): 79–101.

8 See, for example, Robert Hellyer and Harald Fuess, *The Meiji Restoration: Japan as a Global Nation* (Cambridge: Cambridge University Press, 2020); Mark Ravina, *To Stand with the Nations of the World: Japan's Meiji Restoration in World History* (New York: Oxford University Press, 2017).

9 See, for example, Gordon D. Laman, *Pioneers to Partners: The Reformed Church in America and Christian Mission with the Japanese* (Grand Rapids, MI: William B. Eerdmans, 2012); and Hamish Ion, *American Missionaries, Christian Oyatoi, and Japan, 1859–1873* (Vancouver: University of British Columbia Press, 2009). An example of a sesquicentennial history is *Ferisu Jogakuin* (Ferris University, 2022).

10 On Margaret Griffis, see Elizabeth K. Eder, *Constructing Opportunity: American Women Educators in Meiji Japan* (Lanham, MD: Lexington Books, 2003).

11 In 2020, Fukui University, together with Fukui City, the Kusakabe-Griffis Foundation, and Rutgers University, celebrated the 150 years of friendship between Fukui and Rutgers. Although many of the activities were canceled or postponed due to the COVID-19 pandemic, virtual symposiums were held both in Fukui and at Rutgers. Since 2022, student exchange programs and joint virtual class sessions between the two universities have been actively conducted.

Part I

The Bakumatsu Network and the First Japanese Students

1

Guido F. Verbeck

Missionary, Teacher, and Advisor in Bakumatsu-Meiji Japan

JAMES M. HOMMES

To begin the story of Rutgers and Japan, we must begin with the man in the center of a striking 1860s-era photograph taken in the port city of Nagasaki (figure 1.1). This Westerner, surrounded by over forty of his young Japanese samurai students, is Guido Fridolin Verbeck (1830–1898). Born in 1830 in the Netherlands, Guido Fridolin Verbeek moved to the United States in 1852 (altering the spelling of his last name to Verbeck), and seven years later he embarked as one of the first Protestant missionaries to the newly opened mission field of Japan. In a transitional and tumultuous era filled with much tension and hostility, Verbeck gained an unrivaled level of trust and respect, and the Japanese government utilized him as a qualified Western educator, a versatile linguist, and a top government advisor. In 1869, after Verbeck had spent a decade in Nagasaki, his successor, Henry Stout, recognized his impact when he wrote that "the half of his work and his influence has not been told."[1] Similarly impressed with Verbeck's legacy, the Japanese scholar Ogata Hiroyasu, in an essay written in 1961, dubbed him a "founding father" of modern Japan.[2] How did Verbeck, a pioneer missionary to Japan, manage to gain such trust and influence in this formative time? Though there are many factors behind Verbeck's impact in Bakumatsu-Meiji Japan, the most important one was his teaching of many students, who not only

FIGURE 1.1. Guido Verbeck and his students. (Credit: Nagasaki Museum of History and Culture.)

surrounded him in striking photographs but continued to honor their revered teacher throughout his life and beyond.

Undoubtedly, this photograph by Ueno Hikoma is one of the most famous images of Verbeck, in which he and his son William are surrounded by the samurai students from the schools where he taught in Nagasaki. The specific context and date of this photograph remains unknown, and though some scholars conjecture that it was for a farewell party for Verbeck, we simply do not know much about it.[3] What is clear is that this photograph depicts Verbeck, the honored teacher, surrounded by forty-four of his young and eager samurai students, who are utilizing this new medium to capture this moment. Verbeck taught in two schools in Nagasaki (on alternate days): the Hizen (Saga) domain school, the Chienkan, and the Saibikan (or Seibikan), a school for Western learning sponsored by the shogunate. Though this photo was not published or circulated at the time, it first appeared in the magazine *Taiyō* in 1895, and in the twentieth century this iconic photograph became more widely known, with Verbeck often viewed as a catalyst for many of the founders of modern Japan. In his work focusing on this photograph, Yamaguchi Takao simply states that "Verbeck was a very important figure and should be honored as the respected teacher he undoubtedly was."[4] Most of the literature on this photograph focuses on identifying Verbeck's samurai students and often reads like a "who's who" of the Meiji Restoration. Though some of the attempts to identify the samurai in this photo (and in another photo, not shown here, of Verbeck with the Chienkan students) may be mere speculation, most scholars agree that there are various significant figures in these fascinating photos. These figures include two of the sons of the imperial court noble Iwakura Tomomi—for both of whom Verbeck wrote letters of recommendation to study in America—as well as the nephews of Yokoi Shōnan, Yokoi Daihei, and Yokoi Saheita.[5] Many also think they include significant figures from Hizen who were students of Verbeck, such as Ōkuma Shigenobu, Soejima Taneomi, Ōki Takatō, and Etō Shinpei.[6] Though it is difficult to know how much emphasis to place on these photographs, because they do not tell us much specifically about Verbeck's interactions with those students, the fact that these students traveled to Nagasaki to study at a school with the missionary-teacher Verbeck during the tumultuous and dynamic 1860s is significant.

Verbeck as a Missionary-Teacher in Bakumatsu Japan

When Verbeck set out to be one of the first Protestant missionaries to Japan for the Dutch Reformed Church in America, he did not envision teaching as the focus of his missionary plans. Though he received a broad education and was almost thirty years old when he landed in Japan, he was not trained as an educator. Yet, in reference to Verbeck's four decades of work in Japan, one of his missionary colleagues, E. Rothesay Miller, asserted that "among the Japanese, Dr. Verbeck will always be remembered as an educator."[7] Thus, it is no surprise that after his death in 1898, almost thirty of his students from various institutions and time periods raised money to erect a monument on his grave. In addition to being a teacher, Verbeck was one of the most prominent *oyatoi gaikokujin* (foreign employees) who helped with Japan's modernization during this period. Furthermore, as one of the most influential pioneering Protestant missionaries to Japan, Verbeck had an impact on the formation and development of Japanese Protestantism. Yet none of these subsequent roles would have been possible without the respect and recognition he gained as a teacher, particularly in Nagasaki in the 1860s and in Tokyo in the early 1870s.

Though the legacy of his teaching may loom large in assessing his impact, there are relatively few detailed sources regarding his teaching specifically. Even Griffis, in his 1900 biography of Verbeck, writes that he was "always mightier in work than in word," in that he did not write down his class notes, lectures, or sermons. Of these nonexistent sources, Griffis exclaims: "How helpful would they be to those who admired his imitable style, and hearing, despaired."[8] Miller would later describe Verbeck's lectures and sermons as "simply scanty English notes, written and underscored." He supposedly used four ink colors—red, blue, green, and black—and "each color had a distinct meaning to him, but what was written was but an outline of the discourse, which, when spoken, was filled in with the most suitable words . . . so that any one would suppose the whole were carefully elaborated and written out beforehand."[9] So, even if we found his notes, they would probably not shed much light on his effectiveness as a teacher and speaker. Also, the volumes of journals that he kept while in Japan have been lost, and one wonders what insights might have been gained from these, not only on Verbeck's teaching but also regarding his students.[10] Though we have his many letters to the mission board, he rarely goes into much detail about his teaching or his students, perhaps to protect the identity of the students in a time when hostility toward foreigners and Christianity was common,[11] but also because some on the mission board were apt to look at teaching as distracting from language study and more important mission work such as evangelism and Bible translation.[12] However, in many ways, Verbeck, in his four decades in Japan, was always instructing; even after he officially stopped teaching full-time, he still taught Bible classes in his home, delivered lectures for various occasions, and went on preaching tours throughout Japan.

Some of Verbeck's influence as a teacher was simply a result of being in the right place at the right time—in Nagasaki in the Bakumatsu period. When he arrived in Nagasaki, he wrote that the Japanese were "not at all accessible touching religious matters" because of the proscriptions against Christianity, and that missionaries had to gain the "general confidence of the people" and "master the native tongue." Thus, in his words, he "early commenced to give gratuitous instructions at my home in the English language, and various other useful branches." Verbeck acknowledged that "this course . . . led to my being early identified with educational matters, and did much to give shape to my career in this country."[13] He had arrived in Japan just as the ports were beginning to open to foreigners, on the eve of the most dynamic period in the southern corner of Japan, which was burgeoning with young samurai students from the surrounding domains who were eager to learn what the modern West had to offer, things which Verbeck could teach them. By the end of 1863, Verbeck had gained the attention of the Nagasaki governor, who was pleased with the progress of two of his interpreters under Verbeck's tutelage and thus founded a new institution (eventually called the Saibikan or Seibikan) to encourage the study of "foreign languages and science" with Verbeck as the principal.[14] As news of his teaching spread, he was asked to teach and direct another similar school in Nagasaki for the Hizen (Saga) domain, which was eventually called the Chienkan.

It is somewhat surprising that the famous figures who were former students and who are most often associated with Verbeck—like Ōkuma Shigenobu in Nagasaki and Takahashi Korekiyo in Tokyo—did not become Christians, at least officially. In contrast to these famous figures, there were a number of students and individuals that Verbeck taught and interacted with in Nagasaki and elsewhere who joined Protestant churches and other Christian institutions. Though some scholars have demonstrated why Christianity appealed to the samurai class during this time, this aspect of Verbeck's legacy—that is, his impact on the lives of individual Christian believers in the nineteenth century—has been somewhat overlooked and understudied in recent years.[15]

However, in much of the late nineteenth-century missionary literature, Japan was often portrayed as a mission field that had succeeded in gaining highly educated or high-ranking converts to the Protestant faith, and I would argue that this somewhat exaggerated conclusion stems partly from the impact of some of the early conversions of some of Verbeck's samurai students. From the beginning, Verbeck endeavored to teach his students not only Western languages but also Christianity, and so it is no surprise that a number of his students embraced his Protestant faith. This began in Nagasaki, when, in February 1866, Shomura Sukeuemon, a samurai from Higo (Kumamoto) who had studied under Verbeck and the Episcopal missionary Channing M. Williams, was baptized. Though originally attracted by Western military learning, Shomura also took up the study of the Bible.[16] Shortly after this, in June 1866, arguably the most well-known baptisms in Japan in the Bakumatsu period also took place in Nagasaki through one of Verbeck's students from Hizen (Saga), Motono Morimichi, a retainer of a high-ranking official, Murata Masanori (Wakasa-no-kami). Murata had become interested in Christianity when he (or one of his retainers) reportedly found a Chinese New Testament along the beach in Nagasaki and began reading it. Murata Wakasa and his younger brother, Murata Ayabe (who was also a student of Verbeck's), were baptized in secret by Verbeck (along with Motono), though they informed their daimyo about their conversions upon their return to Hizen.[17] In 1868, before leaving Nagasaki for Tokyo, Verbeck also baptized Shimizu Miyauchi, a language teacher, and his associate, Futagawa Itō. Both of these Protestant converts were subsequently arrested for being Christians, and Verbeck later wrote that by the early 1880s, Shimizu had moved to Tokyo and was a member of the prominent Kōjimachi Church there.[18] These early converts, such as Wakasa and Motono, continued to be Christians into the Meiji period, and in 1884, when Verbeck went on a preaching tour to Saga, Henry Stout wrote that "it was a great privilege for Dr. Verbeck to speak to and celebrate the Lord's Supper with a number of the family of Wakasa, who are among the believers."[19] Verbeck's reputation as a winsome advocate of Christianity grew quickly. In 1872, Daniel C. Greene, an early American Board missionary in Japan, found an English-language letter—apparently written by Verbeck in Nagasaki in the early 1860s—urging the "claims of Christianity," which had "quietly circulated among the Japanese" in a time in which Christianity was proscribed.[20] Some of these early conversions through Verbeck's teaching proved to be surprisingly long-lasting. One postwar missionary wrote that a man who attended a church service in 1972 claimed that his family had been Christians for a century largely because of the testimony of Verbeck, who had brought the gospel to his grandfather.[21]

One of the key aspects of Verbeck's background and education, and arguably his greatest asset as a teacher, advisor, and missionary, was his broad language ability. His polyglot Moravian education in his youth in Zeist helped him to become fluent in "four mother tongues," thus providing Verbeck, according to one observer, with "a master-key for both studying and using the language of

Japan with a freedom, accuracy, and scope such as astonished his Japanese audiences and have not been equaled by either missionary or civilian in this country."[22] At every point in his career, Verbeck's language abilities were a key factor in his prominence. In Nagasaki in the 1860s, it was his multilingual skills in Western languages like Dutch, English, German, and French that helped him gain students and recognition by the authorities. By December 1860, a year after he arrived in Nagasaki, he was teaching English to four students in his home, three of whom were government interpreters for whom Verbeck's Dutch background was useful. This was because they had received some instruction in Rangaku, or Dutch studies, to help in their interactions with the Dutch in Dejima (a manmade island in Nagasaki harbor), which, prior to 1859, was the only place foreigners were allowed to reside in Japan. By the end of 1861, Verbeck had a private English class of seven scholars, including three interpreters and four samurai from various domains, and he wrote that his own language study was going slowly because he spent much time teaching English, but that with regard to this teaching, "the general influence cannot fail to be good." He used the Chinese and the English New Testament in his teaching, and in 1862 he established a separate Bible class in his home for four students, though Verbeck admitted that they were there mainly "in consequence of being my pupils in English." Nevertheless, he reported at the end of 1862 that his teaching had "under Providence turned to so good an account."[23] Beginning in 1863, when he was hired to teach in the government-sponsored schools in Nagasaki, his teacher's earnings came at a good time because mission funds were low due to the Civil War at home in America (although apparently Verbeck was not always paid regularly for his teaching by the Japanese authorities in Nagasaki).[24] Because language skills in English and other Western languages were so valued, Verbeck's students were often promoted, and he became known in and around Nagasaki for being an effective teacher. In order to assist in his teaching, Verbeck ordered various items from America through the mission board, such as Chinese and English books on science and other topics, magic lanterns, a microscope, globes and maps, pictures, and even a planetarium, all of which he thought would attract curious students.[25] In Nagasaki, he struggled with having to teach at two different schools, in which instruction was given in several languages and at various levels, during a time of great political tensions, where regular attendance was often disrupted. Although Nagasaki was far from the center of the Tokugawa government, this generally meant that it was safer for foreigners, who were occasionally victims of anti-foreigner violence in the 1860s. This relative safety and reduced hostility in Nagasaki allowed Verbeck more freedom and also gave him connections to some of the increasingly disaffected samurai in many of the domains in southern Japan.[26]

As a man who understood the importance of languages, Verbeck worked very hard to learn Japanese, studying in Nagasaki through a tutor and using the few Dutch or German grammar books and dictionaries that existed.[27] His Japanese language abilities (particularly in speaking) were a result of hard study and living for years among the people of Japan, but he also was particularly gifted, and many Japanese people and foreigners marveled at his skill.[28] Griffis asserts that he was "able to hold his Japanese audiences spellbound for hours. . . . He could use with tremendous effect their own proverbs, gems of speech, popular idioms, and the epigrams of their sages."[29] Unlike some of his contemporary pioneer missionaries to Japan who had some background in Chinese, Verbeck had not studied the Chinese language, which made his progress even more remarkable, and he quickly advanced to translation work.[30] In the 1860s, becoming proficient in Japanese was complicated—having to learn *bungo* (literary Japanese), *keigo* (formal Japanese), and various forms of colloquial Japanese, all of which Verbeck mastered. He supposedly loved to use some phrases in the Nagasaki dialect (such as the ending *degansu*) and even employed humor adeptly. One of his students from Saga, in the 1860s, wrote that in the middle of a discussion about Christianity and God, Verbeck made a joke that contained a pun with the words *okamisama* ("God") and *okamisan* ("wife" or the "missus"), which made them all laugh.[31] In the following story from the 1860s (no doubt passed down by his students), Verbeck was portrayed as one who had great respect and understanding of the Japanese language and traditions:

> One day, there were four young men from Satsuma, who were about to leave to study in the West—one of whom was General Ōyama Iwao (later Field Marshal) who went to visit Verbeck to ask for advice. At this time, after talking about various subjects, Verbeck deliberately added at the end, "No matter how interesting, amusing, or comforting the things are that you find, you must not lose the spirit of Japan (*nihon damashii*)." They replied, "We understand," and someone sang the following: *Japan's precious stone given by God / We must polish until it shines.* According to them, this poem was Verbeck's own work, and he expressly wrote it for them on a poem-card (*tanzaku*) because they wanted a piece of his handwriting.[32]

Though the veracity of the details of this anecdote could be questioned, the fact that this story was passed down and included in a later work by a historian speaks volumes about how his students viewed him and his Japanese language capabilities. Even when he later taught or lectured at various institutions, such as the Peers School (the Kazoku Gakkō, later Gakushūin), Meiji Gakuin, and Union Seminary from the late 1870s, it was his ability to teach his courses in Japanese that distinguished him, a skill that many foreigners and missionaries did not possess at the time.[33] One missionary in Japan, J.A.B. Scherer, wrote that he believed there was "no finer linguist in the Far East" and said that he once heard a Japanese teacher from Saga who had heard a Verbeck lecture say, "He knows more of the language than I do."[34] Even his funeral was unusual for foreigners in that it was conducted in both Japanese and English, with many prominent Japanese pastors participating in the service.[35]

FIGURE 1.2. Guido and Maria Verbeck, 1880s. (Credit: Archives of the Reformed Church in America.)

Verbeck as a Head Teacher and Advisor in Early Meiji Japan

As a result of his connections with his students in Nagasaki, some of whom became important leaders in the Meiji Restoration, Verbeck seems to have been one of the few missionaries who openly supported the Meiji Restoration from the beginning, despite the official neutrality of the United States during the war.[36] Also, there were relatively few foreign employees who worked for both the Tokugawa *bakufu* and the Meiji regime, but Verbeck was one of them. In fact, in a letter in early 1868, Verbeck wrote that revolution was occurring in Japan but that he did not feel like he was personally in danger because he had friends on both sides and that they all understood the "pacific character of the missionary calling."[37] Though this may have been the case, it is more likely that it was his students and the officials who had sponsored and sent them who were his "friends" and who respected him. When Verbeck moved to Tokyo in 1869 at the request of the Meiji government, he did so not only on the basis of his reputation as a knowledgeable and competent multilingual teacher but also as a virtuous and trustworthy figure. Two of the significant early Meiji leaders, Ōkubo Toshimichi and Kido Kōin, recognized these qualities in Verbeck, and in a letter in late 1868, Ōkubo wrote to Kido, "As you know, Verbeck . . . is a knowledgeable and virtuous man and is well acquainted with our Imperial Land. . . . If you hire him and take him under your wing, others will surely want to learn from him at once. Would that not be an excellent outcome? New schools are about to be founded. . . . When that happens you are apt to find him of great use indeed."[38]

Though initially his move to Tokyo was difficult amid the tumultuous changes following the Meiji Restoration, by 1870, he became one of the highest paid *oyatoi* (foreign employees), earning 600 yen a month as the head teacher of the Daigaku Nankō in Tokyo.[39] During this time, he had to deal with an inundation of students and teachers in the dynamic early Meiji years, and these circumstances rendered the quality of education difficult to maintain. Kido Kōin reported that the large number of students were "totally undisciplined," and one student's description of the samurai at the school in 1869 was scathing: "Anyone who wanted to study was scorned as a shilly-shallying fogy. Many students would go off in the afternoons and, depending upon how much money they had, go to . . . a restaurant, drink sake, and summon a geisha, although some went to brothels."[40] In an effort to improve teaching standards, Verbeck helped the government to draft a proposition entitled "Instructions for Hiring Foreigners." As head teacher, Verbeck endeavored to improve teacher standards and hire more professional teachers, writing to Griffis in 1871 that "our staff, I hope, will gradually come up to my 'beau ideal.'"[41] In March 1871, the school had twelve foreign teachers and 994 students and offered instruction in English, French, or German, as well as such Western subjects as physics, chemistry, mathematics, and literature in these languages.[42] Then, in November of that year, the new minister of education, Ōki Takatō (Verbeck's former student from Saga), closed the school for a few weeks while they conducted rigorous examinations and whittled down the student body to 430 students, who were kept under greater control when the school reopened.[43]

Because Verbeck was so well known among his students in both Nagasaki and Tokyo, during this time many of the domains (or prefectures in the Meiji period) entrusted him to find foreign teachers for them. One example was the daimyo Matsudaira Shungaku, who asked Verbeck to obtain a science teacher for his domain of Fukui (Echizen), and thus, William Elliot Griffis, a graduate of Rutgers, was hired. In 1871, the daimyo/governor of Kumamoto in Kyushu inquired as to whether Verbeck could find a "samurai" teacher from the West. Though Verbeck assured him there were no samurai in America, he nonetheless asked the mission board to look for a military man, and eventually Captain Leroy

Lansing Janes, a veteran of the Civil War, was hired for their school, and his students became the core of the Kumamoto Band of Christian leaders.[44]

Even after Verbeck was dismissed from his head teacher/superintendent position in 1873, his reputation for excellence remained. Consequently, in October of that year, Mitsukuri Rinshō, the head of the *Seiin* (Central Chamber) Translation Bureau, urged the Meiji leaders to hire Verbeck as "supervisor of translation and consultant to each bureau on matters relating to foreign countries." Consequently, in December 1873, Verbeck signed a contract agreeing to divide his time equally between translation and answering questions from the legislative section (the *Sain* or the Left Chamber).[45] Though the Japanese authorities knew it might seem inappropriate to hire a foreigner to deal with government matters that were often secret, they viewed such an appointment as indispensable at the time and trusted Verbeck, claiming "there would be no impropriety in hiring a person of splendid character."[46] Undoubtedly, one of the major reasons he was chosen to be an advisor for the new Meiji government in the 1870s was that his former students and others who knew of his reputation were in influential positions and trusted his advice and guidance. As one of the few "general advisors" (*komon*) for the Meiji government in the 1870s, Verbeck's advice was sought regarding a wide variety of topics—teaching and education reform, promulgation of laws and legal counsel, establishment of new political institutions, and many other matters.[47] Tatsumaro Tezuka writes that when Verbeck was appointed a cabinet advisor by Premier Sanjō Sanetomi, he attended a daily cabinet meeting and "took part in several important decisions such as on the approbation of the use of the surname by commoners, on the abrogation of traditional customs of men's topknot hairstyle and sword-bearing, and on the abolition of clans and establishment of prefectures."[48] Verbeck's opinion was also solicited on the choice of models for the new army, and whether to adopt the German, English, or Dutch medical system and language for the Igakkō (medical school).[49] With regard to the latter, Dr. Ishiguro Tadanori, who became head of the Red Cross in Japan, relates how, when he and other doctors had sought to make German the language of the medical school, they were ridiculed by many, but when Verbeck expressed his sympathy with them, it carried great weight because "Dr. Verbeck was already in those times respected and believed in by the people."[50] Though Verbeck's contract as an advisor ended in 1877 and he was replaced by more "specialists" in these areas, that same year he was decorated by the Meiji emperor with the Order of the Rising Sun. When he returned to Japan in 1879 after a year-long furlough in America, he returned as a full-time missionary, believing that, in his words, "My mission is to the Japanese, that I am here to benefit them."[51]

Various Qualities of Verbeck

Though there is little doubt that Verbeck was an influential teacher, advisor, and missionary in Bakumatsu-Meiji Japan, I have often pondered the reasons why he was so highly regarded by his students and others. In other words, other than his ability to speak many Western languages and Japanese proficiently, what qualities did Verbeck possess that resonated with so many of his students and those who interacted with him?

One quality of Verbeck's that appealed to his students was his transnational or cosmopolitan identity—"A Citizen of No Country," as Griffis subtitles his biography—which enabled him to take advantage of his European roots, utilize his American education and training, and embrace his new adopted country of Japan. Uchimura Kanzō, who held Verbeck in high regard, wrote that "the best missionaries are those who have no nationalities to glory in," and Verbeck truly embodied this, distinguishing him from most of the other foreigners in Japan at the time.[52] As someone with a broader life experience than the other American missionaries, he could more readily recognize and embrace what was best in Europe, in America, and also in Japan. Styling himself as an "Americanized Dutchman," Verbeck embraced the best in America, using the Declaration of Independence and the Constitution in his teaching, and he sent many students to study abroad in American educational institutions such as Rutgers. In his work as an advisor to the government, he helped translate from a variety of constitutions as well as political and legal works from various countries in at least four European languages, thus showing his knowledge of, and appreciation for, the traditions and systems of Western Europe. At the same time, he also recognized that Japan had its own strengths, and he took an interest in some aspects of Japanese culture. One small example of this was a keen fascination he developed in Nanga-style painting, where he often visited the painter Kinoshita [Itsuun]'s school in Nagasaki, met with his students, and asked numerous questions about their artwork.[53] As someone who had a broader life experience than many missionaries, he also encouraged his students and the Meiji government leaders to study abroad, to go into the world, and to learn from experience as he had. Further, when he found himself a "stateless" person in 1890—he had no citizenship papers from the Netherlands from four decades earlier, and he had not resided in America long enough to gain citizenship—Verbeck would embrace Japan as his home. Thus, Verbeck became one of the first foreigners to receive a special passport authorized by the emperor granting him full rights and protection under the Japanese government. This last distinctive aspect of Verbeck impressed both Japanese and foreign observers. Sakurai Ōson wrote of Verbeck that "he came before the treaty revisions, and among the foreigners, he alone maintained the special right to live freely on our soil."[54] One symbolic gesture that the Verbeck family made in the 1870s to display their transnational identity was to put up three Christmas trees in their home—one for the family, one for Japan, and one for all the foreigners in Japan.[55] Undoubtedly, students were drawn to this cosmopolitan, knowledgeable "citizen of the world" who truly embraced both Japan and the world.

A second quality of Verbeck that was attractive was his wide knowledge of subjects and range of interests. Although Verbeck, as a seminary graduate and

Protestant missionary, received a quality theological education and training in biblical interpretation and preaching at Auburn Seminary, and eventually an honorary doctorate of divinity from Rutgers, theology was by no means the only area in which "Dr. Verbeck" was trained, or about which he was interested in learning. Verbeck's education included the sciences, having studied to be a civil engineer in Utretcht in the Netherlands and having worked at a foundry in Wisconsin and briefly as an engineer in Arkansas. Even in areas where he had no training, such as medicine and seismography, he made efforts to learn about these subjects. He wrote a brief description of a cholera outbreak in the 1860s and, as mentioned earlier, was instrumental in advising the German system of medicine for Meiji Japan.[56] In a letter he also described a type of seismograph that he constructed "by means of variously constructed pendulums," to measure the direction and force of earthquakes, for which he was later inducted as an honorary member of the Japanese Seismological Society.[57] In addition, Verbeck was knowledgeable about the history and politics of various countries, and one of his prominent students in Tokyo, Takahashi Korekiyo, wrote in his memoirs that "whenever we wanted to know about the circumstances and situations of foreign countries, we asked the teacher Verbeck everything."[58] Benjamin C. Duke also asserts that the Japanese considered Verbeck "a virtual encyclopedia of western knowledge. . . . How Verbeck was capable, and inclined to teach such a wide variety of subjects to his devoted Japanese young samurai shows the mark of the man."[59] In the humanities and music, he loved Shakespeare and German poetry (claiming that German, which his father spoke at home, was his "heart language") and was very gifted musically as well, playing the organ in church in Nagasaki and possessing a good baritone voice for singing.[60] According to his eldest son, William, he was also athletic and enjoyed playing sports and various games, and he "could outrun and outjump any of us. He entered with great zest into all outdoor sports. . . . He played chess and checkers with us, and did everything to amuse and interest us, and in his play we always learned something. He had a great passion for scientific toys . . . our playtime was school, and our schooling under his tutelage was a liberal education."[61] Truly, Verbeck was the model of a well-rounded and curious learner, scholar, and teacher.

A third quality of Verbeck's, which was well recognized by many, was his willingness to work hard. As the head teacher or director of schools first in Nagasaki and then in Tokyo, Verbeck was often overworked by his various responsibilities. When he arrived at the Daigaku Nankō in Tokyo, he had to direct and lead seventeen foreign teachers and seven Japanese teachers, hire new teachers, and develop the curriculum, in addition to all the preparatory work for his own teaching. In one letter from 1869 that he finished writing at 2:00 A.M., Verbeck wrote that he was busy with five and a half hours of teaching at the school, extra tutoring and translation work, and the placing of orders to America for texts, materials, and instruments.[62] During his years as an advisor he also worked extremely hard, and in 1877, in his first letter to the mission board in three years, he admitted to being overwhelmed, claiming that, "Almost daily, questions occur that oblige me to undertake much research and extensive reading." Such hard work certainly took its toll on Verbeck's health, but his willingness to put forth such effort undoubtedly impressed his students and colleagues.[63]

A fourth quality of Verbeck's character that helped him gain trust and respect was his gentleness and generosity with his students. This was particularly important in a time when Japan had been forcibly opened by foreigners, had unequal treaties imposed upon it, and often had to deal with heavy-handed or demanding foreigners, many of them looking to take advantage of the Japanese for monetary gain or personal promotion. Though it is a bit ironic that Verbeck, a Protestant missionary, became so trusted in a time in which Christianity was still technically proscribed, it is also true that Verbeck's missionary identity was somewhat fluid, and technically he was being paid as a teacher or an *oyatoi* during much of this time. In his biography, Griffis describes this servant attitude that Verbeck displayed, whereby he "disarmed the old suspicions, winning new confidence. Becoming the servant of servants, as teacher and helper, he attracted to himself the humble and the great."[64] Though he wanted his students and the Japanese government to accept Christianity and to change the proscriptions against Christianity, Verbeck refused to use his influence to force the issue, choosing instead to work indirectly by encouraging the government to send an embassy to the West—which later came to fruition in the Iwakura Mission—and by sending students to study in America, particularly in Christian institutions such as Rutgers. Even in his individual interactions, he was gentle. When Takahashi Korekiyo, as a young student, decided to leave Verbeck's residence in the early 1870s, largely so that he could have more freedom to carouse with his friends, Verbeck treated him gently, telling him, "If you want to leave to live elsewhere, you are free to do so. And feel free to move back in again if you want." Verbeck then presented Takahashi with his large, leather-bound, annotated family Bible and encouraged him to read it "at least once a day, no matter what happened."[65] Verbeck continued to exhibit these qualities when he became a government employee, and Hazel Jones writes that "Verbeck emerges as the epitome of a trusted [*o*]*yatoi*," those who, in "humility and accommodation," saw themselves as catalysts and guides for modern Japan.[66] Verbeck was generous in his teaching and advising, with his time and his money, and was willing to take time to teach students, not only at various schools but also in his home. He reportedly spent his last moments in Nagasaki talking with a Buddhist priest who had questions about Christianity such that Verbeck almost missed his ship, which was departing for Tokyo.[67] Though he did, on occasion, face some hostility or criticism, Verbeck generously embraced his students and their hopes for the future of Japan and its people. In a brief article on Verbeck's famous student, Okuma Shigenobu, the author wrote of his impact in lofty terms: "He [Verbeck] could use eight languages and he read men. . . . This and the qualities of a willing servant made him a demigod. The young men of the progressive southern provinces flocked to him; he became a trainer of statesmen."[68] As one of the Protestant leaders in Meiji Japan, Uemura Masahisa wrote of Verbeck after his death, "He gave his life for the development of Japan and emotionally enjoyed her development."[69]

Verbeck's Students in Bakumatsu-Meiji Japan and Beyond

Beyond all of these qualities that contributed to Verbeck's effectiveness as a teacher, advisor, and missionary in Japan, the story of his impact is undoubtedly strongly influenced by the caliber and influence of many of the students he taught, as well as their subsequent role in building modern Japan. At places like the Chienkan and the Daigaku Nankō, where he was the director and head teacher, respectively, it is difficult to know how many of the students sat directly under his teaching, like those who came to his home for instruction. But the fact that Christian teachers and missionaries like Verbeck opened up their homes and lives to their students made a huge impression on many of these students. Even while he was an advisor for the government, he still gave lectures in his home. The future political leader Ueki Emori wrote in his diary in January 1877 that he went to Verbeck's home to hear a lecture on the Bible.[70] In reflecting on Verbeck's impact on him, Ōkuma Shigenobu, who later became prime minister and founded Waseda University, wrote that "it was the life of Dr. Verbeck that influenced me more than his teaching."[71] And Verbeck definitely felt mutual respect for, and obligations to, his students, particularly those from his early years. When hired to go to Tokyo to help set up a new school, he was very discouraged about the chaos in the government and the general hostility toward Christianity. He found himself longing to return to Nagasaki, but one of the major reasons why he did not go back there was that at least thirty-six of his former pupils had come to Tokyo after him and "it would not be so easy for them to go back as for me."[72]

Another obligation to his students that Verbeck took seriously was to enable them to study overseas—primarily at American institutions—through letters of recommendation or introduction, believing that these students' prospects, Japan's future development, and the cause of Christianity in Japan would be furthered by such study. Though the students were limited by several stipulations, one of which being that they could not change their religion, there were some who ignored this and were baptized while in the United States.[73] Ishizuki Minoru has calculated that 586 Japanese students were sent to Europe and the United States between 1868 and 1874, and of these students, 223 were sent to the United States.[74] Though New Brunswick was not the only place Verbeck sent recommendations for students, it was certainly the most prominent. As seen throughout part II of this volume, there were several factors that made New Brunswick attractive: It had both a preparatory grammar school and a college; it was Christian in its background and leadership; and as a historical affiliate of the Dutch

Reformed Church (later Reformed Church in America), it had the support of the mission board and many Christian families, with whom some of the Japanese students lived.[75] And though Verbeck was not a graduate of Rutgers, many of his fellow missionaries were, such as his replacement in Nagasaki, Henry Stout, and his colleague in Tokyo, James Ballagh, in addition to William Elliot Griffis and later other *oyatoi* missionary-teachers, such as Edward Warren Clark and Martin Wyckoff.[76]

Not surprisingly, many of the students that Verbeck wrote recommendations for came from the domains in Kyushu, such as Higo (Kumamoto) and Hizen (Saga), the latter of which Verbeck visited at least twice and, in 1868, described as one of his "favorite countries in Japan."[77] In June 1866, Verbeck gave letters of recommendation and introduction for two nephews of the scholar/reformer Yokoi Shōnan from Kumamoto, Yokoi Saheita, and Yokoi Daihei, and the mission board chairman J. M. Ferris took care of them and enrolled them in the Rutgers Grammar School.[78] Later, in 1868, Verbeck wrote a letter in support of a bill in Congress to admit Japanese students, among them Yokoi Saheita and Matsumura Junzō of Satsuma, to the Naval Academy in Annapolis.[79] Verbeck also wrote that he gave letters of recommendation for two young men from Satsuma to study abroad, though he admitted having met them twice only and seemed a bit reluctant to vouch for them.[80] In early 1868, Verbeck sent a recommendation for Egushi Eijirō, a friend of the Yokoi brothers from Higo (Kumamoto), who also studied in New Brunswick.[81] After moving to Tokyo in 1869, Verbeck continued to give introductions for students: In 1869, he reportedly gave one for a man named Kodama, from Chōshū, and for four unnamed young men (including the heir of a prince).[82] In 1870, Verbeck wrote to recommend the sons of the influential court noble Iwakura Tomomi, Tomosada and Tomotsune, who had been Verbeck's students in Nagasaki. They were accompanied by three others—Orita Hikoichi, Hattori Ichizō, and Yamamoto Jūsuke—who also would study in New Brunswick (and Orita became the first Japanese student to graduate from Princeton University in 1876).[83] By 1870, as head teacher of the Daigaku Nankō, Verbeck had written introductions for many students, including Megata Tanetarō, who would serve with the Japanese ambassador, Mori Arinori, in Washington, DC, and later in the Meiji government.[84] By 1871, there were some eighteen Japanese students studying in New Brunswick, many of them with letters of introduction from Verbeck.[85] From 1866 to 1876, approximately forty Japanese students were sent to New Brunswick, with nineteen of those admitted to Rutgers College, though only three of those students graduated.[86] Regardless of the students' performance in the various American institutions, Verbeck trusted that their education and experience would be enlarged by their time in America.

Perhaps the most notable aspect of Verbeck's students is the influence that many of them gained in the government. As Benjamin C. Duke asserts, "It was Verbeck's destiny to provide a foundation in modern government to a great number of Japan's first generation of leaders during the Meiji period."[87] At the beginning of the Meiji Restoration, in May 1868, Verbeck was invited to Osaka by some of the Meiji leaders to talk about revisions to the constitution and other matters. Verbeck expressed an optimism that his former students, particularly Ōkuma Shigenobu and Soejima Taneomi, whom he had seen as "very promising pupils" and who had studied parts of the New Testament with him, would, he believed, "work hard for not only the repeal of the ancient edicts against Christianity, but if possible for the universal toleration in the empire."[88] In 1869, Verbeck sent a proposal to Ōkuma for an embassy to the West, and though he waited for two years for a response, an enthusiastic reply eventually came from Iwakura Tomomi in 1871, who met with Verbeck several times to help plan the embassy.[89] Many of the participants in the Iwakura Mission realized the necessity of removing the proscriptions against Christianity, and prominent leaders, such as Itō Hirobumi, corresponded with Ōkuma and Soejima (who both remained in Japan) about this matter during the trip, urging them to give more freedom of religion.[90] Much later in his life, after Ōkuma had become prime minister and founded Waseda University, he praised Verbeck as one of the key architects of education in modern Japan, stating, "Education made New Japan; he should be remembered as its founder. He was the first great American I ever met in my life."[91] Ōkuma continued to recognize Verbeck's significance for modern Japan. In his proposal to raise funds for a monument over Verbeck's grave after his sudden death in 1898, Ōkuma listed his wide-ranging accomplishments, including his devotion to evangelism, translation work, and his teaching, writing that "there is no need to further eulogize on such matters. There is plenty of evidence throughout his career of his profound learning, gentle manner, and labor with which he gave all on behalf of our nation."[92] There were many other prominent students who had interactions with Verbeck from his days in Nagasaki on whom one could focus, such as significant figures from Hizen (Saga) like Ōki Takatō and Soejima Taneomi and leaders from Satsuma like Ōkubo Toshimichi. Ōki Takatō became education minister in 1871 and was instrumental in establishing the education system in Japan. He later also became chairman of the *Genrōin* and worked on Japan's civil code, was appointed justice minister, and was also president of the privy council. Soejima Taneomi, a revered figure in Saga today, was influential as a diplomat, serving as an interim foreign minister in the 1870s. He resigned from the government in 1873 but returned to government service in 1878.[93]

Though Verbeck arguably had contact with many more students during his three years as head of the Daigaku Nankō/Kaisei Gakkō, and as head teacher had more administrative duties than direct instruction of students, he still taught some important students. One of his most prominent young students in the early 1870s who studied history and read the Bible with Verbeck, and also lived with him for a time, was Takahashi Korekiyo, subsequent finance minister and prime minister of Japan. According to Takahashi's biographer, Richard J. Smethurst,

"Verbeck's teachings had a powerful impact on Takahashi. . . . Takahashi's lifelong magnanimity and his tolerance toward what he saw as the foibles of others (and himself) may well have developed from his ten years of close association with Verbeck."[94] Takahashi was one of Verbeck's most devoted students, even assisting him in personal matters such as procuring a house in Tokyo. And following Takahashi's brutal murder by militarists in 1936, organizers displayed Verbeck's family Bible, a gift from his teacher that Takahashi had always cherished, at a public exhibit held in his honor.[95]

Conclusion

When looking at the life and legacy of Verbeck's four decades in Japan, it is clear that his early years of teaching were critical and that the respect he gained early on from his students and from Japanese officials continued throughout his life. One oft-repeated anecdote from Verbeck's later years in Japan reveals the way that Verbeck's life and legacy were viewed by Japanese observers. One day, as Verbeck was waiting for a train, a young student (*shosei*) asked Verbeck when he had arrived in Japan. "Smiling, Verbeck replied, 'Well, that would be when you were not even born' (using '*degansu*', in the Nagasaki dialect). Verbeck laughed as the questioner stood there dumbfounded."[96] Griffis, in his biography, interpreted this incident merely as an example of Verbeck's sometimes cutting wit, but Uchimura Kanzō focused on the disrespect of the student who displayed such ignorance for a revered teacher and figure who had lived for so long in Japan.[97] When Uemura Masahisa looked at this incident, he highlighted the contrast between the Japanese student and the foreign teacher: "Truly, Verbeck had more knowledge of Japan than many Japanese people."[98] One could attribute this respect to his embracing of Japan and its people for so many years, but I think it was also the influence of his students, and later, colleagues like Uemura, who continued to honor his memory and legacy from his first decades in Japan.

Though Verbeck is perhaps not a household name in Japan today, his legacy and life in service of Japan is still recognized. When I was in Japan in 2015, I was staying in a hotel in Tokyo about three miles (five kilometers) from Aoyama Cemetery, where Verbeck is buried. One of the last mornings I was there, I decided to run to his grave in the foreign section of the cemetery. When I reached his grave, I was surprised to see bright, freshly cut orange and yellow lilies lying on top of the stone monument. I quickly passed by all the other foreign graves and saw that no other grave was adorned with fresh flowers. Why was the grave of Verbeck—a man who had no descendants living in Japan, no Japanese institutions dedicated to or named after him—the only one decorated with a carefully placed fresh bouquet of flowers? We may never know the answer to this question, but the solid legacy of his stone monument—erected through funds raised by his students—is a lasting symbol of the influential teacher, advisor, and missionary that he was during the formative Bakumatsu-Meiji period. Those flowers are also symbolic of the legacy of his teaching and work, which bloomed during his four-decade career in Japan and continued to grow through the impact of those he taught as well as the many lives he touched.

Notes

1 Quoted in Lane R. Earns, "A Miner in the Deep and Dark Place: Guido Verbeck in Nagasaki 1859–1869," *Crossroads*, no. 5 (Autumn 1997): 112.

2 Ogata Hiroyasu, *Kindai Nihon no kensetsu no chichi: Furubekki hakushi* (Tokyo: Waseda Daigaku Shakai Kagaku Kenkyūjo, 1961).

3 Noriko Itoh asserts that it was a farewell party. Noriko Itoh, *Guido F. Verbeck: A Life of Determined Acceptance* (Tokyo: Ayumu Shuppan, 2012), 141. However, this photograph is not in Griffis's 1900 biography of Verbeck, though he does have another well-known photo of Verbeck with twenty-three students from the Chienkan. Verbeck does not mention the photo in his letters, and his diaries have been lost.

4 Yamaguchi Takao, *Nihon no yoake: Furubekki hakushi to bakumatsu no shishi tachi* (Tokyo: Bungeisha, 2009), 16. The literature on these photos is varied, and there is also some debate about the dating and circumstances of the photo. Murase Hisayo, in "Nagasaki ni okeru Furubekki no jinmyaku," *Aoyama Gakuin Daigaku Kirisutokyō ronshū* 36 (2000): 63–94, dates it between December 1868 and the end of January 1869, right before Verbeck left Nagasaki for Tokyo, which seems accurate. Takahashi Shin'ichi believes that the original photograph was owned by Verbeck and that Emma Verbeck took it with her when she left Japan, but that it has been lost.

5 Both sons spent approximately two years studying at the Rutgers Grammar School in New Brunswick, New Jersey.

6 Takahashi Shin'ichi, "Furubekki shashin ni kansuru chōsa kekka" [unpublished and undated document].

7 E. Rothesay Miller, "Resolutions of Respect," *The Japan Evangelist* 5, no. 6 (June 1898): 183. Verbeck died with little money, and the costs of his funeral were defrayed by the Meiji emperor, who also gave him a military escort to accompany his casket for burial.

8 William Elliot Griffis, *Verbeck of Japan: A Citizen of No Country* (New York: Revell, 1900), 27. In contrast to Verbeck, one could say that Griffis was "mightier in word than in work" (with regard to Japan, at least). There are various speeches of Verbeck (particularly graduation speeches for various Christian institutions) that are recorded in various journals, particularly in the 1880s, but it seems that these were transcribed by those who heard them, not written by Verbeck himself.

9 E. Rothesay Miller, "Personal Reminiscences of Dr. Verbeck," *The Japan Evangelist* 5, no. 6 (June 1898): 187.

10 Apparently, both Marius Jansen and I have spent some time searching for these lost journals. F. G. Notehelfer, "Looking for the Lost: Westerners in 19th Century Japan," in *Japan and Its Worlds: Marius B. Jansen and the Internationalization of Japanese Studies*," ed. Martin Collcutt et al. (Tokyo: I-House Press, 2007), 176.

11 In fact, in 1869, the influential figure Yokoi Shōnan, whose two nephews were students of Verbeck's, was assassinated because he was suspected of being a Christian.

12 Verbeck himself may also have prioritized this work at times because, in his last two decades, he spent a large proportion of his time on translation (including, most notably, the Psalms) and on evangelism throughout Japan.

13 Griffis, *Verbeck of Japan*, 144.

14 Robert S. Schwantes, "American Influence in the Education of Meiji Japan, 1868–1912" (PhD diss., Harvard University, 1950), 17. In gratitude, these two interpreters sent Verbeck a young pig as a gift.

15 For the appeal of Christianity to samurai in the nineteenth century, see F. G. Notehelfer, *Kōtoku Shūsui: Portrait of a Japanese Radical* (Cambridge: Cambridge University Press, 1971); and Irwin Scheiner, *Christian Converts and Social Protest in Meiji Japan* (Berkeley: University of California Press, 1970).

16 A. Hamish Ion, *American Missionaries, Christian Oyatoi and Japan 1859–1873* (Vancouver: University of British Columbia Press, 2009), 72.

17 Supposedly the Nabeshima daimyo did punish Wakasa-no-kami by destroying some of his books, but this was a very mild response in a time of harsh proscriptions against Christianity, and he was not removed from his high position in the domain.

18 Ion, *American Missionaries*, 115.

19 Henry Stout to H. N. Cobb, 2 May 1885, Japan Mission of the Reformed Church Archives (hereafter JMRCA). Griffis writes that on a trip to Saga in 1868, Verbeck had also secretly baptized Murata's sister and elderly mother, and that there were four generations of Christians in the Murata family by 1900. Griffis, *Verbeck of Japan*, 179.

20 Evarts Boutell Greene, *A New-Englander in Japan: Daniel Crosby Green* (Boston: Houghton Mifflin, 1927), 98.

21 Richard D. Sytsma, *So I Send You* (unpublished memoirs, 1992), 196.

22 Henry William Rankin, "Political Values of the American Missionary," *American Journal of Sociology* 13, no. 2 (September 1907): 149–150.

23 G. F. Verbeck, 1861 Annual Report, 31 December 1861; 1862 Annual Report (n.d.), JMRCA. In Nagasaki, however, he did not try to overemphasize his Dutch identity, perhaps because he was supported by an American denomination, and his wife was American. Moreover, English was much more popular than the Dutch language, given that two of the major powers were English-speaking.

24 This is something that is overlooked in most other biographical works on Verbeck. Though he was supposed to receive a salary of $4,500 annually from his teaching at both the *bakufu* Saibikan and Hizen's Chienkan, at times he was not paid for months, and Samuel R. Brown continued to periodically send him money throughout the 1860s. He also had to borrow money from the mission board to send his family home on furlough in 1869 and move to Tokyo. The expenses of a growing family (seven children eventually) and the fact that Verbeck tended to be very generous and not terribly good at saving and investing money meant that financial difficulties were a recurring issue in his life.

25 Verbeck to Ferris, 2 April 1860, JMRCA.

26 Verbeck to Peltz, 29 September 1862, JMRCA. However, the atmosphere in Nagasaki was still tense at times. As a result of the British bombardment of Satsuma in 1862, Verbeck was warned by one of his students, Murata Ayabe, and his wife and son went to Shanghai for six months until the tumult and danger subsided. Griffis, *Verbeck of Japan*, 110.

27 G. F. Verbeck, Annual Report for 1861, JMRCA. Verbeck had no prior knowledge of Chinese, but he helped compile and revise dictionaries such as the *Satsuma Japanese-English Dictionary* and later assisted with a French-Japanese dictionary. See Ōhashi Akio and Hirano Hideo, *Meiji Ishin to aru oyatoi gaikokujin: Furubekki no shōgai* (Tokyo: Shin Jinbutsu Ōraisha, 1988), 114–140.

28 Certainly, growing up in a multilingual society in the Netherlands contributed to his ability to learn a new language, but Verbeck, from the beginning, also chose to

mainly live among the Japanese people, not in the foreign communities in the treaty ports, which was in contrast to most missionaries and foreigners at the time.

29 Griffis, *Verbeck of Japan*, 25.

30 Verbeck to Peltz, 4 June 1861, JMRCA.

31 Morita Tadashi, "Nihon no kindaika ni kōken shita Nagasaki no Furubekki senkyōshi: Nihon no kaikoku senkyōshi no rainichi" (unpublished paper, Nagasaki Prefectural Library Archives, 2009), 60. Verbeck visited Saga at least twice, and he would often relax and have tea with various high-ranking members of the domain government, including the Nabeshima daimyo, apparently impressing them with his knowledge and his language skills.

32 Saba Wataru, *Uemura Masahisa to sono jidai*, vol. 1 (Tokyo: Kyōbunkan, 1967), 306. Translation mine. Saba's source is cited as "Dr. Verbeck and the Spirit of Japan" by Yutani Saiichirō.

33 Apparently Verbeck's Reformed colleague, Samuel R. Brown, taught his classes in English, and James H. Ballagh's spoken Japanese was difficult to understand at times. Verbeck's name was well known throughout Japan, and when, in 1877, he joined the staff of the Union Theological Seminary (which was combined with mission school, Meiji Gakuin, at that point), the addition of "Dr. Verbeck" was viewed as bolstering the school's reputation.

34 J.A.B. Scherer, "Recollections of Dr. Verbeck," *The Japan Evangelist* 5, no. 6 (June 1898): 179.

35 See description of the funeral service in C.N., "The Last Scenes," *The Japan Evangelist* 5, no. 6 (June 1898): 191–192.

36 A. Hamish Ion asserts that "only Verbeck among missionaries warmly welcomed the new Meiji government in April 1868 when it came to power." A. Hamish Ion, *American Missionaries, Christian Oyatoi, and Japan, 1859–1872* (Vancouver: University of British Columbia Press, 2009), 75.

37 Verbeck to J. M. Ferris, 28 February 1868, JMRCA.

38 Quoted in Motoyama Yukihiko, *Proliferating Talent: Essays on Politics, Thought, and Education in the Meiji Era* (Honolulu: University of Hawai'i Press, 1997), 95.

39 Hazel Jones, *Live Machines: Hired Foreigners and Meiji Japan* (Vancouver: University of British Columbia Press, 1980), 96; Benjamin C. Duke, *The History of Modern Japanese Education: Construction of the National School System, 1872–1890* (New Brunswick, NJ: Rutgers University Press, 2008), 221. Duke writes that the Japanese government asked Verbeck to translate a book, written for the Centennial Exhibition in Philadelphia, entitled *An Outline History of Japanese Education*. To help later missionaries with language study, Verbeck did write some short articles, such as "What Is the Best Method of Acquiring the Japanese Language" (which he read at the Tokyo Missionary Conference in 1882) and "How to Learn the Spoken Japanese." He also wrote a lengthy work on Japanese verbs, entitled "A Synopsis of All the Conjugations of the Japanese Verbs," published by Kelly and Walsh in Yokohama in 1887.

40 Quoted in Motoyama, *Proliferating Talent*, 120–121.

41 G. F. Verbeck to W. E. Griffis, 7 September 1871, William Elliot Griffis Collection, Special Collections and University Archives, Rutgers University, Libraries, New Brunswick, NJ (hereafter Griffis Collection). He also played a central role in establishing employment standards for foreign teachers and influenced the educational plan (*gakusei*) at the Kaisei Gakkō, issued by the Ministry of Education (Mombushō) in 1872. See Duke, *History of Modern Japanese Education*, 55, and Jones, *Live Machines*, 95.

42 Neil Pedlar, *The Imported Pioneers: Westerners Who Helped Build Modern Japan* (New York: St. Martin's Press, 1990), 128.
43 Schwantes, "American Influence," 36.
44 Fred Notehelfer, *American Samurai: Captain L. L. Janes and Japan* (Princeton, NJ: Princeton University Press, 1985), 105–106, 138.
45 Jones, *Live Machines*, 96–97. His pay for these years as an advisor was reduced to a 400-yen salary. Verbeck translated a wide variety of projects, including parts of the constitutions of various countries, including Spain, Switzerland, Portugal, the Netherlands, Denmark, Italy, Germany, and Austria; legal works, such as the *Code Napoleon*; works by jurists, such as Johan Caspar Bluntschli and Louis Prosper August Eschenbach; and forestry laws and parliamentary rules. Griffis, *Verbeck of Japan*, 280; Ebisawa Arimichi, ed., *Nihon Kirisutokyō kankei wakansho mokuroku* (Tokyo: Bunkodō, 1954) 34–38, 64–68.
46 Jones, *Live Machines*, 96–97.
47 For the Iwakura Mission (1871–1873) many of his students were prominent members, though some sources exaggerated the numbers. The first *Encyclopedia of Missions*, published initially by Edwin Munsell, states erroneously that "over half of its members were his students." Edwin Munsell Bliss, *Encyclopedia of Missions: Descriptive, Historical, Biographical, Statistical* (New York: Funk & Wagnalls, 1891).
48 Tatsumaro Tezuka, "Government-Employed Foreign Missionaries: Verbeck and Thompson," *Tokyo Municipal News*, December 1968, 6.
49 Jones, *Live Machines*, 95.
50 "Baron Ishiguro in *Tenchijin*," *The Japan Evangelist* 5, no. 6 (June 1898): 182–183.
51 G. F. Verbeck to J. M. Ferris, 24 October 1882, JMRCA.
52 Uchimura Kanzō, *Uchimura Kanzō zenshū*, vol. 15 (Tokyo: Iwanami Shoten, 1980–1984), 497.
53 Joshua A. Fogel, *Articulating the Sinosphere: Sino-Japanese Relations in Space and Time* (Cambridge, MA: Harvard University Press, 2009), 40–41. When a few of Kinoshita's students wanted to study art in China, Verbeck helped them secure passage secretly (dressed as Chinese servants or monks) on a Western merchant ship. Though Verbeck was apparently not gifted in painting or art, Verbeck's son Gustave studied art in France and was a gifted artist. In the archives of the Nagasaki Museum of History and Culture, there is a *kakejiku* (a painting on a silk scroll) of Verbeck dressed in Japanese attire, a fascinating and somewhat artistic portrayal of Verbeck in Nagasaki.
54 Susanna Fessler, *Musashino in Tuscany: Japanese Overseas Travel Literature, 1880–1912* (Ann Arbor: Center for Japanese Studies, University of Michigan, 2004), 45. Verbeck, in fact, expressed a desire to become a Japanese citizen, writing, "If there existed in the Empire laws for the naturalization of foreigners, I should under these circumstances gladly avail myself of them." G. F. Verbeck to H. N. Cobb, 3 March 1891, JMRCA. According to Takahashi Korekiyo's memoirs, he once said to him, "I am not serving as a missionary, but I really want to become a Japanese citizen. If I could receive one hundred yen a month from the Japanese government, I could live as a Japanese and support myself in Japan." Takahashi Korekiyo, *Takahashi Korekiyo jiden*, vol. 1 (Tokyo: Chikuma Shobō, 1936), 154.
55 This is from Clara Whitney's diary and is cited in Noriko Itoh, *Guido F. Verbeck—A Life of Determined Acceptance* (Tokyo: Ayumu Shuppan, 2012), 161.
56 Griffis, *Verbeck of Japan*, 24.
57 G. F. Verbeck to J. M. Ferris, 24 October 1882, JMRCA.
58 Translated and quoted in Itoh, *Guido F. Verbeck*, 147.

59 Duke, *Modern Japanese Education*, 44.
60 Griffis, *Verbeck of Japan*, 254.
61 Griffis, *Verbeck of Japan*, 254.
62 G. F. Verbeck, 29 December 1869, JMRCA.
63 G. F. Verbeck to J. M. Ferris, 27 May 1877, JMRCA. There is no question that this work took a toll on Verbeck's health, which deteriorated during the years he worked as an *oyatoi* in Tokyo. In 1873, he took his first furlough to "recover my nerves & elasticity of body and mind" (letter from G. F. Verbeck to J. M. Ferris, 22 February 1873, JMRCA), and in 1878, he explained in a letter that he left Japan because of "so much perplexity, pressure and care, and the state of my nervous system was so disturbed," and, in fact, he asked for a "temporary withdrawal from the Japan field" and only planned to return if his health improved, which, thankfully, it did. See G. F. Verbeck to J. M. Ferris, 18 September 1878, JMRCA.
64 Griffis, *Verbeck of Japan*, 17.
65 Richard J. Smethurst, *From Foot Soldier to Finance Minister: Takahashi Korekiyo, Japan's Keynes* (Cambridge, MA: Harvard University Press, 2007), 45–46.
66 Jones, *Live Machines*, 98–99.
67 Griffis, *Verbeck of Japan*, 174–175.
68 "Oriental Portraits: Marquis Okuma: Japan's Veteran Educator," *The Nation* 107, no. 2788 (December 7, 1918), 702.
69 Quoted in Saba, *Uemura Masahisa*, 289.
70 In Donald Keene, *Modern Japanese Diaries: The Japanese at Home and Abroad as Revealed Through Their Diaries* (New York: Columbia University Press, 1998), 256.
71 Quoted in Frank Cary, *History of Christianity in Japan* (Tokyo: Kyo Bun Kwan, 1959), 341. Although he doesn't discuss Verbeck in his essay, John F. Howes gives examples from other Christian missionaries in "Japanese Christians and American Missionaries," in *Changing Japanese Attitudes Toward Modernization*, ed. Marius Jansen (Princeton, NJ: Princeton University Press, 1965), 337–368.
72 Ion, *American Missionaries*, 75. Also quoted in Griffis, *Verbeck of Japan*, 187–188.
73 Ion, *American Missionaries*, 139.
74 Ishizuki Minoru, "Overseas Study by Japanese in the Early Meiji Period," in *The Modernizers: Overseas Students, Foreign Employees, and Modern Japan*, ed. Ardath W. Burks (Boulder, CO: Westview Press, 1985), 204–205.
75 When the Iwakura Mission was leaving America in 1872, Iwakura Tomomi and Ōkubo Toshimichi sent a letter to J. M. Ferris expressing their gratitude for "the generous conduct exhibited by yourself and other gentlemen in this instance, as well as in all matters of educational interest pertaining to the Japanese youth." See William Elliot Griffis, *Rutgers Graduates in Japan*, rev. ed. (New Brunswick, NJ: Rutgers College, 1916), 36.
76 See, Griffis, *Rutgers Graduates in Japan*, 1–36.
77 G. F. Verbeck to J. M. Ferris, 17 January 1868, JMRCA; G. F. Verbeck to S. R. Brown, 22 January 1869, JMRCA. Verbeck estimated that some forty-six of his students in Nagasaki were from Hizen.
78 G. F. Verbeck to J. M. Ferris, 10 June 1866, JMRCA. Yokoi Shōnan, an influential samurai official from Kumamoto, was assassinated in 1869 by reactionary samurai who suspected him of being a Christian.
79 Ion, *American Missionaries*, 136–137. Yokoi Saheita, however, failing his examinations, soon returned to Japan and died shortly afterward. In contrast, Matsumura succeeded at the Naval Academy, graduating in 1873.
80 G. F. Verbeck to J. M. Ferris, 1 March 1867, JMRCA.

81 G. F. Verbeck to J. M. Ferris, 17 January 1868, JMRCA.
82 G. F. Verbeck to J. M. Ferris, 28 July 1869, JMRCA; G. F. Verbeck to J. M. Ferris, 29 October 1869, JMRCA.
83 G. F. Verbeck to J. M. Ferris, 19 March 1870, JMRCA. Verbeck lists the names of these five young men as "Asahi, Tats, Orita, Hattori, and Yamamoto." The two sons of Iwakura studied in New Brunswick for two years.
84 G. F. Verbeck to J. M. Ferris, 21 September 1870; G. F. Verbeck to J. M. Ferris, 21 November 1870, JMRCA.
85 See photo in Griffis Collection.
86 Edward R. Beauchamp, *An American Teacher in Early Meiji Japan* (Honolulu: University Press of Hawaii, 1976), 16.
87 Duke, *Modern Japanese Education*, 44.
88 Quoted in Griffis, *Verbeck of Japan*, 174–175.
89 See Albert Altman, "Guido Verbeck and the Iwakura Embassy," *Japan Quarterly* 13, no. 1 (January–March 1966): 54–62.
90 Takii Kazuhiro, *Itō Hirobumi—Japan's First Prime Minister and Father of the Meiji Constitution* (London: Routledge, 2014), 30–31.
91 Quoted by Gordon D. Laman, "Guido F. Verbeck: Pioneer Missionary to Japan," *Historical Highlights* 1, no. 4 (Fall 1980): 5.
92 Quoted in Ohashi and Hirano, *Meiji Ishin to aru oyatoi gaikokujin*, 368–369. Translation mine.
93 Although Etō Shinpei was also Verbeck's student and, like Soejima, left the Meiji government in 1873, he is largely known for his involvement in the failed Saga Rebellion in 1874 and was executed after the rebellion was suppressed. When I went to Saga, they did not speak very highly of Ōkuma, largely because he moved to Tokyo and seemed to drop his connections in Saga. Also, Soejima is still respected in Saga as a scholar, as evidenced by his framed calligraphy which was proudly displayed. It is interesting to note how many of the leaders in the tumultuous 1870s died during Verbeck's service as an *oyatoi* in the government. In Verbeck's final year as a government employee (1877–1878), all three of the key leaders—Saigō, Kido, and Ōkubo—died, mainly from the Satsuma Rebellion and its aftermath.
94 Smethurst, *Foot Soldier*, 43.
95 Smethurst, *Foot Soldier*, 315. In the first page of the Bible, Takahashi wrote that he read it to correct his bad habits.
96 Motono Moriyuki, "Kugaku jidai no Morimichi: Furubekki no moto de," *Gaikō Fōramu*, no. 62 (November 1993): 86.
97 Uchimura Kanzō, *Uchimura Kanzō zenshū*, vol. 15, 497. In contrast to Verbeck, Uchimura criticized missionaries who "after spending half their lifetime in this country, they still remain utter strangers to us." *Uchimura Kanzō zenshū*, vol. 22, 381.
98 Quoted in Saba, *Uemura Masahisa*, 307.

2

Envisioning a New Japan

Matsudaira Shungaku, Yokoi Shōnan, and the Bakumatsu Network at the Dawn of the Rutgers-Japan Connection

HARUKO WAKABAYASHI WITH FUJI TAKAGI

> Returning from an errand to the office of the Board of Foreign Missions at 103 Fulton Street, New York, late in the afternoon in the autumn of 1866, I found there a plain looking man and two young men who appeared to be Chinamen. . . . They presented a letter from Rev. Guido F. Verbeck, then at Nagasaki, in which it was said only that they had been a few months in Dr. Verbeck's school, had learned some English there, and picked up more on the long voyage of about six months. *They wished, they said, to study navigation, to learn how to build "big ships" and make*

"big guns" to prevent European powers from taking possession of their country.[1]
—Rev. John Mason Ferris, Board of Foreign Missions of the Reformed Church in America

The two "who appeared to be Chinamen" that John Mason Ferris met in New York were twenty-two-year-old Yokoi Saheita (Ise Satarō, 1845–1875) and his seventeen-year-old brother Daihei (Numagawa Saburō, 1850–1871), who had both left Nagasaki in the fourth month of the second year of Keiō (1866). After reviewing the letter from Verbeck, the Executive Committee of the Board of Foreign Missions decided to find the pair a home in New Brunswick, where they could receive instruction at Rutgers Grammar School. The Yokoi brothers were joined by another of Verbeck's students, Yagi Yasohachi (Kusakabe Tarō, 1845–1870; hereafter Kusakabe) from the Fukui domain in August of the following year. Kusakabe registered as a first-year student at Rutgers College in September 1867 and chose to attend the newly established Scientific School. These first Japanese students were soon followed by the son of Katsu Kaishū (1823–1899), founder of the modern Japanese navy; two sons of Iwakura Tomomi (1825–1883), one of the most powerful figures in early Meiji Japan; and retainers of the Satsuma domain, which had led the overthrow of the Tokugawa regime.

How did these Japanese men get to New Brunswick? As discussed in chapter 1, an obvious answer to this question is their connections to Nagasaki and Guido F. Verbeck. All except for the Satsuma students had studied with Verbeck in Nagasaki; Verbeck introduced them to John Ferris, who then arranged for them to study in the United States. However, these early students also hailed from a vast network of reform-minded men who led Japan through a major transition in the late nineteenth century. The Yokoi brothers were the nephews of the famed Confucian philosopher Yokoi Shōnan (1809–1869), and Kusakabe was a samurai from Fukui, then one of the most influential domains under its former lord, Matsudaira Shungaku (1828–1890). Shungaku and Shōnan were key figures in Bakumatsu history who steered Japan through the Tokugawa's tumultuous final years. Although often dismissed as "losers" who stayed on the Tokugawa side, their networks extended beyond Edo and their home domains to encompass those who eventually led the Meiji Restoration. Shungaku developed close ties with the daimyo of other powerful domains while in Edo and Kyoto and was also known as one of the "four wise lords" of the Tokugawa period, along with Shimazu Nariakira (1809–1858) of Satsuma, Date Munenari (1818–1892) of Uwajima, and Yamauchi Yōdō (1827–1872) of Tosa, with whom he maintained close ties and shared some of his visions for a new Tokugawa regime. He and his retainers reached out to neighboring domains, Kyoto, Nagasaki, and as far as Satsuma, in search of solutions to the challenges faced by their domain and the shogunate. Meanwhile, Shōnan received visitors and students from all over Japan who sought inspiration at his school in Kumamoto. Through this network of scholars, he was discovered by Shungaku and served as the latter's political advisor in Edo and Fukui. His knowledge and curiosity extended beyond Confucianism, and he was well informed about the Western world through translated works and scholars of Western learning. This chapter focuses on the innovations of Shungaku and Shōnan during the Bakumatsu years, the connections through which they exercised their influence, and their vision of a new Japan that sent the first Japanese students to Rutgers.

Shungaku and Shōnan

Let us begin in Echizen Province, Fukui, the hometown of Kusakabe Tarō. Fukui was no ordinary domain; after Tokugawa Ieyasu (1543–1616) claimed victory in the Battle of Sekigahara in 1600 and founded his eponymous shogunate—the *bakufu*—he granted the domain to his second son, Hideyasu (1574–1607), and allowed him to restore his original surname, Matsudaira. Thereafter, Fukui held a uniquely privileged position as a *shinpan*, a collateral domain ruled by relatives of the Tokugawa. Although there were numerous occasions throughout the period in which a deceased daimyo or lord lacked an heir, Fukui maintained its status by inviting outsiders related to the Tokugawa to rule. For instance, when its tenth lord, Munenori, died with no heir, the Echizen Matsudaira house adopted Hitotsubashi Shigemasa, the grandson of the eighth shogun, Yoshimune (1684–1751), who was succeeded by his brother Shigetomi. After three generations, the daimyo again died young and heirless, and he was succeeded by Narisawa, the son of the eleventh shogun, Ienari (1773–1841). When Narisawa died at the age of nineteen in 1838, his heir was selected from the Tayasu family, one of the Tokugawa collateral families in Edo.[2]

Matsudaira Shungaku (Yoshinaga), born in Edo as a son of Tayasu Naritada, was ordered by shogun Tokugawa Ieyoshi (1792–1853) to succeed Narisawa as the sixteenth lord of Fukui at age ten.[3] In this capacity, he implemented radical military and educational reforms in the 1850s and 1860s. The most pressing issue he faced was self-defense against the developing threat from the Western powers, which led him to start training his men in Western warfare even before U.S. commodore Matthew C. Perry's 1853 arrival in Japan.[4] Shungaku also emphasized education and heightening his retainers' morals to build a strong and united political system, and he founded the Meidōkan in 1855 as the domain school.[5] He further carried out drastic economic reforms by advocating the enrichment of domanial finances through interdomain and foreign trade.[6]

Shungaku became not only Fukui's most influential daimyo but also a dominant figure in national politics throughout the Bakumatsu period.[7] The Tokugawa faced a raft of crises in the mid-to-late 1850s: Shogun Iesada was frail and

FIGURE 2.1. Portrait of Matsudaira Shungaku. (Credit: Fukui City History Museum.)

heirless; the *bakufu*'s response to Perry in 1854 sharply divided those who called for expelling the Western barbarians (*jōi*) and those who believed the country had to open up to the same (*kaikoku*); and Japan urgently needed a new political structure that could withstand the rapid pace of domestic and global changes. Shungaku supported Hitotsubashi Yoshinobu (1837–1913), later the fifteenth and the last Tokugawa shogun. He also became a leading advocate of the *kōbu gattai* policy that sought to unite the imperial court and the shogunate, urging a shift from an authoritarian regime run by hereditary vassals to a government that made decisions through a council of top daimyo and talented officials.[8] He further pressed the *bakufu* and the court to open the country and build a strong navy.[9] During the so-called Ansei Purge, Shungaku was forced to resign and placed under house arrest in 1858 by Chief Councilor Ii Naosuke, but he returned after Ii's assassination in 1860 and became chief of political affairs (Seiji Sōsaishoku) in 1862.[10] With Yoshinobu, who was named the guardian of the fourteenth shogun Iemochi (1846–1866), he carried out reforms to rebuild the shogunate in the face of other powerful daimyo and *jōi* activists who sought to expel foreigners.[11]

The mastermind behind Fukui's local and national reform efforts was Yokoi Shōnan, the uncle and guardian of the Yokoi brothers who arrived in New Brunswick in 1866. Shōnan, also known as Heishirō Tokiari, was born in Kumamoto as the second son of a middle-rank samurai of the Higo domain. He had demonstrated academic excellence since childhood and was sent to Edo to study in 1839, but he was forced to return the following year due to a drunken quarrel with a samurai of another domain. Around 1844, he formed a reformist group known as the Jitsugakutō (Practical Studies Party), which criticized the domanial government for exploiting its people for profit and advocated for radical reform. Jitsugakutō had close to fifty members, including Fukui's chief retainer, Nagaoka Kenmotsu, and other local elites.[12]

The connection between Shōnan and Fukui can be traced back to 1849, when Shungaku sent his page, Mitsudera Sansaku, to the Kamigata region in search of a "pure scholar" of neo-Confucianism.[13] Through a connection he made in Kyoto, Mitsudera met a Higo retainer who took him to Kumamoto and introduced him to Shōnan. Impressed by Shōnan's intellect, Mitsudera spent two weeks at Shōnan's academy studying under him. Later, when Shōnan traveled to Kyoto in 1851, he visited Fukui to meet with Mitsudera's teacher at Meidōkan, Yoshida Tōkō. He spent fifteen days in Fukui and is said to have impressed many students, including the future local reformers Murata Misaburō (Ujihisa, 1821–1899) and Mitsuoka Hachirō (later Yuri Kimimasa, 1829–1912).[14] Yoshida Tōkō resigned from teaching in the second month of 1857 (Ansei 4), and in the third month of the same year, Shungaku dispatched Murata to Kumamoto with a personal request for Shōnan to teach at Meidōkan.[15]

But Shōnan struggled in deciding whether to leave his home and family. After his older brother Tokiaki's death in 1854, he had succeeded the Yokoi family and served as the guardian for Tokiaki's two sons, Saheita and Daihei, aged ten and six. He had also remarried the following year after losing his newborn son and his first wife.[16] Jitsugakutō had declined, and his family had moved to the suburbs to lead a quiet and frugal life. Nevertheless, he ultimately accepted Shungaku's invitation and was offered the title of *hinshi* (guest teacher) with a generous stipend.[17] After negotiations between the Fukui and Higo domains, Shōnan finally arrived in Fukui a year later (in 1858). Kusakabe Tarō, who had entered Meidōkan at thirteen, would have been there just as Shōnan took up his post. This marked the beginning of Shōnan's decade-long service as a teacher and advisor to Fukui's reformers and Shungaku himself.[18]

Both Shungaku and Shōnan had supported the anti-foreign policy of *jōi* proponents at the time of Perry's arrival in 1853. Shungaku harshly criticized the *bakufu*'s weak diplomacy, demanding that the shogun reject the request of the United States and prepare to fight under a strong commander-in-chief. To Shungaku and his comrades, this chief would be Tokugawa Nariaki (1800–1860) of Mito, a leading figure in the *jōi* movement. Shungaku revered Nariaki as an ideal leader capable of carrying out urgent reforms within the *bakufu*.[19] He shared this sentiment with Shimazu Nariakira and Date Munenari, which led to his support of Yoshinobu, Nariaki's seventh son, as the shogunal heir.[20] However, Shungaku's (and by extension Fukui's) attitude toward the foreign powers shifted by 1857, when Townsend Harris insisted that Japan sign the Treaty of Amity and Commerce. Fukui official Hashimoto Sanai (1834–1859) submitted a proposal in response to the shogun's inquiry regarding the treaty, which advised Japan to open its doors to the United States and other nations on principle and aspire to wealth through trade. Sanai also advocated the renewal of domestic politics by appointing an "honorable gentleman of wisdom" (suggestive of Yoshinobu) as the shogun's successor, along with other talented men.[21] Sanai, however, was prosecuted and executed in 1859 by Ii Naosuke during the Ansei Purge.

Shōnan's vision clearly aligned with Hashimoto's and Fukui's by early 1857, when Shungaku invited him to Fukui. He, too, had shifted from being a *jōi* advocate to a supporter of opening Japan, or perhaps he had overcome the Sinocentric worldview that saw foreigners, especially Westerners, as barbaric.[22] Like Hashimoto and many innovative thinkers of his time, Shōnan was influenced by *Haiguo tuzhi* (Illustrated treatise on the Maritime Kingdoms), a nineteenth-century Chinese gazetteer compiled by Wei Yuan based on initial translations ordered by Lin Zexu, the special imperial commissioner, as a response to the First Opium War (1839–1842). In addition to maps and detailed descriptions of countries around the world, this work contained abridged translations of British geographer Hugh Murray's three-volume *An Encyclopedia of Complete Description of the Earth, Physical and Political* (1834) and Swiss lawyer Emer de Vattel's *The Law of Nations* (1758).[23] Shōnan also drew inspiration from America's "three major policies" outlined in *Haiguo tuzhi*, as seen in *Kokuze sanron* (Three Theories on National Policy), a record of lectures that Shōnan gave in Fukui in 1860:

> In America three major policies have been set up from Washington's presidency on: First, to stop wars in accordance with divine intentions, because nothing is worse than violence and killing among nations; second, to broaden enlightened government by learning from all the countries of the world; and third, to work with complete devotion for the peace and welfare of the people by entrusting the power of the president of the whole country to the wisest instead of transmitting it to the son of the president and by abolishing the code in the relationship between ruler and minister. All methods of administrative laws and practices and all men who are known as good and wise through the world are put into the country's service and a very beneficial administration—one not completely in the interest of the rulers—is developed.[24]

FIGURE 2.2. Portrait of Yokoi Shōnan by Harada Naojirō, ca. 1891. (Credit: Ota City Katsu Kaishū Memorial Museum.)

Shōnan saw in America an ideal government in three aspects: It took mutual learning and enlightened government, not violence and war, as the nature of nation-to-nation relationships; it chose its top ruler not for his blood but for his wisdom; and it determined its laws and practices for the public good rather than its rulers' interest. He described England and other countries similarly. Crucially, he saw in these Western polities the essence of the "three ancient periods of sage rule in China," which he, as a Confucian scholar, envisioned as an ideal state:

> In England the government is based entirely on the popular will, and all government actions—large and small—are always debated by the people. The most beneficial action is decided upon, and an unpopular program is not forced upon the people. War or peace is decided thusly. . . . Furthermore, all countries, including Russia, have established schools and military academies, hospitals, orphanages, and schools for the deaf and dumb. The governments are

> entirely based on moral principles, and they work hard for the benefit of the people, virtually as in the three ancient periods of sage-rule in China.[25]

Such views led Shōnan to conclude that Japan should open its doors, and he further advocated for completely reforming the Tokugawa shogunate into a meritocratic government run by able men who worked for the good of the people. Hence, he made *kaikoku*, or opening the country, and *kōkyō*, or public good, the fundamental principles of his thought and reforms.[26]

The Bunkyū Reform of 1862

In the seventh month of Bunkyū 2 (1862), Shungaku was appointed to the newly created post of chief of political affairs and Yoshinobu became the shogun's guardian (*kōkenshoku*), as mentioned above. Shungaku had been deposed and confined along with Yoshinobu during the Ansei Purge; after Ii's assassination, in the second month of 1862, the shogunate, under pressure from Satsuma, released both men and returned them to political life. At this time, Shungaku invited Shōnan to his residence in Edo to seek his advice, thereafter making the latter one of his key advisors. This inaugurated a new, brief era of the *bakufu* under Shungaku's leadership.[27]

The shogunal administration under Shungaku and Yoshinobu is often viewed as a forcible creation of Satsuma and the court that achieved little due to opposition within its ranks. However, the role this regime played in central government reforms cannot be overestimated; Shungaku's policies had solid grounds and tacit supporters within the shogunate. The changes that Shungaku, Shōnan, and the reformist leaders of Echizen promoted during this period had a clear vision and roadmap, and in this sense, the shogunate during this period could justifiably be considered the Matsudaira Shungaku administration.[28] The Bunkyū Reform of 1862, as outlined by Yokoi Shōnan, included seven major points:

1. The shogun must first and foremost visit the emperor in Kyoto and apologize.
2. The *bakufu* should abolish the *sankin kōtai* system[29] and establish a new system where each daimyo would have shorter sojourns in Edo and opportunities to opine on national political affairs.
3. The wives and children of daimyo held in Edo should be returned to their home domains.
4. The *bakufu* should abolish the distinction between *tozama* ("outside") and *fudai* (hereditary Tokugawa vassals) daimyo[30] and open administrative offices to men of talent.
5. The *bakufu* should open avenues of communication and conduct fair government together with the daimyo.

6. The *bakufu* should create a navy and strengthen the military.
7. Trade with foreign countries should be conducted under *bakufu* control.[31]

The first point urged the shogun to express reverence to the emperor by reviving a tradition that had ceased since the third shogun Iemitsu; doing so would demonstrate the shift from a "private" government of the Tokugawa family to a "public" government under the emperor. This illustrated the idea of *kōkyō* as government for the public good, which as mentioned above was central to Shōnan's political philosophy.[32] The second and third points reflected Shōnan's critique, advocated by Shungaku, of the *sankin kōtai* system. In *Kokuze sanron*, Shōnan harshly criticizes the Tokugawa for having weakened the domains' economic and military potential by imposing *sankin kōtai* and other duties on them without considering the financial drain this imposed on their people. Abolishing *sankin kōtai* sought to lessen the psychological and financial burden on individual domains. It was also an attempt to reform the authoritarianism of *bakufu* politics by replacing rituals of subjugation with more active and constructive ways for daimyo to participate in national politics.[33]

Points four and five advocated that daimyo and ordinary men of talent participate in national politics.[34] As early as 1857, Shungaku had suggested placing Satsuma, Higo, Uwajima, and other *tozama* daimyo along with the collateral *shinpan* houses (including Fukui) above the chief senior counselor to form a system like Toyotomi Hideyoshi's Council of Five Elders.[35] By giving authority to the "five elders" who belonged to the *tozama* and Tokugawa branches, he sought to break the framework of the Tokugawa system controlled by the chief senior counselor, a position traditionally monopolized by the *fudai* houses. He also wrote an essay around this time in which he proposed to establish an assembly that consisted of an upper house (*harurimon*, or parliament) and a lower house (*konmonsu*, or commons) modeled after the British Parliament. The former would comprise shogunate vassals and daimyo; the latter, noted samurai from various clans. Alternatively, he suggested that the upper house could be made up of lords and samurai from various clans, and the lower house could consist of peasants, townspeople, or commoners. "Public opinion" would be discussed in the assembly, which would serve as the supreme decision-making organ of the national government that even the emperor or the shogun could not sway. Here Shungaku's attitude toward adopting the Western parliamentary system is clear. He undoubtedly had access to the latest overseas information and held a fairly advanced understanding of foreign countries through being surrounded by open-minded men such as Hashimoto Sanai and Shōnan.

Point six stressed the importance of naval defense. Coastal security against the Western powers was Japan's most pressing issue at the time. Within his own domain, Shungaku had begun training his men in Western artillery and building Western cannons and batteries by the mid-1850s.[36] However, Fukui's military reform had centered on the army, and Shōnan broke through this isolationist vision to advocate for a strong navy. In *Kokuze sanron*, he discusses the importance of building a navy as the key to a "strong military" (*kyōhei*).[37] The Bunkyū proposal suggested that the *bakufu* and daimyo should collaborate as equals by contributing capital and human resources to create a powerful national navy.[38]

Lastly, point seven advocated foreign trade under government control. This reflected economic reforms carried out earlier in Fukui under the leadership of Mitsuoka Hachirō and Sasaki Gonroku (1830–1916). The domain had established a "commodities office" (*sanbutsu kaisho*) that purchased local products such as raw silk, which they distributed to agencies in Yokohama and Nagasaki and sold them externally, including to foreign traders.[39] By having the government handle the transactions, the prices of goods could be set to benefit the farmers rather than the merchants. The "rich country policy," in the minds of Shungaku and Shōnan, would first and foremost serve the people and not domanial ruling elites or the Tokugawa.

In sum, Shōnan and Shungaku envisioned a new *bakufu* that would respect the imperial court, rectify its authoritarian attitude, and collaborate with the daimyo to build a wealthy nation and strong military (*fukoku kyōhei*).[40] Reforms were swiftly carried out during the same year: the *sankin kōtai* system was relaxed; the daimyo's residence period in Edo was shortened to one hundred days every three years, and their wives and children were allowed to return to their domains. The shogun's visit to Kyoto was scheduled in the second month of the following year. A dress code reform was issued that abolished elaborate ceremonial clothing. The *bakufu* also began planning to create a navy and appointed Katsu Kaishū as the naval commissioner (*gunkan bugyō*). The following year, in 1864, Kaishū opened the Naval Operation Training School in Kobe, which accepted students from all domains. Soon after, Shōnan entrusted Kaishū with his nephews, Saheita and Daihei, who joined the Naval School as the latter's retainers.[41]

However, the political situation in successive years stymied Shungaku and his fellow reformers. The *bakufu* then confronted a strong *jōi* movement, particularly in Kyoto. Led by an alliance of the Tosa and Chōshū domains, this faction gained the court's support and pressed to "expel the barbarians" immediately. Meanwhile, the *bakufu* had to appease Britain over the Namamugi Incident of 1862 in which Satsuma vassals had killed a British merchant. Ultimately, the shogunate was forced to accept the *jōi* policy the emperor had adopted. Shungaku, in disappointment, resigned as chief of political affairs and returned to Fukui in 1863.[42]

Fukui's Relationship with Satsuma

It is worth noting that Shungaku, until the final moment of the Tokugawa regime, had worked closely with the powerful *tozama* domains, especially with the Shimazu of Satsuma. Their intimate relationship can be seen in the attempted joint coup of 1863. After Shungaku's resignation and return to Fukui, his reformist retainers proposed to send an army of four thousand to Kyoto to convince the court to hold a meeting of the top daimyo to issue an open-door national policy, and they sent envoys to the neighboring Obama and Kaga domains to seek cooperation. Furthermore, a mission of twenty-nine members from Fukui, including Mitsuoka Hachirō, left for Kyushu to meet with members of the Jitsugakutō in Higo; Mitsuoka also went to Satsuma, and both domains agreed to send troops to Kyoto. Shimazu Hisamitsu (1817–1887), the late Shimazu Nariakira's younger half-brother, even sent a letter to Shungaku to confirm his support. At this point, Fukui, Satsuma, and Higo, supported by Shōnan and the Jitsugakutō, had established an allied plot to open the country: They would suppress Kyoto by force and secure a meeting place for the daimyo council to overturn current national policy. However, for Fukui, a Tokugawa collateral domain, this would have been an extreme betrayal of the shogunate. On the cusp of an armed confrontation with the fierce *jōi* faction, Shungaku reversed his position, and the interdomain plan to send soldiers to Kyoto was abruptly abandoned. Its leaders, including Mitsuoka, were punished, and Shōnan, who was believed to have headed the scheme, was sent back to Kumamoto. Ironically, in the eighth month of the same year, Satsuma and Aizu teamed up to expel the Chōshū *jōi* forces from Kyoto.[43]

Fukui and Satsuma also joined hands through a trade agreement as late as 1865. Both domains had been sending envoys to each other to exchange goods as well as information regarding the political and military situation surrounding Chōshū, where a civil war in 1865 had brought anti-*bakufu* forces to power in that domain. Fukui is even known to have requested firearms through Satsuma in 1866.[44] Interestingly, it was just around this time that Kusakabe Tarō, now twenty-one, was sent to Nagasaki to study with Verbeck at the Saibikan. A report that Kusakabe sent to Shungaku in the seventh month of Keiō 2 (1866) reveals that he was in Nagasaki not only to study but also to obtain information on foreign countries and other domains. He mentions the activities of Sir Harry Parkes, the British minister to Japan, Verbeck's comments that Satsuma kept in contact with the French minister, and the close alliance between Chōshū and Satsuma; when Chōshū ships entered Nagasaki, they put up the Satsuma flag. Kusakabe also maintained close communication with Godai Tomoatsu of Satsuma, who informed him of Satsuma's situation and the *bakufu*'s activities abroad.[45] Ties between Fukui and Satsuma, however, unwound amid the turmoil of the Tokugawa's final years.

Fukui's and Satsuma's visions of a new Japan overlapped in certain ways. As chief of political affairs, Shungaku had worked closely with Shimazu Hisamitsu and other powerful daimyo to have Yoshinobu hold council meetings with the major daimyo to discuss and decide core matters of national policy, in particular the country's opening. He saw doing so as a means of allowing capable, powerful daimyo to lead in decision-making, and the councils convened in 1863 and 1867 aligned with this vision. However, their members never agreed on who had the ultimate say: the shogun, the emperor, or the council itself.

Shungaku, as earlier mentioned, envisioned a council based on the British Parliament in which policies were made by participating daimyo and the emperor entrusted the shogun with the authority to finalize decisions.[46] Satsuma, on the other hand, envisioned a nation modeled after the German Confederation, where leading domains retained their sovereignty while Japan engaged outsiders as a nation united around the imperial court, thereby allowing each clan to individually exercise diplomatic power and conclude treaties with foreign countries. The court-centered Council of Lords would form the core of the national administrative structure in emergencies, although each domain would have autonomy in the everyday governance of its own affairs.[47]

This political line, by 1866, was acceptable from Shungaku's point of view, considering the coordination of nationwide issues by the council of daimyo and the peaceful transition of power to the imperial court.[48] After all, it aligned with his proposal to shift the Tokugawa's private rule to collaborative governance. However, this shift that Shungaku and Shōnan envisioned foundered once Yoshinobu succeeded as shogun in 1866. Yoshinobu eagerly sought to restore Tokugawa authoritarianism, which alienated the powerful daimyo, most notably Shimazu Hisamitsu.[49] Satsuma formed an alliance with Chōshū, which abandoned the short-term exclusion of the barbarians and chose to support the emperor as the legitimate ruler of Japan and ultimately to depose the shogun.[50] Meanwhile, Shungaku returned to Kyoto in an effort to convince the shogunate to seek a peaceful resolution with these two domains. However, disillusioned by Yoshinobu, he left Kyoto for Fukui in the eighth month of Keiō 3 (1867); this was only two months before Yamauchi Yōdō of Tosa proposed the *Taisei Hōkan*—the restoration of imperial rule.[51]

Shungaku's position during the Bakumatsu years represented a third alternative for Japan's future: neither sustaining nor overthrowing the Tokugawa regime but reshaping it as a modern institution.[52] Both Shungaku and Shōnan envisioned a new Japan that moved away from an authoritarian government under the Tokugawa and its hereditary retainers to a "public" rule incorporating the imperial court, the powerful daimyo, and men of talent. They also saw the merit of opening the country to the West while boosting its naval defenses. Again, it is important that Shungaku worked closely with Satsuma and other powerful domains from within the Tokugawa to bring it to a peaceful end. In the new Meiji government, he was appointed chief executive of internal affairs, among other cabinet-equivalent posts, and Shōnan was given the title of *san'yo*, or councilor.[53] However, Shōnan was assassinated in 1869 by a radical activist who suspected him of being a Christian, and Shungaku resigned from politics in 1870. After his resignation, he invited William E. Griffis (1843–1928), a Rutgers alumnus, to teach in Fukui.

The First Japanese Students in New Brunswick

The first Japanese students who arrived in New Brunswick left Japan amid the political turmoil outlined above. Yokoi Saheita and Daihei were sent from Nagasaki to New Brunswick in the fourth month of Keiō 2 (1866), while Kusakabe Tarō left from Fukui in 1867, followed later in the same year by Katsu Koroku and his two guardians, Takaki Saburō (1841–1909) and Tomita Tetsunosuke (1835–1916).[54] All these students were linked to the network that had enacted the Bunkyū Reform under Shungaku's leadership, and it is no coincidence that they chose the United States as their destination, given Shōnan's high regard for that nation. That all except Kusakabe had trained with Katsu Kaishū may also have impacted their choice; Kaishū had been a member of the 1860 *bakufu* mission to the United States and seen the country with his own eyes.

Needless to say, their main goal was to gain proficiency in naval management, including building seafaring vessels that matched those of the West. As discussed earlier, Shungaku and Shōnan's prioritization of building a strong navy had led Katsu Kaishū to open the Kobe Naval Training Center. In Shōnan's words, Japan urgently needed knowledge of Western naval methods: "Today we cannot refuse contacts with the various overseas countries which have greatly developed their navigation. In the defense of an island country like ours a navy is of prime importance in our militarization. In Japan up to the present nothing had even been heard of concerning regulations for a navy. Furthermore, nothing had been observed of Western naval methods, so how could we know about their application? Navigation has progressed so much in the world today that we must start the discussion on the importance of a navy."[55]

Saheita and Daihei were well prepared for this endeavor. Even while attending to his heavy political duties, traveling between Kumamoto and Fukui and to Edo, Shōnan had made sure that his two nephews were trained to become proper samurai. The letters he sent to Saheita and Daihei instructed them to take proper care of their swords, guns, armors, and books, to continue their physical training, and to study the Chinese classics with his disciples.[56] Shōnan also provided them with the opportunities to attain a vision that extended beyond one's domain and gain an interest in national politics. For instance, when he was summoned to Edo, Daihei followed him and was permitted to study English at the shogunal Institute for the Investigation of Western Books.[57] The brothers also joined Shōnan in Fukui in 1863, stayed there for several months, and then returned to Kumamoto via Nagasaki on the first Western-style sail ship that the Fukui domain had built. Upon his return to Kumamoto, Saheita served as a liaison between Shōnan, who was in Fukui, and his disciples of the Practical Learning School, for the planning of sending joint troops to Kyoto with the Satsuma domain.[58] When Saheita was twenty and Daihei was sixteen, they joined the newly opened Kobe Naval Training Center led by Katsu Kaishū.[59] Through these experiences, the brothers

FIGURE 2.3. Kusakabe Tarō (*right*) with the Yokoi brothers, Saheita and Daihei (*seated*). (Credit: William Elliot Griffis Collection, Rutgers University Libraries.)

developed an understanding of Western military power and the need for a strong navy, and a sense of mission for Japan as a nation.

By the sixth month of 1865, the Yokoi brothers had moved to Nagasaki and were studying at the school of Western learning with Guido F. Verbeck. Dissatisfied with the *bakufu*-supervised curriculum there, they pleaded with Shōnan to be sent to study in the West. They arrived via Java and the Cape of Good Hope to New York through funds gathered from Shōnan's disciples, with neither having permission from the *bakufu* nor support from their own domain.[60] Saheita's letter addressed to Shōnan's disciples, dated the twenty-seventh day of the fourth month, reveals their strong determination upon leaving for the United States. He writes, "Even in the unlikely event that our life should prove to be a misfortune, we will make sure that one of us will return home to live out his life and to be of some help in the revitalization of our country."[61]

Kusakabe Tarō joined them a year later,[62] arriving in New York on August 12, 1867. He is listed as a first-year student at Rutgers College Scientific School in the fall semester for that year. While it is probable that Shōnan backed his nephews' sojourn in New Brunswick due to his belief in Japan's need for a strong navy, Kusakabe's studies in the United States should be seen within the larger context of Fukui's policies of the time. He came as an official *ryūgakusei* funded by the domain and carried a three-year passport issued by the *bakufu*.[63] Fukui had embarked on a full-scale military reform in the winter of 1867, upon Shungaku's return after his disappointment with Yoshinobu. In addition to its existing military, the domain established two gun corps under the direct control of its daimyo and adopted English-style training for its forces. Furthermore, it sent others besides Kusakabe abroad. At about the same time, Fukui had submitted a formal request to the *bakufu* to send Sasaki Gonroku,[64] who held the key position of the domain's "manufacturing magistrate," to the United States. Accompanied by Yanagimoto Naotarō (1848–1913) as his interpreter, Sasaki left Yokohama in 1867 with the assistance of Eugene Van Reed (1835–1873), a former clerk at the U.S. consulate and a merchant in Yokohama.[65] On their arrival, they contacted Secretary of War Ulysses S. Grant in Washington, DC, to gather data on the military as an institution. They also purchased rifles, looms, and other weaponry. In the meantime, another retainer, Koma Rinnosuke (1848–1911), joined a group of Chōshū students to study abroad. They, with Satsuma's assistance, had departed for England in 1868. Koma is known to have studied mining science at University College London and later joined the Iwakura Mission. A letter he wrote to two Chōshū colleagues and one from Satsuma in New Brunswick shows that he maintained contact with Kusakabe while in England. This underscores how Shungaku dispatched Kusakabe to boost efforts to strengthen Fukui's, and ultimately Japan's, military.[66]

These first Japanese students abroad undoubtedly sought to learn how to build a wealthy nation and strong military as their main purpose for studying in the United States. However, the spirit in which they traveled is equally crucial. A poem that Shōnan sent to his nephews upon their departure reminded them of the ultimate importance of personal righteousness and virtue, and that this journey should also forge a path toward their becoming true gentlemen:

> Reveal the Way of Yao, Shun, and Confucius,
> Exhaust the methods of Western machines.
> Why cease [after attaining] a wealthy nation?
> Why cease [after achieving] a strong military?

What you must do is to lay out the great righteousness over the four seas.
Do not blame those who might go against your heart;
If you blame others, you will lose your virtue.
When you have a goal to achieve, do not trust your heart;
Trusting your heart to be correct may lead to failure.
[Do not forget that] the path of a true gentleman is in moral training.[67]

Shōnan warned his nephews not to be carried away or indulge in the skills of Western technology but to demonstrate the ideal to the world in accordance with Confucian morals. This required the constant cultivation of one's virtues, and Shōnan saw cultivating the spirit as equally important. To him, the way of the samurai was essential to building a nation, and he asserted that "there is no military reform which exceeds the warrior's way (*bushidō*), which is to cultivate that spirit in actual practice."[68] Shōnan believed the Way to be universal, and as earlier mentioned, he saw in the United States an ideal government based on moral principles, which resembled the three periods of sage rule in ancient China, that worked to benefit its people.[69] His vision expressed in the poem he sent to his nephews extended beyond national borders.

The Yokoi brothers and Kusakabe shared the ambition to attain basic knowledge in New Brunswick before entering the U.S. Naval Academy in Annapolis, Maryland, to study related technology, including warship construction. However, things did not go as planned.[70] Daihei, the younger brother, became ill and returned to Japan in July 1869, where he contributed to the founding of a school for Western learning in Kumamoto; however, he died in 1871 before seeing its opening in that same year. Kusakabe also died of illness in New Brunswick in April 1870 at twenty-six, two months before his graduation from college. Saheita, the older brother, was the first Japanese, along with Matsumura Junzō of Satsuma, to be admitted to the Naval Academy by special arrangement of the U.S. Congress.[71] He initially tried to carry out his original aim but headed home in 1871, later returning to the United States but never to the academy.

Saheita's letter to John Ferris is reproduced below. Sent from West Newton, Massachusetts, and dated December 4, 1872, it reflects his deep distress at having lost his brother, his uncle (after Shōnan's assassination in 1869), and his friend Kusakabe:

My dear Sir:
I am also thankful for your kind advice. As you say, I do not wish to discontinue my profession of the naval service, but I have deeply considered about the position which is best for me and our country. I wish to go back to the Naval Academy, but I must study English more at another place. I think to talk and to write the English with facility is more important than any other studies. One thing is that, if I were younger, of course, I would go back to the Naval Academy and study the naval profession, because at first we as a nation wish to

> study about the Navy. It is very important for our country. We got the permission, six of us, to enter the Naval Academy at Annapolis from your government under your kind assistance, and after that we got the appointment from our government. In our first plan with regard to these matters, Kusakabe, myself and my brother entered the school, but both of them could not proceed their design, and they are both dead. I think that [it] is impossible to study the military service when as old as I am. Therefore, my opinion is that I will study English well and I must know about the military system and principle of your government, and I must return to our country as soon as possible and shall help our government, because they do not know any of the laws of the Navy and Army. Such matters are quite a new thing for our people.[72]

Saheita returned to Japan in 1874 and was appointed lesser secretary of the Chamber of Elders in June 1875. However, he, too, died young in October of the same year, aged thirty.

Conclusion

With regard to the early formation of the Rutgers-Japan network, it is important to note that these first students were not isolated individuals but instead belonged to a larger network formed during the Bakumatsu and Meiji periods. Amid major political turmoil, the Yokoi brothers and Kusakabe Tarō were sent to the United States to realize Shungaku and Shōnan's vision of a new Japan. In 1868, just as Yoshinobu, the last shogun, followed the advice of Shungaku and others and returned his power to the emperor amid pressure from the Satsuma–Chōshū alliance, three students from Satsuma joined the Yokoi brothers and Kusakabe in New Brunswick. These young men—Hatakeyama Yoshinari (1842–1876), Matsumura Junzō (1842–1919), and Yoshida Kiyonari (1845–1891)—were among the first fifteen to be sent by the Satsuma domain to England to study at University College London in 1865, after which they joined Thomas Harris's colony in Brocton, New York, and eventually left to study at Rutgers College.[73] Matsumura transferred to Annapolis at the end of 1869 with Saheita and was later joined by Katsu Koroku, who had arrived in New Brunswick the year before. Yoshida moved to Massachusetts in 1869 to attend Wilbraham Academy (now Wilbraham & Monson Academy), studied banking, and joined the Finance Ministry upon returning to Japan in 1870. He returned to the United States in 1872 with the Iwakura Mission. Hatakeyama left Rutgers in 1871 upon receiving a government order to return to Japan; he, too, later returned to Washington, DC, to join the Iwakura Mission.[74] The bustling atmosphere of New Brunswick during their years at the college can be seen in a part of a letter sent by Hatakeyama to the Satsuma domain office in May 1869: "As of now, the son of Katsu (Katsu Koroku), the Echizen student Yagi Tarō (Kusakabe Tarō), the Higo students (the Yokoi brothers), are here, and recently Katsu's disciples Takaki

(Saburō) and Tomita (Tetsunosuke) have also re-entered this town. We are all doing very well and studying. I also hope that the Yokoi brothers will be able to obtain licenses to enter the Navy School as soon as possible."[75]

Yokoi Shōnan's two nephews, Matsudaira Shungaku's retainer, and three Satsuma samurai, along with Katsu Kaishū's son and disciples, were studying and interacting with one another in New Brunswick. In the faraway foreign land of America, the network built by Bakumatsu-era reformers expanded overseas and facilitated Japan's stepping out onto the global stage as a new, modern nation.

Notes

This chapter is based on consultation with and works by Takagi Fuji, in particular *Bakumatsu ishin no kosei 2: Yokoi Shōnan to Matsudaira Shungaku* (Tokyo: Yoshikawa Kōbunkan, 2005) and *Bakumatsu ishinki no Beikoku ryūgaku: Yokoi Saheita no kaigun shūgaku* (Tokyo: Keio University Press, 2015).

1 Excerpted from Ferris's letter to Griffis in 1905; emphasis added. Printed in John M. Ferris, "How the Japanese Came to New Brunswick," *The Japanese Student* 1 (October 1916): 57; reprinted from William Elliot Griffis, *Rutgers Graduates in Japan* (New Brunswick, NJ: Rutgers College, 1916).
2 On the history of Fukui in English, see Kanai Madoka, "Fukui, Domain of a Tokugawa Collateral Daimyō: Its Tradition and Transition," in *The Modernizers: Overseas Students, Foreign Employees, and Meiji Japan*, ed. Ardath W. Burks (Boulder, CO: Westview Press, 1985), 33–68.
3 Shungaku's child name was Kinnojō, and he was given the name Yoshinaga in 1838 on succeeding to the Fukui domain at age eleven. He took the name Shungaku and used this more frequently after 1858; since this chapter focuses on the period after 1858, it refers to him as Shungaku.
4 Takagi, *Yokoi Shōnan to Matsudaira Shungaku*, 27–29.
5 Takagi, 29–33.
6 Takagi, 63–85.
7 Takagi, 18–22.
8 Takagi, 47–54.
9 Takagi, 49–51.
10 Takagi, 55–57.
11 Takagi, 85–94.
12 Takagi, 9–10, 33–47; Takagi, *Bakumatsu ishinki no Beikoku ryūgaku*, 17–19.
13 Takagi, *Yokoi Shōnan to Matsudaira Shungaku*, 6–10.
14 Takagi, 13–16.
15 Takagi, 38–40.
16 Takagi, 38–39. His second wife's sister was married to Tokutomi Ikkei (Sohō's father).
17 His stipend was "50-*nin buchi*" (meaning enough to feed fifty people for a year).
18 Takagi, *Yokoi Shōnan to Matsudaira Shungaku*, 38–45.
19 Takagi, 23–29.
20 Takagi, 21–22.
21 Takagi, 49–51.

22 Takagi, 25–26.

23 Takagi, 26. On the role of *Haiguo tuzhi* in spreading knowledge about foreign nations, see Agawa Shūzō, "*Kaikoku zushi* to Yoshida Shōin: Bakumatsu ni okeru seiyō jijō no juyō ni tsuite," *Chūgoku bunka: kenkyū to kyōiku* 70 (2012): 16–30; and Minamoto Ryōen, "Bakumatsu/Ishinki ni okeru *Kaikoku zushi* no juyō: Sakuma Shōzan o chūshin to shite," *Nihon kenkyū* 9 (1993): 13–25. On *Haiguo tuzhi* in English, see Jane K. Leonard, "Images of Nan-Yang: The Illustrated Treatise on the Sea Kingdoms," in *Wei Yuan and China's Rediscovery of the Maritime World* (Cambridge, MA: Harvard University Asia Center Publications Program, 1984), 93–120; and Osamu Oba, "The Opium War and the *Haiguo tuzhi*," in *Books and Boats*, trans. Joshua Fogel (Portland, ME: Merwin Asia, 2012), 171–184.

24 Yokoi Shōnan and Hanatachi Saburō, *Kokuze sanron* (Tokyo: Kōdansha, 1986), 57–58. Translation based on D. Y. Miyauchi in Yokoi Shōnan and D. Y. Miyauchi, "Kokuze Sanron: The Three Major Problems of State Policy," *Monumenta Nipponica* 23, no. 1/2 (1968): 168–169.

25 Yokoi and Hanatachi, *Kokuze sanron*, 58; Yokoi and Miyauchi, "Kokuze Sanron," 169.

26 On Shōnan's philosophy and *kōkyō*, see Karube Tadashi, "The Confucian Concept of 'Public' and the Adoption of Deliberative Assembly in Japan: Writings of Yokoi Shōnan," *Sungkyun Journal of East Asian Studies* 3, no. 1 (2003): 131–150.

27 Takagi, *Yokoi Shōnan to Matsudaira Shungaku*, 85–86.

28 Takagi, 94. On Shungaku and Shōnan's roles from 1862 to 1863, see Takagi, "Bakumatsu Bunkyū-ki no chūō seikyoku to Echizen-han," *Kindai Nihon kenkyū* 14 (1997): 31–77.

29 The *sankin kōtai*, or the "alternate attendance" system, was a policy set by the Tokugawa shogunate that required daimyo to alternate living for a year in their domain and in Edo. They were also required to leave their principal wife and heir in Edo as "hostages." Its purpose was to maintain political control over the daimyo; it also became a huge financial burden for the daimyo to maintain several residences in Edo and in their domains and to pay for the costly journey to and from Edo.

30 The daimyo during the Tokugawa period were categorized into *shinpan* (collateral; relatives of Tokugawa), *fudai* (hereditary vassals of the Tokugawa from before the Battle of Sekigahara in 1600), and *tozama* (outside; those who became vassals of the Tokugawa only after the decisive Battle of Sekigahara).

31 Takagi, *Yokoi Shōnan to Matsudaira Shungaku*, 89–90; Takagi, *Bakumatsu ishinki no Beikoku ryūgaku*, 28.

32 Takagi, *Yokoi Shōnan to Matsudaira Shungaku*, 90.

33 Takagi, 75–76, 90–92.

34 Takagi, 90.

35 Takagi, 51–53.

36 Takagi, 6.

37 Yokoi and Miyauchi, "Kokuze Sanron," 171–178.

38 Takagi, *Yokoi Shōnan to Matsudaira Shungaku*, 76, 90–94.

39 Takagi, 63–69, 79–85.

40 *Fukoku kyōhei*, or "wealthy nation, strong military," in fact, becomes a rallying cry of the Meiji government along with *bunmei kaika* ("civilization and enlightenment").

41 Takagi, *Yokoi Shōnan to Matsudaira Shungaku*, 86–94; Takagi, *Bakumatsu ishinki no Beikoku ryūgaku*, 45–47.

42 Takagi, *Yokoi Shōnan to Matsudaira Shungaku*, 98–108; Takagi, "Bakumatsu Bunkyū-ki no chūō seikyoku to Echizen-han," 49–52.

43 Takagi, *Yokoi Shōnan to Matsudaira Shungaku*, 109–122. On the attempted coup of 1863, see Takagi, "Bakumatsu Bunkyū-ki no chūō seikyoku to Echizen-han," 53–63.

44 Takagi, *Yokoi Shōnan to Matsudaira Shungaku*, 63–39, 141–155.

45 Murata Ujihisa, *Zoku saimu kiji*, vol. 5 (Tokyo: Nihon Shiseki Kyōkai, 1922), 239; Takagi, *Yokoi Shōnan to Matsudaira Shungaku*, 156.

46 Takagi, *Yokoi Shōnan to Matsudaira Shungaku*, 160–162, 174–179.

47 Takagi, 155–159, 177–178.

48 Takagi, 159.

49 Takagi, 174–175.

50 Takagi, 179.

51 Takagi, 179–182.

52 Takagi, 1–5.

53 Takagi, 193–194.

54 Takagi, 163–171.

55 Yokoi and Hanatachi, *Kokuze sanron*, 72–73; Yokoi and Miyauchi, "Kokuze Sanron," 171.

56 Takagi, *Bakumatsu ishinki no Beikoku ryūgaku*, 21–26. Yokoi Shōnan's letters to his nephews can be found in Yokoi Shōnan and Yamazaki Masatada, *Yokoi Shōnan ikō* (Tokyo: Nisshin Shoin, 1942), 279, 280, 284–285, 293–294, 323–326.

57 Takagi, *Bakumatsu ishinki no Beikoku ryūgaku*, 28.

58 Takagi, 38–39.

59 Takagi, 43–47. In a letter to Kaishū, Shōnan asks him to take his two nephews and another of his disciples as his students and to treat them as vassals. They were later employed as crew members of Kankōmaru, a steamship presented from the king of Holland to the shogunate. Yokoi and Yamazaki, *Yokoi Shōnan ikō*, 441; Katsu Kaishū, *Kaigun rekishi*, vol. 2 (Keisō Shobō, 1973), 177.

60 Takagi, *Yokoi Shōnan to Matsudaira Shungaku*, 163–164.

61 Takagi, *Bakumatsu ishinki no Beikoku ryūgaku*, 65–71; Yamazaki Masatada, *Yokoi Shōnan Jōkan: Denki-hen* (Tokyo: Meiji Shoin, 1928), 897–901.

62 Takagi, *Yokoi Shōnan to Matsudaira Shungaku*, 167.

63 Takagi, 167. By this time, the *bakufu* had officially approved traveling abroad to the treaty countries for the purpose of academic training or commerce; see Ishizuki Minoru, *Seiyō kyōiku no hakken: Bakumatsu Meiji no ibunka taiken kara* (Tōkyō: Fukumura Shuppan, 1985), 98.

64 When William E. Griffis was later invited to Fukui, Sasaki hosted him and became his close friend.

65 Takagi Fuji, "Keiō–ki no Echizen hansei to chūō seikyoku," *Kindai Nihon kenkyū* 16 (1999): 46–48. Van Reed is best known for helping to bring the first Japanese immigrant laborers to Hawaii; he also traded in arms and munitions with Fukui and Satsuma. See John E. Van Sant, *Pacific Pioneers: Japanese Journeys to America and Hawaii, 1850–80* (Urbana: University of Illinois Press, 2000), 97–116; Fukunaga Ikuo, "Eugene Van Reed, An Objective View," *Historical English Studies in Japan* 1986, no. 18 (November 1985): 59–74.

66 Takagi, *Yokoi Shōnan to Matsudaira Shungaku*, 169–170.

67 Takagi, 164.

68 Yokoi and Miyauchi, "Kokuze sanron," 177.

69 Yokoi and Miyauchi, 169.

70 Takagi, *Yokoi Shōnan to Matsudaira Shungaku*, 167–69.
71 Katsu Koroku was admitted two years later in 1871. Ise Satarō's name can be found in the *Annual Register of the United States Naval Academy*, 1872, https://archive.org/details/annualregiste18711872unse/page/16/mode/2up.
72 Takagi, *Yokoi Shōnan to Matsudaira Shungaku*, 168–169. The text is as in the original source.
73 For more on the Satsuma students, see chapter 10.
74 On Hatakeyama's involvement in the Iwakura Mission, see chapter 11.
75 Takagi, *Yokoi Shōnan to Matsudaira Shungaku*, 170–171.

3

Katsu Kaishū as a Shadow Founder of the Japanese *Ryūgakusei* Community in New Brunswick

Katsu Koroku, Takaki Saburō, and Tomita Tetsunosuke

NORIKO OCHIAI AND
YUKAKO OTORI

On the eve of the Meiji Restoration, Katsu Kaishū, a founding father of the modern Japanese navy then serving the Tokugawa shogunate, composed a farewell *kanshi* to his fourteen-year-old son, Koroku. This rhymed prose composed of Chinese characters draws first on his respect for his own father, Kokichi, to bridge the relationship between Kaishū and his son. From there it unfolds with images of life as a voyage across uncharted seas as Kaishū articulates his feelings for Koroku, who was about to depart for the United States. Both father and son knew the boy's journey would be fraught with challenges and dangers. Still, Kaishū wanted Koroku to "kick through the vast ocean and sever yourself from the horde [as you go off] beyond the tall waves."[1] The powerful allure of Western civilization motivated dozens of Japanese men to embark on transoceanic adventures for educational attainment. The last line of the *kanshi* reflects Kaishū's transcultural affinity with the reformist agenda of nineteenth-century liberalism: "Cultivate well the source of your spirit and be determined to attain the true ways from your teachers." He viewed life as a mission that made men responsible for learning and progressing to a higher stage of civilization.

Kaishū rendered his moral and financial support not only to his son but also to many youths who would comprise the first generation of Japanese students in the United States. To this day, he remains famed as a key player of the Meiji Restoration whose mediations facilitated regime change with limited interventions from Western powers.[2] He is much less known for his pragmatic mindset, which oriented him toward helping younger generations navigate through turbulent times marked by political violence, social disorder, and the constant fear of foreign invasion. In Edo, his residence hosted a private school for Rangaku (Dutch studies), where Koroku gained exposure to Western ideas and knowledge at a very young age. Overseas learning was the next step on the teenage boy's intellectual journey.

This chapter illuminates Katsu Kaishū's role in the formation of the Japanese *ryūgakusei*'s community in New Brunswick, New Jersey. This distinguished statesman volunteered to arrange opportunities for Japanese youth to study in the United States, although he himself made only one short visit to San Francisco and never went further east. In 1868, Koroku settled in New Brunswick after a brief stint in Boston, accompanied by two Japanese guardians who were his father's mentees: twenty-eight-year-old Takaki Saburō and thirty-three-year-old Tomita Tetsunosuke. With Kaishū's help, the trio became part of the emerging Japanese community at Rutgers, where a considerable portion of the first generation of Japanese *ryūgakusei* shared the challenge of living abroad. In 1871, they parted ways when Koroku entered the U.S. Naval Academy in Annapolis, Maryland, where the stress of overstudy and overseas living gradually caused the young man's health to deteriorate. His former guardians, Takaki and Tomita, on the other hand, garnered diplomatic posts that allowed them to continue supporting him and other Japanese *ryūgakusei* near and far.

Fathers and Sons

On March 17, 1860, Katsu Kaishū sailed into the San Francisco harbor aboard the *Kanrin-maru*, the first Japanese ship to reach the Americas. It could not have arrived without Lieutenant John Mercer Brooke, whose technical assistance was indispensable for its expedition amid winter storms. Kaishū, "a very small but well formed, wiry & lithe man, with sharp penetrating eye, aquiline nose, [and] rather small chin," gave Brooke a favorable impression. The trained Japanese sailor in his late thirties could easily leap "on the rail or up into the rigging," and amuse others on board with his "humor" and "pleasant countenance."[3] But such friendly interactions hardly occurred during the forty-day voyage because diarrhea left Kaishū in need of medical care. The transoceanic passage involved health

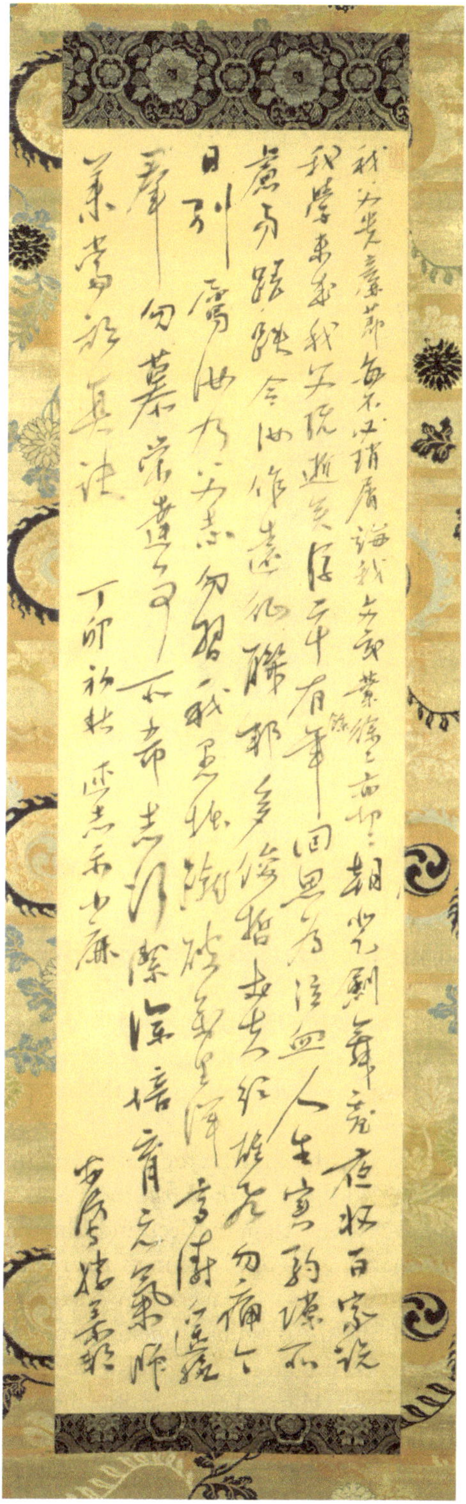

FIGURE 3.1. Calligraphic hanging scroll from Katsu Kaishū to his son, Koroku, 1867. (Credit: Tokyo Metropolitan Edo-Tokyo Museum.)

FIGURE 3.2. Katsu Kaishū, undated. (Credit: William Elliot Griffis Collection, Rutgers University Libraries.)

risks, such as infections, that killed three Japanese sailors upon their arrival in San Francisco.[4]

The *Kanrin-maru*—or more exactly, what it brought from Japan, a country known for its seclusion policy more than two centuries old—piqued the curiosity of San Franciscans, who numbered about fifty-seven thousand at the time. A *Daily Alta California* article urged them to witness the Japanese wonder, asserting that there would not be "another chance of this kind . . . for many years" to come. When local journalists paid a visit to the *Kanrin-maru*, the all-male Japanese crew looked excitedly about the city view from the deck and "showed the most intense curiosity to see our [Americans'] style of writing." Their curiosity could not be fully satiated, as everything they saw in America provided constant and new sources of amusement.[5] While the diplomatic members of the Japanese delegation traveled further east to Washington, DC, to formally ratify the U.S.-Japan Treaty of Amity and Commerce (Harris Treaty) of 1858, the rest, including Kaishū, remained in San Francisco for almost one and a half months. In this booming center of maritime trade, they went through "many confusing and embarrassing moments," according to Fukuzawa Yukichi. This later renowned public intellectual in Meiji Japan, then a youthful samurai serving as an attendant to the *Kanrin-maru*'s captain, recollected one such moment in his autobiography: They underwent uncountable failures on a city street before figuring out how to ride a horse carriage.[6]

Kaishū's trans-Pacific sojourn strengthened his conviction in the critical value of naval force for Japan's sovereignty and modernization. Born in 1823 to the family of a Tokugawa retainer, Kaishū grew into adulthood with little prospect for success under feudal rule, where a son's future hinged on his father's status. His father, Kokichi, had no hope of bureaucratic advancement due to a rebellious youth and a former proclivity for strolling and street fighting, which deprived his son of a head start in life.[7] A window of success for six-year-old Kaishū appeared when he started serving as an attendant to one of the sons of Ieyoshi, the twelfth shogun. Yet, several years later, in 1838, his young master's death foreclosed his advancement within the Tokugawa bureaucracy.

Katsu Kaishū thus had sufficient reason to defy a typical career path for a samurai of his age and rank. He devoted himself to learning Rangaku instead of Jugaku (Confucian studies); the latter was necessary knowledge for promotion within the shogunate, while the former guaranteed nothing but intellectual reward. Kaishū's earliest encounter with Western technologies occurred in Edo when he attended the school of Sakuma Shōzan, a pioneering scholar of Dutch military tactics and technologies in Japan. From there he made inroads into reading Dutch texts, particularly those on naval artillery and gunnery. As more news of the Opium War reached Japan and more foreign ships appeared off its coast on the hunt for whales, the country's need for maritime security grew apparent and urgent in ordinary people's eyes. To that end, in 1850 Kaishū opened a school for Dutch learning, the *Hyōkaijuku*, which developed into a place of communal learning among kindred spirits. That year, his father, Kokichi, died without seeing Kaishū's rise to prominence.

Fortunately for Kaishū, the value of Rangaku skyrocketed in the 1850s, especially after Commodore Matthew C. Perry's arrival at Uraga, a port at the mouth of the Edo Bay, on July 8, 1853. The shock of America's gunboat diplomacy incentivized Kaishū to write in favor of creating a Western-style navy and promoting international trade. Although his proposals wended their way through the Tokugawa bureaucracy, neither the *bakufu*'s top officials nor the era's influential scholars ever agreed on whether and how to open the country to the whole world.

In the meantime, these proposals benefited Kaishū immensely because he gained both recognition from some policymakers and admission to the newly founded Nagasaki Naval Training Center, where a select detachment of Japanese samurai received instructions on navigation, transportation, mechanics, astronomy, and other subjects under Dutch naval officials. Kaishū's portrayal of his life and learning in Nagasaki shows how the city hosted the start of his friendship with one such official, Willem Huijssen van Kattendijke. At the *bakufu*'s request, Kattendijke brought over the corvette *Japan*, renamed the *Kanrin-maru*, with a variety of navigational equipment, and Kaishū learned how to operate a Western-style ship before applying for a trip to the other side of the Pacific Ocean.

From March to May 1860, Kaishū spent a considerable time at the Mare Island Naval Shipyard near San Francisco, where American workers housed the *Kanrin-maru*'s Japanese crew and repaired the vessel for its return journey. His diary contains a rough map of the San Francisco Bay and notes about technological findings, local hospitality, and social interactions among the Japanese crew as well as with locals and naval officers.[8] Today, the Ōta City Katsu Kaishū Memorial Museum exhibits some of the materials that he brought back from the United States, including his portrait photo taken in San Francisco. The black-and-white image shows Kaishū in samurai garb. While his trans-Pacific journey did not instantly change his comportment on the outside, his mind made a huge leap. A man named Thomas Gennett gave him a detailed map of San Francisco showing the city's contours, which undoubtedly satisfied his cartographic inclinations. He demonstrated an avid curiosity as to the political benefit and possibilities of election-based democratic processes after catching a glimpse at the San Francisco City Council. Such encounters paved the way for his political departure from the feudal system, though his personal commitment and emotional attachment to the Tokugawa family continued after the shogunate's demise in 1868.

From the 1860s onward, Katsu Kaishū continued to envision an oceanic future for Japan and worked to build a "national" naval force amid political chaos. Japanese historian Kanazawa Hiroyuki emphasizes Kaishū's obsession with the new concept of the "national," which distinguished him among advocates of increasing Japan's naval force in the late Tokugawa period.[9] At the center of the debate, the *bakufu*'s top officials moved to organize a top-down Western-style navy to restore the regime's influence. Some feudal lords of resourceful domains, such as Satsuma (in the present-day Kagoshima Prefecture), reinforced coastal troops independently from the *bakufu*. In such contexts, Kaishū's emphasis on practical and national approaches appealed to some influential men, including Matsudaira Shungaku, the head of the Fukui domain, and his advisor Yokoi Shōnan, a famous Confucian scholar and political reformer. In 1863, the fourteenth shogun, Tokugawa Iemochi, gave Kaishū permission to create a naval training center in Kobe, which was inaugurated a year later. Much to Kaishū's dismay, the school closed its doors before its first anniversary after political circumstances forced him to resign from his position with the Tokugawa navy, at least temporarily.

In the long run, however, the Kobe Naval Training Center gained importance because of its codevelopment with Kaishū's private school, the Kaigunjuku. The two adjacent schools nurtured a unique intellectual community, and their associates—notably Itō Yūkō, Mutsu Munemitsu, and Sakamoto Ryōma—made remarkable contributions to the country's modernization. These figures are worth mentioning because they prove Kaishū's influence on individuals known for their anti-*bakufu* activities. Sakamoto, for instance, became an intermediary between the Chōshū and Satsuma domains and facilitated their military alliance against the shogunate in 1866.[10] As such, the twin schools under the auspices of Kaishū as a *bakufu* retainer put a throng of young samurai in conversation across differences in feudal ranks, regional backgrounds, and political orientations. While this extensive student body reflected Kaishū's vision for a national navy, its rebellious hue sufficed to make his superiors skeptical about the results of its education, which led to the school's discontinuation.

The premature demise of the Kobe Naval Training Center demonstrates that Kaishū's commitment to education continued even at the risk of undermining his political leverage. That commitment also preceded his involvement with high politics in Tokugawa Japan, which began in 1850 when Kaishū converted his home into the Hyōkaijuku, a place for Rangaku students to live and learn communally. His sons, Koroku and Shirō, born in 1852 and 1854, respectively, grew up in this intellectual community, which gave them early access to Western ideas and practices. By the time Kaishū headed the Kobe Naval Training Center, his private academy had become a popular destination for ambitious Japanese men. Neither his dismissal from the Tokugawa navy nor the demise of the training center reduced his influence among Yōgaku (Western studies) proponents, some of whom chose to expatriate in violation of the *bakufu*'s seclusion policy. In Nagasaki, Rev. Guido F. Verbeck of the Dutch Reformed Church assisted the secret departure of Yokoi Saheita and Daihei, both former students of the Kobe Naval Training Center, to the United States. In the fall of 1866, the Yokoi brothers relocated to New Brunswick, becoming the first Japanese students to enroll at the Rutgers Grammar School.[11]

Kaishū, an ardent advocate for study abroad, was all too excited about the *bakufu*'s decision in the fourth month of 1866 to terminate its long-standing ban on overseas travel, which made it legal for Japanese people to leave the country for educational and commercial purposes.[12] In addition, the *bakufu* announced a competition for scholarships that would cover the education of young samurai in Britain. Kaishū wanted his sons to claim their spots. While waiting for the results of their applications, he proceeded to Miyajima (in today's Hiroshima Prefecture) to negotiate with the Chōshū force. As the Tokugawa shogunate fell into disarray, he ran into a bureaucratic quagmire. When he reached Kyoto on his way back to Edo, two pieces of bad news struck him hard: Shirō's death at age twelve, followed by Koroku's exclusion from the competition for the shogunate's scholarships. The latter's failure had obviously been caused by Kaishū's precarious position in the fractured political landscape. Beset with grief and anger, he decided to send his surviving son to the United States privately and submitted a petition to the *bakufu*. Permission was granted in the second month of 1867, and Kaishū turned for advice to Thomas Walsh, an American merchant based in Yokohama.

As the plan became reality, Kaishū composed the farewell *kanshi* that mingled his feelings for his deceased father, Kokichi, with those for his cherished son, Koroku. He wept "tears of blood" as he continued to mourn Kokichi, and he urged Koroku "not to feel pain over our separation today" because his "wishes [were] to be with" his son across the vast ocean.[13]

Pragmatic Minds

On the morning of August 18, 1867, Katsu Koroku reached the port of San Francisco after twenty-three days on board the *Colorado*. Aged fifteen, he had grown up healthy, though he was only five feet tall according to his passport. In Japan, he was the sixty-third person to receive a passport, which was then issued as a sheet of paper that contained a brief list of identifying information such as the bearer's age, name, height, and facial traits, but not a photo. For instance, Koroku had a "long" face and "ordinary" mouth, nose, and eyes, but it is unclear whether such descriptions were used for inspections. The scant records of his voyage show it was far more comfortable than what his father had endured aboard the *Kanrin-maru* in 1860: Koroku traveled first class, chaperoned by Takaki Saburō and Tomita Tetsunosuke. At the port of San Francisco, the three privileged travelers were unlikely to have been subjected to the demanding inspections that later confronted Asian immigrants at the Angel Island Immigration Station.

One of the first things they did in San Francisco was to westernize their appearance. The trio's arrival was well arranged, so a horse carriage came to pick them up at the pier and took them to the city's burgeoning quarter, where they stayed in a hotel for two weeks, got their hair cut, and bought Western clothes. On September 3, 1867, they boarded a ship to Panama, where they could take the shortest route from the Pacific to the Atlantic by riding the then world-famous Panama Railroad. On September 25, the *Arizona* took the three Japanese passengers to the port of New York. Their long voyage ended in Boston, where they undertook intensive language training with a teacher named Northrup (possibly Birdsey Grant Northrup).[14]

Why Kaishū chose Takaki and Tomita as Koroku's guardians remains unspecified, but reportedly the two avid students of naval science jumped at the opportunity to study abroad when apprised of their mentor's decision. As discussed later, one had previously missed out on an opportunity to visit the United States, and the other had failed in an attempt to smuggle himself out of Japan. A week after the *bakufu* approved Koroku's departure, Kaishū first asked Takaki whether the mentee would be interested in traveling with his son, and in due course, he added Tomita as another guardian.[15] Kaishū's choice was made with consideration as he took pains in persuading Takaki's and Tomita's feudal lords to finance the plan, and his sincere coordination enabled the two not just to leave their native land lawfully but also to receive one thousand *ryō* toward tuition and other expenses. This amount was equivalent to approximately $1,000 at that time and the yearly income of a middle-class *bakufu* retainer.

FIGURE 3.3. Tarō Kusakabe's grave, 1870. Katsu Koroku is seated next to Kusakabe's grave; standing next to him is Takaki Saburō and an unidentified man, and standing on the other side of the grave is Hatakeyama Yoshinari. (Credit: William Elliot Griffis Collection, Rutgers University Libraries.)

On the seventh day of the fourth month in 1867, the Tokugawa shogunate granted Takaki passport number sixty-five, wherein the description of his appearance included that he had a round face and big eyes.[16] Born in 1841 into a samurai family of the Shōnai domain in today's Yamagata Prefecture, Takaki Saburō grew up in Edo, where he received a typical education for boys of his rank. In 1859, he started training with swords under Kaishū's cousin, a connection that probably enabled his entry into the Hyōkaijuku in 1860. Takaki had limited interaction with his Rangaku mentor in the first few years because Kaishū's official duties took him elsewhere in the country, and his private school functioned more as a site of communal learning for young students.[17] Gradually, however, Takaki gained his mentor's recognition, and in 1863, he followed Kaishū and thirteen others to Nagasaki.[18] By then, Takaki had also received an official appointment to the Tokugawa navy's unit in Yokohama (Kanagawa Prefecture), where he possibly learned basic English.

In August 1863, Tomita Tetsunosuke of the Sendai domain (in today's Miyagi Prefecture) joined some ninety students at the Hyōkaijuku, where his friendship with Takaki began and grew rapidly owing to their shared origins in the domains of northeastern Japan (today's Tōhoku region). Much evidence suggests that Tomita, like Takaki, followed an educational path typical for a samurai of his rank. In his twenties, Tomita switched from Jugaku to Rangaku as Japan looked to increase its naval capabilities in the age of maritime empires. Although Kaishū's diary recorded little about his interaction with Tomita before 1868, the young man clearly stood out as a reliable student who sometimes acted as his messenger. Tomita later disclosed that he had twice attempted to leave Japan surreptitiously before Kaishū made his offer in 1867, implying that his mentor knew about his undaunted pursuit of Western knowledge.[19]

Shortly after Takaki and Tomita escorted Koroku to Boston, Katsu Kaishū's political career reached its zenith when he co-orchestrated the peaceful transfer of Edo Castle to the imperial vanguard with Saigō Takamori of the Satsuma domain. On November 9, 1867, the last shogun, Tokugawa Yoshinobu, requested the *bakufu*'s return of its prerogatives to the imperial court. Legally, the Meiji Restoration was complete with the issuance of the emperor's edict in January 1868, which asserted the termination of samurai governance and the resumption of imperial rule. But internal struggles and military clashes dragged on well beyond the legal transition, especially in the northern part of Japan. While the regime change pushed him to the losing side, Kaishū found himself in limbo after his negotiation with Saigō dealt the *bakufu* a final blow. Both the new government and Tokugawa loyalists viewed him with suspicion.

After 1868 dawned, Koroku, Takaki, and Tomita became aware of the revolutionary strife in Japan through American newspapers. The *New York Herald*, for instance, reported the resignation of the Japanese "Tycoon" and the return of power to the "Mikado" on January 2, 1868, based on a telegram from Japan issued almost a month earlier in Yokohama, where the correspondent had heard "many rumors afloat of troubles at Yiato [*sic*], the metropolis of the empire."[20] No substantial updates about Edo appeared in the *New York Herald* as American news reporting at the time focused on commercial interests rather than sociopolitical upheavals. Worried about the situation back home, the three students penned a letter to Kaishū, but it took many months for passengers and letters alike to travel between America's East Coast and Japan.

The inconvenient distance soon generated miscommunication. Several weeks later, the trio sent a follow-up letter, which indicates how the scarcity of information was amplifying their sense of panic. Meanwhile, they relocated to New Brunswick in early 1868, where Takaki and Tomita asked the Yokoi brothers to take care of the teenage Koroku.[21] On August 8, 1868, the two guardians left New York aboard the *Alaska* for Panama and headed to San Francisco, where they stayed longer than expected. Finally, they landed at the port of Yokohama on December 31, after a transit in Hong Kong. Unfamiliar with recent events in Japan, Takaki and Tomita agreed to disguise themselves as merchants, possibly by changing their clothes and hairstyles, as they trekked from Yokohama to Edo, which had been renamed Tokyo.

When they finally reached their mentor's residence in Tokyo, Kaishū did not welcome his faithful disciples. On the contrary, he condemned their presence and had them expelled from his residence. After spending a night at a nearby temple, Takaki and Tomita paid an apologetic visit to him early in the morning and felt his anger modulate into sympathy. Talking with them face-to-face, Kaishū reminded them of their potential contribution to Japan's industrialization. Without much ado, he convinced them to return to the United States as soon as possible. Clearly, Takaki and Tomita took his advice eagerly and seriously, because they willingly returned to New Brunswick.[22] At this time, Katsu secured money to fund his son's education in the United States and entrusted it to Takaki.[23]

Later in March 1869, Koroku reunited with his guardians in New Brunswick, where they became part of a small but vibrant community of Japanese *ryūgakusei*. The trio first boarded with Isaac Bartles and his family at 58 Church Street in New Brunswick. Six other Japanese students resided in two groups at 55 and 62 Church Street, respectively. Those from Satsuma—Hatakeyama Yoshinari, Matsumura Junzō, and Yoshida Kiyonari—occupied the former while those from Fukui—the Yokoi brothers and Kusakabe Tarō—stayed at the latter with Maria Van Arsdale.[24] This arrangement allowed them to converse frequently, and chapter 4 of this book tells more stories of their interactions with American neighbors.

The Meiji Restoration impacted Japanese *ryūgakusei*'s plans and prospects differently depending on their feudal affiliations. On the one hand, the new regime enabled Chōshū and Satsuma students, such as the Japanese residents at 55 Church Street, to be politically ambitious. The Charter Oath, promulgated by the Meiji emperor in 1868, promoted the importation of knowledge from foreign countries. At the other end of the spectrum were those who depended on the shogunate's sponsorship and had no choice but to return home before their funding dissipated.[25] Their futures seemed bleaker than at the time of their departure. The Meiji Restoration placed Koroku, Takaki, and Tomita on the losing side, preventing them from harboring expectations of political success. Unlike official *bakufu* students, they chose to remain in the United States, but financial difficulties loomed as they could not receive further remittances from Japan.

Several months later, their circumstances improved when the Meiji government agreed to finance the study of Japanese students abroad, including those who had left the country before the establishment of the new regime. In July 1869, Takaki and Tomita received 600 Mexican silver dollars to cover their studying and living expenses.[26] Takaki, whom William E. Griffis recollected as a

FIGURE 3.4. Two Japanese in Western dress: Tomita Tetsunosuke (*seated*) and Takaki Saburō (*standing*). (Credit: J. G. Scott, photographer, William Elliot Griffis Collection, Rutgers University Libraries.)

"diligent student," attended the Rutgers Grammar School with students much younger than him.[27] Tomita, less proficient in English, chose to receive individual instruction in nearby Millstone, New Jersey, where he lived with E. T. Corwin and his household consisting of his wife, two children, and a domestic servant. Corwin, the pastor of the Hillsborough Dutch Reformed Church, tutored Tomita for about fifteen months starting in the fall of 1869.[28] Corwin's daughter, Euphemia, later recalled pleasantly her time with Tomita, with whom she sat "at table three times a day."[29]

While language training consumed most of their time and energy, Koroku, Takaki, and Tomita followed political developments in Japan, thanks to Kaishū. By 1867, the Pacific Mail Steamship Company had launched a regular service between San Francisco and Yokohama, and Kaishū took advantage of every possible opportunity to write to his son and mentees.[30] The trio received dozens of letters that kept them updated, despite considerable time lags, about the political climate that forced Kaishū to move back and forth between Tokyo and Shizuoka, where the last shogun lived in confined retirement. Kaishū's letter written shortly before his move to Shizuoka in September 1868 detailed the dissolution of the Northern Alliance that had sought to sustain the old regime in the native domains of Takaki and Tomita. The ensuing letter that he sent from Shizuoka informed the trio of the inauguration of the new era named Meiji.[31] These pieces of information were what Takaki and Tomita sought in 1868 after learning of political turmoil in Japan through American newspapers. If timely communication had been possible then, they would not have made the long journey home.

Kaishū's correspondence became a significant source of information and a tangible sign of emotional support—from home—in New Brunswick, where Japanese students formed a tiny intelligentsia. By 1870, fifty-six Japanese nationals resided in the United States, with eighteen inhabiting New Brunswick and its vicinity. In Shizuoka, Kaishū set out to assist the departure of some young men to the United States, sometimes at the request of their upper-class samurai fathers. In the early 1870s, twenty to thirty Japanese students found themselves in New Brunswick, a considerable proportion of whom were enrolled in Rutgers College or the Grammar School. Some stayed long enough to graduate from either or both schools; others left after several weeks to pursue their interests in places more suitable for them. Though local newspapers broadcasted their dedication to scholarly excellence, language barriers and cultural gaps prevented or considerably hindered their progress. Certainly, they all struggled and needed each other's company, regardless of their former ranks and academic preparation.

In such circumstances, Takaki's experiences seem different from others because his seniority obligated him to guide his younger counterparts. In Shizuoka, in the spring of 1871, Kaishū was preoccupied with finalizing travel arrangements for five sons of former *bakufu* retainers who had the support of the Tokugawa family and Thomas Walsh. In May, these five sons alighted from the Transcontinental Railroad in New York and were met by Takaki, Koroku, and a few others. One of the new arrivals was nineteen-year-old Kawamura Kiyoo, who later spearheaded the *yōga* (Western-style painting in modern Japan) movement in Meiji Japan. In one of his letters to his family, Kawamura described how Takaki came over to help him and his peers in the initial phase of moving into a new culture.[32] Yamakawa Kenjirō of the Aizu domain (in today's Fukushima Prefecture) also noted that Takaki took care of him like a brother during his time in New Brunswick.[33] This future physicist, who later studied at Yale

University, went on to achieve prominence in Japanese academia, serving twice as president of Tokyo Imperial University.

Moreover, Takaki's seniority let him focus on independent learning rather than formal schooling. His attendance at the Rutgers Grammar School did not lead to graduation, let alone to higher education.[34] Unlike Koroku, his two guardians showed no clear intention of pursuing advanced training in naval science. In July 1868, Congress passed a measure that permitted Japanese nationals to attend the U.S. Naval Academy.[35] John Mason Ferris, secretary of the board of foreign missions of the Dutch Reformed Church, had lobbied for this policy and secured the support of Senator Frederick T. Frelinghuysen (R-NJ), a Rutgers College alumnus. After all arrangements were made between the two governments, Yokoi Saheita, the elder of the Yokoi brothers, and Matsumura Junzō of Satsuma entered the prestigious school on December 8, 1869. Koroku sent a letter to his father stating his interest in matriculating at the Naval Academy.[36] By contrast, Takaki, almost thirty, considered himself too old for further schooling, and Tomita was five years older than his colleague.[37]

Rutgers and Beyond

On June 5, 1871, Katsu Koroku departed New Brunswick for Annapolis, and his transition to higher education lessened Takaki's and Tomita's responsibilities as guardians.[38] Tomita seems to have enjoyed greater discretion in choosing where to live and what to learn. As early as November 1870, Tomita entered the Bryant, Stratton, and Whitney Business College, founded in 1856 in Newark, New Jersey. The 1870s saw chains of business colleges thrive in the United States, and by 1880 there were more than 160 such schools across the country, enabling working-class students to receive training in clerical and accounting services.[39] Edmund J. James, a driving force in the founding of the American Academy of Political and Social Science, stated that these schools were "peculiarly American" because of their emphasis on commercial skills and profit-driven management.[40] For Tomita, this type of education fitted his purpose. Still in need of language tutoring, he boarded at the residence of William Whitney, the college's principal. William's wife, Anna, a mother of three children, was willing to help Tomita improve his English.

In the summer of 1871, Takaki moved to Washington, DC, with the intention of attending a business college, but instead he started a diplomatic career.[41] In late February 1871, Mori Arinori also arrived in Washington as the first Japanese minister to the United States. Several months later, Takaki assumed a temporary appointment as his secretary, the second-highest position in the newly established Japanese legation located at the corner of 24th and M Streets. Mori, a former *ryūgakusei* from Satsuma, had spent a couple of years in Britain and the United States before the Meiji government placed him at the forefront of diplomatic efforts. Since Japan had opened up only recently, Mori did his job while learning "the most elementary of the arts of diplomacy": His correspondence with Secretary of State Hamilton Fish indicates that American diplomats coached him about formal protocols and etiquette.[42] Takaki utilized his accounting skills for the legation's operation, helping Mori greatly on a daily basis.[43] Outside official duties, Mori developed cordial relations with Takaki and Tomita. After being called back to Tokyo in 1873, he took the initiative in forming the Meirokusha (Sixth Year of Meiji Society), an academic society for "enlightenment" in Meiji Japan in which Takaki and Tomita took part as overseas correspondents.[44]

The highlight of Mori's diplomacy in Washington was the visit of the Iwakura Mission in 1872, and Takaki was there to assist him. About a week after its members' arrival, they agreed to create a committee to review the status of Japanese students abroad. On March 18, twelve *ryūgakusei*, including Tomita, came to Washington to prepare a report to the Iwakura Mission and the Meiji government. Tomita and Takaki facilitated the discussion about financial issues, possibly because of their expertise and experience in that area.[45] By then, Tomita had taken up an ad hoc appointment in the Japanese consulate in New York, which became permanent in March 1872. Around the same time, Takaki received a formal assignment to the Japanese legation in Washington.

Takaki continued to work in the most convenient position to oversee the life and progress of Japanese students in the United States. Between 1869 and 1879, the Japanese government granted 884 passports to its nationals desiring to travel overseas for educational purposes. Historian John E. Van Sant estimates that "at least 200 but no more than 250 Japanese" attended colleges in the United States during the two decades since 1860, though not all of them graduated with a degree.[46] Another source indicates that, as of 1872, about 200 Japanese *ryūgakusei* studied elsewhere in the United States, with the overwhelming majority supported by the Meiji government. In the Japanese legation, Takaki made the best use of his clerical and accounting skills and became indispensable for its regular business, including the distribution of scholarships to these students.[47]

Hence, Koroku's communication with his former guardians evolved in new ways after his formal enrollment in the U.S. Naval Academy. It took six years for Koroku to fulfill all the requirements for graduation after multiple academic failures and medical leaves.[48] In June 1873, Koroku found himself in Jersey City, where he sent a postcard to Takaki in the Japanese legation, asking for a place to stay during the summer.[49] His personal inquiry reached Takaki, though the subsequent correspondence is lost to history. The young man struggled with not just the school's demanding curriculum but possibly also with its deep-rooted culture of hazing. Koroku, reportedly about five feet tall, was possibly the shortest in his class. In such circumstances, he gained much from the logistical and personal support of the friends who were like his big brothers, even if they no longer lived together.

It is also imaginable that Koroku, Takaki, and Tomita shared the emotional stress of living as persons of color in Gilded Age America. One newspaper article about seventeen-year-old Katsu Koroku, then an incoming student of the Naval Academy, described his complexion as "decidedly yellow." Racism came to the forefront when the correspondent continued to describe his appearance: "He has straight, coal[-]black hair, brown eyes, wide apart, and looks like a mulatto"—a person of mixed ancestry classified as "Black" under America's one-drop rule. Despite this, the article assured readers that Koroku was fond of Americans and their culture.[50] The first generation of Japanese *ryūgakusei* could not evade racial prejudice, whether they were aware of it or not.[51] Perhaps it would have required more translatability between the languages and cultures in which they had grown up and those into which they were thrown upon departure from their homelands for *ryūgakusei* to articulate their unpleasant experiences of racial stereotypes and discrimination. Their encounter with American culture occurred before various efforts to translate Western ideas into Japanese fundamentally changed the narrational norms and conceptual topography of the Japanese language during the Meiji era.[52]

Takaki's and Tomita's official involvement with the diplomatic service continued into the mid-1870s. When Mori left Washington in March 1873, Takaki succeeded him as an interim minister before moving to San Francisco, where he served from December 1873 to 1876 as vice-consul under Charles Walcott Brooke, the first consul of Japan in the port city. In February 1873, Tomita received an appointment as vice-consul in New York and was replaced by Takaki three years later. The two men gained recognition for their work by the Americans who came to know them in person. In October 1876, Brooke met Kaishū during his visit to Japan, spoke highly about Takaki and Tomita, and rewarded their former mentor with glowing words.[53] While the strategic importance of *ryūgakusei* in the bureaucratic organization of Japanese diplomacy remained unequivocal, their destinations became more diverse, reducing the centrality of New Brunswick in their network. By January 1874, the Japanese *ryūgakusei* community at Rutgers had shrunk to eight, including two preparing to return to Japan under governmental order.[54]

The diminution of the *ryūgakusei* community in New Brunswick did not totally disrupt the network that Kaishū, Koroku, Takaki, and Tomita had bridged between Japan and New Brunswick. In August 1875, William and Anna Whitney arrived in Yokohama at Mori's invitation with their fifteen-year-old daughter, Clara, who could not have been more excited to venture on a missionary life among "heathens." But the girl's dream lost its blush as her family was left at a loss after Mori's plan to create a new business college failed. Kaishū volunteered to support the Whitneys, and the American family eventually moved into his compound, where Clara grew into a unique observer of Japanese culture and social life. Her friendship with the Katsu family, in particular with their teenage daughter, Itsu, continued to inform her perspective in lasting ways.

Clara was one of those who noticed something wrong with Koroku after his stressful years in the United States. Koroku graduated from the Naval

Academy and returned home in 1877. On January 8, 1878, she paid a new year's visit and left a short note about his unusual appearance hinting at health problems: "Mr. Koroku was very pleasant, small of stature, slender, with small restless eyes and a queer habit of gulping."[55] That same month, the young man received recognition of his educational attainment through appointment as an officer in the Imperial Japanese Navy. Between 1869 and 1906, twelve Japanese men studied as regular students at the U.S. Naval Academy, of whom only four, including Koroku, finished the course. Yet, his damaged health forced him to take medical leaves in the 1880s and hampered his naval career.

Another friend of Clara in Tokyo was Sugita Nui, whose marriage to Tomita Tetsunosuke heralded a change in Japan's marital norms and customs.[56] In October 1877, the couple's wedding took place in Fukuzawa Yukichi's residence, where the bride and groom signed a contract defining their roles and obligations to each other. This procedure, unheard of in Japan until then, indicates Tomita's heightened sense of individual subjectivity after years in the United States. At the same time, his marriage to Nui reflected traditional matrimony in Japan because it was arranged and officiated during a brief break from his work. A month after their marriage, the newlywed husband left his wife and sailed back to the United States. Later the same year, Takaki returned to Japan for the first time in nine years and married Takashima Suma through arrangement and contract. Unlike Nui, Suma followed her husband to the United States.

On several occasions in the 1880s, Takaki and Tomita appeared in Clara's diary, whose entries captured the daily and emotional aspects of communications between an American girl and a group of Japanese returnees from the United States—a tiny but distinctive community in greater Tokyo at the onset of westernization. In 1880, Takaki terminated his diplomatic career, joined the Yokohama Dōshin Company, and led the development of Japan's raw silk trade. The following year, Tomita returned to Tokyo and relaunched his career in the Ministry of Finance. Clara was fond of Tomita, whose wife Nui had taken care of the Whitney family's daily matters during their earliest days in Japan; she was more critical of Takaki and his wife, Suma, because she viewed their behaviors as Americanized after years of living in the United States. With "a great deal of American life," Suma spoke English "fluently, along and all," using expressions such as "'Good gracious,' 'O Mercy!' 'Not much,' & 'Awful fun,' quite like a native."[57]

Clara's diary also attests to the severity of health problems that many *ryūgakusei* developed during and after their time in the United States. Over time, Koroku's health declined despite his family's dedication to his care and comfort. Clara's brother, Willis, a physician trained at the University of Pennsylvania, helped him recover from recurrent attacks of tuberculosis in May 1884. Clara wrote regrettably that Koroku had "little pleasure in life, being in constant fear of an attack and suffering so acutely during them." Interestingly, the ailing man wanted "some American food," implying that the years away from home had changed his tastes. His affectionate wife, Sakurai Eiko, nicknamed O Tate, came over to the Whitneys' kitchen "to learn how to make" American dishes for her husband. O Tate, however, died earlier than Koroku. On July 17, 1884, the Katsu residence was filled with families, friends, and others coming to pay tribute at her wake. The same day, the newly widowed Koroku underwent three attacks of tuberculosis. Kaishū had "no end of trouble and anxiety," and Clara feared that there might "be a double funeral." On the following day, she and others woke up at five-thirty in the morning, "preparing for poor O Tate's funeral."[58]

After years of suffering, Koroku died in 1892, survived by his father and former guardians. When Edward Warren Clark, a Rutgers alumnus and teacher in Shizuoka, authored Katsu Kaishū's first biography in English at the onset of the twentieth century, he counted Koroku among a possibly long list of Japanese students killed by "over-study" who "sacrificed [themselves] in their ambitious endeavors to attain in a day the intellectual results of centuries of thought and of toil" in the United States and Europe.[59] Many of them found a home in New Brunswick at some point in their trans-Pacific endeavors. About twenty months after Koroku's death, in October 1894, Clark visited Kaishū's residence, seeing "the same, quiet, lovable man as ever,—kind & even giving." The old father felt too "feeble" to dine out but was willing to celebrate this American's twenty-third anniversary of landing in Japan.[60]

Conclusion

Katsu Kaishū's dedication to his son Koroku and other Japanese students contributed to the phenomenal growth of New Brunswick as a hub for Japanese students from the late 1860s to the early 1870s. It was an unusual haven where they found mutual support for making progress while coping with health problems and other troubles. Kaishū, their faraway mentor and generous sponsor, occupies a special place in the history of Japanese *ryūgakusei* to American colleges and other institutions of learning, even though he never traveled to the East Coast, where most of these schools operated in the nineteenth-century United States. As in Koroku's life journey, many Japanese students pursued knowledge at the cost of their well-being, and in doing so, they fulfilled their mentor's expectations one way or another. In his letter to William E. Griffis, Koroku stated that the increase in Japanese *ryūgakusei* would "be a foundation of the Japanese civilization," echoing his father's conviction.[61] In 1899, Kaishū died at age seventy-seven. Those who attended his funeral and prayed for his eternal rest included Takaki and Tomita, whose lives would have been very different without his support and guidance.

Appendix: Poem Sent from Katsu Kaishū to His Son Koroku upon His Departure to the United States, 1867

My father esteemed integrity and did not concern himself with frivolous matters.
He had instructed me both the brush and sword, slowly and earnestly.
In the morning, [I] practiced swordsmanship, at night, [I] mastered the teachings of the countless wise men.
While my studies were still incomplete, my father had passed away.
More than twenty years have passed since then; when I think of him, I weep tears of blood.
Life is fleeting; one fails even as one contemplates.
I send you afar, to a country where there are many who are wise.
As a brave man, [you] must embark [on this journey] with ambitions high.
Do not feel pain over our separation today. Your father wishes to be with you.
Do not be a fool like myself. Kick through the vast ocean and sever yourself from the horde [as you go off] beyond the tall waves.
Do not yearn for success or fame. Your desire must lie in the resolute composure of your aspirations and actions.
Cultivate well the source of your spirit and be determined to attain the true ways from your teachers.
(Tokyo Metropolitan Edo-Tokyo Museum; translation by Haruko Wakabayashi)

Notes

1 Katsu Kaishū to Katsu Koroku, seventh month, 1867. The original letter is part of a collection at the Tokyo Metropolitan Edo-Tokyo Museum (Collection 85200433). The transcription of the entire prose and its translation into modern Japanese can be found in *Katsu Kaishū zenshū*, vol. 20 (Tokyo: Kōdansha, 1976), 305.

2 M. William Steele's unpublished dissertation is the most comprehensive study of Kaishū's role in the Meiji Restoration available in English. "Katsu Kaishū and the Collapse of the Tokugawa Bakufu" (PhD diss., Harvard University, 1976).

3 See George M. Brooke Jr. and Association for Japan-US Amity & Trade Centennial, eds., *Collected Documents of the Japanese Mission to America 1860*, vol. 5, *Brooke Journals* (Tokyo: Kazama Shobō, 1961), 111.

4 "City items," *Daily Alta California*, March 24, 1860, in *Collected Documents of the Japanese Mission to America 1860*, vol. 6, *Selected Press Accounts on the First Japanese Embassy to the United States in 1860*, ed. Association for Japan-US Amity & Trade Centennial (Tokyo: Kazama Shobō, 1961), 48; Kaoru (Kay) Ueda, "Carved in Stone: The Colma Japanese Cemetery Project," n.d., Hoover Institution Library & Archives, accessed July 10, 2025, https://www.hoover.org/library-archives/histories/colma-japanese-cemetery.

5 "City Items. Arrival of a Japanese Steamer," *Daily Alta California*, March 18, 1860, in Association for Japan-US Amity & Trade Centennial, *Collected Documents of the Japanese Mission to America 1860*, vol. 6, 36–37.

6 Fukuzawa Yukichi, *The Autobiography of Yukichi Fukuzawa*, rev. trans. Eiichi Kiyooka, with a foreword by Albert Craig (1960; New York: Columbia University Press, 2007), 112.

7 Katsu Kokichi's autobiography, *Musui's Story*, remains in circulation as a superb description of the lives and circumstances of a struggling samurai in late Tokugawa Japan. Katsu Kokichi, *Musui's Story: The Autobiography of a Tokugawa Samurai*, trans. Teruko Craig (Tucson: University of Arizona Press, 1988).

8 On the *Kanrin-maru*'s visit and the crew's experiences in San Francisco, see Dana B. Young, "The Voyage of the Kanrin Maru to San Francisco, 1860," *California History* 61, no. 4 (Winter 1983): 264–275.

9 Hiroyuki Kanazawa, *Bakufu kaigun no kōbō: Bakumatsuki ni okeru Nihon no kaigun kensetsu* (Tokyo: Keio University Press, 2017).

10 On Sakamoto, see Marius B. Jansen, *Sakamoto Ryōma and the Meiji Restoration* (Princeton, NJ: Princeton University Press, 1961).

11 John E. Van Sant, *Pacific Pioneers: Japanese Journeys to America and Hawaii, 1850–80*, with a foreword by Roger Daniels (Urbana: University of Illinois Press, 2000), 49–50.

12 Katsu Kaishū, diary, seventeenth day of the fourth month, 1866, in *Katsu Kaishū kankei shiryō Kaishū Nikki*, vol. 2, ed. Toshi Rekishi Kenkyūshitu (Tokyo: Tokyo Metropolitan Edo-Tokyo Museum, 2003), 186, https://edo-tokyo-museum.repo.nii.ac.jp/search?search_type=2&q=53. Katsu Kaishū's diary is made available through the repository of the Tokyo Metropolitan Edo-Tokyo Museum.

13 Katsu Kaishū to Katsu Koroku, seventh month, 1867, in *Katsu Kaishū kankei shiryō Kaishū Nikki*, vol. 2.

14 Shiozaki Satoshi, *Amerika chinichi ha no kigen: Meiji no ryūgakusei kōryū tan* (Tokyo: Heibonsha, 2001), 108–109.

15 Takahashi Shūetsu, *Kaishū nikki ni miru bakumatsuishin no Amerika ryūgaku: Nichigin sōsai Tomita Tetsunosuke no Amerika taiken* (Tokyo: Nihon Hyōronsha, 2018), 11–12.

16 Takaki Masayoshi, *Takaki Saburō ō shōden* (Tokyo: Takaki jimusho, 1910), 24–25.

17 Takaki, *Takaki Saburō ō shōden*, 7–11.

18 Takaki Saburō, "Sakamoto Ryōma to Sumō," February 22, 1899, in *Kaishū zadan*, ed. Iwamoto Yoshiharu (Tokyo: Iwanami Shoten, 1983), 283.

19 Tomita Tetsunosuke, "Kuroda san, Itō san," July 18, 1899, in *Kaishū zadan*, ed. Iwamoto Yoshiharu (Tokyo: Iwanami Shoten, 1983), 242.

20 "Telegraphic News from All Parts of the World," *New York Herald*, January 2, 1868.

21 Takahashi, *Kaishū nikki ni miru bakumatsuishin no Amerika ryūgaku*, 155–156.

22 In preparing for another crossing to the United States, however, Takaki and Tomita faced a technical problem: passports. Since the nascent Meiji government prohibited samurai of domains other than the victorious Satsuma and Chōshū to leave the country, they used fake identities to bypass the checkpoint in Yokohama. Takaki, for instance, held a passport issued to Sankichi, a servant of an American named Hepburn (perhaps James Curtis Hepburn or someone related to him). Takaki, *Takaki Saburō ō shōden*, 28–34.

23 Katsu Kaishū, diary, eleventh day of the twelfth month, 1868, in *Katsu Kaishū kankei shiryō Kaishū Nikki*, vol. 3, ed. Toshi Rekishi Kenkyūshitu (Tokyo: Tokyo Metropolitan Edo-Tokyo Museum, 2005), 181.

24 Takahashi, *Kaishū nikki ni miru bakumatsuishin no Amerika ryūgaku*, 139–141.

25 Ishizuki Minoru, *Kindai nihon no kaigai ryūgaku shi* (1972; Tokyo: Chūō kōronsha, 1992), 124–126, 132–134.

26 Mexican silver dollars were widely circulated throughout East Asia. See Steven Bryan, *The Gold Standard at the Turn of the Twentieth Century: Rising Powers, Global Money, and the Age of Empire* (New York: Columbia University Press, 2010), 119.

27 William E. Griffis, *The Rutgers Graduates in Japan* (New Brunswick, NJ: Rutgers College, 1916), 25.

28 Takahashi, *Kaishū nikki ni miru bakumatsuishin no Amerika ryūgaku*, 159.

29 Euphemia R. Corwin to William E. Griffis, 17 January 1917, box 46, folder 58, William Elliot Griffis Collection, Special Collections and University Archives, Rutgers University, Libraries, New Brunswick, NJ (hereafter Griffis Collection).

30 Van Sant, *Pacific Pioneers*, 53.

31 Katsu Kaishū to Katsu Koroku, Takaki Saburō, and Tomita Tetsunosuke, August and September 25, 1868, in Takaki, *Takaki Saburō ō shōden*, 35–42.

32 Kawamura Kiyoo to his family, "Letters of Kawamura Kiyoo, May 22, 1871, and June 16, 1871," in *Kawamura Kiyoo kenkyū*, ed. Takashina Shūji and Miwa Hideo (Tokyo: Chūōkōron Bijutsu Shuppan, 1994), 170–171. The original letters are part of the collection of the Tokyo Metropolitan Edo-Tokyo Museum.

33 Takaki, *Takaki Saburō ō shōden*, 123.

34 Takaki, *Takaki Saburō ō shōden*, 43.

35 J. M. Ellicott, "Japanese Students at the United States Naval Academy," *US Naval Institute Proceedings* 73, no. 3 (March 1947): 303–308.

36 Katsu Kaishū, diary, twenty-first day of the third month, 1869, in *Katsu Kaishū kankei shiryō Kaishū Nikki*, vol. 4, ed. Toshi Rekishi Kenkyūshitu (Tokyo: Tokyo Metropolitan Edo-Tokyo Museum, 2006), 3, https://edo-tokyo-museum.repo.nii.ac.jp/search?search_type=2&q=46.

37 Takaki, *Takaki Saburō ō shōden,* 43.

38 K. Katz [Katsu Koroku] to William E. Griffis, 15 August 1871, box 50, folder 43, Griffis Collection.

39 Benjamin R. Haynes and Harry P. Jackson, *A History of Business Education in the United States* (Cincinnati, OH: South-Western, 1935), 32.

40 Edmund J. James, *Commercial Education* (Albany, NY: J. B. Lyon, 1899), 5.

41 K. Katz [Katsu Koroku] to William E. Griffis, 15 August 1871.

42 Ivan Parker Hall, *Mori Arinori* (Cambridge, MA: Harvard University Press, 1973), 155–160.

43 Takahashi, *Kaishū nikki ni miru bakumatsuishin no Amerika ryūgaku,* 274–276.

44 On the *Meirokusha* and its publication, *Meiroku zasshi*, see *Meiroku Zasshi: Journal of the Japanese Enlightenment*, trans. William Reynolds Braisted (Cambridge, MA: Harvard University Press, 1976).

45 Takahashi, *Kaishū nikki ni miru bakumatsuishin no Amerika ryūgaku*, 245–255.

46 Van Sant, *Pacific Pioneers*, 51.

47 Charles Lanman, *The Japanese in America* (New York: University Publishing Company, 1872), 55.

48 Only twenty-nine of the ninety-four freshmen in the academic year of 1869–1870 graduated in four years.

49 Katsu Koroku to Takaki Saburō, 11 June 1873, private collection.

50 "The Naval Academy," *Baltimore American and Commercial Advertiser*, August 21, 1871.

51 Euphemia R. Corwin thought that the presence of Japanese students in her family "had a decided influence upon me," especially her perspectives on race. When she moved to the south, she realized "how absolutely indifferent" she had "always been

to the color of a person's skin." In her childhood, the Corwin family hosted five Japanese students, including Tomita, for ten years. The family also had "a Korean and Hindu" living with them "at different times." Euphemia R. Corwin to William E. Griffis, 17 January 1917. For more on the Japanese students at Corwin's residence, see chapter 6.

52 See, for instance, Douglas R. Howland, *Translating the West: Language and Political Reason in Nineteenth-Century Japan* (Honolulu: University of Hawai'i Press, 2001).

53 Katsu Kaishū, diary, tenth day of the tenth month, 1873, in *Katsu Kaishū kankei shiryō Kaishū Nikki*, vol. 6, ed. Toshi Rekishi Kenkyūshitu (Tokyo: Tokyo Metropolitan Edo-Tokyo Museum, 2017), 94, https://edo-tokyo-museum.repo.nii.ac.jp/search?search_type=2&q=42.

54 "State and County Items," *Matawan Journal*, January 3, 1874.

55 Clara A. N. Whitney, *Clara's Diary: An American Girl in Meiji, Japan*, ed. William Steele and Tamiko Ichimata (Tokyo: Kodansha International, 1979), 158.

56 Nui's great-grandfather was Sugita Genpaku, one of the first Japanese physicians who studied Western medicine.

57 Clara A. N. Whitney, diary, January 9 and 20, 1879, box 2, Clara Whitney Papers, Library of Congress, Washington, DC.

58 Whitney, *Clara's Diary*, 330, 333.

59 Edward W. Clark, *Katz Awa: "The Bismarck of Japan" or the Story of a Noble Life* (New York: B. F. Buck, 1904), 18.

60 Edward Warren Clark to William E. Griffis, 26 October 1894, box 46, folder 44, Griffis Collection.

61 K. Katz [Katsu Koroku] to William E. Griffis, 15 August 1871.

Part II

The Japanese Students in New Brunswick and Beyond

4

A Comparative Study of New Brunswick and Boston as Hubs for Japanese *Ryūgakusei*

SATOSHI SHIOZAKI

In 1866, the Tokugawa shogunate lifted the ban on Japanese people traveling overseas. Prior to this, in fact, domains such as Satsuma and Chōshū had secretly sent students to Europe and the United States, and individuals like Niijima Jō had smuggled themselves out of Japan. However, the numbers of *ryūgakusei*, here referring to students studying abroad in Europe and the United States, increased significantly as a result of this new permission, and so did the number of their destinations, particularly in the latter. The purposes of Japanese travelers to the United States at that time included studying, working, seeking political refuge, and even performing acrobatics. In 1867, direct ship service between Yokohama and San Francisco began, and the U.S. Transcontinental Railroad opened in 1869. Due to these developments, the trans-Pacific journey via San Francisco and New York became the main route to the eastern United States and even Europe.[1] Some Japanese who chose the United States as their place of study stayed in the gateway city of San Francisco, but most went to New York and New England on the East Coast.

Among the Japanese aboard the *Colorado*, which departed Yokohama on August 14, 1867, Takahashi Korekiyo and Suzuki Tomoo of the Sendai domain remained in San Francisco, whereas Katsu Koroku, the son of noted shogunal retainer Katsu Kaishū, transferred with two companions, Takaki Saburō and Tomita Tetsunosuke, to a ship bound for Boston via Panama (as discussed in chapter 3), along with another six from the Fukuoka domain led by Hiraga Isosaburō.[2] Although both groups were on the same ship from Yokohama to San Francisco, they do not appear to have had exchanges, possibly because each knew an American in Boston to rely on and because of the rarity of interdomain exchanges during the Tokugawa period.[3]

In 1868, Katsu Koroku and his companions moved to New Brunswick, New Jersey.[4] At Rutgers College and the Rutgers Grammar School, where Katsu studied, his peers included Satsuma students, such as Hatakeyama Yoshinari, Matsumura Junzō, and Yoshida Kiyonari, who had moved from England to the United States mainly for financial reasons. Takaki also studied at the Grammar School, whereas Tomita studied for some time with Rev. E. T. Corwin in Millstone and then went to Bryant, Stratton, and Whitney's Business College in Newark. Katsu later went on to the U.S. Naval Academy with Matsumura. Meanwhile, the Fukuoka students in Boston probably turned to Aaron Davis Weld French, a trader whose acquaintance they had made in Japan.[5] Inoue Yoshikazu went to Harvard Law School, and Honma Eiichirō went to the Massachusetts Institute of Technology (MIT). Thus, although the Fukuoka students and Katsu's group arrived in San Francisco on the same ship and subsequently moved to Boston, they never studied in the same schools.

At times, these two groups had interactions. As mentioned in chapter 3, when Tomita Tetsunosuke and Takaki Saburō learned of the overthrow of the Tokugawa shogunate, they left Katsu Koroku in the care of the Yokoi brothers of the Kumamoto domain, who lived in New Brunswick at the time, and briefly went back to Japan. When Tomita and Takaki returned, they visited the Fukuoka students in Boston with Katsu. Perhaps their Fukuoka counterparts wanted to hear from them about Japan's situation in the turbulence of the Meiji Restoration.[6] At the end of the Tokugawa period, *ryūgakusei* were sent independently by domains or individuals and had few exchanges after arriving at their destinations. However, Japan's critical situation at the end of the Tokugawa period, the crisis of the Restoration, and the associated loss of remittances for their study abroad gradually promoted more interactions among the different groups.

Boston and New Brunswick were not the only places where Japanese students in the United States enrolled during the late nineteenth century. About twenty Japanese students are known to have studied at the City College in San Francisco between 1867 and 1870, although their names are mostly unknown.[7] Others studied in New Haven, a city in coastal Connecticut, and Hartford, the state's capital, as well as in the inland Massachusetts municipalities of Monson and Amherst. Students in Boston, Connecticut, and New Brunswick frequently contacted each other as needed by letters, telegraph, and visits on weekends and summer breaks to actively exchange information on schools and other affairs.[8]

In this chapter, I compare the various trajectories and environments in the lives of *ryūgakusei* in New Brunswick and Boston and explore the roles that these locales played in the history of cultural exchange between Japan and the United States. I also compare New Brunswick with Brooklyn, New York, where many of these students temporarily enrolled as an extension of their education in the former, and Monson, located halfway between Boston and New Brunswick, which received such students from 1866 at Monson Academy, an institution that served as a grammar school for Yale University.[9]

New Brunswick, New Jersey

Below is an excerpt of the first two-thirds of the description of the grave of Kusakabe Tarō in New Brunswick, who studied and died of illness there, from an anonymous article that appeared in the December 16, 1872, issue of *The Far East*, an English-language newspaper published in Yokohama.[10] The text clearly and concisely expresses the characteristics of New Brunswick as a hub for Japanese students:

> The number of Japanese students within the United States, though not exactly known, cannot fall far short of two hundred. They are scattered about in different places, generally avoiding the large cities as places of residence. Six are in the U.S. Military Academy of West Point, another half dozen are in the U.S. Naval Academy, Annapolis. Several are in San Francisco, at Monson, Mass, and about a dozen in or around Washington, D.C.; but (1) *the general rendezvous and abiding place of most of them*, is at New Brunswick, N.J. To this said old city, they first went on reaching America, and they consider it (2) *a sort of head-quarters.* (3) *The efficient Grammar School and* (4) *the Rutgers Scientific College* of that place seem to be the chief attractions; for the classical course is not approved by the Japanese, and it is doubtful whether more than two or three of all those who have studied in the United States have been graduated from a full college course. (5) *From 20 to 30 usually live in New Brunswick.* They are (6) *very popular with the citizens and students.* The Junior Prime Minister Iwakura's three sons are being educated there, and (7) *sundry "princes," hatamotos, etc., were drilled in the rudiments of English education at the same school.* Among these (8) *pilgrims to the shrines of knowledge*, more than one has paid the forfeit of life to his too (9) *intense love of study.* Some who have failed in health, have returned to their native country, among whom is Asahi, the eldest son of Iwakura. Two, however, have died and are buried in the Willow Grove Cemetery in New Brunswick. The Imperial Government purchased a burial lot, the deed of which is held in trust by the Trustees of Rutgers College. (emphasis and numerals added)

The following summarizes the key points about New Brunswick italicized in the quoted text:

FIGURE 4.1. Japanese students at Rutgers, 1871. (Credit: William Elliot Griffis Collection, Rutgers University Libraries.)

1. It was the general place of residence for Japanese students in the United States.
2. It was a sort of headquarters for such students.
3. Its chief attractions were its "efficient" Grammar School and Rutgers
4. Scientific College.
5. Around twenty to thirty Japanese students usually lived there.
6. These students were very popular with local citizens and fellow students.
7. Various sons of aristocrats received basic English education at Rutgers.
8. The Japanese students were seen as pilgrims seeking knowledge.
9. These students had an intense love of study.

I will first discuss how these points apply to New Brunswick and then compare them with Boston. The numbers of Japanese students who studied in New Brunswick from the late 1860s to the end of the 1870s are listed in table 4.1. Because the school catalog for Rutgers College Grammar School (RCGS) for that period has yet to be found, I have made rough estimates based on Japanese historical documents.[11] The numbers in table 4.1 verify the fifth point in the quoted excerpt from *The Far East* that "from 20 to 30 usually live in New Brunswick." The only school that had more than twenty Japanese students in one year was the private Brooklyn Polytechnic Institute (BPI; now the New York University Tandon School of Engineering) between September 1872 and June 1873. As I discuss later, there are no cases of such a large number of Japanese students

Table 4.1

Japanese students in New Brunswick by academic year: Number of Japanese students in Rutgers College / number of Japanese students in Rutgers College Grammar School; students who resided in New Brunswick for multiple years are counted for each year

September 1866–June 1867	0 / 2	total 2
1867–1868	1 / 5	total 6
1868–1869	4 / 6	total 10
1869–1870	2 / 16	total 18
1870–1871	1 / 26	total 27
1871–1872	3 / 29	total 32
1872–1873	2 / 19	total 21
1873–1874	5 / 9	total 14
1874–1875	4 / 1	total 5
1875–1876	3 / 0	total 3
1876–1877	2 / 0	total 2
1877–1878	2 / 0	total 2
1878–1879	1 / 0	total 1
1879–1880	0 / 0	total 0

NOTE: See appendix 4A for individual names.

studying in Boston and the surrounding area in a single year, even at several schools, colleges, and graduate schools combined. The number of Japanese students declined sharply after 1873–1874 when the Meiji government ordered all overseas students to return to Japan in 1873.

These students lived in lodgings around the college or in the principal's dormitory of the Grammar School, so New Brunswick was almost certainly their "abiding place." The diaries and memoirs of Nagai Kyūichirō, a student from the Nagoya domain, and Orita Hikoichi of Satsuma, who studied nearby at The College of New Jersey (TCNJ; later Princeton University), show that Japanese students on the East Coast spent long breaks, such as summers and weekends, in New Brunswick—an area of "general rendezvous"—at each other's boarding houses.[12] In particular, those from nearby Millstone, Princeton, Newark, and Brooklyn frequently interacted with one another.

The expression "a sort of head-quarters" in the second point is difficult to comprehend. In many cases, *ryūgakusei* first came to New Brunswick, where they listened to advice from seniors and other enrolled students or briefly attended classes before deciding whether to stay or transfer. It may also refer to the fact that Hatakeyama Yoshinari and Yoshida Kiyonari, both current or former New Brunswick residents, managed the tuition fees paid to foreign students by the Ministry of Education. In any case, the term "head-quarters" is not entirely clear, but it is a fact that the earlier batches of Japanese students who had studied in New Brunswick since the late 1860s were relied upon as guides. Yoshida, who moved from New Brunswick to Massachusetts and then to Connecticut, and Orita, who was nearby in Princeton, had lived in the United States for many years and attended college there, so they had a good relationship with many *ryūgakusei* and engaged them in discussions and correspondence.

Regarding the third point about "the efficient Grammar School," no historical records to date suggest that RCGS surpassed other schools in terms of its curriculum, facilities, or instructors. In addition, many of those who attended the Grammar School chose to attend Rutgers College, although a few graduates went on to schools like Yale College, Harvard College, TCNJ, the U.S. Naval Academy, or the U.S. Military Academy. However, extant primary sources suggest that Japanese students found the Grammar School attractive. For example, Tsuda Seiichi and Hayashi Gensuke from Kumamoto arrived in San Francisco at the end of 1869, from which they planned to head to the United Kingdom to study, but when they stopped by New Brunswick, they were told that "the academic situation in this area is extremely convenient, and the teachers are accustomed to Japanese people and are very kind to us," a consultation that led to their decision "not to go to England for a while, but to stay here for a year or so to study."[13] The benefit of kind teachers used to teaching Japanese students surely proved attractive. Yamakawa Kenjirō from the Aizu domain later recalled that "Hatakeyama Yoshinari, who had been in the country for some time, was a very kind man and took good care of us newcomers. I remember there would be 30 or 40 Japanese students there at one time because he took care of students from Japan."[14] The presence of a senior student like Hatakeyama, who studied at the college on the same campus, spoke fluent English, and had long lived abroad, must have been a great blessing for the newcomers from Japan.

Another important point is that very few U.S. colleges at that time had grammar schools affiliated with institutes of higher education. According to the memoir of Ogawa Zenkichi, a student from Nagoya who tried to enter TCNJ through Mori Arinori with a fellow *ryūgakusei* named Ōsawa found his English skills inadequate for attending the college, despite having received private instruction.[15] As TCNJ did not have a grammar school, Ogawa and Ōsawa moved to the one in New Brunswick and continued their studies there, and they were able to qualify for admission to Rutgers College in 1873. They were surely drawn to the "efficient" prospect of entering a college on the same campus after a year or two of study at the Grammar School, where they knew how things were done and how to get along.

As for the fourth point, the president of TCNJ described Rutgers as "an excellent college in New Brunswick run by a few Dutch people."[16] The college had been gaining national renown as a small but excellent educational institution run by the Dutch Reformed Church, a minority Christian denomination in the United States. By the time the Japanese students reached New Brunswick, they had grown keenly aware of the crucial progress of science and technology through witnessing the development of San Francisco, Chicago, and New York City.

Students in the science curriculum, unlike their counterparts in the classical courses, were exempt from Greek and Latin classes, and this was a big attraction for many *ryūgakusei*. Although the school's facilities and curriculum did not seem particularly advanced, the absence of certain requirements made it convenient for them to study there.

When the Yokoi brothers arrived in New Brunswick in 1866, some landlords and landladies were reluctant to accept Japanese students in their boarding houses, partly because they confused the latter with Native Americans. There were no dormitories in New Brunswick, so Japanese students had to rent places to live. However, as their number increased, it became clear that they were serious, studious, and followed rules, and more boarding houses were opened to them, which provides some proof of their acceptance by local residents. Nagai, Ōtsuka, Tajiri, and others attended Sunday school at a local church, and they also interacted with American families through Rutgers College faculty members, such as David Murray. One student, Matsudaira Tadaatsu, had a relationship with the daughter of a bookdealer in the city and married her. The Japanese students were interviewed by the local Trenton and New Brunswick newspapers,[17] and articles from this period about Japanese students studying at Rutgers institutions could be found in the *Targum*, the Rutgers College student newspaper. Ogawa Zenkichi and Hara Yasutarō played football with American students, and Katsu went to watch a game.[18] The school's small size fostered a sense of community among its Japanese and American students and their peers at the Grammar School.

The seventh point indicates that the sons of feudal lords and shogunal officials studied together. Most students were from Satsuma, but the rest came from a wide range of backgrounds. Many were from the northeastern Tohoku domains that had fought against the new government forces during the Bakumatsu civil war. There were also a small number of shogunal vassals and court nobles, along with students from the merchant class, the Mitsui family's scions, and a group of attendants who interacted with students from the samurai clans.

The eighth and ninth points, respectively, describing the Japanese students as "pilgrims to the shrines of knowledge" and having an "intense love of study," seem somewhat exaggerated. The former may refer to their willingness to travel from San Francisco to the eastern United States by the Transcontinental Railroad to study in New Brunswick. The article is written in reference to Kusakabe Tarō, who died of illness before graduating from Rutgers College, but he was not the only Japanese student who died during his American sojourn: Kitō Ichisuke and Kunitomo Takinosuke were buried in Monson Cemetery, and Nawa Michikazu was buried in Boston. Still others died from illness or suicide while pursuing their studies in unfamiliar environments—Obata Jinzaburō and Hirosawa Kenzō in Brooklyn, Hasegawa Kijirō in Albany, and Matsukata Sosuke in Farmington, Connecticut, to name a few. Many Japanese students died due to health problems caused by excessive study, on ships returning to Japan earlier

FIGURE 4.2. Street where Kusakabe Tarō lived with landlady Maria Van Arsdale at 62 Church Street, New Brunswick, on the lower part of the street. (Photo by George H. Pound, William Elliot Griffis Collection, Rutgers University Libraries.)

than planned, or they returned to their hometowns and succumbed to illness or injury first sustained in the United States.

Although not mentioned in *The Far East* article, the quiet environment and relatively low cost of study in New Brunswick, despite its proximity to the metropolis of New York, may have been one of the reasons why it drew flocks of Japanese students. In his November 14, 1870, entry, Ikagawa Motoi, a resident of Brooklyn, estimated the cost of study to be $2,000 or more per year in New York City, $1,200 in Brooklyn, $800–$900 in New Brunswick, and $400–$500 in Michigan.[19] It is unclear whether this is the total cost of studying abroad or only tuition, but it does give an idea of the different resources required to study in each region.

While New Brunswick is described here as a "shrine" of knowledge, it was not always a suitable place for Japanese students to study. An increasing critical mass of their compatriots became a negative factor in learning English. As they spent their days immersed in English during classes, they found it hard to resist using their native tongue with fellow countrymen after school. Nagai Kyūichirō and Ōsawa Yoshio, along with Tajiri Inajirō, sometimes met other *ryūgakusei* as part of their English study to read English books together.[20] However, Nagai Kyūichiro's diary in New Brunswick shows that they visited each other's lodgings on a daily basis. It was probably rare for Japanese students to communicate with each other in English. On the other hand, Kawamura Kiyoo and other *ryūgakusei* sent by the former shogunal Tokugawa family in 1871 studied at New Brunswick for about two months, but because they felt that being surrounded by the twenty-six or twenty-seven Japanese students there would interfere with their studies, they transferred to Flatbush Academy in Brooklyn, which was also connected to the Dutch Reformed Church.[21] The Mitsui sons were supposed to receive on-the-job training at a U.S. bank, but their English skills did not reach that level even after two and a half years of study, probably due to the fact that they studied in a school with many Japanese students.[22] Considering that Kanda Naibu, Kudō Seiichi, Orita Hikoichi, and others taught by Edward T. Corwin, a pastor of the Dutch Reformed Church in Millstone—an area somewhat isolated from the greater Japanese community in New Brunswick—were all able to go on to college, studying in New Brunswick may not have been "efficient."[23] Many *ryūgakusei* like Yamakawa Kenjirō, who was determined to go to Yale University Scientific School, ended up moving to schools with fewer Japanese students.

Boston and Its Vicinity

When I was researching Boston as a mecca for Japanese students, it surprised me to see how many of them had studied at Harvard University and MIT, which I thought of as elite schools equivalent to the University of Tokyo in Japan. Some of the well-known names in Japanese history, such as Kaneko Kentarō, Komura Jutarō, and Megata Tanetarō, attended these U.S. schools.[24] There were also Japanese students who lived in Boston and were friends with then popular American poet Henry W. Longfellow, who expanded the scope of their interest in American *Japonisme* through connections with intellectual and cultural figures, such as Edward Morse and Ernest Fenollosa. Among these, I identified Gilbert Attwood, a money changer, banker, and independent scholar of Japan, as a bridge between the *ryūgakusei* and Boston intellectuals.[25]

Saitō Shūichirō and Kaneko Kentarō published and presented English translations of classic Japanese stories like *Chūshingura* and *Musume Setsuyō* in the United States while studying. The students in Boston also participated in Alexander Graham Bell's historical experiments with the telephone, and the Iwakura Mission's reception in the city in the summer of 1872 was a great success and attended by the writer/philosopher Ralph Waldo Emerson and the physician/poet Oliver Wendell Holmes Sr. Boston, a city of learning and trade with the Orient, allowed the Japanese students there to interact with a unique local set of intellectuals and wealthy traders. It was the setting for exchanges between Niijima Jō and Alpheus Hardy, a wealthy trader who sponsored Niijima's studies there. Edward Kinsley, a trader and family friend of Mori Arinori, led Mori, a frequent visitor to Boston, into the city's intellectual circle and paved the way for *ryūgakusei* to study in its public schools.[26] Aaron Davis Weld French, a trader with Japan and China, led students he had met in Nagasaki to Boston. Thus, Boston holds a notable place in the history of U.S.-Japan cultural exchange, having once hosted elite Japanese students who made their mark on history in later years.

Let us now analyze Boston and its suburbs based on the key points in the excerpt from *The Far East* article on New Brunswick above. With regard to Boston as an "abiding place," the colleges and graduate schools around Boston where Japanese students studied included Harvard College, Harvard University Law School, Harvard University Scientific School, MIT, Boston University Law School, and Tufts College. Next, the private academies and public schools where Japanese students studied prepared them to enter colleges and graduate schools mainly around Boston; these secondary schools included the Public Grammar School and the English High School in Boston, Chauncey Hall School, Allen's English School, Worcester Polytechnic Institute, Williston Seminary, and Highland Military Academy, all of which may be considered as counterparts to "the efficient Grammar School" found in New Brunswick. Unlike New Brunswick, which had only one college and an affiliated grammar school, Boston, a much larger city with an easy access to suburbs, had a wide array of secondary schools for students who intended to attend colleges in the area.

Table 4.2 shows the length of time Japanese students studied at these universities and private academies and the number of Japanese students in each year, including special students.

Boston had seventeen students in 1871–1872, or about 50 percent of the thirty-two in New Brunswick in the same year, but the number is enough to consider it an "abiding place." However, the total enrollment in the school at any given time, even at its peak, did not reach "20 or 30 Japanese students." Meanwhile, the ratio of students who studied at colleges and graduate schools to the number of students who studied at private academies and other secondary schools was 30 to 113 in New Brunswick but 48 to 55 in the Boston area, which is high even if data on secondary education is omitted. In addition, the fifth point of being "very popular with the citizens and students" is also true, probably due to the abovementioned interactions with Boston's elite community.

There are two peaks in the arrivals of Japanese students. The first peak is from 1871 to 1874, which is around the same period as New Brunswick and reflects the rush of *ryūgakusei* from Japan. The second peak, from 1875 to 1877, excludes New Brunswick, largely due to the number of students who came to the United States on Kaisei Gakkō loan scholarships, students such as Komura, Saito, and Kikuchi. After the order for *ryūgakusei* to return to Japan in 1873, government-sponsored study abroad was offered only to a small elite. The first of these dispatched students came in 1875 after having received higher education in English

Table 4.2
Japanese students in Boston and its vicinity by academic year: Number of Japanese students in colleges or graduate schools / number of Japanese students in private academies or public schools

1868–1869	0 / 4	total 4
1869–1870	0 / 3	total 3
1870–1871	2 / 3	total 5
1871–1872	4 / 13	total 17
1872–1873	4 / 10	total 14
1873–1874	6 / 7	total 13
1874–1875	2 / 6	total 8
1875–1876	8 / 3	total 11
1876–1877	9 / 2	total 11
1877–1878	7 / 1	total 8
1878–1879	3 / 1	total 4
1879–1880	4 / 1	total 5

NOTE: See appendix 4B for individual names.

at Daigaku Nankō and its successor, Kaisei Gakkō (now the University of Tokyo); students at the highest level were not required to attend grammar school or private academies for admission to colleges and graduate schools after their arrival in the United States. American and British teachers on the faculty of Nankō and Kaisei provided "an education comparable to American colleges."[27] Students who had to start from primary or secondary education upon arrival in the United States were limited to those of private means.

The increasing preference of *ryūgakusei* for law schools also led to an increase in the number of Japanese students studying law in Boston and its suburbs. Because there were no law schools in the vicinity of New Brunswick, they studied at Columbia, Yale, Harvard, and the universities in Boston. These students were certainly "pilgrims to the shrines of knowledge" who possessed an "intense love of study," as seen in the cases of Kaneko Kentarō and Komura Jutarō, whose overreading led their ophthalmologist to intervene.

As a place of "general rendezvous," Boston was the northernmost hub of the *ryūgakusei* community. Geographically speaking, transportation to and from the city cannot be said to have been convenient, but it had good rail access to places like New Haven (Connecticut), Albany (New York), the area along the Connecticut River where private academies were scattered, and western Massachusetts. A large number of *ryūgakusei* came and went in this area; Gilbert Attwood, who obtained information about Japan from them, said that many came to his office on State Street in Boston to read Japanese newspapers.

Lastly, Boston could also be identified as "a sort of head-quarters" for *ryūgakusei* because Mori Arinori, Japan's first minister to the United States who

FIGURE 4.3. Hiraga Isosaburō (*center*) with Honma Eiichirō and Inoue Rokusaburō, two of the first Japanese students in Boston. Photo by Edward L. Allen, late nineteenth century. (Credit: Museum of Fine Arts, Boston. Charles Bain Hoyt Fund, 2002.237.)

was posted in 1871, frequently visited Boston to supervise them, and Megata Tanetarō, who returned to Japan after graduating from Harvard Law School, came back to Boston to oversee students on Ministry of Education loan scholarships.[28] Some intellectuals and Americans who supported Japan, such as Gilbert Attwood and Edward Kinsley, may also have taken care of *ryūgakusei* in Boston.

In sum, although Boston had fewer *ryūgakusei* than New Brunswick, it effectively took over the function of a hub for these students.[29] Those who studied at universities, graduate schools, and other higher education institutions formed the core of the population in this area.

Brooklyn, New York, and Monson, Massachusetts

Most of the *ryūgakusei* who went to New Brunswick were Grammar School students. It is thus worth comparing the areas where the private academies at which they studied to prepare for college were located, so this section focuses on Brooklyn, New York and Monson, Massachusetts.

In Brooklyn, many of these students attended BPI, and their numbers are shown in table 4.3. The school was an eight-year institution, with the first four years in the Academic Department and the next four in the Collegiate Department. The latter curriculum had four courses: classical or preparatory, scientific, liberal, and commercial, which resembled the relationship between the Grammar School and Rutgers College. Once enrolled, students received individualized instruction based on their progress in a "special student" system. If judged able to keep up with the group classes, they were placed in a class appropriate to their ability.

Obata Jinzaburō of the Nakatsu domain chose the school because its principal, Cochran, had formerly headed a teacher training college and knew how to tailor the education offered to the needs of individual Japanese students.[30] Ikagawa Motoi from the Fukuyama domain wrote in a travel diary at the time that "Prince Kachōnomiya wanted to go there because it is a very famous school and excels in the field of politics and law."[31] This referred to Kachōnomiya Hirotsune, the first *ryūgakusei* to enroll at the school, who spent the first two years of his education there as a special student. In the third year, Egi Takatō and Satō Momotarō entered the liberal course, and Obata, previously a teacher at Keiō Gijuku, was in the third class from the bottom.

Many of the *ryūgakusei* who entered this school came in groups. In 1870–1871, a group of six came with Prince Kachōnomiya, and in 1872–1873, a group of three came with Ii Naonori of the Hikone domain, and seven students were sent by the Ministry of the Japanese Navy. The navy students in particular must have

Table 4.3
Japanese students at the Brooklyn Polytechnic Institute by academic year: Number of Japanese students in the Collegiate Department / number of Japanese students in the Academic Department

1870–1871	0 / 6 (Special students)	total 6
1871–1872	0 / 15 (Special students)	total 15
1872–1873	2 (Liberal course) / 20 (13 special students)	total 22
1873–1874	2 (Liberal course) / 4	total 6
1874–1875	2 (Liberal course) / 0	total 2

NOTE: See appendix 4C for individual names.

chosen the school in view of the field training it provided at the Brooklyn Navy Yard. Since Kachōnomiya's group landed in San Francisco on October 16, they would have arrived in New York at the end of October. Since classes would have already started and there were many Japanese students in New Brunswick, it must have been difficult to secure lodgings for the group in the city. It is possible that they chose to study at a reputable school in Brooklyn not too far from New Jersey and New York City, where John Mason Ferris of the Reformed Church Board of Foreign Missions, who had helped many *ryūgakusei*, was. Incidentally, Kachōnomiya was the first *ryūgakusei* from the royal family, and he used the alias Azuma Takahiko. Local reports and descriptions of Japanese students indicate that he made friends not only with his compatriots but also with others around him.[32]

According to the diary of Nagai, who attended the Grammar School in New Brunswick, it took two hours each way between New Brunswick and Brooklyn by train and boat, and the *ryūgakusei* came and went via New York.[33] It is safe to assume that Brooklyn and New Brunswick were within the same sphere of life for these students. New Brunswick's boarding situation, BPI's flexible special student system, and the geographical relationship with the Brooklyn Navy Yard may have attracted *ryūgakusei* to briefly attend BPI; many of those finished after only one year of study.[34]

Monson Academy is the alma mater of Samuel R. Brown, who was sent to Japan by the Dutch Reformed Church in 1859. Brown, a native of East Windsor, Connecticut, went on to Yale College and subsequently to Union Theological Seminary. In 1863, he began teaching English in Yokohama, and one of his students is said to have been Yoshihara Shigetoshi of Satsuma; he may also have taught another Satsuma student, Kitō Ichisuke, who went to Edo. Brown had already introduced Chinese students to Monson Academy, and it is likely that he recommended the school to the Satsuma students because of its experience in teaching Asian students and its quiet environment away from urban hustle and bustle. The number of its enrolled *ryūgakusei* by academic year is given in table 4.4.

Monson Academy, where Japanese students began studying in 1866, has as long a history of ties with *ryūgakusei* as New Brunswick. However, because it does not have an affiliated college, no Japanese students enrolled after 1873–1874, when all *ryūgakusei* were ordered to return home.[35] The lack of a college meant the lack of senior students to whom newcomers could turn. Perhaps this is related to why, with the exception of Nakahara from Chōshū, all of Monson's Japanese students were from Satsuma or Kumamoto. The relative homogeneity among the Japanese students here stands in contrast to their diversity in New Brunswick.[36] Of the students who went on to college, three went to Yale, one to the U.S. Naval Academy, and one to Massachusetts Agricultural College.

What stands out about Monson is the attention paid to Japanese students by local newspapers, starting with a detailed interview with Satsuma students who

Table 4.4
Number of Japanese students at Monson Academy by academic year

1866–1867	6
1867–1868	5
1868–1869	3
1869–1870	1
1870–1871	4
1871–1872	5
1872–1873	4
1873–1874	3

NOTE: See appendix 4D for individual names.

entered Monson Academy in 1866. Unfortunately, it was Kitō's suicide by hanging that made their existence widely known. Many *ryūgakusei* had lost their lives to tuberculosis, but Kitō was the first and last to commit suicide. The Satsuma students were impressed by the warm cooperation of school officials and residents in the search for Kitō, who had gone missing, and in the preparation and execution of his funeral.

At that time, it was common for even private secondary academies to require a thesis or oral examination at graduation, similar to universities. The English papers read for this occasion by Tanegashima Keisuke, Tsuda Seiichi, and Kunitomo Jirō appeared in full in major local newspapers such as the *Springfield Republican* and the *Hartford Courant*.[37] Such readings were also required at both Rutgers Grammar School and Rutgers College, but only the title of Hattori Ichizō's graduation thesis was published in the local New Jersey newspaper, which may reflect differing levels of intellectual interest in the local communities of Monson and New Brunswick. Because Monson Academy did not have an affiliated college, its atmosphere was more relaxed. In contrast to Brooklyn, most students stayed in school for two or three years, and none stayed for only one year.

Conclusion

This chapter has conducted a comparative examination of New Brunswick and Boston as hubs for Japanese *ryūgakusei* based on nine points. It confirms that similar conditions existed in both places despite differences in the quality of the educational institutions and the number of years they were attended. In addition, since the overwhelming majority of *ryūgakusei* in New Brunswick studied at Rutgers Grammar School, comparisons were further drawn with Brooklyn Polytechnic Institute in New York and Monson Academy in Massachusetts to clarify these schools' characteristics.

In the case of Brooklyn, New York City's location across the river attracted Japanese arrivals that New Brunswick alone could not accommodate, namely the

Kachōnomiya, Ii, and navy groups. The students in Brooklyn were very active in interacting with their counterparts in New Brunswick, and together they formed a kind of Japanese community in the suburbs of New York. The length of their stay was relatively short because of the BPI's flexible "special student" program, and the school also provided English language instruction in preparation for on-the-job training at the nearby Brooklyn Navy Yard.

Monson Academy was a place where students preparing for Yale University could devote themselves to their studies in a quiet environment. Japanese students had studied in Monson as early as in New Brunswick, and perhaps reflecting the intellectual bent of the former's residents, local newspapers carried articles about the Japanese students and even published their English readings for their graduation ceremonies. For reasons unknown, almost all Monson Academy students were from Satsuma and Kumamoto, giving the impression that the school was more closed than the New Brunswick academy. The unique environments in Brooklyn and Monson enabled Japanese students to study in either place under special conditions; comparing New Brunswick to these two locales highlights the former's openness and the diversity of its Japanese students. On the other hand, because Boston had more colleges and graduate schools than New Brunswick, more Japanese students received higher education there after they had completed their initial studies in the country or in Japan. In sum, it seems that Boston had fully succeeded New Brunswick as a hub for Japanese students by the mid-1870s, but it is necessary to provide a broader context.

Although this chapter has focused on students who moved from Japan to New Brunswick, we must not forget their counterparts who moved in the opposite direction, namely Rutgers College graduates and teachers who traveled to Japan. In addition, many missionaries were sent to Japan by the Dutch Reformed Church to teach in Nagasaki and elsewhere, although not all those dispatched were Rutgers College graduates. Guido F. Verbeck, who wrote letters of introduction to Ferris in New York, was appointed in October 1870 to the position of vice principal of Kaisei Gakkō (formerly the shogunate-run Kaiseijo), which had briefly been called the Daigaku Nankō in December 1869; the school was the predecessor of the University of Tokyo. Verbeck served as Kaisei's vice principal from October 1870 to 1873 and worked to improve its regulations and educational content. In 1872, he invited William E. Griffis, a graduate of Rutgers College who had taught at the Meishinkan in Fukui, to teach chemistry classes. Meanwhile, Griffis recommended and brought in Edward Warren Clark, a graduate of Rutgers College, to teach at the Shizuoka Gakumonjo until it closed, after which Clark taught science at Kaisei Gakkō from December 1873 to December 1874. In June 1873, David Murray, a Rutgers College professor who had taught the early overseas Japanese students, was appointed superintendent at the Ministry of Education, in which capacity he advised on educational affairs. Murray's invitation to Japan may have been at least indirectly influenced by students who had studied at Rutgers College, such as Hatakeyama Yoshinari.[38]

In other words, as if to offset the decrease in the flow of people from Japan to New Brunswick, the movement of Rutgers graduates, faculty, and related personnel in the opposite direction occurred at about the same time, and Kaisei Gakkō appeared to be the Japanese equivalent of Rutgers College and the Grammar School. Students who had received English education at Kaisei Gakkō and the former Nankō, including Komura, Saitō, and Kikuchi, were sent to Europe and the United States by the Ministry of Education as loan scholarship students in 1875. The Nankō students sent to the United States in 1870 were Megata, Hasegawa Kijirō, Matsumoto Sōichirō, and Katsuki Keigorō. Records show that Megata studied at Harvard University Law School in Boston, and Matsumoto studied at Rensselaer Polytechnic Institute in Troy near Albany in New York. Edward S. Morse and Ernest Fenollosa also came from Boston in 1877 and 1878, respectively, to teach at the University of Tokyo, and they greatly influenced U.S.-Japan cultural exchanges; however, they did not form deep relationships with their students in Japan.

The seeds sown by the Yokoi brothers and Kusakabe Tarō, the first *ryūgakusei* to be dispatched to New Brunswick, encouraged the dispatch of Rutgers-affiliated personnel to Japan. These exchanges sowed seeds that bore fruit in Boston and elsewhere in the United States, creating benefits that returned to Japan and contributed to its rapid modernization in a variety of fields. The achievements of the two-way exchange between Japan and the United States pioneered by those affiliated with Rutgers and the broader New Brunswick college and grammar school community, backed by the Dutch Reformed Church, shine brightly in the history of Japanese overseas students.

Appendix 4A: Last Names of the Japanese Students Who Studied in Rutgers College or Rutgers College Grammar School in New Brunswick, New Jersey

Rutgers College / Rutgers College Grammar School (Total, Pre-Meiji Affiliation in Brackets)

1866 September–1867 June
Yokoi brothers (2) [KUMAMOTO 2]

1867–1868
Kusakabe / Katsu, Takaki, Tomita, Yokoi brothers (6) [FUKUI 1 / KUMAMOTO 2, SENDAI 1, SHŌNAI 1, BAKUSHIN (TOKUGAWA VASSAL) 1]

1868–1869
Kusakabe, Matsumura, Hatakeyama, Yoshida / Katsu, Takaki, Yokoi brothers, Shiramine, Sugano (10) [SATSUMA 3, FUKUI 1 / KUMAMOTO 2, TOSA 1, NAGAOKA 1, SHŌNAI 1, *BAKUSHIN* 1]

1869–1870
Kusakabe, Matsumura / Hashiguchi, Hirayama, Maruoka, Shimazu, Hayashi, Tsuda, S. Yokoi, I. Hattori, Kodama, Mōri, Orita, Sugano, Takaki, Katsu, Iwakura brothers (18) [FUKUI 1, SATSUMA 1 / SADOWARA 4, KUMAMOTO 3, CHŌSHŪ 3, SATSUMA 1, TOSA 1, SHŌNAI 1, *BAKUSHIN* 1, *KUGE* (nobility) 2]

1870–1871
Hatakeyama / I. Hattori, Mōri, Kodama, Kunishi, Mogami, Taneda, Tanimoto, K. Hattori, Takaki, Nara, Nanbu, Sugano, Yamakawa, Tokura, Shiramine, Matsuda, Asano, Hayashi, Katsu, Kawamura, Nakura, Ono, Ōkubo, Takemura, Iwakura brothers (27) [SATSUMA 1 / CHŌSHŪ 4, SATSUMA 3, SHŌNAI 2, MORIOKA 2, TOSA 1, AIZU 1, OKAYAMA 1, NAGAOKA 1, MATSUYAMA 1, *BAKUSHIN* 8, *KUGE* 2]

1871–1872
I. Hatttori, Shiramine, Hatakeyama / Andō, Mogami, Tajiri, Taneda, Tanimoto, Nagai, Ogawa, Ōsawa, Nara, Nanbu, K. Toda, U. Toda Ujitomo, Nishikimi, K. Hattori, Takaki, Matsuda, Tokura, Kokushi, Ōtsuka, Yamakawa, Hara, Sugano, Katsu, Iwakura brothers, Minamiiwakura, Mitsui Family (36) [CHŌSHŪ 1, NAGAOKA 1, SATSUMA 1 / SATSUMA 5, NAGOYA 3, ŌGAKI 3, MORIOKA 2, SHŌNAI 2, MATSUYAMA 1, OKAYAMA 1, CHŌSHŪ 1, SAGA 1, AIZU 1, TANBA 1, TOSA 1, *BAKUSHIN* 1, *KUGE* 3, MERCHANT 7]

1872–1873
I. Hattori, Ōtsuka / Matsudaira brothers, Yamaguchi, Matsukata, Shibayama, Ogawa, Ōsawa, Takaki, K. Hattori, Nishikimi, Ū. Toda, Hara, Nishikikōji, Shido, Mitsui Family 7 (23) [CHŌSHŪ 1, SAGA 1 / UEDA 3, SATSUMA 2, NAGOYA 2, SHŌNAI 2, ŌGAKI 2, TANBA 1, *KUGE* 1, MERCHANT 7, unknown 1]

1873–1874
Ogawa, Ōsawa, I. Hattori, Ōtsuka, Hara / Matsudaira brothers Takaki, Taku, Mitsui Family 5 (14) [NAGOYA 2, CHŌSHŪ 1, SAGA 1, TANBA 1 / UEDA 2, SHŌNAI 1, MERCHANT 5]

1874–1875
I. Hattori, Kudō, Taku, Hara / Matsudaira Tadanari (6) [CHŌSHŪ 1, SAGA 1, TANBA 1, *BAKUSHIN* 1 / UEDA 2]

1875–1876
Matsudaira Tadanari, Taku, Kudō (3) [UEDA 1, SAGA 1, *BAKUSHIN* 1]

1876–1877
Matsudaira Tadanari, Kudō (2) [UEDA 1, *BAKUSHIN* 1]

1877–1878
Matsudaira Tadanari, Kudō (2) [UEDA 1, *BAKUSHIN* 1]

1878–1879
Matsudaira Tadanari (1) [UEDA 1]

Appendix 4B.1: Last Names and Total Number of Japanese Students in Colleges, Universities, or Graduate Schools in the Boston Area (Including Its Vicinities) by Enrolled Years

1870–1871	2	Honma, Yuji
1871–1872	4	Honma, Tominaga, Yamada, Yuji
1872–1873	4	Honma, Inoue, Megata, Yamada
1873–1874	6	Honma, Hotta, Inoue, Megata, Nagai, Nawa
1874–1875	2	Maruoka, Mori Haruyoshi
1875–1876	8	Dan, Isawa, Kikuchi, Komura, Mitsuoka, Mori Haruyoshi, Saito, Uesugi
1876–1877	9	Dan, Isawa, Kaneko, Kikuchi, Komura, Mitsuoka, Mori Haruyoshi, Saitō, Uesugi
1877–1878	7	Isawa, Kaneko, Kikuchi, Komura, Nakayama, Saitō, Uesugi
1878–1879	3	Kurino, Nakayama, Uesugi
1879–1880	4	Kikkawa, Kurino, Nakayama, Uesugi

Appendix 4B.2: Names of the Colleges, Universities, and Graduate Schools Where Japanese Students Enrolled in the Boston Area, Their Names, Their Pre-Meiji Affiliations, and Enrolled Years

Boston University College
Uesugi Katsuyoshi of YONEZAWA (1875–1876, 1876–1877, 1877–1878, 1878–1879, 1879–1880)

Boston University Law School
Nawa Michikazu of CHŌSHŪ (1873–1874)
Kikuchi Takeo of MORIOKA (1875–1876, 1876–1877, 1877–1878)
Saitō Shūichirō of TAKEFU (1875–1876, 1876–1877, 1877–1878)

Bridgewater Normal School
Isawa Shūji of TAKATŌ (1875–1876, 1876–1877)

Harvard College
Kikkawa Chōkichi of IWAKUNI (1879–1880, 1880–1881, 1881–1882, 1882–1883)

Harvard University Law School
Yamada Ineyasu of KURUME (1871–1872, 1872–1873)
Inoue Yoshikazu of FUKUOKA (1872–1873, 1873–1874)
Megata Tanetarō of SHIZUOKA (1872–1873, 1873–1874)
Komura Jutarō of OBI (1875–1876, 1876–1877, 1877–1878)
Kaneko Kentarō of FUKUOKA (1876–1877, 1877–1878)
Nakayama Kanrokurō of SHIMOUSA (1877–1878, 1878–1879, 1879–1880)
Kurino Shin'ichirō of FUKUOKA (1878–1879, 1879–1880, 1880–1881)

Harvard University Scientific School
Maruoka Takeo of SADOWARA (1874–1875)
Isawa Shūji of TAKATŌ (1877–1878)

Massachusetts Agricultural University
Yuji Sadamoto of SATSUMA (1870–1871, 1871–1872)
Hori Seitarō of CHŌSHŪ (unknown, 1874–1875?)

Massachusetts Institute of Technology
Honma Eiichirō of FUKUOKA (1870–1871, 1871–1872, 1872–1873, 1873–1874)
Tominaga Fuyuki of BAKUSHIN (1871–1872 nondegree)
Mori Haruyoshi of TOSA (1874–1875, 1875–1876 nondegree, 1876–1877 nondegree)
Dan Takuma of FUKUOKA (1875–1876, 1876–1877, 1877–1878)
Mitsuoka Takeo of FUKUI (1875–1876, 1876–1877)

Tufts College
Nagai Kyūichirō of NAGOYA (1873–1874)
Hotta Akira of SAKURA (1873–1874)

Appendix 4B.3: Last Names and Total Number of Japanese Students in Private Academies and Grammar Schools in the Boston Area (Including Its Vicinities) by Enrolled Years

1868–1869	4	Hanabusa, Honma, Inoue, Tsuge
1869–1870	3	Honma, Inoue, Yamada
1870–1871	3	Inoue, Shimazu, Yamada

1871–1872	13	Akabane, Hayashi, Hirayama, Hotta, Inoue, Irie, Kodama, Kondō, Megata, Onodera, Shimazu, Shirane, Shimizu
1872–1873	10	Dan, Kaneko, Karahashi, Kikkawa, Ono, Ōzeki, Saisho, Seya, Tanaka, Yokoi Saheita
1873–1874	7	Dan, Kaneko, Kikkawa, Maruoka, Mitsuoka, Tanaka, Ueda
1874–1875	6	Dan, Kaneko, Kikkawa, Mitsuoka, Tanaka, Ueda
1875–1876	3	Kaneko, Kikkawa, Ueda
1876–1877	2	Kikkawa, Nanbu Nobukata
1877–1878	1	Kikkawa
1878–1879	1	Kikkawa
1879–1880	1	Nakahara

Appendix 4B.4: Number of Japanese Students Who Studied in Private Academies and Grammar Schools in the Boston Area (Including Its Vicinities) by School Name

Chauncey Hall School (Boston)

1871–1872 1
1873–1874 1
1874–1875 1
1875–1876 1
1876–1877 2
1877–1878 1
1878–1879 1
1879–1880 1

English High School of Boston

1875–1876 1

Highland Military Academy (Worcester, MA)

1869–1870 3
1870–1871 3
1871–1872 6

Louise Grammar School of Boston

1868–1869 2

Mt. Pleasant Classical Institute (Amherst, MA)

1868–1869 2

Philip Grammar School of Boston

1873–1874 1
1874–1875 1

Phillips Academy (Andover, MA)
1865–1866 1
1866–1867 1

Rice Grammar School of Boston
1872–1873 4
1873–1874 3
1874–1875 2

Roxbury High School of Boston
1875–1876 1

The West Newton English and Classical School (West Newton, MA)
1871–1872 3
1872–1873 1

Williston Seminary (Easthampton, MA)
1871–1872 1
1872–1873 4

Appendix 4C: Names and Their Pre-Meiji Affiliation of the Japanese Students Who Studied in Brooklyn Polytechnic Institute by Enrolled Years

1870–1871 (Special students)
Azuma Takahiko (Kachōnomiya Hirotsune) of KYOTO
Egi Takatō of FUKUYAMA
Fujimori Shūichirō of MORIOKA
Ikagawa Motoi of FUKUYAMA
Magome Tamesuke of BAKUSHIN
Yanagimoto Naotarō of FUKUI

1871–1872 (Special students)
Azuma
Egi
Fujimori
Hayashi Kyūshirō of BAKUSHIN
Hirosawa Kenzō of CHŌSHŪ
Ikagawa
Matsuda Shinsai of MATSUYAMA
Obata Jinzaburō of NAKATSU
Okudaira Masayuki of NAKATSU
Sakai Tadakuni of HIMEJI
Satō Momotarō of SAKURA
Takasu Kuzuma of HIMEJI

Takemura Kingo of BAKUSHIN
Yamada Tetsuji of NAGOYA
Yanagimoto

1872–1873

Liberal Course
- Egi
- Satō

Fourth Grade
- Kōno Michikato of MATSUYAMA

Third Grade
- Hayashi
- Hirosawa
- Matsuda
- Obata
- Okudaira

Second Grade
- Takasu

Special Students
- Ii Naonori of HIKONE
- Ii Naoyasu of HIKONE
- Kawakami Fusanobu of HIKONE
- Kazuye Tadakuni of HIKONE
- Kunitomo Takinosuke (NAVY)
- Matsuda Masanori (NAVY)
- Murase Tamekichi (NAVY)
- Nishimura Sutezō of HIKONE
- Saigō Koreichi of SATSUMA (NAVY)
- Sakai
- Shiramine Shunme of NAGAOKA (NAVY)
- Sone Naonoshin (NAVY)
- Tsumura Fukuhiro (NAVY)

1873–1874

Liberal Course
- Matsuda
- Satō

Fourth Grade
- Takasu

Third Grade
- Okudaira
- Saigō

First Grade
- Sakai

1874–1875
Liberal Course
Egi
Satō

Appendix 4D: Names and Pre-Meiji Affiliations of the Japanese Students in Monson Academy by Enrolled Years

1866–1867
Ashiwara Shūhei (Kitō Ichisuke) of SATSUMA (E)
Hisamatsu Shōzō (Enatsu Kizō) of SATSUMA (E)
Kudō Jūrō (Yuji Sadamoto) of SATSUMA (E)
Ōhara Reinosuke (Yoshihara Shigetoshi) of SATSUMA (E)
Shimada Kan'ichi (Nire Kagenori) (E) of SATSUMA (E)
Yoshida Hikomaro (Tanegashima Keisuke) of SATSUMA (E)

1867–1868
Hisamatsu (E)*
Kudō (E)*
Ōhara (CL)
Shimada (E)*
Yoshida (CL)

1868–1869
Kudō (E)
Ōhara (CL)
Yoshida (CL)

1869–1870
Yoshida (CL)

1870–1871
Kudō (E)
Nada Jirō of KUMAMOTO (CL)
Nakahara Kuninosuke of CHŌSHŪ (E)
Tsuda Seiichi of KUMAMOTO (CL)

1871–1872
Ikeda Inosuke of SATSUMA (E)
Iwao Saburō of KUMAMOTO (CL)
Nada (CL)
Nakahara (CL)
Tsuda (CL)

1872–1873
Ikeda (CL)

Iwao (CL)
Yoshida Keizō of SATSUMA (E)
Yuji Sadanori of SATSUMA (E)

1873–1874
Ikeda (CL)
Nada (E)
Yoshida (E)

* Shimada, Hisamatsu, and Kudō were with Thomas Lake Harris from November 1867 to April 1868. There are two other students, whose records of their enrollment in Monson Academy were not found, but some sources showed they stayed in Monson for a while. Their names are Uesugi of YONEZAWA and Kunitomo of NAVY.
CL = Classical Department; E = English Department.

Notes

This chapter was originally written in Japanese and is edited and translated here by Haruko Wakabayashi.

1 The Yokoi brothers from the Kumamoto domain departed Nagasaki and arrived in New York via Java, Indonesia, and Europe. They departed on June 11, 1866, and arrived in New York in November of the same year, so it took them six months to reach the United States. About a year after they arrived, Kusakabe Tarō from the Fukui domain also sailed from Nagasaki on February 13, 1867 (Japanese calendar), and reached the United States via Java, arriving in New York on August 12; his trip also took nearly half a year. The direct Yokohama–San Francisco route took about three weeks to cross the Pacific Ocean, and the transcontinental railroad connected San Francisco and New York in about two weeks. The first Japanese to travel to the United States by the direct Yokohama–San Francisco service, as confirmed by Japanese and U.S. newspaper articles, arrived in San Francisco in March 1867 and carried Ono Tomogorō and other members of the *bakufu* envoys. The second group sailed aboard the *Colorado*, which departed Yokohama on May 25, 1867, and included Sasaki Gonruk (Sasaki Gonroku from Fukui), Yangimoto (Yanagimoto Naotarō from Fukui), Nomura (Nomura Ichisuke from Satsuma), Higo (Higo Jūrō from Satsuma), Mura Kami (Tanimoto Michiyuki from Satsuma), Drozo (unknown), Kinzo (Takeuchi Kenzō from Satsuma), and Ghozje (unknown). Also on board was the Dutch Reformed Church missionary Rev. Samuel Robbins Brown and his wife and daughter, who were returning home temporarily. Since the Transcontinental Railroad had not yet opened, they took the Panama Isthmus crossing route from San Francisco via Aspinwall to the eastern United States. See Takagi Fuji, *Bakumatsu ishinki no Beikoku ryūgaku* (Tokyo: Keio Gijuku University Press, 2015), 80–81, 154–155.

2 Takahashi Korekiyo's autobiography states that "Among the first-class-cabin Japanese passengers were five or six students from the Fukuoka domain, led by Hiraga Isosaburō"; see Takahashi Korekiyo and Uetsuka Tsukasa, *Takahashi Korekiyo jiden* (Tokyo: Chūō Kōronsha, 1976), 40. They were Hiraga, Inoue, Honma, Funakoshi, Aoki, and Matsushita, who traveled on to study in Switzerland. According to the Fukuoka domain's historical records, "Also on the same ship were Katsu Kaishū's heir,

Katsu Koroku; Tomita Tetsunosuke, Takahashi Wakiji (Korekiyo), and Suzuki Rokunosuke (Tomoo) of the Sendai domain; Takaki Samurō of the Shōnai domain; Itō Shirō and Koba Eijirō of the Satsuma domain; and a certain Nakao of the Hiroshima domain." The source of this information is unknown; see Ōkuma Asajirō, "Bakumatsu Fukuokahan yōkō no senku, Matsushita Naomi gaiseki 3," *Tsukushi shidan* 46 (1929): 30. A total of fifty-one Japanese were on board, including about thirty members of Hayatake Torakichi's troupe of acrobats. The Swiss consul Brennwald accompanied the Fukuoka students, though his diary does not mention Katsu's party; see Yokohamashi Furusato Rekishi Zaidan and Burenwarudo Nikki Kenkyūkai, eds., *Suisu shisetsudan ga mita bakumatsu no Nihon, Burenwarudo nikki 1862–1867* (Tokyo: Bensei Shuppan, 2020). This group arrived in San Francisco on September 14 and departed on September 18 to arrive in Panama on October 1 and New York on October 9. There are no historical records for Katsu's group after they landed in San Francisco.

3 Although there are no records that indicate rifts between domains, tensions can be inferred from the lack of descriptions of mutual exchanges of information. It seems that the ice gradually melted after their arrival in the United States.

4 No record indicates why they moved from Boston to New Brunswick; since they had already moved to New Brunswick in February 1868, their stay in Boston would have been five months at most. See Takahashi Shūetsu, *Kaishū nikki ni miru bakumatsu ishin no ryūgaku, Nichigin sōsai Tomita Tetsunosuke no America taiken* (Tokyo: Nihon Hyōronsha, 2018), 84.

5 French was also involved with Japanese students living in New Brunswick, lending about $2,000 without interest to Satsuma students who were having trouble making ends meet due to the lack of remittances from Japan, but in this case his first name is William. Further research is needed to identify French in Boston and French supporting Satsuma students. Regarding French, I received valuable information from the researcher Miyoshi Akira.

6 See Ōkuma, "Bakumatsu Fukuokahan yōkō no senku," 30–31.

7 Its principal at the time was Peter V. Veeder, pastor of the Napa Presbyterian Church, who taught in Japan from 1871 and knew James H. Ballagh of the Reformed Church. For more on the Japanese students in San Francisco, see Shiozaki Satoshi, "A Report on a Survey of Historical Documents Related to Japanese Residents in San Francisco during the Bakumatsu and the Meiji Restoration Period (Mainly 1866–1870)," *Jinbun, shizen, ningenkagaku kenkyū* 51 (2024): 116–144. The article focuses on "Kaneko" in Takahashi Korekiyo, *Takahashi Korekiyo jiden* (Tokyo: Chūō Kōronsha, 1996).

8 Specific information can be found in the diary and letters of Orita Hikoichi and in the letters of Yoshida Kiyonari.

9 Although studies on Japanese students in the United States are rapidly increasing due to the development of the digital age and research by scholars in Japan and the United States, many important historical documents have not yet been discovered, such as the list of Japanese students at the Rutgers Grammar School, and exchanges between researchers in Japan and the United States have been insufficient. I am very happy that Haruko Wakabayashi of Rutgers University has made every effort to facilitate the interaction of Japanese and U.S. researchers in bringing this book to fruition, and I have striven to incorporate the latest findings in this chapter in hopes of contributing to the advancement of future research.

10 "The Japanese Burial Lot at Willow Grove Cemetery, New Brunswick, New Jersey, U.S.," in *The Far East: An Illustrated Fortnightly Newspaper*, vol. 3, *Yokohama, June 1, 1872–May 17, 1873* (Tokyo: Yūshōdō Shoten, 1999), no. XIV, December 16, 1872, 160.

11 The number of students enrolled at the college includes all those who were accepted, but it is unclear whether they actually studied at the college or not. Thirteen Japanese students were enrolled at Rutgers College from 1866 to 1880. Hada estimates that at least twenty-three Japanese studied at New Brunswick before the Meiji Restoration and about thirty-four from 1868 to 1874; see Hada Sekio, "Nihon no kindai kyōiku to Ratogāsu Karejji," *Nihon Daigaku Jinbun Kagaku Kenkyūjo kenkyū kiyō* 27 (1983): 127. Katsu Koroku's article in the *Cincinnati Daily Gazette* on August 24, 1871, states that there were about thirty Japanese in New Brunswick before June 1871. Eleven Japanese thought to be living in New Brunswick at the time, one of whom was named Nishikikōji, attended the funeral of Mitsui Takaharu in January 1873. The names of Hattori Ichizō and Hara Yasutarō repeatedly appear as Japanese students who cared for the sickly Takaharu. See Mitsui Hachirōemon Takamuneden Hensan Iinkai, eds., *Mitsui Hachirōemon Takamune den* (Tokyo: Tokyo University Press, 1988), 690–692.

12 Orita Hikoichi traveled from New York City to New Haven with Nawa Michikazu of the Chōshū domain from July 11 to 19, 1873, and met Nanbu Hidemaro of the Morioka domain. In Boston, they stayed at Nagai Kyūichirō's lodgings and enjoyed sightseeing in the city with Kuroda Nagatomo of Fukuoka. On his way home, he went to the Japanese consulate in New York and stayed with Hara Yasutarō of the Tanba domain in New Brunswick, and he later visited Kanda Naibu at Corwin's house in Millstone. Itakura Shōzō, *Ichimai no shōzōga: Orita Hioichi sensei no kenkyū* (Kyoto: Sankō Dōsōkai, 1994), 107–108.

13 Letter from Tsuda to his father, March 18, 1870, in Nōda Masuki, *Baikei Tsuda sensei densan* (Kumamoto: Tsuda Seiichi Sensei 25-kai Tsuitōkai, 1933), 43. A letter dated January 15, 1870, from Ise Satarō (Yokoi Saheita) at the U.S. Naval Academy in Annapolis to Mrs. Van Arsdale mentions an "unexpected arrival of his friends, Tsuda and Hayashi, who "were going to England, but since they come to this country they want to stay here, so they do not intend to go to England, and they will study in New Brunswick." He further asks her to take care of them: "I am very sorry that they can not speak." See box 158, folder 2, William Elliot Griffis Collection, Special Collections and University Archives, Rutgers University Libraries, New Brunswick, NJ.

14 In addition to personal guidance in English study, it was a great relief to have compatriots, in emergency situations, like Hattori Ichizō and Hara Yasutarō, who as mentioned above cared for Mitsui Takaharu when his health failed. See Yamakawa Danshaku Kinenkai, ed., *Danshaku Yamakawa sensei ikō* (Tokyo: Yamakawa Danshaku Kinenkai, 1937), 47–48.

15 A private memoir by Ogawa Zenkichi shown to the author by Mr. Yoshihara Shigekazu.

16 Takagi, *Bakumatsu ishinki no Beikoku ryūgaku*, 148. In dealing with the history of U.S.-Japan exchange during the Bakumatsu and early Meiji era, one may overestimate the status of the Dutch Reformed Church in the United States. Takagi points out that its marginality may have limited New Brunswick students' and officials' relationships with the outside world.

17 *New Republic*, July 7, 1870. Also printed in the *New York Sun*, June 3, 1870, under the heading "Japanese in College."

18 A private memoir by Ogawa Zenkichi shown to the author by Mr. Yoshihara Shigekazu.

19 Ikagawa Motoi, "Tōyō kikō," *Hiroshima kenshi kindai shiryōhen* 4 (1976): 617–618.

20 Setoguchi Ryūichi, "Nagai Kyūichiro to Senshū Daigaku sōritsushatachi," *Senshū Digakushi kiyō* 3 (2011): 55–79.

21 Takashina Shūji and Miwa Hideo, *Kawamura Kiyoo kenkyū* (Tokyo: Chūō Kōron Bijutsu Shuppan, 1994), 80.

22 Mitsui Hachirōemon Takamuneden Hensan Iinkai, *Mitsui Hachirōemon Takamune den*, 97–98.

23 For more on the Japanese students who studied with Rev. Corwin in Millstone, see chapter 6.

24 Shiozaki Satoshi, *America chinichi-ha no kigen* (Tokyo: Heibonsha, 2001).

25 Shiozaki, *America chinichi-ha no kigen*. Takagi notes that "New Brunswick was a newly emerging industrial city and had not developed an upper class of brahmins and others who combined wealth and honor, as was the case in Boston"; see Takagi, *Bakumatsu ishinki no Beikoku ryūgaku*, 148.

26 Kuniyoshi Sakae, *Mori Arinori ga kirihiraita Nichibei gaikō, shodai chūbei gaikōkan no chōsen* (Tokyo: Bensei Shuppan, 2018). Kinsley worked as an importer for the firm Horswell, Kinsley, and French in Boston. This French might be related with Aaron Davis Weld French.

27 In the April 1875 "Annual Report of Tokyo Kaisei Gakkō," the principal, Hatakeyama, reported to the Ministry of Education that "the methods of teaching, the progress of students, etc., are not so different from those of Western schools." A chemistry teacher named Atkinson also reported that in advanced mathematics, such as calculus, his students were at the same level as those at the U.S. Military Academy. See Ishizuki Minoru, *Kindai Nihon no kaigai ryūgakushi* (Tokyo: Chūō Kōronsha, 1992).

28 Megata was also a member of a study group called the "Japanese Law Company," formed in 1875 by Japanese students at Columbia University Law School in New York. Their meetings were apparently held in New York City.

29 The funeral of Nawa Michikazu was held in Boston in 1873. Since Nawa was the adoptive father of Hattori Ichizō of Rutgers College, many Japanese students from New Brunswick and elsewhere, including Hattori, would have attended the funeral. Dan says that many Japanese students moved to Boston at that time. See Ko Dan Danshaku Denki Hensan Iinkai, eds., *Danshaku Dan Takuma den* (Tokyo: Ko Dan Danshaku Denki Hensan Iinkai, 1938).

30 Nishizawa Naoko, "Obata Jinzaburō no America ryūgaku," *Kindai Nihon kenkyū* 14 (1997): 148.

31 Ikagawa, "Tōyō kikō," 618.

32 Shiozaki Satoshi, "Bakumatsu ishin zai Burukkurin Nihonjin ryūgakusei kanren shiryō shūsei oyobi kōsatsu," *Gogaku kenkyū* 116 (2007): 150–151. See also *Brooklyn Daily Union*, April 19, 1871.

33 On November 25, 1871, Yamada Tetsuji visited New Brunswick from Brooklyn and stayed at Nagai's house; on Thanksgiving Day, November 30, he met the Saga domain students in New York and then went to Brooklyn to visit Yamada and Andō; on December 2, at the same hotel in Brooklyn, he visited Nanbu Hidemaro and Shiramine.

34 Not much is known about whether the Japanese students from this school went on to higher education or transferred to other schools. Kachōnomiya went to the U.S. Naval Academy in Annapolis in June 1872, and Egi went to Columbia University Law School. Navy personnel apparently received on-the-job training at the Brooklyn Navy Yard or were tutored by officials there.

35 Uesugi Katsukata from the Yonezawa domain and Kunitomo Takinosuke from the Japanese Navy also lived in Monson but did not enroll in Monson Academy. For more on Kunitomo, see Shiozaki Satoshi, "Beikoku ni nemuru ichi Nihonjin

ryūgakusei Kunitomo Takinosuke no bohi kara manabu reimeiki Nihon kaigun to Beikoku tono kakawari," *Seien* 806 (2016): 30–32.

36 Monson seems to have had good access to Boston, and Tanegashima Keisuke from Satsuma appears several times in documents related to Fukuoka students in Boston.

37 Shiozaki Satoshi, "Bakumatsu ishinki, Beikoku Nihonjin ryūgakusei ni yoru eibun hasshinrei no kōsatsu, Chūtōgakkō (Monson Academy) sotsugyōshiki de rōdokusareta ingurisshu supīchi o shiryō toshite," *Gogaku kenkyū* 127 (2012): 1–43.

38 For more on Murray's appointment and accomplishments as the superintendent of the Ministry of Education, see chapter 11 by Haruko Wakabayashi and chapter 12 by Benjamin Duke (ed. Fernanda Perrone) in this volume.

5

Rutgers in the Nineteenth Century

FERNANDA PERRONE

In 2025, Rutgers, the State University of New Jersey, is a comprehensive public research university with over 69,000 students in three New Jersey cities.[1] In the mid-nineteenth century, however, Rutgers was a small private men's college affiliated with the Dutch Reformed Church, which became a welcoming home for the early international students to come from Japan. Although some Japanese students only stayed at Rutgers for a short time, it became a hub from which they branched out to other institutions in other parts of the country. This chapter explores the history of Japanese students at Rutgers during the early Meiji period.

Origins

In 1766, Rutgers was chartered as Queen's College, one of eight colleges founded in the American colonies before the Revolutionary War. Named after Queen Charlotte, the consort of the English King George III, the college opened in 1771 in rented rooms in a local tavern. New Brunswick was a bustling market town in central New Jersey settled in 1681 by the Dutch. Queen's College was founded to train ministers for the Dutch Reformed Church in the American colonies, sparing them the long and dangerous voyage back to the Netherlands. The college president and more than a quarter of the founding trustees were ministers of the Dutch Reformed Church. Despite these sectarian influences, Queen's

College was not fully under ecclesiastical control. Its avowed purpose was "the Education of Youth in the Learned languages and in the Liberal and Useful Arts and Sciences." There were no religious restrictions on the faculty or students.[2] In 1812, the college advertised that students "may expect to be treated with becoming Candor, without any Discrimination with Respect to their religious sentiments." Possibly in response to this advertisement, Samuel Judah, the first Jewish graduate, became a member of the Class of 1816.[3] It would be many years before more non-Christian students came to Rutgers, and these would be of the Buddhist faith.

Part of the reason for the college's open policy, however, was that it was badly in need of students and funds. In fact, Queen's College closed several times during the first fifty years of its existence. The connection with the Reformed Church, however, proved to be an important support for the struggling institution, as did the affiliated Rutgers Grammar School, which still attracted students while the college was closed. When a permanent home for the college, an imposing federal-style building known as Old Queens, was erected in 1809, the Grammar School shared the space. They were joined by a theological seminary, first established in New York, which moved to New Brunswick in 1810. In 1825, Queen's College was renamed Rutgers College in honor of trustee and philanthropist Henry Rutgers.

The years leading up to the U.S. Civil War saw modest growth and prosperity for Rutgers College. In 1830, a new building, today known as Alexander Johnston Hall, was constructed for the Grammar School. A second academic building, Van Nest Hall, was completed in 1848. The new building became the home of the geological museum and Professor Louis Beck's chemistry laboratory, significant in the development of science education at the college. Crowding in Old Queens, however, continued to be a problem.

Most students of the antebellum period came from Dutch families residing in New Jersey and New York and were members of the Dutch Reformed Church, one of the United States' smallest Protestant denominations. During this period, a lively student culture began to develop on campus. Intellectual life centered on the student literary societies, the Philoclean and the Peithessophian, which held spirited debates and public speaking contests, wrote essays, and created their own library. Students formed their own clubs and societies. The first Greek-lettered secret society or fraternity, Delta Phi, was approved in 1845,[4] although fraternities were not officially recognized by the trustees until 1864. At that point, three new chapters were founded—Chi Phi in 1867, Beta Theta Pi in 1871, and Chi Psi in 1879, bringing the total to seven. None of the chapters had their own houses, but they rented rooms for gathering in New Brunswick. By 1879, over half of the students were fraternity members.[5]

Rutgers in the 1860s

The U.S. Civil War (1861–1865) had a profound and devastating effect on all aspects of American society. Higher education lost students and momentum, although the effect was much more pronounced in the South where much college property was destroyed. At Rutgers, enrollment decreased to a low of sixty-four students in 1863–1864; approximately 160 Rutgers students and alumni served in various capacities during the war, and seventeen died.[6] During the war, however, the U.S. Congress was able to pass the Morrill Land Grant Act of 1862, which provided funding for individual states to establish collegiate programs in such "useful arts" as agriculture, mechanics, mining, and military instruction.[7] This act would have far-reaching effects on the development of state-supported education, particularly in the areas of science, agriculture, and vocational subjects. While some states used the windfall to found new colleges, Rutgers professors successfully lobbied the New Jersey legislature to designate the existing institution in New Brunswick as the land-grant recipient. The Rutgers Scientific School was founded in 1864. Most students from Japan would enter this new program.

In the years following the Civil War, the United States rapidly developed from a sleepy, predominantly agricultural society to an industrial and commercial world power. Advances in transportation, technology, and communication fueled a growing economy. Millions of immigrants flocked to U.S. shores, leading to an explosion of the urban population and growing ethnic, linguistic, and religious diversity. The higher education sector expanded as well. The period from 1860 to 1890 saw an increase in the number of institutions of higher education and a growing diversification of the curriculum—particularly in the fields of teacher education, applied sciences, engineering, and agriculture—and new opportunities for women.[8]

Rutgers itself was transformed from a small church-affiliated institution to what historian of education Ben Justice has termed a multipurpose college.[9] Between 1840 and 1870, Rutgers gradually and amicably separated itself from the Dutch Reformed Church, known from 1867 as the Reformed Church in America. The construction of Hertzog Hall in 1856 removed the theological students physically from the college. By 1867, the separation was complete, although Rutgers remained Dutch Reformed in character.[10] Indeed, the new president, Dr. William H. Campbell (1862–1882) was a Reformed Church minister and professor at the theological seminary. He had served as principal of Erasmus Hall in Brooklyn and Albany Academy and held pastorates in New York City and upstate New York. Campbell believed that education should be firmly based on Christian principles, introducing a compulsory Bible class on Sunday before regular religious services. This course was only discontinued in 1893 under President Austin Scott.[11]

Campbell has been called "the first effective head" of the institution.[12] Under Campbell, Rutgers would begin to assume the contours of a modern academic institution. Under his leadership, the college's assets increased fivefold. He hired an outstanding faculty, including David Murray and Isaac Hasbrouck in mathematics, Francis C. Van Dyck in chemistry, and George Atherton in history. It was under Campbell's leadership that the first Japanese students would come to Rutgers. Campbell would emerge as a key figure in the Rutgers–Reformed Church–Japan network. Like Campbell, David Murray (1830–1905) was a member of the Reformed Church and served as principal of Albany Academy. He would later emerge as another key figure in the network.[13] This dynamic group developed the curriculum of the new scientific school, reintroduced modern languages for both scientific and classical students, and dropped the requirement of Latin and Greek after the sophomore year.[14] Gradually the traditional classical curriculum was being replaced. Academic standards improved, as evidenced by the establishment of the Phi Beta Kappa Society, the national honor society, in 1869.

William Campbell was also a successful fundraiser who enhanced the physical plant of the college. In 1866, a donation from New York City businessman Daniel S. Schanck funded the construction of an observatory, which boasted telescopes, clocks, and a revolving roof. Another science building, Geological Hall, was built in 1872 to give instruction in agriculture, engineering, and military tactics. The new building had an armory in the basement, facilities for physical sciences on the first floor, and a large museum on the second floor. The college next received a bequest from Mrs. Sophia Astley Kirkpatrick of New Brunswick to build a combined chapel and library, which was dedicated in December 1873. This freed up space in the Queen's building, which had housed both the chapel and the library. The new building had a chapel in the front, a library in the rear on the second floor, and classrooms and offices on the first floor.[15] Whereas previously students were required to attend Sunday services at churches in New Brunswick, now attendance at services in the chapel was mandatory.

The city of New Brunswick became increasingly industrialized during this period, and its busy railroad tied it to the nearby commercial centers of New York and Philadelphia. Immigrants, primarily working-class Roman Catholics from Ireland and Germany, staffed the factories and labored as domestic servants for the city's prosperous middle class. The African American population—about five percent of the city's approximately 11,000 residents—tended to be relegated to the worst jobs.[16] At this time, middle-class New Brunswick residents lived in the downtown area, side by side with factories and commercial establishments, since the outer areas of the city had yet to be developed. It was here that most of the Japanese students lived. Rutgers had no dormitories until the erection of Winants Hall in 1890. Students either lived at home or in boarding houses certified by the college. A few students planning to enter the church, like William Elliot Griffis of the Class of 1869, were permitted to live at the New Brunswick Theological Seminary in Hertzog Hall.

The young men at Rutgers College enjoyed their years in this lively city. Under Campbell's leadership, the college grew from seventy-nine undergraduates in 1862 to 194 in 1872. By the late 1860s, an intricate student culture had developed.

FIGURE 5.1. View of Rutgers College and grounds, New Brunswick, New Jersey, 1879. (Credit: Photo Engraving Co., New York, William Elliot Griffis Collection, Rutgers University Libraries.)

The students established new organizations like the *Targum* newspaper in 1869 and the *Scarlet Letter* yearbook in 1871. William Elliot Griffis, a founder of both of these publications, emerged as an honor student and class leader. The *Targum* was initially published by the fraternities in 1869 as an annual. In January 1869, it was transformed into a monthly paper, which "also sought to awaken interest of Alumni in Alma Mater to bring the college before the public."[17] One of the *Targum's* early successful campaigns was to adopt scarlet as the college's official color, although it was not ratified by the trustees until 1900. The students were still interested in producing an annual: the *Scarlet Letter* continued to be published by the fraternities until it was taken over by the junior class in 1913.

College sports were growing in popularity; for example, the Rutgers Boating Association was founded in 1867. In the next two years, a six-oared boat, the *Henry Rutgers*, was purchased, and a boathouse was constructed. Baseball at Rutgers College was initially informal. The college team played Princeton in 1866, losing with the seemingly incredible score of forty to two. The Rutgers Baseball Club was founded in 1870. For many years, the students had played a loosely defined game that resembled soccer. There was no limit to the number of participants. The ball could be batted with the hands as well as kicked, and considerable physical contact was allowed. In Princeton, a similar game was popular. In early autumn 1869, Rutgers organized a team of twenty-five players and invited Princeton to play a series of three games. The first game at Rutgers took place on November 6, 1869, with Rutgers winning six to four. It is now known as the first intercollegiate football game.[18] Recent graduate William Elliot Griffis wrote about Rutgers's victory in the *Targum*.

As at Yale and other nineteenth-century colleges, students identified with their class year—freshman, sophomore, junior, and senior—and interclass rivalries and freshman hazing were common.[19] It was fashionable for mid-nineteenth-century undergraduates to carry canes. Freshmen were initially not

FIGURE 5.2. Rutgers Grammar School, undated. (Credit: William Elliot Griffis Collection, Rutgers University Libraries.)

permitted this privilege, resulting in "cane wars"—pitched battles on the campus lawn as freshmen tried to wrest the prize away from their sophomore classmates. The worst battle apparently took place on September 22, 1869.[20] The Faculty Minutes reported many minor (and major) infractions of discipline. For example, in April 1868, the faculty attempted to discover who had "fired the privies," or blown up the toilets.[21] In March 1869, Simeon E. Buchnall, a senior from the Scientific School was "admonished for visiting billiard saloons," and "his guardians . . . [were] informed."[22] This was the atmosphere that the first Japanese students encountered upon their arrival in New Brunswick in 1866.

The Rutgers Grammar School

The very first Japanese students in New Brunswick, the brothers Yokoi Saheita and Yokoi Daihei, did not go to Rutgers College at all but instead attended the Rutgers Grammar School, which was founded in 1768 in New Brunswick with the purpose of preparing students for the colonial colleges. By 1770, the school and the college were joined.[23] In the early nineteenth century, the school and college shared a building where the school continued to function during periods when Queen's College was closed. The new Queen's Building (1809) was planned to house both the college and school. In 1830, a new building was erected for the Grammar School, originally a two-story building on the corner of College Avenue and Somerset Street. The Grammar School used the two rooms on the first floor while those on the second floor were used by the college literary societies.[24] By the 1840s, the school was primarily a day school, although twelve boarders were living with the rector.[25] In the early 1860s, the school building was improved and renovated, and an additional building was purchased for boarders. At that time, the school had eighty-eight students, although the rector, Cornelius Crispell, believed it could accommodate 150 students.[26] Lack of students was likely a motivator for the school to accept students from Japan.

Under Crispell, numbers increased to 112 students in 1866, the year of his resignation. Crispell was replaced by Alexander McKelvey, who taught at the college and also served as librarian. McKelvey resigned after one year because of his college responsibilities. It was McKelvey, however, who welcomed the Yokoi brothers upon their arrival in New Brunswick. DeWitt Ten Broeck Reiley was appointed to replace McKelvey. Reiley was a Rutgers graduate, an ordained minister and staff member at Rutgers College, where he taught classical languages. He served as rector from 1867 to 1874, and after a two-year hiatus, he accepted the post again in 1876, serving until 1883. Reiley continued to attract larger numbers of students, including a significant number from Japan.[27]

According to the Rutgers Grammar School catalog of alumni, sixteen Japanese students attended from 1866 through 1899.[28] The directory only lists those, including deceased students, for whom the school had a record when the directory was published in 1923; for instance, the Yokoi brothers and Katsu Koroku are not listed. Among the students of the 1870s was Hattori Ichizō from Chōshū, who graduated from the Grammar School in 1871 and went on to Rutgers College. Back in Japan he became vice president of language at the preparatory school of Tokyo University, vice president of Tokyo University and dean of the law department, and later governor of several prefectures.[29] Hara Yasutarō graduated in 1873 and was later a paymaster in the Japanese Navy. The two sons of Iwakura Tomomi—Tomosada, known as Asahi, and Tomotsune, known as Tats—accompanied by Hattori Ichizō, Yamamoto Jūsuke, and Orita Hikoichi had arrived in New Brunswick in 1870, where they studied at the Grammar School. The son of Katsu Kaishū, Katsu Koroku, who ultimately graduated from the U.S. Naval Academy in Annapolis (Maryland), matriculated at the Grammar School along with his companion Takaki Saburō (1841–1909) from Tsuruoka. Matsudaira Tadanari, lord of the Ueda clan after the early death of his father, graduated from the Grammar School in 1875 and went on to Rutgers College. Matsumura Junzō from Satsuma, who later transferred to the Naval Academy, and Shiramine Shunme from Niigata were also alumni of the Grammar School.

In the 1870s, the Rutgers Grammar School included several departments. The primary department was for students between six and twelve years of age. The secondary department had three sections: the "classical school for the preparation of boys and young men to the entry of any college"; "practical and scientific studies required to enter various Technical and Scientific Schools"; and a sequence of courses aimed at "meeting demands of Modern business life."[30] Course offerings included arithmetic, geography, English, U.S. history, natural science, writing, composition, letter writing, declamation, military drill, German, industrial design, Greek, bookkeeping, industrial drawing, drafting, physiology, commercial law, U.S. Constitution, algebra, geometry, botany, chemistry, geology, zoology, Roman history, and antiquities. The school offered military drill "as a means of promoting health, improving the figure and personal carriage, aiding discipline, and securing order, regularity, and a *habit* of prompt and unquestioning attention and obedience to proper authority."[31] Students boarding at the rector's house were required to attend preaching in the college chapel, unless their parents directed otherwise. Bible class was held at the rector's house on Sundays.[32] The Yokoi brothers were among the students who boarded with the rector. John Mason Ferris accompanied them to New Brunswick, met Alexander McKelvey, and arranged for their admission, room, and board at the rector's home.[33] At the Grammar School, the Yokoi brothers worked on improving their English and took basic courses to prepare them for college study.

The First Japanese Students at Rutgers College

New Brunswick was the destination of choice for Japanese students during the early Meiji period. Of the fifty-five Japanese listed in the 1870 census, ten lived in New Brunswick and were students at Rutgers.[34] The early Japanese at Rutgers College faced many challenges, as evidenced by the experience of the very first Japanese student at Rutgers College, Kusakabe Tarō. The first hurdle was finding a place to live. Unlike the Grammar School, Rutgers College had no facilities for boarding students. Reputedly, at some boarding houses, Irish maids refused to serve the Japanese students.[35] Despite the existence of prejudice, some Japanese students forged bonds with their landladies. While on vacation in Lake George, Kusakabe Tarō corresponded with his landlady, Maria Van Arsdale, whose boarders included Takaki Saburō and the Yokoi brothers, who had moved out of the rector's house.[36] Numagawa Saburō (Yokoi Daihei) wrote to Mrs. Van Arsdale after he was forced to return to Japan because of illness, "The doctor did not like to write this letter but I told him I must write a letter to my American home. . . . I often think about New Brunswick and hope that I shall be able to go over and to see you again."[37]

A second challenge concerned the new and evolving curriculum of the Rutgers Scientific School, to which Kusakabe, like most of the Japanese students, applied. Upon its opening in 1865, only seven students, instead of the expected thirty, enrolled. With so few students, the planned curriculum was shelved and the science students were forced to follow a curriculum similar to that of the classical students. The scientific school had two divisions—engineering and mechanics, and chemistry and agriculture. At this time, however, all scientific school students followed a single three-year curriculum, which included French, German, rhetoric, elocution, composition and speech, history, political economy, the U.S. Constitution, moral and mental philosophy, mathematics, chemistry, physics, and zoology, along with specialized courses in mechanics, engineering, and military engineering and field fortification.[38] From 1866, science students were required to participate in military drills, although apparently, under the supervision of history professor George Atherton, the training was not rigorous and students did not wear uniforms.[39] Arriving in New Brunswick in 1867, Kusakabe Tarō followed this eclectic and unfamiliar curriculum, making his academic success still more astonishing.

At first, the science students were known as the "Scientifs" by the classical students. They were initially not well integrated into the college, holding their own commencement in 1868, at which they received the Bachelor of Science degree. After a few years, however, they were invited to join the literary societies and fraternities, and they participated in the regular commencement exercises.[40]

Kusakabe entered Rutgers College in the summer term of 1867. American colleges did not necessarily correspond to the Japanese educational calendar, so the existence of the summer term contributed to Rutgers's appeal.[41] Candidates for admission had to be sixteen years of age and had to submit testimonials of a good moral character to the college president. Examinations for admission included tests in arithmetic, algebra, plane geometry, English grammar (including spelling) descriptive geography, physical geography, and U.S. history.[42] Rutgers' admission policies were fairly flexible, however, as shown by the experience of the Japanese students. Hatakeyama Yoshinari and Yoshida Kiyonari from Satsuma, who arrived in September 1868, were "admitted to the Third Scientific Class" (sophomore year) with a caveat that Hatakeyama "must have a tutor."[43] Hatakeyama struggled academically over the next few months, ultimately withdrawing in December 1868 to study privately.[44] Yoshida left after approximately one term of study.[45] In September 1870, Hatakeyama was "admitted to the Freshman Class as an irregular student with the privilege of the Latin and Greek lecture rooms and the omission of mathematics for this year."[46] Hatakeyama ultimately left in 1871 without graduating when he was ordered to return to Japan; while in Europe he was called to join the Iwakura Embassy.[47]

In 1864, a new and complicated system of numerical grading was introduced. By the 1870s, most students were doing very well. In a typical year, slightly more than half the students achieved an average of over ninety percent, and only two scored below eighty percent. Although those who failed a single class were supposed to repeat the entire year, in reality the students were often able to retake the examination and usually passed. At a time when, like other colleges, Rutgers struggled to find enough students, the college could ill afford to be too exacting.[48] Kusakabe's 95.2 percent average needs to be seen in light of what we would term grade inflation.[49] Nevertheless, it does not take away from the very real challenges of language, culture, and illness, which he overcame to place first in his class.

As the number of students increased, the curriculum of the Rutgers Scientific School was extensively revised in 1871. There were still two courses, one oriented toward engineering and one toward chemistry, but students did not elect a specialization until junior year. Admission requirements were raised to include plane geometry, U.S. history, and physical geography, in addition to grammar, spelling, geography, arithmetic, and algebra.[50] In the new curriculum, the course of study was lengthened from three to four years, and the number of courses required each term was reduced from six to five and in some cases to four. In the senior year, the number of required humanities and social science courses was also reduced.[51]

Many Japanese students developed close relationships with their teachers, who took a keen interest in these first international students. After leaving the Grammar School to return to Japan, Iwakura Asahi wrote to Rutgers College history professor George Atherton, "I think so much of New Brunswick as I have been there so long and I get home sick very often."[52] Many faculty members spent extra time tutoring Japanese students. Ise Satarō (Yokoi Saheita) reported to Mrs. Van Arsdale that during the summer of 1869, he spent every day studying with mathematics professor Isaac E. Hasbrouck.[53]

Mathematics professor David Murray and his wife, Martha, frequently invited Japanese students to their home and included them in activities with Martha's extended family.[54]

This closeness with faculty members and local citizens drew some of the Japanese students to Christianity. As has been mentioned, all students were required to attend religious services. Indeed, some Japanese students converted to Christianity and took part in religious life at Rutgers. As can be seen in chapter 10, Hatakeyama Yoshinari and Yoshida Kiyonari had experienced an unusual form of Christianity at the Brotherhood of the New Life community in Brocton, New York. Nevertheless, both Hatakeyama and Yoshida were baptized in the Reformed Church while in New Brunswick. Yoshida even wrote asking Ferris if he could take John Mason as his baptismal name, but, not receiving a reply in time, settled for John Wesley instead.[55] Hatakeyama was likely influenced by the Murrays in choosing to be baptized in the Second Reformed Church, where Martha Murray was a Sunday school teacher.[56] As David Murray wrote, "While in New Brunswick, he became convinced of the truth of the Christian religion and was baptized. In the belief and practice of this faith with earnest but unostentatious fidelity he continued until his death."[57]

These developing networks would prove to be important in times of crisis. In 1868, civil war broke out in Japan, ultimately leading to the restoration of the Meiji emperor. The Japanese students at Rutgers were deeply concerned over events at home. As Hatakeyama explained in a letter to Ferris, "I am very anxious to hear from Japan; but rather sorry that even we do not see any news of Civil War in Japan lately. I hope however you not be anxious about the miserable state of our country."[58] Most pressingly, financial support for the students dwindled in the chaos of war and change of government. At this time, members of the Reformed churches organized a fund for the students' support, much of which was later paid back.[59] Thanking Ferris for forwarding a check from a supporter, Hatakeyama wrote, "I am very sorry that I was compelled to make that request to yourself and the other gentlemen. I was never in such an awkward situation. If I had not met such friends it would not be possible for me to remain in this country and gain knowledge. I thank God he sent me here."[60]

After the Meiji Restoration, the new government ordered students sent abroad by the shogunate to return to Japan, although most did not comply with this dictate.[61] Foreign students were placed under the Gakusei, which launched an investigation into the status of Japanese nationals studying abroad, ultimately issuing rules and providing financial support.[62] Some Japanese already abroad were made government-sponsored students retroactively. The number of Japanese students increased under the new regulations. In December 1873, however, the government, concerned about growing costs and the poor performance of some students, decided to abolish the system of government support of overseas students and ordered them to return home. This time the order was enforced.[63] After 1873, the number of Japanese students at Rutgers declined. Those who remained were reliant on private funding.

Student Life at Rutgers College

What was life at Rutgers like for the Japanese students? Besides their studies, many participated in cocurricular activities, student clubs, and athletics. The literary societies from the earlier part of the century were not as popular but continued to attract students until the 1890s.[64] Utsuka Nagateru of the class of 1876, "Kanichiro Taku" of the class of 1877, and Kudō Seiichi of the class of 1878 were all members of the Philoclean Literary Society,[65] and Kusakabe Tarō was a member of the Scientific Literary Society. Since all students were required to take classes in rhetoric and elocution, the literary societies gave them a chance to practice public speaking, which must have been a challenge for Japanese speakers still learning a new language. Some of them nevertheless excelled. In 1874, Hattori Ichizō received honorable mention in a debate of the Peithessophian Society, where he claimed that having only two political parties was undemocratic.[66] Hattori was selected to give an oration in Japanese at his commencement in 1875. His subject was "The Order of Progress."[67]

Hattori Ichizō was particularly active on campus. Nicknamed Ike Hattori, he was associate editor of the *Targum* his first term and became senior editor in his second term, 1875. The yearbook dubbed him one of the "Targumatical Collaborateurs." He was vice president of the scientific class of 1875, member of the Rutgers Microscopical Society,[68] and one of the few Japanese who belonged to a fraternity. As a member of Alpha Sigma Chi, he participated in their intriguingly named "Thumpus," where he was dubbed "Guzzler of the Funds."[69]

Matsudaira Tadanari of the class of 1879 was also active on campus. Appointed scientific class poet in his first year,[70] he was a member of the Philoclean Society for three years. This wealthy student designed his own Philoclean pin, a crescent

FIGURE 5.3. Hattori Ichizō, ca. 1871. (Photo by D. Clark Studio, William Elliot Griffis Collection, Rutgers University Libraries.)

made of platinum, set with a diamond star. His graduation thesis was on Japanese bronze.[71] In his graduation year he served as class secretary of the Scientific Section, and although not technically a Christian he was a member of the Rutgers College branch of the American Bible Society. In a "class statistics" section, the 1879 yearbook lists his weight as 105 pounds, his height as five feet seven inches, his age as twenty-four, and his political affiliation as Republican. Under religion, he listed "prefers Christianity." His future occupation was undecided, his nickname was Matsie, and his favorite song was "Heathen Chinese," suggesting he felt no affinity with the Chinese immigrants who were flocking to the United States during this period.[72]

Some of the Japanese students participated in college sports. Matsumura Junzō reportedly liked to play football.[73] Hattori Ichizō joined the recently founded baseball club and became vice president of the Rutgers College Baseball Association.[74] Japanese students did not participate in certain activities, however. No one joined the glee club, drama society, horse-riding club, whist club, or any of the eating societies. Most likely these activities were deemed too frivolous, costly, or too much of a distraction from academic study. The drama society was a challenge for non-English speakers; it was unlikely that Japanese students owned horses in the United States or knew how to play whist (a card game); and the eating societies, which met in various restaurants in New Brunswick, might have been socially awkward for Japanese students.

Furthermore, there is little evidence that the Japanese students joined in the raucous student pranks of the day. Matsudaira Tadanari cosigned a letter to Professor George H. Cook, stating "we acted no part in the disorder created in your class room and discountenance the same."[75] Matsudaira and several other Japanese students, however, were at Rutgers College during the "Cannon War." In 1875, nine members of the class of 1877 were selected to go to Princeton to repossess a Revolutionary War cannon that supposedly was taken from Rutgers years before by Princeton students. On April 25, 1875, the students walked to neighboring Milltown loaded down with ropes, shovels, pickaxes, a crowbar, and other equipment. Arriving at the farm of a Mr. Vanderbilt, they hired horses and a wagon. They reached Princeton at one o'clock in the morning in pitch darkness. The cannon was deeply buried, so it took the students quite a while to unearth it. At one point, they laid flat on the ground to avoid Princeton students getting off a late train. It was dawn by the time they lifted the cannon into the wagon. It was so heavy that the horses could only walk, and they did not get back to New Brunswick until ten o'clock. When they arrived, they buried the cannon in a coal yard and then removed it to the cellar of a house on Paterson Street. That night's work was the beginning of a long controversy about the ownership of the cannon. Rutgers professors investigated and came to the conclusion that it had never belonged to Rutgers at all, and it was returned to Princeton.[76]

Although there is no evidence that any of the Japanese students participated in the prank, Matsudaira Tadanari was involved in another scandalous incident. His younger brother Tadaatsu, who studied in New Brunswick for a short time, remained long enough to fall in love with and marry Carrie Sampson, the daughter of a local bookseller. Apparently Tadanari, who had been head of the Ueda clan since the age of nine following the death of his father, disowned his brother. Matsudaira Tadaatsu transferred to the Worcester Free Institute (later Polytechnic) and then to Harvard University. Remaining in the United States, he had a career as an engineer and started a family before his early death in 1888.[77] His son, Matsudaira Kinjiro, the first known Asian-American elected official, became the mayor of Edmonston, Maryland.[78]

Relatively few Japanese students actually graduated from Rutgers College in the nineteenth century. In the 1870s, there were only three: Hattori Ichizō in 1875; Kudō Seiichi, one of Edward Corwin's students, in 1878; and Matsudaira Tadanari in 1879. Hattori and Kudō, along with Kusakabe, were all inducted into the Phi Beta Kappa Society (Kusakabe posthumously).[79]

Many Japanese attended Rutgers for a period of time and either transferred to another institution or went back to Japan. Of Hatakeyama's fellow students from Satsuma, Matsumura Junzō transferred to the U.S. Naval Academy, completing the four-year course and graduating in 1873.[80] He became a rear admiral in the Japanese Navy.[81] Yoshida Kiyonari (Nagai) left after a few months. According to the Faculty Minutes, "Nagai should drop his present studies and class and prepare to enter the sophomore class next September and it was resolved that he be allowed to attend such lectures as he chooses without being required to recite."[82] While at Rutgers, however, Yoshida was placed in charge of the financial affairs of the Japanese students on the East Coast. Upon his return to Japan sometime in 1869, he served in the Ministry of Finance and later returned to the United States as an ambassador.[83] Shiramine Shunme left Rutgers after one term and transferred to the Brooklyn Collegiate and Technical Institute.[84] In Japan, Shiramine became a shipbuilder in Kanagawa and was decorated by the emperor for patenting a folding boat for the Japanese Navy.[85] Utsuka Yasuhiro attended Rutgers for four terms but left to study privately with Isaac Hasbrouck.[86] From the class of 1877, Hara Yasutaro and "Kanichero Taku" both left after several terms.[87] Ogawa Yoshi, also part of the class of 1877, entered but never matriculated, leaving to study in the Brooklyn Navy Yard.

Furthermore, many of the Japanese students who came to New Brunswick did not attend Rutgers College at all. Some attended the Grammar School or studied with private tutors like Edward Corwin; others were visitors from other schools and colleges, or from Japan. Prince Shimazu of the *daimyo* family of Sadowara arrived in New Brunswick with three attendants in December 1869. Writing from Millstone where he was staying to try to recover his health, Kusakabe explained to Ferris, "The Prince and his party have arrived at New Brunswick on the last saturday, [*sic*] and are now staying at Hotel, but they will move somewhere else as soon as we find good boarding places. . . . In regard to their studies I think, it is better for them, that Soogiwoora or I, myself will teach them on some primary branches until be able to go to school . . . at present condition they all know hardly, how to pronounce the 24 characters."[88] The Japanese students clearly knew each other and formed a network to look out for other Japanese. This network originated in New Brunswick but extended far beyond.

Conclusion

In conclusion, the experience of the Japanese students at Rutgers was mixed. Of the many Japanese nationals who came to New Brunswick during the 1860s and 1870s, a relatively small number attended Rutgers College and an even smaller number graduated. Many Japanese attended the Rutgers Grammar School, studied with private tutors, or simply visited with their countrymen. Academically and socially, Rutgers College presented a somewhat challenging environment for Japanese students. The science curriculum, which most of them followed, was still being refined during this period. On the other hand, Rutgers administrators were fairly flexible, and often the special needs of Japanese students could be accommodated. The small college did not have any residence halls, so the Japanese students were forced to find private landlords who would accept them. Like many colleges of its time, Rutgers had mandatory religious services in which the Japanese students were expected to participate. Student life was lively at this small college. The Japanese students arrived at a time when new clubs, societies, and athletics were beginning to flourish, and they participated to some extent. This all-men's college boasted a raucous social life characterized by elaborate pranks, which had less appeal for the Japanese. Those students who stayed at Rutgers for four years, however, appear to have been active and valued members of their classes, a relationship which endured long after graduation.

Notes

1 "About Rutgers," Rutgers, the State University of New Jersey, accessed January 2, 2025, https://www.rutgers.edu/about-rutgers.
2 Thomas J. Frusciano, Benjamin Justice, Marie Logue, Barry V. Qualls, and Linda Stamato, *Rutgers: A 250th Anniversary Portrait* (London: Third Millennium Publishing for Rutgers, the State University, 2015), 18–20.
3 Frusciano et al., *Rutgers: A 250th Anniversary Portrait*, 229.
4 Frusciano et al., 31–34.
5 Richard P. McCormick, *Rutgers: A Bicentennial History* (New Brunswick, NJ: Rutgers University Press, 1966), 106.
6 Frusciano et al., *Rutgers: A 250th Anniversary Portrait*, 34.
7 John R. Thelin, *A History of American Higher Education*, 2nd ed. (Baltimore, MD: Johns Hopkins University Press, 2011), 76.
8 Thelin, *A History of American Higher Education*, 75, 96.
9 Frusciano et al., *Rutgers: A 250th Anniversary Portrait*, 35.
10 Frusciano et al., 34.
11 McCormick, *Rutgers: A Bicentennial History*, 82, 114–115.
12 McCormick, 83.
13 On David Murray, see Benjamin Duke, *Dr. David Murray: Superintendent of Education in the Empire of Japan, 1873–1879* (New Brunswick, NJ: Rutgers University Press, 2019).
14 Duke, *Dr. David Murray*, 83–97.
15 Frusciano et al., *Rutgers: A 250th Anniversary Portrait*, 36–38; McCormick, *Rutgers: A Bicentennial History*, 102.
16 John P. Wall, *Chronicles of New Brunswick, N.J., 1667–1931* (New Brunswick, NJ: Thatcher-Anderson, 1931), 437.
17 McCormick, *Rutgers: A Bicentennial History*, 105–106.
18 Frusciano et al., *Rutgers: A 250th Anniversary Portrait*, 161–162; McCormick, *Rutgers: A Bicentennial History*, 104–105.
19 Thelin, *A History of American Higher Education*, 94.
20 Frusciano et al., *Rutgers: A 250th Anniversary Portrait*, 159.
21 Rutgers College Faculty Minutes, 30 April 1868, Special Collections and University Archives, Rutgers University Libraries, New Brunswick, NJ (hereafter SC/UA).
22 Rutgers College Faculty Minutes, 12 March 1869, SC/UA.
23 Frank V. Sperduto, *A History of Rutgers Preparatory School*, vol. 1 (Somerset, NJ: Rutgers Preparatory School, 1967), 3–13.

24 Sperduto, *A History of Rutgers Preparatory School*, 57.
25 Sperduto, 68.
26 Sperduto, 79–81.
27 Sperduto, 81–82.
28 William P. Kelly, *Alumni and Students of the Rutgers Preparatory School* (Somerset, NJ: Rutgers Preparatory School, 1923–1925).
29 Marilyn Bandera, "Hattori Ichizō," in "A Case Study in Educational Motivation: Ryugakusei and Rutgers College, 1866–1895" (master's thesis, University of Hawaii, 1970), unpaginated biographical appendix.
30 *Catalogue of Rutgers College Grammar School* (New Brunswick, NJ: Terhune & Van Anglen's Press, 1878), 7.
31 *Catalogue of Rutgers College Grammar School*, 15–16.
32 *Catalogue of Rutgers College Grammar School*, 20.
33 John M. Ferris, "How the Japanese Came to New Brunswick," in William Elliot Griffis, *The Rutgers Graduates in Japan*, rev. ed. (New Brunswick, NJ: Rutgers College, 1916), 32–33.
34 John E. Van Sant, *Pacific Pioneers: Japanese Journeys to America and Hawaii* (Urbana: University of Illinois Press, 2000), 55.
35 Ferris, "How the Japanese Came to New Brunswick," 33.
36 Kusakabe Tarō to Maria Van Arsdale, 19 July 1869, box X, William Elliot Griffis Collection, SC/UA (hereafter Griffis Collection).
37 S. Numagawa to Mrs. Van Arsdale, box 158, folder 3, Griffis Collection.
38 McCormick, *Rutgers: A Bicentennial History*, 91; *Rutgers College Catalog, 1867–68* (Newark, NJ: Starbuck, Jennings, & Bros., 1868), 33.
39 McCormick, *Rutgers: A Bicentennial History*, 115.
40 McCormick, 92.
41 Bandera, "A Case Study in Educational Motivation," 20–21.
42 *Catalogue of the Officers and Students of Rutgers College, 1869–70* (New Brunswick, NJ: Terhune and Van Anglen, 1869).
43 Rutgers College Faculty Minutes, vol. 4, 22 September 1868, 600, SC/UA.
44 "Soogiwoora Kozo," Rutgers College Faculty Minutes, 22 December 1868, SC/UA; Bandera, unpaginated biographical appendix.
45 Rutgers College Faculty Minutes, 22 February 1869, SC/UA.
46 Rutgers College Faculty Minutes, vol. 5, 23 September 1870, 298, SC/UA.
47 See chapter 11 on the Iwakura Mission.
48 McCormick, *Rutgers: A Bicentennial History*, 108.
49 Rutgers Scientific School Records, vol. 1, 18, SC/UA.
50 McCormick, *Rutgers: A Bicentennial History*, 92.
51 *Catalogue of the Officers and Students of Rutgers College 1871–72*, 1871.
52 K. Asahi to George Atherton, 3 May 1872, box 158, folder 4, Griffis Collection. The fact that Asahi, who did not attend Rutgers College, knew George Atherton shows how interlinked the Grammar School and the College were at this time.
53 Ise to Mrs. Van Arsdale, 25 August 1869, box 158, folder 3, Griffis Collection.
54 Duke, *Dr. David Murray*, 32–34.
55 Iwoske Nagai (Yoshida Kiyonari) to J. M. Ferris, 20 November 1868, box 159, folder 2, Griffis Collection.
56 Duke, *Dr. David Murray*, 38.
57 Quoted in Duke, *Dr. David Murray*, 64.
58 Kozo Soogiwoora [Hatakeyama] to J. M. Ferris, 28 September 1868, box 159, folder 2, Griffis Collection.

59 Gordon D. Laman, *Pioneers to Partners: The Reformed Church in America and Christian Mission with the Japanese* (Grand Rapids, MI: William B. Eerdmans, 2012), 66.
60 Kozo Soogiwoora [Hatakeyama] to J. M. Ferris, 3 November 1868, box 159, folder 2, Griffis Collection.
61 Ishizuki Minoru, "Overseas Study by Japanese in the Early Meiji Period," in *The Modernizers: Overseas Students, Foreign Employees, and Meiji Japan*, ed. Ardath W. Burks (Boulder, CO: Westview Press, 1985), 166.
62 James Thomas Conte, "Overseas Study in the Meiji Period: Japanese Students in America, 1867–1902" (PhD diss., Princeton University, 1977), 45–49.
63 Ishizuki, "Overseas Study," 167–169.
64 McCormick, *Rutgers: A Bicentennial History*, 106.
65 *Scarlet Letter*, May 1874 and 1875, SC/UA.
66 *Targum*, December 1874, SC/UA.
67 *Targum*, October 1875, SC/UA.
68 *Scarlet Letter*, 1875, SC/UA.
69 *Scarlet Letter*, 1875, SC/UA.
70 *Targum*, October 1875, SC/UA.
71 *Targum*, March 1879, SC/UA.
72 *Scarlet Letter*, 1877 and 1879, SC/UA.
73 Griffis, *The Rutgers Graduates in Japan*, 12.
74 *Scarlet Letter*, May 1874, SC/UA.
75 Box 158, folder 14, Griffis Collection.
76 Class of 1877 History, Class Histories, Alumni Class Files, box 3, SC/UA.
77 See Iinuma Nobuko, *Ōgon no kusabi: Umi o watatta rasuto purinsu Matsudaira Tadaatsu* (Nagano-ken Matsumoto-shi: Kyōdo Shuppansha, 1996).
78 "Kinjiro Matsudaira: Mayor of Edmonston, Maryland," Discover Nikkei: Japanese Migrants and Their Descendants, May 2021, https://discovernikkei.org/en/journal/2021/5/5/kinjiro-matsudaira/.
79 Box 158, folder 31, Griffis Collection; and *Scarlet Letter*, 1875, SC/UA. Some sources claim that Kusakabe received his degree posthumously, but he is not included in the list of graduates of 1870.
80 Box 158, folder 33, Griffis Collection.
81 Griffis, *The Rutgers Graduates in Japan*, 23.
82 Rutgers College Faculty Minutes, 22 February 1869, SC/UA.
83 Griffis, *The Rutgers Graduates in Japan*, 23.
84 *Scarlet Letter*, 1872, SC/UA.
85 Griffis, *The Rutgers Graduates in Japan*, 23–24.
86 Griffis, 24.
87 Griffis, 24.
88 Kusakabe Tarō to John Ferris, 12 December 1869, box 159, folder 2, Griffis Collection.

6

Rev. Edward T. Corwin and the Japanese Students at the Hillsborough Reformed Church at Millstone

HARUKO WAKABAYASHI

> Blessed be the tie that binds
> Our hearts in Christian love
> The fellowship of kindred minds
> Is like to that above.[1]

As discussed in the previous chapters, dozens of Japanese students arrived in New Brunswick from the late 1860s to the 1880s through introductions from their missionary teachers in Nagasaki and Yokohama or through the network of their peers who had earlier settled in the area. However, these young men would not have thrived in this foreign land without the acceptance and support of the local community. Most of them lived in boarding houses run by the residents of New Brunswick, many of whom were members of the Reformed Church. Furthermore, not all of them attended Rutgers College or the Rutgers Grammar School; many who needed to develop adequate fluency in English chose instead to study with private tutors.

This chapter focuses on the small group of students who studied under Rev. Edward Tanjore Corwin (1834–1914), the pastor of Hillsborough Reformed Church at Millstone. They took instruction and had room and board in Corwin's

FIGURE 6.1. Hillsborough Reformed Church, Millstone, 1931. (Credit: Sinclair New Jersey Collection, Rutgers University Libraries. Photo by C.R.W.)

parsonage, a sleepy rural community of farmlands and forests about ten miles west of New Brunswick. As a mentor and a tutor, Corwin established caring relationships with these students who aspired to study in the United States, as did his wife, Mary, and their two children, Euphemia (Effie) and Charles (Charlie), and members of his church and local community. Meanwhile, the bonds the students formed with their fellow Japanese in New Brunswick and its vicinity provided constant support in their times of need. The accounts of their experiences in Millstone reveal and enrich our understanding of how these young men far from home fostered communal ties as they strove to fulfill their duty and fit into an alien culture.

The First Japanese Students at Millstone: Kusakabe Tarō and Tomita Tetsunosuke

The Hillsborough Reformed Church at Millstone was founded in 1766, the same year that Queen's College (now Rutgers) was established. Built in 1851, the parsonage is located across the street south from the church, sitting on three acres bordered to the east by the Millstone River and to the west by Millstone River Road (formerly Main Street).[2] Edward T. Corwin, best known as a historian of the Reformed Church, served as its pastor from 1863 to 1888 and lived there with his wife and their two children.[3] He left few records of the Japanese students who came under his tutelage, except for a letter to William Elliot Griffis he wrote on November 17, 1905.[4] In this letter, Corwin recalls knowing thirty to forty Japanese students. Of those he sponsored—Tomita Tetsunosuke, Orita

Hikoichi, Kanda Naibu, Saisho Chōhachi, and Kudō Seiichi—he writes, "They were all gentlemen, not objectionable, courteous in the extreme, fond of croquet, rode with me daily, regular at church, and generally at prayer meeting; always present at family worship; eager to learn, and grateful as they could be for everything. Our relationship with them was a very pleasant chapter in our life."[5]

Effie Corwin also remembered the Japanese students fondly:

> The Japanese who were in New Brunswick frequently came out to spend a day at our house, and especially in cherry-time. There were about a dozen cherry-trees in the parsonage yard, and the Japanese were always delighted to see their native fruit, and to climb the trees where they would eat their fill. . . . The Japs who lived with us became very skillful croquet players. . . . It seemed to me that our summer evenings were always spent on the croquet ground in front of the house and I can see the Japanese running over the ground after the ball, and hear father's hearty boyish laugh ringing out on the evening air.[6]

For the Japanese students, Millstone, which was a short train ride away from New Brunswick, became a sanctuary from the city. How they came to be acquainted with Edward T. Corwin remains unknown, but their letters and diaries and the Corwins' letters offer glimpses of their life in Millstone and reveal a portrait of Corwin untold in church records.

The first Japanese students who attended Rutgers College were also the first to meet the Corwins at Millstone. Effie, in her letter to Griffis, recalls two young men visiting her father when she was about five years old.[7] They were Yokoi Saheita and Kusakabe Tarō, the first Japanese students to enter Rutgers Grammar School and Rutgers College, respectively. Their visit to Millstone is mentioned in a July 1869 letter that Saheita wrote to his brother Daihei, who had returned to Japan due to illness.[8] Here Saheita mentions that on June 25, he and Kusakabe took the train from New Brunswick at 9:00 A.M. and arrived at Millstone at 9:30. From there, they walked to Corwin's house, where the minister entertained them with food and drink, and from 10:30, they enjoyed the country landscape on a carriage ride along the canal. Afterwards, they had a long afternoon conversation with Corwin, took a walk in the village, and returned after dinner to their home in New Brunswick around 8:00 P.M. Their peer, Hatakeyama Yoshinari, also made visits to Millstone. Hatakeyama's letter of August 11, 1869, mentions staying with Corwin for a few days and being taken to the Annual Bible Society Meeting in Somerville, of which he wrote as follows: "It was interesting & grant [*sic*] meeting so that I was truly pleased to have attended it. I enjoyed exceedingly in visitation of Rev. C. at Millstone where I spend [*sic*] *two* nights."[9]

For Kusakabe, Millstone became one of his last homes in the United States. He moved there by mid-September 1869 to recuperate from his illness and commuted to New Brunswick for a while. In a letter dated September 20 of the same year, he writes:

> I have left New Brunswick on the last Friday and now am boarding with Mr. Van Nuys, whose house is situated on about two blocks distance from depot so that it will be quite convenient for me to catch train on every morning even in the winter time. Mrs. Van Nuys is very kind lady and takes great care about my food and room &c. knowing my sickly condition. The place is, of course as you already know, very quiet but since I do like such a place I will succeed very well without any trouble.[10]

In the rest of the letter, Kusakabe expresses hopes of recovering and continuing his studies. However, ill health compelled him to take leave from Rutgers in December, and in April he moved back to New Brunswick, staying at Hatakeyama's boarding house on French Street, to prepare to head home. Unfortunately, he passed away there on April 13, 1870.[11]

Tomita Tetsunosuke was the first to study extensively with Corwin. According to Corwin, Tomita stayed with him from the fall of 1869.[12] As discussed in chapter 3, Tomita arrived in New Brunswick in 1868, accompanying Katsu Koroku, the son of Katsu Kaishū, together with Takaki Saburō. While Katsu and Takaki both entered Rutgers Grammar School, Tomita's English was apparently insufficient, and his advanced age of thirty-three years at the time may also have been an issue. Effie, in her letter to Griffis, attests to this, "While he [Tomita] was too old to acquire the language so well, he was a very fine man and we remember him with great pleasure."[13]

At Millstone, Corwin often made the Japanese students translate the Bible and works, such as *The Pilgrim's Progress*, which by then had already been translated into Chinese, from Chinese into English.[14] Effie remembers one instance of Tomita walking back and forth in their front yard, reading about Christian falling into the Slough of Despond[15] and then asking her father, "I do not quite understand about this mud into which Christian fell. Does it mean that it was mud up here (tapping his forehead)?"[16] In another instance, a student translating a section in the New Testament that said "whosoever shall say to his brother, Thou fool, shall be in danger of the council," startled her father by translating "council" as "Congress." Thus did Tomita and his peers train under Corwin, whose methods seemed effective, as many of his Japanese students went on to study in college, among whom was Tomita, who moved on to Whitney Business College in Newark after fifteen months.

Orita Hikoichi

The second Japanese student who studied with Corwin was Orita Hikoichi[17] (1849–1920), who arrived in New Brunswick in 1870, accompanying the sons of

FIGURE 6.2. Orita Hikoichi, 1876. (Credit: Historical Photograph Collection: Alumni Photographs series, AC058, Princeton University Archives, Department of Special Collections, Princeton University Library. Photo by D. Clark.)

Iwakura Tomomi, Tomosada (1851–1910), and Tomotsune (1853–1890).[18] Orita, a native of Satsuma, was appointed a page to the daimyo Shimazu Mochihisa at age thirteen; in 1868, while in Kyoto with Mochihisa, he "received orders to serve Lord Iwakura [Tomomi] . . . and served him day and night."[19] Later that same year, Iwakura entrusted his two sons to Orita, and the three left for Nagasaki to study with Guido F. Verbeck at Chienkan, a school for western learning founded by the Saga domain. They spent only a short time with Verbeck, since the latter left Nagasaki in April 1869 to serve the new Meiji government by heading a school in Tokyo; nevertheless, he assisted the young men with their plans to study in the United States. He wrote the following letter to John M. Ferris, dated March 19, 1870:

> Dear Brother,
>
> This is simply to say that this trip brings five promising young men, who will probably call on you. I crave your kind advice and directions on their way to N. Brunswick. Their names are: Asahi, Tats, Orita, Hattori, & Yamamoto.
>
> The first two have been my and later Mr. Stout's scholars. They are sons of one of the first houses in the Empire, as their many good manners will show. Hattori is a fine fellow too. Altogether I think them the most promising of any

that have come yet. They will of course be well provided with funds. Two or three of the company speak English nicely.

Hoping that they will not cause you much trouble, & under obligation for any kindness shown these young men, I remain,

Very truly yours,
G. F. Verbeck[20]

"Asahi" and "Tats" referred to the respective aliases used by Iwakura Tomosada and Tomotsune. It is unclear why Hattori (Ichizō, 1851–1929) and Yamamoto (Jūsuke, 1847–1901), natives of Chōshū, came with the Iwakura brothers, but both had also studied in Nagasaki under Verbeck. All four, except Orita, were admitted to Rutgers Grammar School upon arrival in New Brunswick. The Iwakura brothers enrolled for two years, whereas Hattori and Yamamoto, who seem to have been better prepared, went on to college after a year—Hattori to Rutgers and Yamamoto to Rensselaer Polytechnic Institute in Troy, New York.[21] Orita, in the meantime, chose to receive private tutorship from Corwin. According to Corwin, he went to Millstone in the spring of 1870, and after two years of intensive studies there, he was admitted to the College of New Jersey (now Princeton University).[22]

Orita's diary reveals glimpses of his simple life in Millstone from January to August 1872.[23] On most days, he went to the post office for mail, recited his lessons, read books, and took a short walk in the afternoon. On Sundays, he attended morning service at church, studied the Bible in the afternoon, and attended prayer meetings. He read *Caesar*, picked up news at the post office through browsing the *Tribune*, and bought books from Tibbal & Co. in New York. The diary also tells us that he paid $120 to Corwin for board and tuition for ten weeks. Most notably, however, we learn that even while Orita was in Millstone, he stayed well connected with a wider Japanese community. His numerous exchanges of letters and visits to New Brunswick and New York attest to an active network of Japanese students in those areas, of which Millstone had become a part.

It is thus unsurprising that Orita kept in close contact with the Iwakura brothers and their entourages even after moving to Millstone. He exchanged letters with both Asahi and Tats occasionally, as well as with Yamamoto, with whom he had traveled from Japan.[24] He also corresponded with "Minami," or Iwakura Tomoyoshi (1842–1879), the half-brother of Asahi and Tats.[25] While Minami is overlooked by most studies on Japanese students in New Brunswick, official Japanese records indicate that he studied in the United States from 1871 to 1872, and Orita's diary further attests to his residence in New Brunswick. Another figure, "Hara," referring to Hara Yasutarō (1847–1936), received his government order to study in the United States in February 1871.[26] Hara is known to have served Iwakura in Kyoto, where Orita would have met him before coming to the United States; incidentally, Hara is mentioned most frequently in Orita's diary. Minami and Hara's arrival in New Brunswick in the spring of 1871 would have freed Orita from his accompaniment of Asahi and Tats and allowed him to focus on his own studies with Corwin.

Orita's relationship with the Iwakura brothers and his Satsuma connections led him, in 1872, to partake in the momentous arrival in the United States of the Iwakura Mission, a 150-strong imperial embassy headed by Iwakura Tomomi. As recounted in chapter 11, many of the students who were studying or had studied in New Brunswick were recruited to assist the embassy.[27] Furthermore, many of the mission's key personnel hailed from Orita's native Satsuma, including Mori Arinori, Japan's first ambassador to the United States, and Hatakeyama, who had studied at Rutgers College and was appointed third secretary to the embassy upon its arrival in Washington, DC. The first reference to the embassy in Orita's diary appears on the seventh day of the twelfth month (January 16, 1872), when he read about its arrival in San Francisco in the *Tribune*.[28] He then learned that Ōhara Reinosuke (Yoshihara Shigetoshi, 1845–1847)[29] and Hatakeyama, both from Satsuma, were returning to the United States from Europe to join its staff.[30] Soon after, Tats left with Hara for Chicago to meet his father, who arrived there on February 26.[31] Upon their return to New Brunswick, Orita visited them and "heard great many news from them about the embassy."[32]

Around this time, Asahi had become ill and was set to return to Japan in May or June.[33] It is unclear whether this illness prompted Orita's visit to Washington, or if he had already planned his trip; in either case, he traveled to Washington on March 19, immediately went to see Iwakura Tomomi, explained Asahi's condition, and received permission for him to return to Japan.[34] On the next day, he "spent the whole day talking with my friends," and on March 21, he visited the Capitol with Matsumura (Junzō, 1842–1919) and Iwashita (Chōjūrō, 1853–1880).[35] From March 22 to 25, he spent time in Philadelphia with Iwakura, Takahashi (Shinkichi, 1843–1918),[36] Yoshida (Kiyonari, 1845–1891), Hatakeyama, and others, visiting Independence Hall, the library and museum, the zoo, and Fairmount Park. It is highly possible that these visits were preliminary inspections for the mission's visit to Philadelphia later in June. On March 25, he left Philadelphia around 11:00 A.M., stopped briefly in New Brunswick, and then returned to Millstone at 2:30 P.M., writing in his diary that he "was very tired after a long trip."[37]

Asahi left for Japan the following month after visiting Washington, DC. Tomita, who was headed for "some official business" in San Francisco, had arranged the trip to take Asahi with him.[38] Before leaving New Brunswick, he visited Millstone.[39] According to Orita, "Mr. Asahi came here about half past 2 o'clock, & received from here a book, *Life and Resources in America*,[40] which I bought. He went down to New Brunswick by 4 o'clock train, so I went there with him. He is going back to Japan starting New York on the 18th."[41] Orita went to New York to see Asahi and other friends at the St. Nicholas Hotel on the 17th; however, Asahi postponed his departure due to a cold, eventually departing from San Francisco on May 16.[42] Meanwhile, Tats also decided to leave New Brunswick to study in Europe, and he left the United States with his father and the embassy in August of that year.[43] Orita joined the embassy for the last time on August 1, visiting many sites in New York before their departure for Boston that afternoon. In the evening, he went to a theater, of which he wrote, "It was a finest time, since I came to this country. Yamamoto and Kunishi went to Europe. Mr. Minami will go back to Japan."[44] Minami's return to Japan concluded Orita's commitment to the Iwakura brothers.

Orita's accounts of his interactions with the Iwakura brothers and mission members demonstrate his strong ties to the Iwakura family and his Satsuma colleagues. His connections ultimately brought more Japanese students to Millstone, some of whom, like him, stayed and studied with Corwin. In March, he received a letter from Mogami Gorō (another Satsuma student who had been studying in the United States since 1870) asking if "Soske Matsgata" (Matsukata Sosuke, 1850–1872),[45] who had come with the embassy, could stay with him in Millstone. While Matsukata ended up choosing not to stay in Millstone, two months later, on May 3, Orita was unexpectedly visited by more fellow Satsuma students: Ichiki Sōsuke[46] and Saisho Chōhachi,[47] who had just arrived as two of the eleven students sent by the Hokkaido Development Commission (Kaitakushi) to study in the United States. They were accompanied by Tajiri Inajirō (1850–1923),[48] who was then studying at the Rutgers Grammar School.[49] After catching up on news from home, Saisho expressed his wish to stay at Millstone, and Corwin agreed.[50] A month later, on June 10, Kudō Seiichi also began boarding there.[51] Kudō had come to the United States with Ichiki and Saisho as a Kaitakushi student; he studied with Corwin until August 1874 and then entered Rutgers. According to Corwin, he "began to study for the ministry, but got off the track and in Junior year, shifted to the Scientific course; but finally, graduated in both Classical and Scientific Courses. I doubt if he ever went below 100 in Mathematics, and stood very high in all branches."[52] Kudō graduated in June 1878. Saisho stayed with Corwin for a few months during the summer and went on to the West Newtown English and Classical School in Newtown, Massachusetts.[53] According to Effie, he was "the only one of the five who was not a desirable student. He was very hot-tempered and father found him unteachable, so that he did not remain with us as long as some of the others."[54]

When Orita left Millstone to start at the College of New Jersey (Princeton University) in August 1872, Kudō and Saisho accompanied him; they "drove to Princeton about 12 miles distant, taking with me all trunks and boxes."[55] Corwin remembers Orita fondly as having been "prepared by me" to enter Princeton, and that Orita was baptized in 1876 by Dr. McCosh while at Princeton,[56] where he graduated in 1876 before returning to Japan the same year.

Kanda Naibu

Another notable student who studied with Corwin was Kanda Naibu (1857–1923),[57] who, according to Corwin, went to Millstone "in the spring of 1871, aged 14, a splendid fellow." He had been born into a family that served the Tokugawa house as the shogunal "Controllers of Noh actors," and in 1868 he was adopted by Kanda Takahira, a scholar of Dutch learning and a teacher of Western mathematics and sciences known for his progressive views and contributions to English education in Japan.[58] Kanda first attended Kaiseijo, the school of foreign studies established by the shogunate that became the forerunner of Kaisei Gakkō, Daigaku Nankō, and the present-day University of Tokyo. He attended Daigaku Nankō at the age of twelve after studying at a private academy in Osaka. In 1871, he was entrusted to the care of his adoptive father's colleague Mori Arinori, who was leaving to assume his ambassadorship in Washington, DC.[59] Their party left early that same year from Yokohama and, according to Kanda's diary, arrived in San Francisco on February 16.[60] Upon arrival on the East Coast, Kanda was received by Corwin in Millstone.

Why Corwin? This choice may have been due to Mori's connections with Iwakura and Orita. Orita had already been studying with Corwin by then, and Asahi was among those who accompanied Kanda to Millstone.[61] On the night of their arrival, Asahi slept at Corwin's house,[62] and he visited Millstone at least once with his brother while Kanda was there.[63] The Rutgers link also mattered. Griffis mentions Mori and Kanda's adoptive father among the "men of new Japan" who welcomed him upon his arrival in Tokyo in early 1871. He writes of a "delightful call on Mr. Kanda, the ex-President or Speaker of the House of Assembly," and that his son, "a bright lad," was to accompany Mori to the United States.[64] Griffis also calls Mori a great friend of Iwakura whose sons Griffis knew at Rutgers; Mori apparently called on Griffis, from whom he "received letters of introduction to my friends in America."[65]

Thus began Kanda's life in Millstone. Lessons began three days after his arrival, on Thursday, March 9. His diary, written in English, contains an entry for this date: "From this morning began to learn several books from Mr. Corwin. History of US every day. And one day Geography and one day Grammar, learn by heart. Beside those Arithmetic and Composition, and Letterwriter."[66] He also studied the Old and New Testaments and the history of Christ and received lessons in shorthand and phonography. Mori, now in Washington, had instructed him to send a letter and "any composition, or record of any thing which I saw, and any which I hear, or visit" to him every month.[67] Obeying these instructions, Kanda wrote as follows:

> Millstone, N. J., April 17th, 1871
>
> Dear Sir,
>
> I have seen your letter written about me to Mr. Orita some days ago, but I did not hear or see anything until day before yesterday, to be the subject of the composition, and I was troubled to make it. Then a joyful thing took place, as follows; our kind teacher went to New York on Wednesday last week, and he

FIGURE 6.3. Kanda Naibu, 1879. (Credit: Naibu Kanda, Amherst College Class of 1879, Biographical File, Archives and Special Collections, Amherst College.)

had been told us that if Mr. Orita and I will go to New York on Thursday, he will lead us to many places, which we had been talking about. For the above reasons Mr. Orita and I went to New York on that day, and we were lead [*sic*] to several places from nine o'clock to four o'clock. I wrote composition on other sheet of paper, but I could not mention my true thoughts exactly, because of my imperfect knowledge in the English language.

Yours very truly,
N. KANDA[68]

Corwin had taken him and Orita to New York on April 13, and they visited the Trinity Church, which Kanda described as a site "where great many warrior's graves are placed, and steeple of about 365 or 370 feet high, and we went up to the top of it, and looked all over N.Y." They also went to the U.S. Treasury, the Custom House, and the Tract Society, where he saw men making bibles, all "made by means of machinery," and they were given "a sheet of bible for blind and piece of printing letter covered with copper."[69] On this visit, he penned essays titled "Trinity Church, New York" and "The Tract Society," and he also wrote various other texts during his time in Millstone and later when he furthered his studies at Amherst.[70]

Kanda's diary and letters, being that of a teenager, paint a rich, colorful picture of life at Millstone. He spent much time with Effie and Charlie Corwin, and he befriended neighborhood boys with whom he played croquet until dark, picked cherries, rode boats, and fished.[71] Corwin also occasionally took him to the nearby schoolhouse, where he met more boys.[72] In his letter to his father, dated June 20, 1871, he writes, "I am not homesick at all, because there are many boys in the neighboring house, and we play ball or croquet when we get very tired of studying."[73]

Kanda also describes annual festivities. On June 21, he attended the commencement of Rutgers College: "We got into Church with professors and ministers who graduated some time ago. It was first time for me to see such a grand review. Every student that delivered his speech gets many baskets of flowers from young ladies."[74] Of the fireworks on July 4, he writes, "As I got up, I heard noise of shooting pistols and setting off fireworks all over the Millstone, on account of the coming of the same day of when Declaration of Independence was issued from Independent Hall in Philadelphia in 1776. We fired Mr. Corwin's pistol at the mark fastened to a tree. We have set off great many fireworks at our dooryard. Tonight there was a great festival on Methodist Church over river. Today many cannons are shoot [*sic*] in the cities."[75] Another major event was Mr. and Mrs. Corwin's Tin Wedding Party, held on July 25 and attended by about two hundred people who brought gifts and enjoyed a spread of ice cream, cakes, and fruits.[76]

Kanda's diary further provides a glimpse into the social life surrounding the church in late nineteenth-century America. He regularly attended Sunday schools and the weekly prayer meetings held in the evening. He was also invited to the weddings and funerals of "black people," and he wrote about the funeral of a black woman on May 13: "This black woman was very kind one and she died on about Wednesday night suddenly, she was quite old. Everybody think of her." This event indicates the church's engagement with the African American community in the area.[77] Most importantly, Kanda found connections to his home country, perhaps unexpectedly, through the church's global enterprise: foreign missions.

One such example was the "Mite Society" meetings held by neighboring families. These were gatherings organized mainly by women in which "mite," or penny, boxes were circulated to collect donations for various causes.[78] The idea was based on the biblical tale of a widow's mite—a small sum of money—and female giving, and it allowed women with no income of their own to support church activities, particularly foreign mission work, by contributing a penny a month. According to Hillary Kaell, the practice of mite boxes reached its zenith after the 1870s development of well-organized women's mission boards.[79] Children were encouraged to take part as well, because these boxes served as didactic tools "to cultivate intellectual, moral, and fiscal practices within [middle class] children," who were taught that "every mite-box is a tiny bank for 'your Lord's money,' which is used for heathen children."[80] On April 20, the Corwins were invited to Mr. Blackwell's house next door, "where many gentlemen and ladies were talking in one room, and the boys and girls playing games in another." Another meeting took place on May 18, at Mr. Schenck's house, where attendees played a game called "Copenhagen." Kanda's accounts suggest that children, who also attended these gatherings, are likely to have been made aware of the importance of foreign missions.[81] One cannot help but wonder how a Japanese boy in his early teens would have felt, because his companions were being told of the needy children of Asia, seeking to be saved, both physically and spiritually, by their generosity.

Kanda also had opportunities to personally meet figures directly or indirectly involved in missions to Japan. Heavy rain prevented him from attending the farewell meeting in Brooklyn for Mrs. Pruyn, Mrs. Pierson, and Miss Crosby, who were departing for such a mission;[82] but on June 2, he drove to Raritan "about six miles off to Mr. Rev. Lafevre's house, and I and Mr. Orita went to Mr. Stout's parent's house from thence."[83] This Mr. Stout referred to Henry Stout (1838–1912), the missionary in Nagasaki who had taught Orita and the Iwakura brothers. Another important figure mentioned in Kanda's diary is "Mrs. Dremus," of whom he wrote on June 8, "Mrs. Dremus came to Parsonage this morning and brought with her many pictures of peoples and places pertaining to the religious events. She is a president of that woman missionary society." Kanda was referring to Sarah Platt Doremus (1802–1877), who founded the Woman's Union Missionary Society for Heathen Lands, the first American nondenominational women's missionary society that aimed to send Christian women as teachers and missionaries to Asia. Doremus's work and support allowed the aforementioned three women—Mary Pruyn, Julia Crosby, and Louise Pierson—to be dispatched to Yokohama, Japan, where they founded the American Mission Home, an orphanage and school for mixed-race children and girls, later renamed the Doremus School (the present-day Kyōritsu Gakuen).[84] Kanda's diary fragments show how the intricate ties of foreign missions to the domestic sphere encouraged the faithful to open their doors to Japanese students, many of whom had come to the United States after receiving a missionary education.

Kanda's stay at Millstone was eventful but brief. On June 25, Mori Arinori paid an unexpected visit to Millstone. According to Kanda, he had come "to talk with our teacher about me, that he will send me to some other place to prepare for entering a college."[85] Effie remembered the occasion vividly: "While Baron

Kanda was at our house, Mr. Mori with eleven other men came out to visit him. These twelve dignified Orientals arose when mother came into the room and remained standing until she was seated. It was [a] perfectly natural occurrence for them, but rather an unusual one for mother."[86] This, she added, was a scene that had always been a pleasure for her mother to recall.[87]

Kanda departed two months later on August 26, 1871. He traveled first to Washington, DC, to see Minami, Asahi, and Mori, after which he briefly returned to Millstone and New Brunswick, where he stayed with Hatakeyama at the latter's boarding house and then left for Amherst on August 30. He entered Amherst College in 1875 and returned to Japan upon graduating in 1879.

Conclusion

The four students who studied with Corwin—Tomita Tetsunosuke, Orita Hikoichi, Kanda Naibu, and Kudō Seiichi—pursued further learning in the United States after leaving Millstone and became prominent figures in their respective fields.[88] Tomita, after graduating from Bryant, Stratton, and Whitney's Business College in Newark, was appointed as Japan's first vice-consul to New York in 1872, and he later became the consul general to Shanghai and secretary to the Japanese Legation in London. Upon his return to Japan in 1881, the Ministry of Finance appointed him the first vice-governor of the Bank of Japan, an institution he later served as its second governor in 1888. He is best known for facilitating the development of financial institutions in Japan.[89]

Orita Hikoichi became the first Asian student to graduate from Princeton in 1876 and subsequently served for almost three decades as principal of the Osaka Middle School, which later became the Third Higher School (present-day Kyoto University).[90] He was instrumental in developing Japan's systems of modern secondary and higher education. As noted earlier, he was baptized while at Princeton and continued to practice his faith by attending the church in Tsukiji when he was in Tokyo, approved an active Christian organization at the Third High School, and served on the board of the Okayama Orphanage founded in 1877 by Ishii Jūji, a fellow Christian.[91] Orita's accomplishments are noted in his own report to Princeton dated May 27, 1906: "The most important work to promote the welfare and standing of our country is to produce useful men in every direction. Toward such an aim I believe I am doing good."[92]

Kanda Naibu returned to Japan after graduating in 1879 from Amherst, where he had been baptized in 1878. He taught English and history at the institution that became the First Higher School, later assuming a professorship at the University of Tokyo. From 1893 to his death in 1923, he taught at the Tokyo School of Commerce (present-day Hitotsubashi University). He devoted his life to English education, publishing numerous dictionaries and textbooks, and he is also known for supporting the YMCA's founding in Japan.[93] His son, Tateo, continued his legacy by studying at Oxford and Heidelberg (Germany), becoming a scholar of linguistics and biblical studies, and helping to found the International Christian University in Japan.

Kudō graduated as one of the top ten students from Rutgers College in 1878 and was inducted into the Phi Beta Kappa Society. As Corwin noted, he had initially aspired to become a clergyman when he started at Rutgers, but he returned to Japan in 1879 and became one of the first Japanese tutors to offer a specialized course in geology at Sapporo Agricultural College (present-day Hokkaido University).[94] He later held professorships at Rikkyō University and Senshū University, and he significantly boosted the development of science and English education in Japan.

Effie recalled in her letter how her father used to say that "he was the foreign missionary and mother was the domestic missionary; and Kanda used to call mother his American mother." Indeed, the Corwins' mission successfully fostered Christian faith among Japanese men who became influential figures, particularly in the field of education. While Corwin and the Millstone community undoubtedly had an immense impact on these young men, they too left their own mark on that milieu, at least on one young girl who happened to be there. Effie fondly remembered Kanda, to whom she and her brother were very much attached: "He was only a boy and the most courteous and charming playmate we ever had." Furthermore, she continued, "I am sure . . . that the presence of these Japanese in our family for ten years during my childhood had a decided influence upon me in some ways. I never realized until I came to live in the south how absolutely indifferent I have always been to the color of a person's skin. No doubt, sitting at table three times a day with some of the dark-skinned races had an effect upon me in that way."[95]

The Japanese men who stayed in Millstone kept in touch with Corwin even after they left the United States. In a 1905 letter to Griffis, Corwin mentions that Tomita sent him photos of his family in 1896 and "a photo of himself in his civil official robes" around 1901. Orita visited Millstone in 1876 before he returned to Japan; Kanda called on the Corwins during his world tour from 1901 to 1902 and even went to see Effie, who was then at the Union Theological Seminary Library.[96] The lasting bonds that spanned the Pacific are aptly captured in the hymn, "Blest Be the Tie That Binds," quoted at the beginning of this chapter, which Orita proposed to sing with the Corwins when he made his final visit to the family in 1876.[97] Its final verse reads as follows:

> When we asunder part,
> It gives us inward pain;
> But we shall still be joined in heart,
> And hope to meet again.[98]

The ministers and members of the Reformed Church in America welcomed young strangers from a distant land with Christian spirit, and these Japanese students returned their hospitality with honor and respect. Their ties were undoubtedly blessed.

Notes

I thank Rev. Dr. Fred D. Mueller, former pastor of the Hillsborough Reformed Church, for generously sharing his research findings on Corwin and the Japanese students, in particular the letters from Edwin and Euphemia (Effie) Corwin to William E. Griffis held in the William Elliot Griffis Collection of the Special Collections and University Archives of Rutgers University Libraries (hereafter Griffis Collection).

1 The Hymnal Committee of Reformed Church in the United States, *The Hymnal of the Reformed Church* (Philadelphia: Publication and Sunday School Board of the Reformed Church in the United States, 1920), no. 420, Dennis S. M., arr. by Lowell Mason from Hans Nageli, 1845, accessed July 13, 2022, https://archive.org/details/hymnalofreformedoorefo/page/n361/mode/2up.

2 This house still stands and serves as the parsonage where Rev. Fred Mueller lived until his retirement in 2023.

3 His many works include the *Manual of the Reformed Protestant Dutch Church in North America* (1859; 4th ed., 1902) and *A History of the Reformed Church Dutch* (1895). The entry in his *Manual*, which lists all RCA clergy up to that point, is as follows: "Corwin, Edward Tanjore, b. in N.Y.C., July 12: Coll. of the City New York, 53, N.B.S. 56, L. Cl. Bergen, Resident Graduate at N.B.S. 56, 57. Paramus 57–63, Hillsborough (Millstone), 63–88; also Instructor in Hebrew and O.T. Exegesis in N.B.S., Nov. 83–May, 84, Rector of Hertzog Hall, 88–95; Instructor in Heb. and O.T. Exegesis, Jan.–Mar., 89, Jan. and Feb., 90, Sept., 90–May, 91; Instructor in N.T. Exegesis, Jan.,–May, 92; Greenport, Columbia Co., N.Y., 95–97; General Synod's Agent in Holland, for collecting ecclesiastical documents relating to America, Aug. 21, 97–Nov. 13, 98; editing said ecclesiastical documents (as well as others obtained by J. Romeyn Brodhead in 1841–4), for the State of New York, July 1899—D.D. by R.C. 1872; President of General Synod, 1891." *Manual* 4, 394–395; *Manual* 5 (Charles Corwin, 1922) includes his death on June 22, 1914, and his receipt of a Litt.D. from Rutgers in 1911.

4 According to Mueller, the minutes in the Millstone consistory—the local church governing body made up of the minister (who serves as president), elders, and deacons elected from the congregation—mention a Japanese student only once in all of those years.

5 E. T. Corwin to W. E. Griffis, 17 November 1905, box 46, folder 58, Griffis Collection. This and the letters from Euphemia Corwin in the Griffis Collection were discovered by Mueller during his research fellowship at the New Brunswick Theological Seminary.

6 Euphemia K. Corwin to W. E. Griffis, 3 February 1917, box 46, folder 58, Griffis Collection.

7 Effie assumes that these two youths—the first Japanese she ever saw—were the Yokoi brothers, because she remembers "Ise" (Saheita's alias in the United States) as a "peculiar little Japanese name," but Saheita's letter cited above proves that they were in fact Saheita and Kusakabe. Effie's letter to Griffis, 3 February 1917, box 46, folder 58, Griffis Collection.

8 The letter is cited in Takagi Fuji, *Bakumatsu ishinki no Beikoku ryūgaku: Yokoi Saheita no kaigun shūgaku* (Tokyo: Keio University Press, 2015), 111–115.

9 A copy of this letter can be found in one of Hatakeyama's notebooks, currently in the archives of Shōko Shūseikan, Kagoshima Prefecture. Inuzuka Takaaki, "Honkoku: Sugiura Kōzō nōto," *Kagoshima Kenritsu Tanki Daigaku kiyō* 15 (1987): 122–124.

10 Transcript of a letter from Kusakabe addressed to "Sir" from East Millstone, 20 September 1869, box, 159, folder 1, Griffis Collection. Hatakeyama mentions Kusakabe's move to Millstone in his letter to Yoshida Kiyonari dated October 9, 1869; see also Takagi, *Bakumatsu ishinki no Beikoku ryūgaku*, 162.

11 Takagi, *Bakumatsu ishinki no Beikoku ryūgaku*, 164. Kusakabe's funeral was conducted in New Brunswick, and his grave can be found in the Willow Grove Cemetery there.

12 E. T. Corwin to W. E. Griffis, 17 November 1905. Hatakeyama's letter dated October 9, mentioned above, also says that Tomita went to study English with "Bro Corwin." Takahashi Shūetsu, *Kaishū nikki ni miru bakumatsu ishin no Amerika ryūgaku: Nichigin sōsai Tomita Tetsunosuke no Amerika taiken* (Tokyo: Nihon Hyōronsha, 2018), 176. See also Griffis's mention of this in *The Rutgers Graduates in Japan, an Address Delivered in Kirkpatrick Chapel, Rutgers College, June 16, 1885, by William Elliot Griffis, of the Class of 1869* (New Brunswick, NJ: Rutgers College, 1916), 22.

13 Euphemia K. Corwin to W. E. Griffis, 17 January 1917, box 46, folder 58, Griffis Collection.

14 *Pilgrim's Progress*, translated into Chinese by Rev. W. E. Burns, 1839, can be found in box 144, folder 18, Griffis Collection.

15 The Slough of Despond is a deep bog into which Christian falls on the way from the City of Destruction and from which Help saves him in John Bunyan's allegorical story, *Pilgrim's Progress* (1678). See "Slough of despond," *Merriam-Webster*, accessed November 9, 2023, https://www.merriam-webster.com/dictionary/slough%20of%20despond.

16 Euphemia K. Corwin to W. E. Griffis, 17 January 1917.

17 According to Mueller, in 1993, Orita's descendants contacted the Reverend Allen Buurma, who served as Millstone's pastor from 1979 to 2001, and came on a de facto pilgrimage to see where their ancestor lived, during which they also honored Rev. Corwin and the church who had cared for him. They had discovered Orita's diary from this period, in which he recorded his daily life from 1870 to 1872 in Millstone and from 1872 to 1876 in Princeton. The extensive correspondence between Rev. Buurma and Orita's descendants is housed in the archives of the Hillsborough Reformed Church at Millstone.

18 Iwakura Tomomi (1825–1883), a leading figure of the Meiji Restoration, served as an advisor to Emperor Kōmei and won the trust of Emperor Meiji. Within the newly established Meiji government, he played a central role as minister of the right (minister of state). See chapter 11 on the imperial embassy to the United States and Europe that he led from 1871 to 1873.

19 Yan Ping, *Sankō no mihatenu yume: Chūtō/kōtō kyōiku seiritsu katei to Orita Hikoichi* (Kyoto: Shibunkaku Shuppan, 2008), 18–19.

20 Guido F. Verbeck's letter to John Ferris, 19 March 1870, Reformed Church in America Archives.

21 On Hattori's life at Rutgers, see chapter 5.

22 E. T. Corwin to W. E. Griffis, 17 November 1905. It is unknown why Orita did not stay in New Brunswick. Scholars have suggested the difficulties of finding boarding

for all five of them in New Brunswick or that Orita's insufficient English barred him from admission to the Grammar School because Verbeck's letter mentions that only "two or three of them speak English nicely."

23 A copy of Orita's diary is currently held by the Mudd Library at Princeton University. It covers his five-year sojourn in the United States, from January 1, 1872, to December 31, 1876, and is mostly written in English. This chapter focuses on the entries between January 1, 1872, when the diary begins, to August 30, 1872, when he leaves for Princeton. Orita Hikoichi, *Diary* (hereafter Orita, *Diary*), 1872–1876, AC#033 box 1, Seeley G. Mudd Manuscript Library, Princeton University, Princeton, NJ. All quotes from this diary are reproduced as they appear in the original text.

24 Interestingly, Hattori is seldom mentioned in his diary.

25 As the child of a mistress, Tomoyoshi was sent at an early age to Kōfukuji, the temple where he became a monk. In 1868, he returned to secular life and established the Minami-Iwakura house in 1869. Both Griffis and Charles Lanman mention "Minami," another of Iwakura's sons, as having attended Rutgers. However, his name does not appear in any of the school's records, and he is thus excluded from many extant studies on Japanese students in New Brunswick. William E. Griffis, *The Rutgers Graduates in Japan*, rev. and enlarged and republished at the 150th anniversary of the College (New Brunswick, NJ: Rutgers College, 1916), 13; Charles Lanman, *The Japanese in America* (London: Longmans, Green, Reader, and Dyer, 1872), 12. According to the *Daijōkan Kōbunroku* (Compiled records of the Grand Council of State), Minami studied in the United States from the third month of Meiji 4 (1871) to the tenth month of Meiji 5 (1872). *Kōbunroku* 94 (n.d.): 46, Japan Center for Asian Historical Records, National Archives of Japan, accessed February 20, 2024, https://www.digital.archives.go.jp/img/3047610.

26 *Daijō Ruiten: Grand Council of State Categories of Regulations*, vol. 1, no. 120; case no. 024 (Meiji 4.2.27), "Order Issued to Hara Yasutarō of Tokyo Prefecture to Study in the United States," Japan Center for Asian Historical Records, National Archives of Japan, accessed May 15, 2024, https://www.digital.archives.go.jp/img.pdf/1360175.

27 On the Japanese students' involvement with the Iwakura Mission, see also Haruko Wakabayashi, "Iwakura Mission and the Network of Japanese Students in the United States," *Journal of American-East Asian Relations* 31 (August 2024): 278–307.

28 Orita, *Diary*, 12/7 (January 16, 1872). Orita continued using lunar calendar dates (month/day) until 1/29 (March 8, 1872) and switched to using the Gregorian calendar from March 9; dates in parentheses indicate the Gregorian dates.

29 Yoshihara was a native of Satsuma who had studied with Samuel R. Brown in Yokohama and came to the United States as a member of the second Satsuma student group in 1866. He attended Monson Academy and in 1870 entered Yale Law School. However, he was sent to Europe in the same year to observe the Franco-Prussian War, during which time he was called back to the United States to serve as the mission's secretary.

30 The news reached him on 12/11 (January 20); on 12/21 (January 30), he saw Soogiwoora (Hatakeyama)'s name in the *Tribune*, and a few days later, on 1/2 (February 10), he received a letter, "a very long one," from Soogiwoora. Orita, *Diary*, 12/11 (January 20), 12/21 (January 30), and 1/2 (February 10).

31 On 1/14 (February 22), he received a letter from Tats, "who is awaiting his father in Chicago." On 1/18 (February 26), he received a letter from Hara in Chicago, and on

the following day, he read in the *Tribune* that the embassy had arrived "yesterday." Orita, *Diary*, 1/14 (February 22), 1/18 (February 26), 1/19 (February 27).

32 Orita, *Diary*, March 16, 1872.

33 Orita, *Diary*, March 14, 1872.

34 Orita, *Diary*, March 19, 1872.

35 A native of Satsuma who had been studying in France since 1866 and joined the mission in 1872, entering the Army Ministry upon his return to Japan.

36 A native of Satsuma who compiled an English-Japanese dictionary in 1868 with assistance from Verbeck and who studied in the United States for four years from 1870. *Jinji kōshinroku* database, 4th ed. (January 1915), https://jahis.law.nagoya-u.ac.jp/who/docs/who4-5537.

37 Orita, *Diary*, March 20–25, 1872.

38 This is mentioned in a letter from Yamamoto, who had gone to Washington, DC, with Asahi. Orita, *Diary*, April 6, 1872.

39 Orita also mentions in his diary (April 19, 1872) that "I handed Mr. Hiraga's letter and presents to Mr. Corwin." "Mr. Hiraga" may refer to Hiraga Yoshitada, a member of the mission dispatched by the Department of Justice; if so, said "letter and presents" could have been sent on Iwakura's behalf as thanks to Corwin for looking after the Japanese students.

40 Mori Arinori, *Life and Resources in America* (Washington, DC, 1871). See John Van Sant, ed., *Mori Arinori's Life and Resources in America* (Lanham, MD: Lexington Books, 2003).

41 Orita stayed in New York until April 19 but chose to go back to Millstone: "Of course, I wished to stay there until he will start thence, nevertheless I am very busy at present so I left there, saying farewell to him, accompanying with Messrs Minami & Kunishi, & home half past 6 P.M."

42 Orita received a letter from Asahi in San Francisco on May 17 that said he had gotten very sick on the way and therefore had to wait for the next steamship on the sixteenth. The letter from Hara he received on May 25 included a letter from Asahi written on the thirteenth in San Francisco; we may hence assume that Asahi managed to take the steamboat that left San Francisco for Japan on or around May 16; Orita, *Diary*, May 17 and 25, 1872. A letter from Asahi to George Atherton, dated May 3, 1872, in the Griffis Collection, expresses his regrets that he could not return to continue his studies (box 158, folder 4). He returned to Japan on the third day of the fifth month, Meiji 4 (June 8, 1872). *Daijō Ruiten: Grand Council of State Categories of Regulations* 2, no. 248, case no. 059, "Iwakura Tomosada and Three Others Return to Japan from Respective Countries," Japan Center for Asian Historical Records, National Archives of Japan, accessed May 15, 2024, https://www.digital.archives.go.jp/img/1385319.

43 Orita, *Diary*, June 5, 1872. On this day, Orita heard from Minami that Tats was expecting to go to Europe with his father and would probably not return to the United States; he further learned that Yamamoto would also go to Europe; Orita, *Diary*, July 29, 1872. Tats (i.e., Tomotsune) became the first Japanese student to attend Oxford University. See "Oxford and Japan: 150th Anniversary of the Admission of the First Japanese Student at Oxford," June 20, 2023, *Archives and Manuscripts at the Bodleian Library: A Bodleian Library Blog*, Oxford University, https://blogs.bodleian.ox.ac.uk/archivesandmanuscripts/2023/06/20/oxford-and-japan-150th-anniversary-of-the-admission-of-the-first-japanese-student-at-oxford/.

44 Orita, *Diary*, August 1, 1872. Official records show that Minami returned to Japan in the tenth month (November) of 1872.

45 Another native of Satsuma who seems to have gone to Philadelphia instead. Orita's diary entry for March 23 mentions seeing him when he visited Philadelphia with the mission members; Orita, *Diary*, March 23, 1872. On June 17, however, he is informed that "Matsgata is very sick vomiting blood, so I with Saisho went to Philadelphia, starting here 4 P.M. meeting Mogami at N.B. and we arrived Phila before 9 P.M. & I was extremely glad to see Matsgata that he was a little better, but he was very weak, & I took care for him all the night." On another note, he mentions that Wyckoff, who was preparing to go to Japan to teach, came to see him; Orita, *Diary*, June 17, 1872. Unfortunately, Matsukata died two months later, on August 13, aged twenty-two. On August 15, Orita "went to N.B. half past 6 A.M. I saw Arima & others. They told me that Matsgata died last Tuesday, & that Mogami and others brought his body here to bury at New Brun today. It was a very sad matter, although we could not help it. The funeral service took place at Miss [Drummond?] by Dr. Steele, after that we buried him in the semitary [*sic*] near Mr. Kusakabe's place"; Orita, *Diary*, August 15, 1872. Matsukata's grave, like Kusakabe's, is at the Willow Grove Cemetery in New Brunswick.

46 The son of Saigō Takamori's younger sister; he studied in the United States with Saigō's son, Kikujirō, from 1872 to 1874, later taught at schools in Kagoshima, and was captured and executed during the Satsuma Rebellion (Seinan War) of 1877.

47 Little else is known of Saisho other than that he was a native of Satsuma; he may have been related to Saisho Atsushi (Chōzō), also from Satsuma, who fought with Saigō and Ōkubo to overthrow the Tokugawa shogunate. Atsushi became the second governor of Sakai Prefecture in Osaka. "Meiji jidai shoki ni okeru Ōsaka-fu no rekishi," *Osaka ākaibuzu* 46 (2014): 2–25, Osaka Prefecture Archives, https://archives.pref.osaka.lg.jp/search/information.do?method=initPage&id=70.

48 Tajiri had been in the United States since the spring of 1871. According to his biography, published in 1933, he briefly studied in a school in New York and then at the Rutgers Grammar School, before moving to Hartford, Connecticut. The mission called on him to serve as a supervisor and teacher to its female students, including Yamakawa Sutematsu and Tsuda Umeko. Tajiri studied at Yale from 1874 to 1879, and upon returning to Japan, he founded what is now Senshū University with Sōma Nagatane, Megata Tanetarō, and Komai Shigetada (who reputedly studied at Rutgers College), whom he had met while in the United States. Tajiri Sensei Denki Oyobi Ikō Hensankai, ed., *Hokurai Tajiri sensei-den*, vol. 1 (Tokyo: Tajiri Sensei Denki Oyobi Ikō Hensankai, 1933), 21–26. On Tajiri's contributions to the Matsukata financial reform, see Steven J. Ericson, *Financial Stabilization in Meiji Japan: The Impact of the Matsukata Reform* (Ithaca, NY: Cornell University Press, 2020), 42–50.

49 Almost fifty Japanese were on board the *Amerika-gō*, the ship that brought them from Yokohama to San Francisco, including sixteen sent by the Hokkaido Development Commission (five of whom were to study in Europe), fourteen sent by the Agricultural Promotion Bureau (*kannōryō*), seven from the Mitsui Corporation, and a group of government officials led by Yoshida Kiyonari. Orita in his April 19 diary entry mentions seeing in the paper that a steamship had arrived at San Francisco from Yokohama carrying forty students and Yoshida; Orita, *Diary*, April 19, 1872. See Shiozaki Satoshi, "1872 nen 3 gatsu 26 nichi Yokohama hatsu San Furansisuko yuki, Amerika-gō Nihonjin tokōsha no chōsa: senkō kenkyū happyōgo shihanseiki no kanren kenkyū seika no matome," *Takushoku Daigaku ronshū: Jinbun, shizen, ningenkagaku kenkyū* 44 (2020): 75–107; Nishioka Toshio, "Meiji 5

nen 2 gatsu 18 nichi Yokohama hatsu no Amerikagō de tokō shita ryūgakusei tachi," *Eigakushi kenkyū* 1994, no. 26 (1993): 159–172.

50 "I learned much home news from Ichiki, was very glad that my relatives were all well. Saisho wished to stay with me, so I asked Mr. Corwin. He answered to take him. About a half past 6 P.M. we went to the depot where we found Saisho's trunks, so we sent them home. Ichiki & Tajiri went back about 9 o'clock." Orita, *Diary*, May 3, 1872.

51 On June 8, Saisho went to New York to tell Kudō that he could stay in Millstone; the latter came to Millstone on June 10.

52 E. T. Corwin to W. E. Griffis, 17 November 1905.

53 Shiozaki, "1872 nen 3 gatsu 26 nichi Yokohama," 86.

54 Euphemia K. Corwin to W. E. Griffis, 17 January 1917.

55 Orita, *Diary*, August 30, 1872.

56 Corwin mentions in his letter that Orita was baptized as a Christian, probably in the spring of 1876, without joining a specific church. E. T. Corwin to W. E. Griffis, 17 November 1905.

57 Mueller recalls one of Kanda's descendants visiting him at Millstone in 2016: "The mysterious figure appeared in work clothes at my study and claimed to be a descendant of Naibu. He holds a Juris Doctor from Harvard Law School. Having completed law school and taught, the descendant of Naibu decided that life was not for him, that he was at heart a farmer, so he linked up with the Amish in Pennsylvania where he did farm work every chance he got. Hence his clothing! He asked for some time and produced a few pages copied from a book. The pages were from a book about his ancestor, Naibu Kanda, who met Corwin and studied with him, living in his home."

58 Ueda Tatsunosuke, "Naibu Kanda, 1857–1923," in *Memorials of Naibu Kanda*, ed. Kanda Memorial Committee (Tokyo: Tōkō Shoin, 1927), 3–33, 4–6.

59 Ueda, "Naibu Kanda," 7.

60 Ueda, 10–11. Also Kanda Naibu, *Diary*, n.d., 1871 (hereafter Kanda, *Diary*), with all quotes reproduced according to the original. The diary is now part of the Kanda Naibu Collection in the Hitotsubashi University Library.

61 Also Nawa Dōichi, who had also traveled with Mori from Japan, and a certain Kinashi.

62 Kanda, *Diary*, March 6, 1871.

63 Kanda, *Diary*, June 17–19, 1871.

64 William E. Griffis, *The Mikado's Empire* (New York: Harper and Brothers, 1876), 400.

65 Griffis, *The Mikado's Empire*, 399. He further writes that Mori and Sameshima Naonobu (1845–1880) "stood so high in the confidence of Iwakura that they were dubbed, in the political slang of the capital, 'the legs of Iwakura.'"

66 Kanda, *Diary*, March 9, 1871.

67 Kanda, April 10, 1871. Mori had written a letter to Orita with these instructions for Kanda.

68 Letter included in Kanda Memorial Committee, *Memorials of Naibu Kanda*, 281. This compilation states that this letter was found in draft form, among other letters, in the notebook Kanda used during this period; they are reproduced in *Memorials of Naibu Kanda* as originally written.

69 Kanda, *Diary*, April 13, 1871. Kanda went to New York again on May 1, with Corwin, Effie, and Orita. They visited City Hall, the college "where my teacher used to go when he was young," and the Young Men's [Christian] Association "where

gymnastic place was built, and many newspapers are placed, and pictures are too, and those things are made for young men, to prevent them from bad habit, or house." See Kanda, *Diary*, May 1, 1872.

70 These writings, along with sixteen essays Kanda wrote in his notebooks between 1871 and 1876, are included in Kanda Memorial Committee, *Memorials of Naibu Kanda*, 87–120. Two of these, "George Washington" and "Christmas," were published in Lanman, *The Japanese in America*, 141–144, 162–164. Lanman's book also contains an essay titled "Japanese Costume," not included in Kanda Memorial Committee, *Memorials of Naibu Kanda*, 119–122.

71 Croquet, a popular backyard sport of the period, is frequently mentioned along with fishing and boating as other common pastimes. On May 16, 1871, for example, Kanda mentions catching many fish using "crazy bait" which made the fish drunk; they also occasionally went to catch catfish and eels, and he describes sailing down the river as "very pleasant, and good exercise." Kanda, *Diary*, April 17, 1871.

72 See, for example, Kanda, *Diary*, March 25 and 26, 1871.

73 Kanda Memorial Committee, *Memorials of Naibu Kanda*, 283.

74 Kanda, *Diary*, June 21, 1871.

75 Kanda, *Diary*, July 4, 1871.

76 Kanda, *Diary*, July 25, 1871.

77 Kanda, *Diary*, April 5, June 24 (weddings); May 13, June 5 (funeral). See also J. W. Beardslee, "The Reformed Church in America and the African-American Community," *Reformed Review* 46, no. 2 (December 1992), https://repository.westernsem.edu/pkp/index.php/rr/article/view/1211.

78 Hillary Kaell, "Evangelist of Fragments: Doing Mite-Box Capitalism in the Late Nineteenth Century," *Church History* 86, no. 1 (May 2017): 86–119, https://doi.org/10.1017/S0009640717000014.

79 Kaell, "Evangelist of Fragments," 95.

80 Kaell, 95–96; Karen Li Miller, "The White Child's Burden: Managing the Self and Money in Nineteenth-Century Children's Missionary Periodicals," *American Periodicals* 22, no. 2 (August 2012): 151, https://doi.org/10.1353/amp.2012.0013.

81 Miller, "The White Child's Burden," 139–157.

82 The party was held at the Church of Pilgrims in Brooklyn on May 17. See Kanda Memorial Committee, *Memorials of Naibu Kanda*, 283.

83 Kanda, *Diary*, June 2, 1871.

84 Sakata Masao, "Yokohama Kyoritsu Gakuen and the Three Women Missionaries," website of the United Church of Christ in Japan, accessed March 11, 2024, https://uccj.org/knl/9764.html.

85 Kanda, *Diary*, June 25, 1871.

86 Euphemia K. Corwin to W. E. Griffis, 3 February 1917.

87 Euphemia K. Corwin to W. E. Griffis, 3 February 1917.

88 Saisho's whereabouts remain unclear.

89 On Tomita, see Takahashi, *Kaishū nikki ni miru bakumatsu ishin no Amerika ryūgaku*.

90 On Orita, see Yan Ping, *Sankō no mihatenu yume: Chūtō/kōtō kyōiku setsuritsu katei to Orita Hikoichi* (Kyoto: Shibunkaku Shuppan, 2008); and Itakura Sōzō, *Ichimai no shōzōga: Orita Hikoichi sensei no kenkyū* (Tokyo: Sankō Dōsōkai, 1993).

91 Yan, *Sankō no mihatenu yume*, 72.

92 *Record of the Class of 1876 of Princeton College*, Class Reunion Books Collection, Princeton University Libraries. Cited in Yan, *Sankō no mihatenu yume*, 72.

93 On Kanda, see Ueda, "Naibu Kanda, 1857–1923," 3–33.

94 "Sapporo Nōgakkō no secchi (1876–1886)," in *Hokudai hyakunenshi tsūsetsu*, 61, accessed February 18, 2024, http://hdl.handle.net/2115/30013. Kudō also taught geology, astronomy, chemistry, history, and English.

95 She spent most of her career as the librarian at Berea College in Kentucky.

96 E. T. Corwin to W. E. Griffis, 17 November 1905; letter from Euphemia K. Corwin to W. E. Griffis, 3 February 1917. Effie remembers the visit being in 1898 or 1899, writing that Kanda "gave me a visit which I enjoyed greatly"; Corwin correctly dates it between 1901 to 1902.

97 E. T. Corwin to W. E. Griffis, 17 November 1905. In Orita's diary, he mentions that he went to Millstone and stayed for one night on August 14; his entry for August 15 reads "Good bye to the Corwins." Orita, *Diary*, August 14–15, 1876.

98 The Hymnal Committee of Reformed Church in the United States, *The Hymnal of the Reformed Church*.

Part III

The American Teachers in Japan

Griffis, Wyckoff, and Clark

7

"Well of Blessing"

Griffis in Fukui

FERNANDA PERRONE

William Elliot Griffis spent approximately eleven months in Fukui, from March 4, 1871, to January 22, 1872. Griffis's experience in Fukui profoundly influenced his views about Japan and laid the foundation for his reputation as a "Japan hand." In the long years after his departure from Fukui, Griffis kept in touch with contacts there, which laid the foundation of his Rutgers-Japan network. In addition to enabling Griffis's own writing and research, the network facilitated international exchange and encouraged international understanding. It can be seen as an early precursor of Eisenhower's People-to-People program. In his writing, Griffis would come back again and again to his time in Fukui until his triumphant return to the city in 1927, the year before his death. His diary and letters paint a picture of an inland city far removed from Western influences, describing funerals, festivals, agriculture, fishing, and other aspects of everyday life. Griffis gives a remarkable description of a society in transition as Fukui transforms from a feudal principality to a modern Japanese prefecture. Naturally curious and already exposed to Asia through the Japanese students at Rutgers, Griffis proved to be the ideal narrator of the Western experience in early Meiji Japan. Although Griffis was initially unimpressed with Fukui, by the end of his stay, his thinking had evolved to claim that he had learned the "truth" in Fukui, which he called a "well of blessing" (the literal translation of Fukui).

FIGURE 7.1. William Elliot Griffis, ca. 1865. (Credit: William Elliot Griffis Collection, Rutgers University Libraries. Photo by J. G. Scott.)

Griffis's Early Life

William Elliot Griffis was born in Philadelphia, Pennsylvania, on September 17, 1843, the fourth child of John Limeburger Griffis and Anna Maria Hess. His father was a prosperous coal trader whose business had taken him to Europe, Africa, and Asia. The Griffis children enjoyed a happy, middle-class childhood, attending local primary schools. They were members of Presbyterian John Chambers's First Independent Church of Philadelphia, where Anna Griffis taught Sunday school. After years of prosperity, however, John Griffis's coal business suffered badly in the financial panic of 1857. Despite graduating from the prestigious Central High School at the age of sixteen, rather than going to college, Griffis apprenticed as a jewelry designer to the firm of Carrow, Thibault & Company. With the outbreak of the U.S. Civil War, he joined the Home Guard, serving in the Spencer Miller Howitzer Battery and the Philadelphia Zouaves. He later enlisted in the 44th Pennsylvania regiment of militia, where he was made a corporal.[1]

Griffis arrived at Rutgers College in New Brunswick in 1865, planning to become a minister. He was awarded a scholarship and permitted to live in Hertzog Hall, the only building where housing was available, at New Brunswick Theological Seminary. At Rutgers, Griffis followed the classical curriculum, although he took chemistry and natural history,[2] and became a campus leader, serving as a founder of the college newspaper, the *Targum*, and the yearbook, *The Scarlet Letter*. He was an excellent student who won several prizes and was inducted into the Phi Beta Kappa Society. It was at Rutgers that Griffis encountered some of the first Japanese students to come to the United States: the Yokoi brothers from Kumamoto and Kusakabe Tarō from the province of Echizen or Fukui.

The Opportunity of a Lifetime

After graduation from Rutgers, Griffis enrolled in the seminary while teaching part-time at the Rutgers Grammar School to earn extra money. In September 1870, the rector of the Grammar School wrote to Griffis that Rutgers President Campbell had just shown him a letter asking for a young man, single and not a minister, to go to Japan to teach the natural sciences and organize educational work in general.[3] He was offered a generous salary of $2,400 (later raised to $3,600), a house, and a horse.

This offer came from Matsudaira Mochiaki, the daimyo of Fukui, Kusakabe's home province. Mochiaki was the adopted son of Matsudaira Shungaku, a progressive and pro-Western leader who was influenced by Hashimoto Sanai and the Yokoi brothers' uncle, Yokoi Shōnan. Although Matsudaira Shungaku had stepped down during the Ansei Purge, which resulted in Hashimoto's execution, he still served as an advisor while his son carried on his progressive policies.[4] Under Hashimoto and Shōnan's influence, a domain school for educating young samurai, the Meidōkan, was established in 1855. At first teaching the Confucian classics and the military arts, the curriculum later included medicine and Dutch studies. Later, the Institute for the Study of Western Books, Military Training, and Mathematics was established. Renamed the Meishinkan (House of Enlightenment and Innovation), the school has been considered as "the origin of all kinds of educational activities in modern Fukui prefecture."[5]

Griffis was excited by the opportunity, not least because he badly needed money to help his family. At first, however, he was reluctant to accept and in fact refused the offer. He had recently become engaged to Ellen G. Johnson, a young woman from Upper Red Hook, New York, whose brother was a college friend of Griffis. Sometime between September 15 and 17, when Griffis visited Ellen in Upper Red Hook, something happened, leading him to write to his sister, "there is no present likelihood that E[llen] and I will ever be husband and wife."[6] With encouragement from friends and mentors, Griffis made the decision to accept the Japanese offer.[7]

Two months later, he left Philadelphia by train for the long journey to Japan, traveling by transcontinental railroad and steamer to Yokohama. Arriving in late December, Griffis spent a few months in Tokyo before setting out for the interior. He reached Fukui on March 4, 1871, after a twelve-day journey ending with a trek through snow-covered mountains. His entry to Fukui was certainly dramatic, with the snow, the poor roads, and stops in remote villages. As he wrote in his diary, "Arose, dressed and ready for breakfast, when an officer from

Fukouwi arrived, bringing congratulations, and a present of a brace of fine ducks and a box of Jap bon-bons. Walked 12½ miles to-day, and stopped for the day at Foochow—a large town, where an officer sent specially from Fukoui, met me. . . .[8] When he finally arrived, the European-style house being built for him was not ready, so Griffis was put up "in two large rooms of an old yashiki of some officer. One room about 16 feet square, very high ceiling, serves as my bedroom, another little cosy one of 16 × 10 feet serves as my study and eating room."[9] On his first day, accompanied by his interpreter, Iwabuchi, whom he had brought from Tokyo, he visited Prince Matsudaira. He also had a visit from Kusakabe's father, whom he presented with Kusakabe's Phi Beta Kappa Society key and from whom he received a gift of oranges.[10]

First Impressions of Fukui

Griffis was initially appalled by Fukui: "I was amazed at the utter poverty of the people, the contemptible houses, and the tumble-down look of the city. . . . I realized what a Japanese—an Asian city—was. All the houses of wood, the people poor, the streets muddy, few signs of wealth, no splendid shops."[11] Griffis was surprised to find the Meishinkan a thriving school with fifty instructors and eight hundred students. The school was in the castle, lying "inside the innermost of the 3 circuits of walls and moats. Some of the rooms are gorgeously decorated in gold and lacquered designs."[12] There was one other English-speaking teacher, Alfred Lucy from the British Isles, who taught English. Griffis described him as "a rather quiet young man of about my own age, and is a smart fellow with a head packed full of information, and talks the Japan language fluently, having been in Japan five years."[13] The school had a fairly good library of Dutch, English, and American works, including Kusakabe's books from Rutgers.[14]

Griffis's first order of business was to design and equip a Western-style chemistry laboratory. Griffis supervised the construction of the laboratory, worked with local craftsmen to build apparatus, and ordered equipment from Yokohama and the United States. The chemistry lab was completed at the end of May, but unfortunately the apparatus ordered from the United States did not arrive until September.[15] In the classroom, working with an interpreter, Griffis set up his large science classes using more advanced students as teaching assistants.[16]

Griffis filled his time with reading, writing, ordering books and equipment, teaching, and preparing for his classes. He taught chemistry and physiology for four hours a day, except on Sundays. He had fewer than ninety pupils divided into four classes.[17] Griffis also held evening classes in his own house three or four evenings a week. On Mondays, he lectured on physiology to an audience from the medical school and hospital; on Wednesdays, he read Hume's *History of England* with six of the most advanced pupils; on Thursdays, he lectured on the governments of the world and the laws of "civilized countries"; and on Fridays, he read German with six medical students. He also taught German and French

FIGURE 7.2. Griffis's "new chemical laboratory" (*left*). (Credit: William Elliot Griffis Collection, Rutgers University Libraries.)

three times a week to a class of fifteen very young boys whom he had picked out from a small school nearby.[18] Before leaving for Japan, Griffis had arranged to be a correspondent for several newspapers and magazines, including the Reformed Church's *Christian Intelligencer*.[19] Only a few days after his arrival, he wrote his first piece for the *Intelligencer* tellingly entitled "How could a nineteenth century New Yorker live in the twelfth century?"[20]

One challenge was adjusting to Japanese food. Griffis noted that he ate rice every day, didn't eat bread because he couldn't get any butter, and had delicious fresh fish "never more than 8 hours out of the water, and better than I have ever tasted." He supplemented his diet with a stock of canned meats and fruits from Yokohama, and lettuce and radishes from his garden.[21]

Griffis and Lucy were occasionally entertained by Prince Matsudaira or other local officials. In April, they were invited to the Prince's summer mansion, where they were served a Western-style meal with chairs, a table, plates, knives, and forks. The meal ran to ten courses and included beer and wine.[22] Griffis used this opportunity to describe "our glorious country with its free schools, free institutions, where labor with the hands was not a disgrace, where our chief magistrate came from the people, where we educated our women as highly as ourselves."[23] Despite his fascination with Japan, Griffis was highly critical of the feudal society he observed in its last years. He was particularly concerned about the status of women, noting that when eating with a Japanese family, wives and daughters always occupied a back room, never eating or mingling with the male guests.[24]

In his free time, Griffis was determined to learn and experience what Japan had to offer. He wrote, "Mr. Lucy does not go out much, or at least only to go gunning in the country and suburbs, while I go everyday in the streets, and where I can see human life, and study custom and character." While Griffis and Lucy hunted, planted a garden, and often had dinner together, Griffis did more exploring with his interpreter Iwabuchi and Sasaki Gonroku, the officer assigned to look after the foreign teachers, who had been to the United States and spoke English well. They made numerous expeditions into the Japanese countryside, visiting paper-making villages, tea houses, temples, shrines, an oil press, and a sake distillery.[25] Griffis also made longer expeditions, for instance to Mikuni, the seaport of Fukui, where he watched women diving for shellfish. Of that he wrote: "These women form a sort of guild, and always dive in couples or fours. Men are never allowed to dive with them. They strip, except a waist-cloth, and dive in the sea, several hundred yards from lands. Through a glass, I watched them diving for over an hour, swimming like mermaids, and bringing up the spoils of the deep."[26]

In another memorable trip, Griffis visited Yamanaka, about forty miles from Fukui. On the way, he passed tea plantations and had views of the "great blue Japan Sea." At Yamanaka, he took a bath at the natural hot sulfur baths of the city. The town was known for the manufacture of lacquered wooden work, so he bought dishes for his new house.[27] He took another trip by river to the Sea of Japan, describing "the usual river scenes such as women washing cloths [*sic*], dipping up water, children playing and bathing, cranes by the score, and occasionally pairs or trios of stately storks five feet high, hawks, cormorants, and a species of tall, snow-white birds."[28] Another highlight was a seven-day visit to Hakusan, or Mount Haku, a dormant volcano on the border of the prefectures of Gifu and Ishikawa, which was believed to be sacred. En route Griffis and Iwabuchi stayed the night in a Buddhist temple at Katsuyama. "The streets were jammed and packed with people eager to scan the TO-JIN [foreigner] from crown to sole." Griffis wanted to measure the height of Hakusan, coming to the conclusion that it was about two-thirds the height of Mount Fuji. On the way back, Griffis was attacked by fleas one night and descended the mountain in pouring rain.[29]

Loneliness

Although Griffis was fascinated by life in Fukui, he also felt lonely and isolated. He looked forward to letters from home, which sometimes took weeks or even months to arrive. He tried to help his family financially; however, he was determined to settle the debts he had incurred from his education at Rutgers and in coming to Japan, and as he noted, his expenses for servants and food were heavy.[30] Griffis constantly asked his family to send items from home that he used for his teaching, attesting to the difficulty of finding what he needed in Tokyo or Yokohama. In one letter he asked Maggie for fifteen copies of a simple, cheap German primer, twenty copies of a French primer, and copies of sheet music for

American popular songs. He asked his father to send "printed information, samples etc. about any and every kind of arts, manufactures, machines, specially of Gas works, pipes, metres etc., and if he could send a burner (best kind) by mail, it would be good. Directions etc. concerning the manufacture of patent fertilizers, poudrette, etc. will be useful and turned to good account. Also concerning sugar-refining, etc."[31] Griffis did, however, send presents of silks, lacquer and other articles to his mother, aunt, and sisters.[32]

Griffis occasionally received letters from the growing Rutgers-Japan network, particularly from his friend Edward Warren Clark, who was making his own plans to come to Japan. Four young men from Higo (Kumamoto Prefecture), one of whom was a cousin of Yokoi Daihei, who had returned home suffering from consumption, came all the way to Fukui to study with Griffis. Griffis wrote that Numagawa Saburō (Yokoi Daihei's assumed name) "coughs so badly, that he could not write me a letter, but he sent these three students here, as soon as he knew I was here. A few days ago, he sent another of his cousins to me, with thanks and kind memories." Katsu Kaishū, the father of Rutgers Grammar School student Katsu Koroku, sent Griffis Japanese netting, which he sent home, with his picture and a letter of thanks.[33]

Griffis's loneliness increased particularly after the departure in July 1871 of Lucy, whose contract was not renewed. Lucy moved to Tokyo and then to Aomori, where he helped introduce English methods of agriculture and stock-raising, eventually ending up as a farmer in South Africa.[34] Griffis and Lucy were never close friends. Griffis wrote, "Besides, Mr. Lucy, although a pleasant gentleman[,] is not according to my tastes in many respects. He does not live in my world, and the mould of our thoughts is entirely different."[35] When Lucy left, however, Griffis wrote, "Now I have no live thing of foreign birth or nature, except my flowers from home, and a cactus."[36] Part of Griffis's ambivalence toward Lucy came from the fact that like many other Western men in Japan, Lucy had taken a temporary Japanese wife. Griffis explained to Maggie that he had "put her away" just before Griffis arrived, but when Lucy left Fukui, Griffis noted that he took his wife (or possibly another woman) with him.[37]

Griffis himself fought against loneliness and temptation during the time he was in Fukui. He wrote, "My saddest and sorest need is for something to love, something to caress, or at least some congenial soul and prescience [*sic*]. The temptations to a lonely man here, are fearful, dare not have any idle moments."[38] In August, his interpreter Iwabuchi got married, which Griffis feared would take away yet another companion. "Iwabuchi's marriage, taking away much of his close connection with me, leaves me more lonely than ever."[39]

Griffis kept relentlessly busy; his new Western-style house was ready in September, and he moved in. On September 22 he wrote in his diary, "Afternoon the new foreign houses thrown open to public inspection—grounds crowded, and houses jammed, refreshment-sellers, and clog-check men did a thriving business."[40] In fact, two houses were built side by side for the foreign teachers.

FIGURE 7.3. Griffis's Western-style house (*left*), Fukui, 1871. (Credit: William Elliot Griffis Collection, Rutgers University Libraries.)

Griffis moved in the next day, where he was joined by three students who lived with him—Nakano, whom Griffis also refers to as his assistant; Ōiwa; and Honda.[41] Later they were joined by Carl Kasahara and Motoyama, one of the students from Higo mentioned above; and Imadate Tosui, who would later accompany Griffis to the United States. At home in the evenings, Griffis gave additional instruction in American history, Bible study, and other subjects, despite the fact that Christianity was still technically illegal in Japan. One method that Griffis used in teaching was to ask his students to write essays in English about Japanese history, customs, and geography, with titles such as "The Province of Echizen." Motoyama wrote an essay about Japanese money. Griffis later incorporated this material into his books about Japan.

In his new house, Griffis looked forward to having a new servant, whom he planned to hire in advance. "My new servant will be a girl of about 17, who will wait on the table, and take care of my room specially."[42] In the event, Griffis felt forced to send the woman away. "The young girl of 18, whom I took for a servant to wait specially upon me, proved to be very faithful, diligent and pleasant in every way, anticipated my every want, and made my house almost as comfortable as a home. I liked her very much. All of which to a sometimes weary and home-sick young man must necessarily be a strong temptation in his lonely hours. I found after two weeks, that she made too much comfort for me, and was too attractive herself. After having her 11 days, I sent her away, before temptation turned into sin."[43] After this experience, Griffis was convinced that sending for his brothers to join him in Japan, as he had periodically discussed with his family, would be a mistake. "I am sure you see now the madness, the folly of sending anyone here, but one clothed in the whole armor . . . though an inactive and idle life at home is bad, yet a life of sin here is worse."[44]

Transition and Transformation in Fukui

While Griffis was busy teaching, Japanese society was undergoing a profound transformation. The new Meiji government began to replace the feudal system with a federal structure, meaning that Fukui became a prefecture rather than a principality. In July, Griffis wrote in his diary, "Proclamation from Imperial Gov. dispencing [*sic*] with officers and reducing incomes—excitement among thousands of families all over Japan."[45] Soon after these events, the Meiji government decreed the end of the *Han* system and the removal of the feudal lords to Tokyo.[46] Griffis recounted Matsudaira's departure in early October in his diary. "Morning bright and fair, prince left for Yedo escorted by over 1,000 men, nearly all Fukuwi turned out to see him, and soon we were in a province without a prince."[47] In a passage describing Matsudaira's departure from Fukui in *The Mikado's Empire*, Griffis wrote, "The whole city seems to be astir to-day. The streets are crowded with citizens in their best clothes, and thousands are in from the country. They have come to see their prince for the last time. It is a farewell gathering. Many hundreds of old men, women, and children are weeping."[48]

Griffis was already witnessing the practical result of this change as students and teachers left for Tokyo, noting in his diary, "Exodus of Fukuwi students still continues."[49] Officials like Griffis's friend Sasaki, "whose house was an open place always to me," were called to Tokyo.[50] The new regime brought changes in the education system: the fencing, wrestling, and riding schools were dispensed with, mathematics was made compulsory for all, and a total of thirteen schools were organized in the city. Griffis noted that all classes can now attend the schools previously restricted to samurai and samurai's sons. He reported that women's education was being discussed in Tokyo. In Fukui, the castle was gradually dismantled as old walls were leveled and moats filled in.[51] Deprived of many of his English-speaking friends, Griffis "attacked Japanese language. So far since I came to Japan, I had done almost nothing at the language, being too busy with other things, and having no special need to learn it. But finding it impossible to get my lectures translated (written) and being put to inconvenience in other ways, I have resolved to go manfully at the language. Of course I have gradually picked up a great deal, and have trained my ears to distinguish & my brain to think in Japanese."[52]

By late November, "at least 700 men have made exodus from Fukuwi alone, since March, the retired prince, all the former chief officers and scores of the most talented young men have gone. . . . Of course I have lost some good scholars."[53] Griffis was thinking strategically, however, noting that "in the development of the future, it is better as it is, i.e. to have my chief friends, and those I most influenced by my reiterated opinions & principles in the Imperial Government, as high officers, instead of their being petty local dignitaries."[54] Griffis was clearly thinking beyond Fukui at this point, imagining he would have influence on the former local officials as they moved into positions in the new government.

As Griffis reported, "A few months ago, I wrote to the Department of Education, urging them to adopt a National System of Education and the establishment of several Polytechnic or Scientific schools in various chosen parts of the country."[55] Apparently, the Department of Education in Tokyo wrote to officials in Fukui, asking if Griffis could be transferred to Tokyo, but they refused. Griffis wrote to Guido Verbeck, declaring his willingness to come to Tokyo. Griffis's lobbying ultimately resulted in an invitation from the Department of Education to serve as professor of chemistry and natural philosophy in the new polytechnic that was shortly opening.[56] Murata Ujihisa, the chief education officer in Fukui, was not pleased about Griffis ending his contract two years early. Griffis wrote, "I had two interviews in the Gov't office each nearly two hours long, in which Murata used all his keen mind to frame unnumbered arguments to deter me from my purpose and keep me in Fukuwi."[57] After protracted negotiations, Griffis received permission to leave Fukui. He somehow also convinced Murata to provide an escort of an officer, pay all expenses for his journey, and continue his salary until a new contract was made. A grand going-away party was held where Griffis was showered with presents.[58] Finally, on another snowy day in late January 1872, Griffis left Fukui, writing, "I now bid farewell to this 'well of blessing,' the scene of a year's severe toil, deep thought, bitter loneliness, occasional temptation, wondrous experience and calm joy, with not a little sorrow."[59]

Griffis's Life After Fukui

When Griffis arrived in Tokyo, however, the polytechnic was not ready to open, so he busied himself with reading and writing. Several of his Fukui students joined him in Tokyo, where they shared a vacant samurai house: Carl Kasahara, Griffis's favorite pupil; Casper Nakazawa; Griffis's assistant, Nakano; Motoyama; Ishida; and Yamagata. Without his generous salary from Fukui, Griffis became more concerned about money. He was able to secure a contract for a series of English-Japanese grammar books with the Bancroft Company from San Francisco. He also began work on what would become *The Mikado's Empire*, incorporating many of his experiences from Fukui. After many months of waiting, Griffis found employment teaching physics, chemistry, and law at the Daigaku Nankō, one of the predecessors of Tokyo University. He was

FIGURE 7.4. Griffis with students from Fukui who lived with him in Tokyo: Carl Kasahara, Casper Nakazawa, Nakano, Motoyama, Ishida, and Yamagata. (Credit: William Elliot Griffis Collection, Rutgers University Libraries.)

joined by his older sister, Maggie, who kept house for him, tutored students, and eventually gained an appointment at the first government school for girls.

Griffis and his sister left Japan in 1874—Griffis was in a dispute with the Kaisei Gakkō (the old Nankō) about his contract; Maggie, on the other hand, was offered the opportunity to set up a Western-style teacher training school for women, but being a dutiful sister, she accompanied her brother to the United States.[60] Back at home, Griffis completed what would be his signature work, *The Mikado's Empire*, first published in 1876. In 1877, Griffis entered the Union Theological Seminary in New York and was ultimately ordained as a minister in the Reformed Church. After graduation from Union Theological Seminary, Griffis served as a pastor of three churches—the First Reformed Church of Schenectady, New York (1877–1886); Shawmut Congregational Church in Boston (1886–1893); and the First Congregational Church in Ithaca, New York (1893–1903). In 1879, Griffis married Katherine Lyra Stanton (1855–1898) of Schenectady and the couple had three children. After Katherine's early death, Griffis married Sarah Frances King Griffis (1868–1959) of Pulaski, New York, in 1900. In 1903, Griffis retired from the ministry to devote himself full time to his research on East Asia. Griffis would spend the rest of his life writing, lecturing, and collecting material about Japan, writing more than twenty books, hundreds of magazine articles, newspaper editorials, and reference book contributions. As will be seen below, he did not return to Japan until 1926, over fifty years after his original stay.

Martin N. Wyckoff

Griffis did not abandon Fukui in 1872—he arranged for another friend and Rutgers graduate, Martin N. Wyckoff, to take his place at what had become the Fukui middle school. A few years younger than Griffis, Wyckoff graduated from Rutgers in 1872, so he would have known Kusakabe Tarō and the other Japanese students there. He set out for Japan almost immediately after commencement, accompanying Maggie on her way to join her brother in Tokyo. In Fukui, Wyckoff taught English and French, and he continued the physics and chemistry courses taught by Griffis. He used Griffis's grammar books and the scientific apparatus Griffis had left behind. Wyckoff was less lonely than Griffis because he was anticipating the arrival of his fianceé, Anna Baird. Griffis met her ship in Yokohama in June 1873 and found her a place to stay while she waited for Wyckoff to arrive. The young couple was married in Griffis's house in Tokyo.

The centralization and reorganization of Japanese education at this time, however, impacted Wyckoff as it had Griffis in Fukui. Murata himself left for Tokyo not long after Griffis's departure and was joined by five other officials from Fukui. The situation in Fukui, both within and outside the schools, had become unstable. The educational system was merged with that of a neighboring city, Tsuruga, where decisions were made. Tomita, the director of the school, was removed as a result of a petition sent to Murata by the lower teachers, who had apparently been dissatisfied for some time. As Wyckoff explained to Griffis, "The business of the school is to be done in future according to the voice of the teachers, who are to meet together for that purpose."[61] At the same time, there was an uprising among the farmers, forcing Wyckoff and his fellow teacher Mudgett, who were living in Griffis's old house, to stay in the castle for a few days. Wyckoff explained that the uprising had to do with "forbidding Buddhist priests to speak from house to house and in their temples, and changing some of their ceremonies."[62] Ultimately, six of the mob's ringleaders were decapitated.[63]

Wyckoff was determined to expose his students to Christianity. Asking Griffis to send Bibles, he started a Bible study class for twenty-two boys. "I feel almost afraid when I think of so many souls entrusted to my teaching."[64] The school officials became concerned about Wyckoff's religious instruction. "The feeling toward religion is changing greatly among officers here, but they are afraid to do much, because of the lower classes, who are all Buddhists and this Ken [prefecture] is the most strongly Buddhist."[65] Although Christianity was no longer illegal in Japan at this point, the prefectural office had not removed the posted edict against Christianity until "the present disturbances quiet a little." Wyckoff was asked not to teach the Bible publicly, although he was permitted to instruct privately.

By September, Wyckoff was seriously considering leaving Fukui, noting that funds were in short supply. Two girls' schools in Fukui had merged, and the authorities were preparing to tax the middle school.[66] More changes would follow. In December, the German section was separated from the school and turned over to the medical institution since all of the students studying German were planning to become physicians. The teachers were unhappy about the resulting drop in their salaries. Wyckoff continued to teach chemistry for four hours a day.[67] He reflected on the challenges of being a *yatoi* (a foreign worker employed by the Japanese government): "My experience is that they [the Japanese] don't want any more foreign advice than they can put in practice as their own original ideas. They want advantage of all the foreigner knows, but they also want to do [things] themselves."[68] Wyckoff felt powerless to influence developments at the school, explaining that the school building was being moved to the prefectural offices. There would be no laboratory in the new building, and Griffis's chemical apparatus was put in storage.[69] Wyckoff noted that Griffis's friend Sasaki had been forced to resign because of some difference of opinion with the Tsuruga leadership. "All our old Fukui men are getting out of Kencho. Muratta at Tokio Tomita, at Gifu Ken, and all the rest of any importance out of office."[70]

In February 1874, Wyckoff heard from the Ministry of Education that they "cannot listen to the idea of keeping a teacher here," because of the cost of paying a foreigner.[71] Although the new director, Kobayashi, tried to plead his case, by May 1874, Wyckoff was writing to Griffis that the middle school in Fukui was to be closed or merged with the new normal school. He was offered a ten-month contract, which he respectfully declined.[72] Instead, Wyckoff accepted a two-year position to teach physics, chemistry, and English at the Niigata School for Foreign Languages.[73] He went back to the United States in 1877 but returned to Japan in 1881, where he would have a long and distinguished career as a teacher and administrator at Meiji Gakuin University.[74] His textbook, *English Composition for Beginners Prepared for Japanese Students*, published by the Maruzen Company in 1885, was reissued several times. Martin Wyckoff died of a heart attack in 1911 at the age of sixty-one. He was buried in the mission cemetery of Zuishōji, a temple of the Ōbaku sect near Meiji Gakuin University.[75]

Griffis's Japanese Network

Martin Wyckoff became one of the members of Griffis's Rutgers-Japan network. Writing to Griffis in Tokyo, he remarked, "If you see the Prince, Murata, or Sasaki, give them my regards, please."[76] Throughout his long life, Griffis remained in contact with many of the Japanese students at Rutgers, foreign workers in Japan, and friends from Fukui, as revealed by the hundreds of letters in the William Elliot Griffis Collection at Rutgers University. Many of the young men whom Griffis knew in early Meiji Japan went on to have distinguished careers. Several of his Fukui students emerged as fine scholars—Sengaku Ryō, Nanbu Kyūgo, Nakae Iwatarō, Yamada Tō, and others went on to contribute to the development of science and technology in the Meiji and Taishō periods.[77] Amenomori Nobushige, Griffis's student in both Fukui and Tokyo, became a friend and biographer of Lafcadio Hearn. In addition to Amenomori, Griffis kept in touch with many of his friends and students from Fukui. The Griffis Collection contains letters from Carl Kasahara, who later became the manager of Kobe Pier Limited; Griffis's assistant, Nakano; and even Education Officer Murata.

Matsudaira Keimin, a son of Matsudaira Shungaku, was an important correspondent. Matsudaira Keimin was made a viscount in 1906 in gratitude for his father's service to the country. In 1917, he wrote to Griffis asking him to write his recollections of his father, whom he hardly remembered.[78] In response, Griffis wrote a lengthy description: "Seen in the perspective of nearly fifty years, Echizen Shungaku—'the old prince,' as we foreigners used to call him—looms as one of the great men of his era and not least among the makers of the New Japan.... This feudal ruler labored for the welfare of all his people, in developing resources, promoting education, science, hygiene, and sound philosophy through reform."[79]

Rutgers professor and curator Ardath Burks once described Griffis as a "saver of string." Indeed, Griffis's most enduring legacy is his archival collection of over 250 boxes, which were donated to Rutgers after his death. Griffis continued to collect materials about Fukui through his friends and correspondents long after his sojourn of 1871–1872. He acquired a series of mounted albumen photographs of Fukui dated 1900, which included photographs of the moat and castle, shrines and temples, schools, and street scenes. Griffis also owned a set of photographs in postcard format, probably from the 1910s or 1920s, as well as various miscellaneous photographs. He obtained a 1915 map of Fukui, which someone had annotated, showing where his house was and the location of churches, which of course was important to Griffis.

With his second wife, Frances, Griffis finally returned to Japan, making a six-month trip in 1926–1927, about a year before his death. Arriving in Tokyo, they undertook a two-thousand-mile journey to the four major islands of Japan (Hokkaido, Honshu, Kyūshū, and Shikoku), Korea, and Manchuria. Griffis delivered over 250 speeches. The highlight of the trip, however, was a triumphant return to Fukui. Griffis wrote, "I was particularly delighted with my reception in Fukui ... it consisted of four glorious days. The whole town was decorated and more than ten thousand students were kind enough to come out to welcome me."[80] He visited the prefectural offices, schools, factories, his old house, and the Fukui College of Technology and Normal School, making speeches everywhere. Intriguingly, he met with the "Tuesday Club," a men's organization that discussed improving social life through having parties without geishas.[81] Clearly, Griffis was still a figure of significance in Fukui that many years later. Not long after his trip, while in Florida, Griffis died on February 5, 1928.

Conclusion

In conclusion, what was Griffis's Fukui legacy? His eleven months in Fukui in 1871–1872 was a life-changing, life-defining experience. It shaped Griffis's view of Japan and his own place in relation to that country. While Griffis advanced the Westernization and modernization of education in Fukui, his career in Tokyo was less successful. Griffis's greatest impact, however, was as a writer and lecturer about Japan, an identity that was forged in Fukui. Griffis's most famous and influential book, *The Mikado's Empire*, was shaped by his time in Fukui, which in turn would shape the view many Americans had of Japan. Before leaving Fukui, Griffis wrote in his diary. "Yet these people are just like ourselves, their hearts the same as ours. Their emotions and traits, both noble and despicable, are twin to those which belong to mankind between the Alleghanies [*sic*] and the Atlantic. This is a trite truism. Yet in its truth consists its novelty. When men of differing climes and nations see behind each other's mail of codes, manners, education, and systems their common humanity, the hope of their dwelling in peace as children of one Father is no longer a chimera."[82] Griffis would come back to Fukui time and time again in his writings. His contacts in Fukui formed the basis of a network of students, teachers, missionaries, government officials, and countless others, which played an important role in building the relationship between the United States and Japan, and which continues to this day.

Notes

1 Ebenezer Mack Treman and Murray E. Poole, *The History of the Treman, Tremaine, Truman Family in America*, part 2 (Ithaca, NY: Press of the Ithaca Democrat, 1901), 1528.
2 Rutgers College Scholarship Record, Liberal Arts, Special Collections and University Archives, Rutgers University Libraries, New Brunswick, NJ (hereafter SC/UA).
3 Frances Yeomans Helbig, "William Elliot Griffis: Entrepreneur of Ideas" (master's thesis, University of Rochester, 1966), 53.
4 Kanai Madoka, "Fukui, Domain of a Tokugawa Collateral Daimyō: Its Tradition and Transition," in *The Modernizers: Overseas Students, Foreign Employees, and Meiji Japan*, ed. Ardath W. Burks (Boulder, CO: Westview Press, 1985), 56–61.
5 Kanai, "Fukui, Domain of a Tokugawa Collateral Daimyō," 57–59.
6 W. E. Griffis to Maggie Griffis, 21 and 26 September 1870, box 132, folder 7, William Elliot Griffis Collection, SC/UA (hereafter Griffis Collection).
7 Edward Beauchamp, *An American Teacher in Meiji Japan* (Honolulu: University Press of Hawaii, 1976), 24.
8 W. E. Griffis, diary, 3 March 1871, box 16, Griffis Collection.
9 W. E. Griffis to Maggie Griffis, 9 March 1871, box 132, folder 8, Griffis Collection.
10 W. E. Griffis, diary, 5 March 1871, box 16, Griffis Collection.
11 Quoted in Joseph M. Henning, *Interpreting the Mikado's Empire: The Writings of William Elliot Griffis* (Lanham, MD: Lexington Books, 2021), 45.
12 W. E. Griffis to Maggie Griffis, 28 April 1871, box 132, folder 8, Griffis Collection.
13 W. E. Griffis to Maggie Griffis, 12 March 1871, box 132, folder 8, Griffis Collection.

14 Quoted in Beauchamp, *An American Teacher*, 39.
15 W. E. Griffis to Maggie Griffis, 24 September 1871, box 132, folder 8, Griffis Collection.
16 Motoyama Yukihiko, "The Educational Policy of Fukui and William Elliot Griffis," in Burks, *The Modernizers*, 280–288.
17 W. E. Griffis to Maggie Griffis, 9 March 1871.
18 W. E. Griffis to Maggie Griffis, 28 April 1871.
19 Helbig, "William Elliot Griffis," 55.
20 Beauchamp, *An American Teacher*, 36.
21 W. E. Griffis to Maggie Griffis, 10 June 1871, box 132, folder 8, Griffis Collection.
22 W. E. Griffis to Maggie Griffis, 2 April 1871, box 132, folder 8, Griffis Collection.
23 W. E. Griffis to Maggie Griffis, 3 April 1871, box 132, folder 8, Griffis Collection.
24 W. E. Griffis to Maggie Griffis, 12 May 1871, box 132, folder 8, Griffis Collection.
25 W. E. Griffis, diary, 24 March 1871.
26 W. E. Griffis to Maggie Griffis, 17 May 1871, box 132, folder 8, Griffis Collection.
27 W. E. Griffis to Maggie Griffis, 12 July 1871, box 132, folder 8, Griffis Collection.
28 W. E. Griffis to Maggie Griffis, 12 August 1871, box 132, folder 8, Griffis Collection.
29 W. E. Griffis to Maggie Griffis, 28 August 1871, box 132, folder 8, Griffis Collection.
30 W. E. Griffis to Maggie Griffis, 26 March 1871 and 10 April 1871, box 132, folder 8, Griffis Collection.
31 W. E. Griffis to Maggie Griffis, 12 May 1871.
32 W. E. Griffis to Maggie Griffis, 17 May 1871.
33 W. E. Griffis to Maggie Griffis, 23 May 1871, box 132, folder 8.
34 William Elliot Griffis, *The Mikado's Empire* (New York: Harper and Brothers, 1876), 533; Hamish Ion, *American Missionaries, Christian Oyatoi and Japan* (Vancouver: University of British Columbia Press, 2009), 156.
35 W. E. Griffis to Dear Ones at Home, 6 June 1871, box 132, folder 8, Griffis Collection.
36 W. E. Griffis to Maggie Griffis, 5 July 1871, box 132, folder 8, Griffis Collection.
37 W. E. Griffis to Maggie Griffis, 5 July 1871.
38 W. E. Griffis to Maggie Griffis, 25 June 1871, box 132, folder 8, Griffis Collection.
39 W. E. Griffis to Maggie Griffis, 13 August 1871, box 132, folder 8, Griffis Collection.
40 W. E. Griffis, diary, 22 September 1871, box 16, Griffis Collection.
41 W. E. Griffis to Maggie Griffis, 24 September 1871.
42 W. E. Griffis to Maggie Griffis, 17 August 1871, box 132, folder 8, Griffis Collection.
43 W. E. Griffis to Maggie Griffis, 9 September 1871, box 132, folder 8, Griffis Collection.
44 W. E. Griffis to Maggie Griffis, 3 December 1871, box 132, folder 8, Griffis Collection.
45 W. E. Griffis, diary, 18 July 1871.
46 Beauchamp, *An American Teacher*, 62.
47 W. E. Griffis, diary, 2 October 1871, box 16, Griffis Collection.
48 William Elliot Griffis, *The Mikado's Empire*, 10th ed., vol. 2 (New York: Harper and Brothers, 1903), 535.
49 W. E. Griffis, diary, 8 September 1871, box 16, Griffis Collection.

50 W. E. Griffis to Maggie Griffis, 28 October 1871, box 132, folder 8, Griffis Collection.
51 W. E. Griffis to Maggie Griffis, 28 October 1871.
52 W. E. Griffis to Maggie Griffis, 28 October 1871.
53 W. E. Griffis to Maggie Griffis, 26 November 1871, box 132, folder 8, Griffis Collection.
54 W. E. Griffis to Maggie Griffis, 26 November 1871.
55 W. E. Griffis to Maggie Griffis, 10 January 1872, box 132, folder 8, Griffis Collection.
56 W. E. Griffis to Maggie Griffis, 10 January 1872.
57 W. E. Griffis to Dear Ones at Home, 20 January 1872, box 132, folder 9, Griffis Collection.
58 W. E. Griffis to Dear Ones at Home, 20 January 1872.
59 W. E. Griffis to Dear Ones at Home, 22 January 1872, box 132, folder 9, Griffis Collection.
60 On Margaret Griffis, see Elizabeth K. Eder, *Constructing Opportunity: American Women Teachers in Early Meiji Japan* (Lanham, MD: Lexington Books, 2003).
61 M. N. Wyckoff to W. E. Griffis, 5 March 1873, box 56, folder 69, Griffis Collection.
62 M. N. Wyckoff to W. E. Griffis, 5 March 1873.
63 M. N. Wyckoff to W. E. Griffis, 9 April 1873, box 56, folder 69, Griffis Collection.
64 M. N. Wyckoff to W. E. Griffis, 24 March 1873, box 56, folder 69, Griffis Collection.
65 M. N. Wyckoff to W. E. Griffis, 9 April 1873.
66 M. N. Wyckoff to W. E. Griffis, 19 September 1873, box 56, folder 69, Griffis Collection.
67 M. N. Wyckoff to W. E. Griffis, 3 December 1873, box 56, folder 69, Griffis Collection.
68 M. N. Wyckoff to W. E. Griffis, 23 December 1873, box 56, folder 69, Griffis Collection.
69 M. N. Wyckoff to W. E. Griffis, 9 and 25 March 1874, box 56, folder 69, Griffis Collection.
70 M. N. Wyckoff to W. E. Griffis, 9 February 1874, box 56, folder 69, Griffis Collection.
71 M. N. Wyckoff to W. E. Griffis, 26 February 1874, box 56, folder 69, Griffis Collection.
72 M. N. Wyckoff to W. E. Griffis, 6 May 1874, box 56, folder 69, Griffis Collection.
73 Tatsumaru Tezuka, "Martin N. Wyckoff," newsletter, unpaginated (Tokyo: Tokyo Metropolitan Historiography Institute, 1966).
74 Meiji Gakuin, *Meiji Gakuin: A Century at a Glance* (Tokyo: Meiji Gakuin, 1977).
75 Tezuka, "Martin N. Wyckoff."
76 M. N. Wyckoff to W. E. Griffis, 26 February 1874.
77 Motoyama Yukihiko, "The Education Policy of Fukui and William Elliot Griffis," in Burks, *The Modernizers*, 294–295.
78 Matsudaira Keimin to William Elliot Griffis, box 51, folder 64, Griffis Collection.
79 William Elliot Griffis, "Echizen Shungaku," unpublished, ca. 1920, box 78, folder 7, Griffis Collection.
80 Quoted in Beauchamp, *An American Teacher*, 140–141.
81 W. E. Griffis, diary, 28–29 April 1927, box 36, Griffis Collection.
82 Quoted in Henning, *Interpreting the Mikado's Empire*, 74–75.

8

Edward Warren Clark in Shizuoka, 1871–1873

A. HAMISH ION

Edward Warren Clark's (1849–1907) life and adventures in early Meiji Japan as witnessed in his eponymous book for Christian youth or in his letters to his friend and fellow Rutgers graduate, William Elliot Griffis (1843–1928), show an exuberance, a zest for life with an added touch of puerile naivete.[1] James Hamilton Ballagh (1838–1920), a Dutch Reformed missionary and 1860 Rutgers graduate, described Clark as "Our irrepressible [*sic*] friend" in October 1894 when he revisited Yokohama for the first time in nineteen years as the tour leader of a group of American women.[2]

The focus of this chapter is Clark in Shizuoka, which he christened "the St. Helena of Tycoonism."[3] It was where he lived and taught Western studies in English and French between 1871 and 1873. In the early 1870s, Shizuoka was by no means a simple provincial town in a prefecture well known for its mandarin oranges and tea. Shizuoka was the ancestral home of the Tokugawa shogun, and it was there that Tokugawa Yoshinobu (1837–1913), the last shogun, retired following the Meiji Restoration. Many of his former retainers followed him there into semi-exile, and approximately six thousand ex-Tokugawa samurai were living in Shizuoka and its vicinity when Clark was there. Clark did much to develop the teaching of English in the region. Even though Christianity was officially prohibited, he also laid the foundational work for one of the earliest groups of Japanese Protestant Christians (the so-called Shizuoka Band) to emerge in provincial Japan following the Yokohama Band, the latter being the first group of Japanese Protestant converts in the treaty port, which had coagulated around Ballagh in 1871 and 1872.[4] Clark's Christian belief was a vital part of his makeup, and he was fortunate when he landed in Yokohama that there was an openness to Christianity, despite its prohibition, in part due to the ideology of *risshin shusse* (rising in the world), which drove ambitious youth in Meiji Japan to seek success through education, in general, and, in particular, Western studies.[5] This resonated especially with a group of young Japanese who sought to become "masters of English" and saw the acquisition of English language as the key to acquiring Western knowledge.[6]

The study of Clark in Shizuoka is also a pertinent one given the current academic interest in the role of religion in the political, diplomatic, economic, and social transformation of Japan in the early Meiji period.[7] As an individual Christian teaching in provincial Japan as it began to transform, the boyish Clark was "one American whose influence far surpassed that normally wielded by so young a man."[8] He served between 1871 and 1875 as a walking encyclopedia of things Western for those Japanese, especially Nakamura Masanao (Keiu, 1832–1891), whose acquaintance he made in Yokohama, Shizuoka, and Tokyo.[9] By chance or by providence—as a sincere Christian layman like Clark might wish to think of it—much of his influence in Shizuoka[10] stemmed from the fact that he was "friend and spiritual counsellor"[11] to Nakamura, a leading progressive intellectual in the early Meiji period, and through his translations and writings, a significant opinion maker.[12] Nakamura was the key example of Clark's impact on the intellectual world of a rapidly changing Japan in the first half of the 1870s. Clark's influence on Nakamura took place largely during the halcyon first year that Clark was teaching in Shizuoka when Nakamura was working on his translation of John Stuart Mill's *On Liberty*.[13] Clark wrote the English-language introduction to Nakamura's bestseller, which was published in 1872. To Nakamura, Christianity was seen as the essence of Western civilization, and that to gain equality with the great Western powers, Japan ought to adopt Christianity.[14] F. G. Notehelfer has pointed out that also some intellectuals with a samurai background "whose moral system was undercut by the destruction of the feudal system, turned to Christianity precisely because it offered a means of preserving those values—loyalty, single-mindedness of purpose, sincerity etc.—that lay at the core of the former warrior ethos."[15] Importantly, while other Japanese converted to Christianity before him, Nakamura became "the first prominent Meiji figure to profess the Christian faith openly" when he was baptized on Christmas Day in 1874.[16] Ohta Akiko has suggested that Nakamura "became a Christian as part of his quest for a 'spirit' or a moral philosophy (*shin*), which would meet the needs of the dramatically changing society in Japan."[17] Why this stress on the centrality of Christianity in Western civilization? One reason was that Christian missionaries endorsed this view (as Clark also did) and certainly did not try to contradict any Japanese who held such an idea.[18] More importantly, as Kiri Paramore has pointed out, "The idea of 'civilization,' key to the Western empires' arguments of justification for their unequal treatment of Asian countries in nineteenth-century trade and diplomacy, were also heavily reliant on religious ideas."[19] Religious freedom, which entailed free access and legal privilege for Christian missionaries, was a crucial demand in the treaty negotiations which institutionalized the unequal treaties between the Western powers and Japan. The use of religion by the new Meiji government after 1868 to serve its own ends is clearly seen in its exploitation of Shinto and Buddhism to counter the growth of Christian influence after the removal of the proscription edicts from public view in 1873.

In microcosm, Clark's experience in Shizuoka offers an example of how Western ideas crossed over the cultural divide and took root in provincial Japan. For foreign ideas to transcend cultural barriers, they must resonate with perceived needs or aspirations within the different culture. However, only those ideas—amid the veritable smorgasbord of Western knowledge and ideas that Clark brought with him to Japan—that resonated with already held Japanese views were accepted by them; those that did not were discarded. There was a selectivity in which ideas the Japanese chose, over which Clark or other Westerners of his ilk, who were largely ignorant of Japanese society and sensitivities, had very little control. Happily, for Clark his arrival in Japan coincided with an important intellectual debate over the meaning and limits of liberty as well as the role of religion in the transformation of Japanese society. While religion continued to play a significant part in the rapid development of Japanese society, it was Buddhism and Shintoism, rather than Christianity, that the Japanese ultimately selected for that part.

The Rutgers Connection and Clark's Appointment in Shizuoka

Clark was born in Portsmouth, New Hampshire, in 1849, the son of Rufus Wainwright Clark (1813–1886), a Dutch Reformed minister famed for his oratory and who, as a prolific author of Christian tracts, ultimately became the minister of the prestigious First Reformed Church in Albany, New York, in 1862. Because of his youth and sheltered background, it would seem unlikely that Clark would become at twenty-two a pioneer in the introduction of Western studies and Christianity into provincial Japan. It was even more unusual perhaps because Clark was hampered from an early age by an eye injury which would pain him for the rest of his life (although poor eyesight also did not deter Lafcadio Hearn (1850–1904), the journalist and author, from going to Japan). It was at Rutgers where Clark studied chemistry and biology, and where he first met William Elliot Griffis, a meeting that would change the trajectory of his life.[20] Their friendship was further cemented during the summer of 1870 when Griffis joined Clark and his father for part of their study trip to Europe and Geneva. It was while at Rutgers that Clark, like Griffis, first became interested in Japan because of his contact with Japanese students, who were studying at Rutgers College or at the Rutgers Grammar School. The notion of going to Japan had for both Griffis and Clark "so lit our imagination, at the outset, and caused our dreams to run wild in fairy-land, and our poetic fancies to soar to marvellous heights."[21] The exotic and romantic appeal of Japan gradually wore off once Clark was on Japanese soil, but life there always was an adventure for him. For Griffis, the reassurances of his fellow Rutgers graduate, the missionary James Ballagh, who was on sabbatical in the United States in late 1870, that he would be in no personal danger in Japan and that three years of teaching there would stand him in good stead on his return to the United States were possibly significant in reinforcing his determination to set out for Japan.[22] What Ballagh encouragingly wrote to Griffis could equally apply to Clark. Ballagh hoped that the experience of living and teaching in Japan "would be decisive as to your future course. Indeed I feel morally certain you will be a Missionary"[23] Clearly, Ballagh believed that there was a Christian motivation behind Griffis's going to Japan (as there certainly was in Clark's later case), but the hopeful expectation that Griffis would become a missionary did not materialize, although both he and Clark would both become clergymen on their return to the United States.

Clark left the United States for Japan in October 1871 without any job awaiting him there, but not before he had gone into debt buying chemistry and other scientific equipment that might prove useful in teaching science. Unlike Griffis who was cautious in spending money, Clark was free with it, for he was $500 in debt to his father for his passage to Japan and had paid a further $200 for chemicals and another $100 for their shipping to Yokohama.[24] Later in Shizuoka, Clark would seemingly spare no expense to entertain on quite often a grand scale. The difference between the free-spending Clark and the tightfisted Griffis was that Clark came from a financially comfortable background, whereas Griffis's family had suffered a financial crisis in 1857 that delayed his further education until he obtained a church scholarship to attend Rutgers in 1865.[25] Clark had originally hoped to escort Mrs. Mary Putnam Pruyn (1820–1885), a member of Clark's father's congregation at the First Reformed Church in Albany, when she went to Yokohama in early 1871 as a missionary with the Woman's Union Missionary Society of America for Heathen Lands (WUMS);[26] however, financial restraints prevented Clark from going to Japan with Mrs. Pruyn and her companions.

In going to Japan, Clark had been encouraged by his Japanese friends from Rutgers, including Hatakeyama Yoshinari (known as "Kozo Soogiwoora," 1842–1876) whom Clark thought was "a noble fellow, & one of my best friends."[27] Hatakeyama was being recalled to Japan by the Meiji government, and Clark had tried to convince him to accompany him across the prairies and the Pacific and thus back to Japan, but Hatakeyama was adamant in his desire to return via Europe, the Middle East, and India. It was not only with well wishes from Hatakeyama and presents from other Japanese friends that Clark set out to Japan, but also with lots of letters of introduction of which the most valuable were written by his Japanese friends, including most of those Japanese students with a Rutgers connection then in the United States.[28] Thus, Clark was furnished with introductions not only to Japanese high officials like Iwakura Tomomi (1825–1883), whose son—known at Rutgers as Kotarō Asahi—was one of Clark's many Japanese friends, but also to many lesser figures living in Tokyo, Kagoshima, and Shizuoka. On his way out, Clark learned happily that Griffis had arranged with Katsu Kaishū (Awa, Rintarō, 1823–1899) for him to take up a teaching post in Shizuoka, at the Gakumonjo.

Shizuoka Gakumonjo was a school established by the Tokugawa family to help provide education in Western studies for the sons of ex-Tokugawa samurai.[29] Even though it had lost political power because of the Meiji Restoration, the Tokugawa family initially hoped that it might retain its former control of Japan. Katsu Kaishū and other Tokugawa elders thought that by educating the sons of ex-samurai in Western science, at least some of the former Tokugawa influence in Japan could be regained. Moreover, as the demand for experts in Western studies increased, there would be employment opportunities for these young men. In recognizing the future need for Western-studies specialists, the progressive spirit of the Tokugawa exiles in Shizuoka prefecture was clear, albeit directed toward the restoration of their own power rather than the good of all Japan. For this reason, in the autumn of 1868, the Tokugawa family established the Numazu Heigakkō (Military Academy at Numazu) some fifty kilometers from Shizuoka, with the leading Western-studies scholar, Nishi Amane (1829–1897), as its first headmaster.[30] With less overtly militaristic aims in mind, the Tokugawa authorities also founded in late 1868 the Gakumonjo in Shizuoka. In November 1868, it began teaching classes in English, French, German, and Dutch. Among the leading teachers were Tsuda Mamichi (1829–1903), Mukōyama Kōson (1826–1897), Nakamura Keiu (1832–1891), and Toyama Masakazu (1848–1900).[31] By 1871, the Gakumonjo was the higher education center of a network of eight or nine junior schools that the Tokugawa family had established in Shizuoka Prefecture.[32] Entry to the school was restricted to those of the samurai class, and, importantly, tuition was free.[33]

Since the founding of the Gakumonjo in 1868, the Tokugawa authorities had wanted to hire a Western teacher.[34] After all, the school had been founded to teach Western subjects—English, French, German, Dutch, mathematics, and Western science—as well as traditional Chinese studies. The need for a Western professor became increasingly acute as the Gakumonjo expanded. Indeed, by November 1871, it had grown to such an extent that it had been divided into four different schools: the Shōgakujo, the Denshūjo, the Shūgakujo, and the Shizuoka Honkō (the old Gakumonjo). What these divisions meant in practical terms was that Western subjects were now being offered from primary school to the highest academic level, to students ranging from young boys to mature men in their thirties. Compounding educational problems posed by expansion was the simple reality that English had replaced Dutch as the major language of Western studies.

The shortage of English-language teachers was clearly illustrated in 1871 by the fact that the Tokugawa authorities sent Sugiyama Magoroku (1856?–1876)[35]—the son of Sugiyama Sanpachi, a Dutch-learning scholar who was a key figure in Western studies at the Gakumonjo—to learn English in Yokohama instead of continuing his Dutch studies.[36] In addition to learning English, Sugiyama Magoroku converted to Christianity and became a member of the Yokohama Christian Band in 1872. Sugiyama did not stay in Yokohama long after his baptism, for by September 1872, he was teaching at the Gakumonjo in Shizuoka alongside his father and Nakamura Keiu, of whom the younger Sugiyama was a *deshi* (disciple). Already Toyama Masakazu,[37] an English-language specialist who would become a very prominent figure in the Meiji educational world, had been called away from the school by the Foreign Ministry before being sent to the United States for further education. Sugiyama was obviously badly needed back in Shizuoka.[38]

Clark's arrival was welcomed with much enthusiasm. However, as Yamamoto Yukinori has pointed out from entries in Katsu Kaishū's diary, the hiring of Clark involved considerable discussion among Tokugawa officials in Shizuoka and Katsu prior to Clark's arrival.[39] As Clark already had letters of introduction to Katsu, including one from his son, Katsu Koroku (1852–1892), a student at Annapolis whom Clark knew from Rutgers, Clark was pleased to accept this appointment. Yet, causing more trouble for Katsu and the Tokugawa officials in Shizuoka, Clark delayed the signing of his teaching contract because he found that the Japanese Foreign Affairs Department, which ratified all contracts with foreigners, had included a clause which prevented him from teaching Christianity. Clark refused to sign unless he was allowed to teach the Bible. This was an unprecedented move, because Griffis and other Western teachers had never contested the ban on teaching Christianity.[40] Despite this fact, Clark had Katsu's support to remove the offending article three of the English-language copy of his contract.[41] Outside of his contract, one of the difficulties that Clark encountered—according to one of Griffis's former students at Fukui—was finding an adequate interpreter willing to go with him to Shizuoka, and failing to find one he ended up having to content himself with a bad one.[42] The need for a good interpreter to make living in an isolated provincial city more pleasant had been one of the points Ballagh had made to Griffis before setting out to Japan and Fukui.[43]

In late October 1871, as he contemplated teaching in Shizuoka, Clark trusted that the educational authorities there had not misplaced the confidence they may have placed in him. However, Clark was perhaps surprisingly confident in his own ability to succeed, for he wrote, "I know to some extent now through my experience with the Japs in America about what the Japanese wish to have taught them & I know also by teaching some in Albany for some time past about what

FIGURE 8.1. Clark with his Bible class: "pupils in the 70s—many now prominent in Japan." (Credit: William Elliot Griffis Collection, Rutgers University Libraries.)

the average number of students are capable of, in the present stage of education in Japan. I think that by coming up with a better understanding of the Japs & of their language & by studying up on my own weak points I can manage to go along successfully."[44] On November 27, 1871, with contract in hand and chemistry equipment being shipped, porters, and accompanying Shizuoka officials (including Nakamura) assembled, Clark set off at a leisurely pace down the Tōkaidō for Shizuoka, with notable stops to see the Daibutsu at Hase and the lake at Hakone.[45]

Taking five days to cover the ninety-mile journey to Shizuoka, Clark and his party were met four miles outside of Shizuoka by the chief officer of the Gakumonjo school, where Clark was to teach, and by local officials. They were mounted on jet-black ponies for the grand entry into Shizuoka and then across a deep moat into the old castle grounds, where they stopped before the governor's residence where some twenty men of obvious rank were standing on the porch waiting to greet Clark. Afterward, Clark was taken to Ren'eiji temple, where Katsu Kaishū had arranged for Clark to live.[46] He would begin teaching on December 25, 1871. Clark thus became part of an important educational endeavor sponsored by the Tokugawa authorities.

Clark and Nakamura Keiu

The well-known Confucian scholar Nakamura Keiu (Masanao, 1832–1891), who had recently supervised a group of Tokugawa bakufu students in Britain

(1866–1868), was among the first Japanese people whom Clark met when he arrived in Yokohama. Because Nakamura played a crucial role in the success of Clark in Shizuoka, it is useful to investigate in detail their relationship from its beginnings in Yokohama and its development in Shizuoka.[47]

By the time Clark reached Japan, Mary Pruyn and her two companion WUMS missionaries had established the American Mission Home on the Yokohama Bluff, where Clark was able to stay. It was there, in October 1871, that he met Nakamura and Hitomi Fujitarō, who had come to accompany him to his new job in Shizuoka.[48] Clark later described Nakamura at their first meeting as "one of the officers sent from the province where I am going; and although he was the most noted scholar of Chinese literature in Japan, he was as simple as a child, and quite amusing in his use of broken English."[49] Nakamura, however, was apparently so impressed by Clark that he declined an offer by Iwakura Tomomi to join his eponymous diplomatic mission to the West because, according to Clark, "In as much as his habits of study and retirement were well-known, and especially as his Province had now engaged 'so excellent' (?) [*sic*] an American teacher, he would beg to forgo his trip around the world, and stay at home and study."[50] Nakamura asked Mrs. Pruyn for permission to stay there while final arrangements were being made for Clark's journey to Shizuoka, because he wanted to see how foreigners lived and to learn about Christianity.[51] He stayed for nearly two weeks and took advantage of the available help with English to work hard on his translation of John Stuart Mill's *On Liberty*.[52] He was obviously happy with the help and the experience, for he paid Mrs. Pruyn twenty-five dollars upon his departure for Shizuoka.[53]

At the end of 1871, Nakamura wrote another important piece: a memorial to the Meiji emperor, titled *Taiseijin no Jōsho ni Gisu* (Memorial on the imitation of Westerners),[54] urging the toleration of Christianity and the adoption of Christianity by the Japanese emperor to benefit Japan.[55] The background to the memorial lay in the imprisonment of sixty-seven *Kirishitans* in what is now Saga Prefecture in early October 1871.[56] The piece first appeared in an English summary in the *Japan Weekly Mail* on May 11, 1872, with S. R. Brown, the pioneer Dutch Reformed missionary in Yokohama, translating Nakamura's *kanbun* text into English.[57] The publication undoubtedly helped boost the morale of the newly baptized members of the Yokohama Band, but it also played into the broader question of the toleration of Christianity that the Iwakura Embassy would face in 1872–1873 upon its journey to the United States and Europe. Indeed, when it appeared in the original in the *Shinbun zasshi* in August, it was the first time that ordinary Japanese heard that the Nihon Kirisuto Kōkai, the first Japanese Protestant church in Yokohama, had been established in February 1872 (according to lunar calendar dating).[58] How much influence Clark had on Nakamura's writing of this memorial is difficult to ascertain, but it is noteworthy that Clark and Nakamura were both in Shizuoka in December 1871 when Takahashi contends it was written. On the other hand, it was Samuel Robbins Brown who translated Nakamura's Japanese original into English and saw it published in the *Japan Weekly Mail*, so it might well be the missionaries in Yokohama who were the decisive influence on Nakamura in the case of the memorial.

In the English version, Nakamura, writing under the guise of a subject of a foreign power, warmly praised Japan for the reforms adopted by the new regime but wondered why Christianity was still banned as an "evil sect." He went on to say that the wealth and power of the Western nations was in their religion, stating that "the condition of Western countries is but the outward leaf and blossom of their religion, and religion is the root and foundation on which their prosperity depends."[59] Nakamura reasoned that if Japan was to become strong like the Great Powers, then it must tolerate Christianity. The appeal for the acceptance of Christianity was made as a patriotic gesture that could materially benefit Japan, for Western religion was utilitarian and practical in nature and the reason behind Western strength.

Nakamura's memorial was bitterly attacked by an article in the *Japan Herald* as "presumptuous, impertinent, and utterly opposed to the facts."[60] Griffis saw Nakamura's rather naive memorial as a means of bringing attention to Christianity and hopefully bringing about religious toleration.[61] It certainly attracted attention. In late June 1872, the *Japan Weekly Mail* referred to the controversial debate on the Christian question that the memorial had provoked.[62]

Nakamura's understanding of Christianity continued to advance as is clearly seen in a letter that he wrote in early 1873 to Ballagh looking for advice and help with the question of personal faith. Nakamura wrote that "I dare to say (though I am not assuming) that I was thinking Christianity is very useful for promoting this world in the purest & the highest state, & did not see that I am needed for it personally."[63] He continued, "but now by your letter & Mr. Clark's talkings etc., I feel the kingdom of God is at hand & my faith becomes more stronger," and he had been particularly touched that "Mrs. Pruyn Dr. Brown & others prayed for me on my beleaf [*sic*]. I am very thankful for their kind wishes to my insignificant man. You called me Brother & hope I shall be duly so called by you & others, by & by."[64] It was quite clear that Nakamura was familiar with the Yokohama missionaries and was thinking about becoming a Christian, and Clark was a catalyst in drawing him to this point.

After a visit to see Clark in Shizuoka in early 1872, Griffis mentioned that Nakamura was Clark's right-hand man who was at that time printing his translation of *On Liberty*.[65] It is curious that Griffis saw Nakamura's relationship with Clark as being his "right-hand man," given that—as Ōta Aito stressed—there was an eighteen-year age difference between the two, for Nakamura was forty and Clark just twenty-two.[66] Nevertheless, they got along extremely well. Nakamura and Clark helped each other: Clark helped Nakamura with his translations and in return received help with his Bible classes and teaching.

Both Clark and Nakamura thought liberty was intimately connected to Christianity. In his introduction to Nakamura's translation of *On Liberty*, Ōta

Aito stressed that Clark saw liberty as connected to freedom of religion—a freedom that was not present in Japan during the feudal period.[67] Douglas R. Howland noted that Clark saw that "liberty in its highest sense must have limitations," condemning the licentious delusion of unrestricted false freedom. Clark believed that by following "the example of the 'true liberator' of mankind, the Messiah who came to 'unchain the captive, not from a temporal, but from a spiritual despotism.' Key to this true freedom is the capacity to love."[68] Howland also points out that Nakamura, in his translation, followed this line of argument, stating that "Whereas Mill's text concerns the limits of government, the problem for humankind, Nakamura adds, is to emulate God's limitless love for man. The difference between God's limitless love for man and mankind's limited institutions, Nakamura implies, highlights the rightful limitations on man's control over others, for liberty ultimately refers to Christian promise and responsibility—self-development to the glory of God."[69] Whether John Stuart Mill himself saw a connection between liberty and Christianity is a moot point. However, the importance of Clark's influence on Nakamura's growing understanding of Christianity during this period should not be underestimated.[70]

Teaching in Shizuoka

When Clark arrived in Shizuoka in late 1871, he was welcomed with enthusiasm, for the Tokugawa authorities had achieved their goal of hiring and bringing to the city a foreign teacher. Clark was expected to work hard, and he certainly did. In Shizuoka, Clark taught English and chemistry, and as a bonus for his employers, he was able to teach French. In early 1872, Clark wrote about teaching at the Gakumonjo: "With an institution of nearly one thousand students, under the supervision of a single Foreigner with fifty Japanese assistants to direct and instruct: with classes in various scientific departments, both theoretical and practical; with interpreters to be drilled, regulations to be made and enforced, experiments prepared, and lectures given through the three-fold medium of English, French and Japanese you may believe I had my hands full."[71]

Certainly, Clark was busy with classes.[72] One result of his multiple teaching activities was that he became extremely reliant on his Japanese assistants—particularly Henry Satoh (Satō Kenri, 1859–1926),[73] a ten-year-old student whose favorite subject was English (which he concentrated on learning at the expense of other subjects), who wrote that he advanced rapidly up three classes in a year. With his superior knowledge of English, he outshined his Japanese English teachers until he reached the apex of achievement by becoming the interpreter in the English class led by Clark himself.[74] Satoh's rapid promotion to Clark's English course does suggest that the standard of English-language teaching was not very high outside of Clark's own classes. Indeed, Satoh alludes to a very different kind of school than the disciplined institution that Clark described.

The fact that he was much in demand for teaching secular subjects did not deter Clark from propagating Christianity. Indeed, the first Sunday that he was in Shizuoka, Clark conducted a Bible class with Nakamura acting as interpreter. At the end of the class attended by "as earnest and intelligent body of young men as it was ever my privilege to address,"[75] he handed out copies of the Scriptures, which he had brought with him from Yokohama. After a time, the Japanese organized themselves into their own Bible classes. Clark was not prevented by his contract from propagating the Gospel, and he was also fortunate in being on good terms with the authorities in Shizuoka. The very positive and supportive atmosphere in which Clark found himself in early 1872 also aided the success of his Bible classes. In addition to Nakamura, Clark was aided by Shimojō Isaotarō (1854–1874), his best interpreter, who was described by Griffis as "one of the sweetest and gentlest spirits that ever quitted or tenanted a human form."[76] Clark wrote about him that "he was acute in science as well as in religion, nor could I have expounded the intricacies of chemistry and physics without his aid. No experiment was so difficult or dangerous, but he was willing to stand with me 'behind the gun' and take his chances."[77] Clark was an advocate of explosive bangs in teaching chemistry. For the young students in Shizuoka, Clark's Bible classes offered another opportunity to hear English. Such an opportunity, given the nature of the school, was important for those serious about mastering English. However, Hiraiwa Yoshiyasu (1857–1933),[78] who was a student of Clark when he taught at the Kaisei Gakkō in Tokyo, thought Clark to be an inspiring teacher of chemistry but disappointing when it came to explaining Christianity. Initially, Hiraiwa was attracted to Clark's Bible class because Clark played the organ, which he had never heard before.[79] (Clark, it seems, relied heavily on props to draw skeptical students into his Bible class.)

The first months in Shizuoka seem to have been enjoyable, providing Clark with outlets for youthful exuberance and pranks. He galloped his pony from the Ren'eiji temple complex, where Katsu arranged for him to live in one of temple buildings, one and a half miles to the school in the old castle grounds; undertook explosive demonstrations in chemistry class which startled both his interpreter and students; hunted boars and fowls in the countryside; and entertained high officials.[80] Both at the Ren'eiji temple and later when he moved for greater security reasons to a specially built and furnished Western-style house in the old castle grounds, Clark entertained lavishly and often. On Christmas Day in 1872, for example, he held an open tour of his new house for several hundred people, followed by a magnesium stereopticon show of famous places in the United States and Europe, and then he served a turkey dinner to a more select group of forty in his home.[81] The culinary, engineering, and natural wonders of the West and its civilization came together with his underlying promotion of Christianity.

Clark also had Western visitors; his friend Griffis stayed with him in Shizuoka twice, James Ballagh visited and joined him in climbing Mount Fuji, and Mary Pruyn[82] of the WUMS came to see him. All of them were impressed. While he

FIGURE 8.2. Edward Warren Clark, "Shizuoka fūkei" (Scenes from Shizuoka), 1873. (Credit: Special Collections, Waseda University Library.)

makes no mention of other Westerners living in Shizuoka[83] (unlike the case of Griffis in Fukui), Clark was not isolated, for he had the constant attention of his main interpreter, Shimojō,[84] and a cook, Sentarō (1831–1874), the Japanese Sam Patch (the first famous American daredevil) who had previously served Ballagh and before him John Goble, the Baptist missionary. Sentarō not only spoke colloquial American English, albeit quaintly, but also was able to cook sumptuous Western-style meals[85] for the numerous guests.

Furthermore, Clark was not out of reach of the Western community in Yokohama and, in comparison with Griffis in Fukui, not as isolated or remote from a familiar Western outside world. On one occasion, to see a dentist to get a tooth pulled, Clark even returned to Yokohama, from where he was also able to order canned Western foods for his table. Lake Hakone, which many foreigners visited for supposedly health reasons in the summertime, was half the distance to Yokohama. And not to be completely dismissed was the companionship of the young son of Ōkubo Ichiō (1817–1888), who was the governor of Shizuoka when Clark arrived. He became a close friend, and his ten-year-old son lived with Clark.[86] Ōkubo's friendship with Clark is significant because he became lord mayor of Tokyo in 1872 during the time missionaries first began to proselytize there. As Griffis noted in *The Mikado's Empire* in describing a visit to Shizuoka at the beginning of February 1872, "Clark is extremely fortunate in having so many cultivated gentlemen, famous characters and educated, intelligent helpers."[87] By late 1872, however, Clark was increasingly disillusioned with the school. He lamented in a letter to Griffis that he was lonely because so many friends had left Shizuoka for Tokyo and that the school was in a "chaotic, or rather the 'Japonic' state, which are synonymous terms in which the school has been for a long time past," which left him quite disgusted with everything.[88] Nakamura had left in late 1872 to live in Tokyo, where he proceeded to establish his own private school, the Dōjinsha, in Koishikawa ward. In leaving Shizuoka, Nakamura was merely joining the "brain drain," which also included Clark's favorite interpreter, Shimojō, and his two best French-language interpreters, in going to Tokyo, where there were better employment opportunities. Part of the reason for the exodus was that major changes in regional government had meant the end of direct Tokugawa rule in Shizuoka. Moreover, the centralization of education under the Meiji government meant that the Gakumonjo was being closed. In June 1873, amid the chaos of a school that was being run down, Clark was offered the opportunity to take charge of the entire school, but he angrily refused—even though this position might have allowed him to institute reforms for which he had been advocating for over a year.[89] Disillusioned after his experience at the school over the previous year, Clark's days in Shizuoka were numbered, and like for so many of his friends and students, Tokyo beckoned with a post alongside Griffis at the Kaisei Gakkō.

The Shizuoka authorities, however, hoped to open a new small private school, the Shizuhatasha, under the aegis of Hitomi Fujitarō, to take the place of the Gakumonjo, and they were fishing for a foreign teacher to replace Clark. It so happened that Henry Loomis (1839–1920), an American Presbyterian missionary, and George Cochran (1834–1901),[90] a Canadian Methodist missionary, visited Clark in Shizuoka in October 1873, just at the time when Clark was preparing to leave Shizuoka. Hitomi asked Cochran to become the foreign teacher.[91] However, Cochran declined the offer because he would not be able to move from Yokohama to Shizuoka for some time, but realizing the great possibilities for evangelistic work that the Shizuoka school offered, he suggested that his married medical missionary colleague, Davidson McDonald (1836–1905), would respond favorably if asked.[92] So, it was McDonald who went to Shizuoka, where he taught for almost four years at the Shizuhatasha from April 1874, with Sugiyama Magoroku as his first interpreter and an initial class of ten students. Like Clark, McDonald gave Bible classes; his first Bible class, which consisted of a reading of the Lord's Prayer, was attended by seventeen people.[93] Among those who attended were Sugiyama (later Tsuchiya) Hikoroku (1856–1930), Sugiyama Magoroku's younger brother, Tsuyuki Seiichi, Yamanaka Emu (1850–1928),[94] and Muramatsu Ichi, all of them students at the Shizuhatasha who had been formerly students of Sugiyama Magoroku at the Gakumonjo.[95] In October 1874, McDonald baptized his first eleven converts, which included the abovementioned people and Henry Satoh, and formed a Methodist class with Tsuyuki as class leader and Yamanaka as assistant leader. Thus was laid the foundation of the Shizuoka Christian Band from among Clark's former students. By July 1876, it was reported that five hundred people gathered on

Sunday evenings "to receive the 'bread of life' sent down from heaven."[96] By 1877, McDonald had baptized more than 120 people, of whom some sixty-five maintained a connection with the Shizuoka church.[97] As in Clark's time, the lure of Tokyo drew many away from Shizuoka.

McDonald built on the educational and Christian foundations that Clark had established in Shizuoka. There is a clear line from the Gakumonjo of Nakamura and Clark to the students of the Shizuhatasha who formed the core of the Shizuoka Christian Band. Without the help of Clark, the course of the development of the Christian movement in Shizuoka would have been very different. The opportunity to learn English and Western science that Clark and later McDonald offered[98] gave their samurai pupils the chance to acquire new practical skills that made them employable and useful in the new Meiji Japan. They, too, in provincial Shizuoka could become "masters of English."

Conclusion

The idea of Christianity as the essence of Western civilization, which Clark espoused, resonated with the view that Nakamura articulated in his writings during the early 1870s. They were both concerned with the meaning of liberty, though at different levels. Nakamura also had other interests that echoed those of Clark and the women missionaries of the WUMS: education, for example—especially *female* education.[99] His prestige was such that he could influence his students toward Christianity through his writings and personal conduct to the extent that Clark could never have achieved by himself, even with the prop of his magnesium stereopticon.

By the late 1870s, however, new arguments imported from the West, especially those relating to evolution and scientific skepticism, were added to the well-stocked arsenal of traditional ones available to the opponents of Christianity and seriously challenged the link between Christianity and Western civilization and progress.[100] Likewise, both Buddhism and Shintoism, which appeared to be in decline when Clark first came to Japan, were utilized by the Meiji government by the end of the 1870s to counteract the growth of Western religion. Furthermore, while those popular mass religions were gaining strength, the Confucian moral code, which the conservative Nakamura hoped to improve by grafting supposedly superior Christian morals to it, was in decline as its samurai adherents were relegated to history.

Clark, however, seemed to be unconcerned about the challenge that Darwinian evolutionary ideas posed to Christianity, and he never questioned the interpretation that Christianity was at the root of Western prosperity. He emerges as an irrepressible young man who achieved a regional impact that few Americans could claim and whose adventures in Shizuoka showed that life in Japan was quite enjoyable.

Notes

1 See, for instance, the joy that Clark expressed on his arrival in Japan, in Clark to Griffis, 26 October 1871, box 46, folder 41, William Elliot Griffis Collection, Special Collections and University Archives, Rutgers University Libraries, New Brunswick, NJ (hereafter Griffis Collection). Clark wrote three books: *Life and Adventures in Japan* (New York: American Tract Society, 1878); *From Hong Kong to the Himalayas: or Three Thousand Miles Through Asia to India* (New York: American Tract Society, 1881); and *Katz Awa, "the Bismarck of Japan"; or, the Story of a Noble Life* (New York: B. F. Buck, 1904). Unless otherwise cited, all references to Clark's books are to *Life and Adventures in Japan* (Metraux edition, cited below). Clark also wrote articles in newspapers and journals, including *The New York Evening Post, The Brooklyn Daily Argus, The New York Daily Tribune,* the *Albany Evening Journal,* the *International Review,* and *The Far West.* Some fifty of his letters from Japan appeared in the *New York Evangelist,* and at least fifteen in the *Albany Evening Journal.* See Daniel A. Metraux, "First Introduction: Japanese American Relations in the Meiji Era: Conflicting Misconceived Images," in *E. Warren Clark's 1878 Life and Adventure in Japan*, ed. Daniel A. Metraux and Jessica Puglisi (San Jose, CA: Writers Club Press), 3–22, 19; F. Calvin Parker, *The Japanese Sam Patch: Saga of a Servant* (Notre Dame, IN: Cross Road Books, 2001), 147. As seen in Metraux's work, there has been a strong interest in the impact of Clark's writings on the image of Japan in the United States during the Gilded Age.

2 See Ballagh to Griffis, 28 October 1894, in *Japan Through Western Eyes* (Marlborough, UK: Adam Matthew, 2000), part 3, microfilm reel 27: Correspondence Japan A–B. Parts of the Griffis Collection were microfilmed and published as part of the set *Japan Through Western Eyes: Manuscript Records of Traders, Travellers, Missionaries & Diplomats, 1853–1941.*

3 See *The Rutgers Graduates in Japan*, address given on June 16, 1885, by W. E. Griffis (New Brunswick, NJ: Rutgers College, 1916), 11, Griffis Collection.

4 Contemporaneous to Clark's activities in Shizuoka were Ballagh and Yokohama Christian Band members' evangelistic efforts in Shizuoka Prefecture. See Andrew Hamish Ion, "Seeding the Wheat Among the Tares: James Ballagh and Protestant Beginnings in the Hakone, Mishima and Numazu Regions," *Meiji Gakuin Daigaku Kirisutokyō Kenkyūjo kiyō* 45 (December 2012): 187–228. For the Yokohama Christian Band, see Hamish Ion, *American Missionaries, Christian Oyatoi and Japan 1859–1873* (Vancouver: University of British Columbia Press, 2009), especially 218–263.

5 See Satoru Saito, *Detective Fiction and the Rise of the Japanese Novel, 1880–1930* (Cambridge, MA: Harvard University Asia Center, 2012), 7.

6 The age of the "masters of English" ran from 1868 to 1878 with its peak in 1871–1872, benefiting from the desire of the Meiji government to learn from abroad and fueled by the activities of *oyatoi gaikokujin* like Clark and Griffis at educational institutions at home and overseas study by Japanese, see Ōta Yūzō, *Eigo to Nihonjin* (Tokyo: Kōdansha Gakujutsu Bunko, 1995), 70–78.

7 See, for instance, Jason Ananda Josephson, *The Invention of Religion in Japan* (Chicago: University of Chicago Press, 2012); Trent E. Maxey, *The "Greatest Problem": Religion and State Formation in Meiji Japan* (Cambridge, MA: Harvard University Asia Center, 2014); Michel Mohr, *Buddhism, Unitarianism, and the Meiji Competition for Universality* (Cambridge, MA, Harvard University Asia Center, 2014); Richard M. Reitan, *Making a Moral Society: Ethics and the State in*

Meiji Japan (Honolulu: University of Hawai'i Press, 2010). See also Kiri Paramore, *Ideology and Christianity in Japan* (London: Routledge, 2009), especially chapter 6; Kiri Paramore, *Japanese Confucianism: A Cultural History* (Cambridge: Cambridge University Press, 2016), especially chapters 4–6.

8 Quoted in Parker, *The Japanese Sam Patch*, 150; see also A. Hamish Ion, "Edward Warren Clark and Early Meiji Japan: A Case Study of Cultural Contact," *Modern Asian Studies* 11, no. 4 (1977): 572. Ardath Burks recognized Clark as an important interpreter of Japan to the West, see Ardath W. Burks, "Legacy: Products and By-Products of Cultural Exchange," in *The Modernizers: Overseas Students, Foreign Employees, and Meiji Japan*, ed. Ardath Burks (Boulder, CO: Westview Press, 1985), 365. For Clark's troubled life after returning from Japan, see Richard Candee, "E. Warren Clark (1849–1907): 'Noted Traveller and Lecturer on Oriental Topics,'" *The Magic Lantern Gazette* 24, no. 1 (Spring 2012): 3–20.

9 Clark was also a bird in flight, for he, like Griffis and many other foreign *oyatoi* employees, was a contract worker and only in Japan for a relatively short time. There were other walking encyclopedias from whom Nakamura at different times took ideas: Henry Faulds (1843–1930), the United Presbyterian Church of Scotland medical missionary, concerning schooling for the blind; George Cochran (1834–1901), the Canadian Wesleyan Methodist missionary who taught at Nakamura's Dōjinsha school in Koishikawa, Tokyo, and baptized him in 1874; Walter Dening (1846–1913), the ex-missionary educator and author; and the women missionaries belonging to the Woman's Union Missionary Society (WUMS) at the American Mission Home regarding women's education. However, Clark was the first Westerner to have extended close contact with Nakamura and was responsible for introducing him to Cochran.

10 For a study of Clark's influence on the formation of the Shizuoka and Koishikawa Christian Bands, see A. Hamish Ion, "Edward Warren Clark and the Formation of the Shizuoka and Koishikawa Christian Bands (1871–1879)," in *Foreign Employees in Nineteenth-Century Japan*, ed. Edward R. Beauchamp and Akira Iriye (Boulder, CO: Westview Press, 1990), 171–189. See also Andrew Hamish Ion, "Shizuoka Christians and Tokyo Evangelism in the early 1870s," *Meiji Gakuin Daigaku Kirisutokyō Kenkyūjo kiyō* 37 (March 2005): 251–297.

11 Douglas R. Howland, *Translating the West: Language and Political Reason in Nineteenth-Century Japan* (Honolulu: University of Hawai'i Press, 2002), 106–107. Clark himself noted, "Nakamura himself was my most intimate friend in Shidzuoka" [*sic*]. Clark, *Katz Awa*, 17.

12 Akiko Ohta, "Nakamura Masanao (Keiu), 1832–91: Translator into Japanese of Samuel Smiles's *Self Help*," in *Britain & Japan Biographical Portraits*, ed. Hugh Cortazzi, vol. 4 (London: Japan Library, 2002), 215–223.

13 Clark mentions that Nakamura had begun translating *On Liberty* when staying with him at the American Mission Home in Yokohama prior to making the journey to Shizuoka. See Clark to Griffis, 24 November 1871, box 46, folder 42, Griffis Collection. See also Yokohama Kyōritsu Gakuen 120 Nen no Ayumi Henshū Iinkai, *Yokohama Kyōritsu Gakuen 120 Nen no Ayumi* (Yokohama: Yokohama Kyōritsu Gakuen, 1991), 40–43. Nakamura sent Griffis some copies of his translation, see W. E. Griffis, journal, 30 May 1872, loose sheets, box 17, folder 11, Griffis Collection (hereafter W. E. Griffis, journal). Clark's relationship with Nakamura sets him apart from Griffis, who had no similar intimate connection with a Japanese intellectual of equal standing.

14 Nakamura's interest in Christianity had been stimulated when he lived in London in charge of a group of twelve Japanese students sent over to study there by the

Tokugawa shogunate in 1866. He had been struck by the high moral standards of English people which he felt were rooted in Christianity. The impact of the Christianity he had seen in England is evident in an article entitled "Keiten Aijin Setsu" ("Revere God and love man"), which was published in Shizuoka in 1868. See Ogihara Takahashi, *Nakamura Keiu to Meiji keimō shisō* (Tokyo: Waseda Daigaku Shuppanbu, 1984), 214. See also Takahashi Masao, *Nakamura Keiu* (Tokyo: Yoshikawa Kōbunkan, 1966), 60, 65.

15 F. G. Notehelfer, *Kōtoku Shūsui: Portrait of A Japanese Radical* (Cambridge: Cambridge University Press, 1971), 74.

16 Parker, *The Japanese Sam Patch*, 197.

17 Ohta, "Nakamura Masanao (Keiu)," 219.

18 As Joseph M. Henning has argued, "to Clark and his evangelical brothers and sisters, Christianity and civilization were inseparable." Joseph M. Henning, *Outposts of Civilization: Race, Religion and the Formative Years of American-Japanese Relations* (New York: New York University Press, 2000), 36.

19 Kiri Paramore, *Japanese Confucianism*, 142. As late as 1889, Paramore has argued, Itō Hirobumi (1841–1909), the Meiji statesman and a major proponent of the Meiji Constitution, believed Christianity was a key element in Western statecraft and that Western nations used "religious elements for control and mobilization of the citizenry, so the structure of the Japanese state must therefore also deploy religion centrally."

20 Clark left Rutgers in 1869. It is a moot point whether he graduated.

21 Clark to Griffis, 17 October 1871, box 46, folder 41, Griffis Collection.

22 Ballagh to Griffis, 28 September 1870, in *Japan Through Western Eyes*.

23 Ballagh to Griffis, 28 September 1870.

24 Clark to Griffis, 26 October 1871.

25 Fernanda Perrone, "The Rutgers Network in Early Meiji Japan," *Rikkyo American Studies* 39 (March 2017): 79–101, 87.

26 Clark to Griffis, 26 October 1871.

27 Clark to Griffis, 26 October 1871.

28 Clark to Griffis, 26 October 1871.

29 Iida Hiroshi, *Shizuoka ken eigaku shi* (Tokyo: Kōdansha, 1967), 11.

30 Thomas R. H. Havens, *Nishi Amane and Modern Japanese Thought* (Princeton, NJ: Princeton University Press, 1970), 72. See also Yoneyama Umekichi Sensei Denki Kankōkai, *Yoneyama Umekichi sensei zenshū*, vol. 1 (Tokyo: Aoyama Gakuin Shotōbu, 1960), 189. For Nishi Amane and the Numazu Heigakkō, see 193–197. By 1871, the military school had been moved to Tokyo and absorbed by the Meiji government.

31 Iida, *Shizuoka ken eigaku shi*, 12–13.

32 Yamamoto Yukinori, "Shizuoka han oyatoi gaikokujin kyōshi: E. W. Kurāku: Shizuoka Bando seiritsu no haikei," *Kirisutokyô shakai mondai kenkyû* 29, no. 3 (1981): 135–136.

33 Henry Satoh, *My Boyhood: A Reminiscence*, 2nd ed. (Tokyo: Japan Times, 1921), 76.

34 Yamamoto, "Shizuoka han oyatoi," 122.

35 For a brief biographical note on Sugiyama, see *Nihon Kiristutokyō rekishi dai jiten* (Tokyo: Kyōbunkan, 1988), 717.

36 Ōta Aito, *Meiji Kirisutokyō no ryūiki—Shizuoka bando to bakushintachi* (Tokyo: Tsukiji Shokan, 1979), 18.

37 For a brief biographical note on Toyama Masakazu (1848–1900), see *Nihon Kiristutokyō rekishi dai jiten*, 962. Toyama had already studied in England between 1866

and 1868 among the scholars who went abroad with Nakamura. In 1872, the Meiji government sent Toyama to high school and then to the University of Michigan. He returned to Japan to teach at the Kaisei Gakkō and later in his career became president of Tokyo Imperial University.

38 While he was in Yokohama, Sugiyama was also associated with the American Mission Home, where he, Kumano Yōshichi, and Momoe Kyōkichi (Masaki Mamoru)—two former samurai from Ōmura—were students of Mrs. Louise Henrietta Pierson (1832–1899) of the WUMS. Momoe proved to be a government spy, but Kumano remained a Christian and later taught at Meiji Gakuin, the Presbyterian and Reformed Church mission school in Tokyo.

39 Yamamoto, "Shizuoka han oyatoi," 114–154.

40 Griffis pointed out that his own teaching contract for the school in Fukui said nothing about religion and gave him "perfect freedom" from all duties on Sunday and "absolute liberty" to do anything he wished, including teaching the Bible in his own house. See William Elliot Griffis, *The Mikado's Empire* (New York: Harper & Brothers, 1876), 402. See also Yamamoto, "Shizuoka han oyatoi," 128–129.

41 Yamamoto, "Shizuoka han oyatoi," 130. See also Clark, *Life and Adventure in Japan*, 29–30; and Clark to Griffis, 27 November 1871, box 46, folder 41, Griffis Collection.

42 Ideura to Griffis, 1 December 1871, box 49, folder 55, Griffis Collection.

43 Ballagh to Griffis, 28 September 1870, box 45, folder 47, Griffis Collection.

44 Clark to Griffis, 26 October 1871.

45 For a description of the journey from Yokohama to Shizuoka, see Clark, *Life and Adventure in Japan*, 34–44.

46 Parker, *The Japanese Sam Patch*, 155–156. The close connection between Ren'eiji temple and Katsu is seen in the fact that Katsu's mother and younger sister were buried in the temple's cemetery. See Ōta Aito, *Meiji Kirisutokyō no ryūiki*, 26.

47 Nakamura is important for his translations of Samuel Smiles's *Self-Help* and John Stuart Mills's *On Liberty*. He was also famous for his educational work, which included founding the Western Studies Dōjinsha school in Tokyo (1873), and his advocacy for educational opportunities for women and for the blind. He was a member of the leading intellectual learned society the Meirokusha (Society of Meiji Six). Nakamura was one of the first prominent Japanese intellectuals to convert to Christianity.

48 The American Mission Home was situated next door to the home of Samuel Robbins Brown (1810–1880) on Yokohama Bluff, and the religious links of the Home through Mrs. Mary Pruyn, the senior of its three missionaries, were strongly directed toward the Reformed Church.

49 Clark, *Life and Adventure in Japan*, 31.

50 Clark to Griffis, 27 November 1871.

51 For Nakamura's positive view of the work of the three WUMS missionaries at the American Mission Home, see Takahashi, *Nakamura Keiu*, 85–90.

52 Nakamura's translation was published in Shizuoka in early 1872. It became a major bestseller and exerted considerable influence on the political thinking in Japan, especially on the Popular Rights Movement in the 1880s. Hirakawa Sukehiro has pointed out that through their writings, "Fukuzawa [Yukichi] showed the world of wisdom to the young men in the Meiji era. Keiu truly saw the world of virtue was good." Hirakawa Sukehiro, *Ten wa tasukeru mono o tasuke: Nakamura Masanao to "Saigoku Risshi Hen"* (Nagoya: Nagoya Daigaku Shuppankai, 2006), 5.

53 Parker, *The Japanese Sam Patch*, 150.

54 See *Nihon Kiristutokyō rekishi dai jiten*, 813. It was published in English in its entirety on May 18, 1872. The memorial appeared in its original form in *Shinbun zasshi*, no. 56, in August 1872. Takahashi Masao hazards the guess that it was originally written in December 1871. See also Takahashi, *Nakamura Keiu*, 286.

55 Ozawa Saburō, *Nihon Purotesutantoshi kenkyū* (Tokyo: Tōkai Daigaku Shuppankai, 1964), 228–229, 243–247.

56 Kirishitan is the term used for Japanese Catholic Christians converted by Portuguese and Spanish missionaries in the sixteenth and early seventeenth centuries. Takahashi, *Nakamura Keiu*, 95.

57 Ozawa, *Nihon Purotesutantoshi kenkyū*, 244.

58 Takahashi, *Nakamura Keiu*, 97. It was March 10, 1872, according to the Western calendar.

59 Otis Cary, *A History of Christianity in Japan: Protestant Missions* (New York: Fleming H. Revell, 1909), 75.

60 W. E. Griffis, "Journal," 30 May 1872, loose sheets, box 17, folder 11, Griffis Collection. Grace Fox, in her study of Anglo-Japanese relations, noted that copies of Nakamura's memorial were given to Ernest Satow, an interpreter at the British Legation, by Kido Kōin and Itō Hirobumi, who both stated privately that the anti-Christian prohibition must be lifted soon. See Grace Fox, *Britain and Japan 1858–1883* (Oxford: Clarendon Press, 1969), 499.

61 Griffis, "Journal," 30 May 1872.

62 Griffis.

63 Nakamura to Ballagh, February 1873, in Yokohama Gaikō Shiryōkan, Japan Mission of the Reformed Church of America, microfilm, vol. 45, Reformed Church in America Archives, New Brunswick, NJ.

64 Nakamura to Ballagh, February 1873.

65 Griffis, "Journal." See also Ōta Aito, *Meiji Kirisutokyō no ryūiki*, 36.

66 Ōta, *Meiji Kirisutokyō no ryūiki*, 24.

67 Ōta, 48.

68 Howland, *Translating the West*, 107.

69 Howland, 107.

70 Yamamoto noted that there were three stages in Nakamura's developing interest in Christianity: The first stage was from 1868 to the end of 1871 the second stage from the end of 1871 to 1874, and the third stage from 1874. The first stage saw Nakamura publish "Keiten aijin setsu" ("Revere God and love man") in 1868, in which the impact of Christianity as Nakamura had seen it in England was evident. The second stage started with Nakamura's chance meeting with Clark and saw the drafting of Nakamura's memorial to the emperor, and later in Shizuoka with the publication of *Jiyū no ri*. It also covered Clark's Bible classes not only in Shizuoka but also later at Nakamura's Dōjinsha school in Koishikawa, Tokyo, when Clark was teaching at the Kaisei Gakkō. The third stage was marked by Clark's departure from Japan and George Cochran's taking up residence at the Dōjinsha and baptizing Nakamura on Christmas Day, 1874. See Yamamoto, "Shizuoka han oyatoi," 145–146.

71 Clark, *Life and Adventure in Japan*, 41–42.

72 Yamamoto, "Shizuoka han oyatoi," 134.

73 For a short biographical note on Satō, see *Nihon Kiristutokyō rekishi dai jiten*, 579.

74 Henry Satoh, *My Boyhood*, 77.

75 Ion, "Edward Warren Clark and Early Meiji Japan," 563.

76 Quoted in Parker, *The Japanese Sam Patch*, 156. Shimojō came from a family of doctors belonging to Himeji han, and he studied at the Shizuoka Gakkō, the

Daigaku Nankō, and various other schools, including those of Fukuchi Gen'ichirō and Mizukuri Juku. After he stopped being Clark's interpreter, he attended the ninth class at the Kōgaku (engineering school) but died shortly after at the age of twenty. Nakamura, in his epitaph to Shimojō, stressed the influence of Christianity on Shimojō as the young man faced death. See Yamamoto, "Shizuoka han oyatoi," 144–145.

77 Clark, *Katz Awa*, 18.

78 For a short biographical note on Hiraiwa, see *Nihon Kiristutokyō rekishi dai jiten*, 1172.

79 Kuranaga Takeshi, *Hiraiwa Yoshiyasu den* (Tokyo: Kyōbunkan, 1938), 21–23.

80 Parker provided an excellent account of Clark's daily life and activities when living in the rat-infested Ren'eiji temple compound. See Parker, *The Japanese Sam Patch*, 155–165.

81 Parker, 168–170.

82 During Pruyn's visit, Clark organized at his house an evening of Japanese traditional music and dance for her, which she found strange but enjoyed. See Mrs. Mary Pruyn, *Grandmamma's Letters from Japan* (Boston: James H. Earle, 1877), 135–137.

83 The closest was Goodman and then William Keeping, an Englishman with a Japanese wife, who taught at the Shōgakkō affiliated with the Numazu Heigakkō.

84 Clark expressed great concern when he learned that Shimojō was very sick with consumption in Tokyo and in the hospital, and another of his "runaway" students who had been with Nakamura in London was dangerously ill with fever at home in Tokyo. Moreover, Sugiyama, who was acting as his interpreter at a musical "concert" with some Japanese musicians at Clark's residence, had fainted and had to be carried upstairs and put to bed. All this led Clark to exclaim, "The Japs are a weakly set, there is no mistake; & how they are going to get physically better, on the strength of rice & slops, is more than I can see." Clark to Griffis, 1 February 1873, box 46, folder 42, Griffis Collection.

85 Unfortunately, Sentarō was unable to make custard like Margaret Griffis's "celestial" custard. Clark to Griffis, 26 September 1873, box 46, folder 43, Griffis Collection. Sentarō later would die of beriberi, a disease caused by a thiamine deficiency, which eating brown rice rather than polished white rice might have prevented. See Parker, *The Japanese Sam Patch*, 188.

86 Clark, *Katz Awa*, 14–15.

87 Griffis, *The Mikado's Empire*, 548.

88 Clark to Griffis, 26 October 1872, box 46, folder 42, Griffis Collection.

89 Clark to Griffis, 9 June 1873, box 46, folder 43, Griffis Collection.

90 For short biographical notes on Loomis and Cochran, see *Nihon Kiristutokyō rekishi dai jiten*, 1510 and 518, respectively.

91 George Cochran letter, 21 January 1874, *Wesleyan Missionary Notices Canada Conference, New Series*, no. 23, May 1874.

92 George Cochran letter, 21 January 1874. See also Ōta, *Meiji Kirisutokyō no ryūiki*, 94. For a short biographical note on McDonald, see *Nihon Kiristutokyō rekishi dai jiten*, 1312. See also Nihon Mesojisuto Shizuoka Kyōkai rokujūnen shi hensan iinkai, *Nihon Mesojisuto Shizuoka Kyōkai rokujūnen shi* (Shizuoka: Nihon Mesojisuto Shizuoka Kyōkai, 1937), 4–6; Iida, *Shizuoka ken eigaku shi*, 29–33.

93 Nihon Mesojisuto Shizuoka Kyōkai rokujūnen shi hensan iinkai, *Nihon Mesojisuto Shizuoka Kyōkai*, 12.

94 For a short biographical note on Tsuchiya and Yamanaka, who both became influential Methodist pastors in later life, see *Nihon Kiristutokyō rekishi dai jiten*, 887 and 1441, respectively.

95 Nihon Mesojisuto Shizuoka Kyōkai rokujūnen shi hensan iinkai, *Nihon Mesojisuto Shizuoka Kyōkai*, 12. See also Kuranaga Takeshi, *Kanada Mesojisuto Nihon dendō gaishi* (Tokyo: Kanada Gōdō Kyōkai Senkyōshikai, 1937), 94–95.
96 Amenonori to Griffis, 23 July 1876, in *Japan Through West Eyes*, part 3, microfilm reel 27.
97 Yamamoto Yukinori, "Yamaji Aizan to Kirisutokyō: Meiji 20 nendai o chūshin toshite," *Kirisutokyō shakai mondai kenkyū* 26 (December 1977): 102–162.
98 For the subjects and textbooks used by McDonald at the Shizuhatasha, see Iida, *Shizuoka ken eigaku shi*, 31.
99 See chapter 15 for more on missionary involvement in female education.
100 See Ōta Yūzō, *E. S. Mōsu: "Furuki Nihon" o tsutaeta shin-Nichi kagakusha* (Tokyo: Liburo Pōto, 1988), 40–44. See also Helen Ballhatchet, "The Religion of the West Versus the Science of the West: The Evolution Controversy in Late Nineteenth Century Japan," in *Japan and Christianity: Impacts and Responses*, ed. John Breen and Mark Williams (Basingstoke, UK: Macmillan, 1996), 107–121.

9

Fukui's Role in the Career of William Elliot Griffis

JOSEPH M. HENNING

William Elliot Griffis, a Rutgers College alumnus, both benefited from and contributed to his alma mater's trans-Pacific network. Hired to teach in Japan via Rutgers connections, he spent the rest of his life publicly promoting the U.S.-Japan friendship to American audiences. Of the three and a half years that he lived in Japan, he taught in Fukui for only ten and a half months (see chapter 7). His time in that provincial city, however, returned dividends to him throughout the rest of his life. When he began publishing newspaper and magazine articles about Fukui shortly after his arrival there in 1871, its people and customs gave him a wealth of material to describe and analyze for the American public. His observations proved popular: most of his earliest writing appeared in the religious press but soon began to reach the wider audiences of high-profile secular magazines. After he returned to the United States in 1874, his writing career flourished further with the lasting success of his first book, *The Mikado's Empire.*[1] In the following decades, he continued to publish articles and books about Japan while serving as a clergyman and then after retiring from the pulpit, when he devoted himself full-time to writing and lecturing. He thus built a career as an authority on Japan that spanned nearly sixty years, an achievement that no other American could rival.

Griffis's time in Fukui made that career possible. Living in the remote domain, he saw not only feudalism in operation but also its fall—a rare experience for foreigners in Japan. He used this distinction initially to establish his credentials as an authority on Japanese society, culture, and politics. Even when he finally exhausted his supply of firsthand observations to recount, he never stopped reminding readers of his unusual status as an American eyewitness to Japan's transformation. He also emphasized the significant role that Fukui and its leaders had played in the reforms of the Bakumatsu and early Meiji eras. Underscoring the historical importance of Fukui enabled him to share in the spotlight that he cast on the city. Despite observing Japan from a distance in his later years, he wrote that his previous residence in Fukui and his proximity to its leaders gave him a unique perspective on the continuing development of Meiji and Taishō Japan. In doing so, Griffis crafted an enduring professional reputation as an expert who understood both traditional and modernizing Japan. The months that he spent in Fukui first launched and then sustained his long career.

Griffis as a Writer

Before his departure for Japan, Griffis started his writing career by publishing in religious newspapers, a popular medium with many readers in the nineteenth-century United States. His first article on Japan, "The Japanese Students in America," appeared without a byline in August 1870 in the *Independent*, a Congregational weekly published in New York City with a large general audience. In the article, Griffis identified only Kusakabe Tarō (see chapters 2 and 4) by name and praised him as having "the keenest intellect and most insatiable desire for knowledge."[2] Although this piece appeared anonymously, in the following year the *Independent* began printing articles with Griffis's byline. His work and the *Independent* were a good match: One of its editors wrote to him that "you seem to know very well what we want, not descriptions of places and things so much as records of progress in civilization and religion."[3] From 1871 to 1879, Griffis published twenty articles about Japan in the *Independent* under his name.

Griffis arrived in Japan in December 1870 and reached Fukui in March 1871. His first article from Japan and then his first from Fukui appeared soon thereafter under the pseudonym "Curio" in the *Christian Intelligencer*, a New York City weekly paper published by the Dutch Reformed Church, with which Rutgers College had been affiliated until 1867. Earlier, Griffis had signed "Curio" to articles on other topics in the *Christian Intelligencer*.[4] In "First Glimpses of Japan," which appeared in its March 2, 1871, issue, he described his initial impressions of Yokohama and Tokyo. He did the same for Fukui in an article titled "In the Heart of Japan." It appeared in the April 27, 1871, issue, but Griffis had written it on March 13, only nine days after his arrival there.[5]

While in Fukui until January 1872, Griffis continued to write and published at least one dozen articles; of these, two appeared in the *Independent* and six in the *Christian Intelligencer*. He also began to reach beyond the religious press, publishing at least two essays in the *Home Journal*, a New York City weekly.

While one of these appeared under "Curio," the other appeared under his name.[6] Also from Fukui he contributed two articles, both titled "A Philadelphian in Japan" and signed with his initials, to one of his hometown daily newspapers, the *Philadelphia Evening Telegraph*.[7]

When Griffis left Fukui to teach in Tokyo, he continued to contribute essays to these four newspapers. He aspired, however, to become a regular correspondent for the literary monthly *Lippincott's Magazine*, which frequently featured travel essays. He wrote to his sister Martha that "if I could only take time to *finish* and polish my scribbling, I could do well at magazine writing."[8] He soon did: In 1873, he enjoyed his first major successes when *Lippincott's* and *Appletons' Journal*, a popular weekly, began printing work under his byline. The August issue of *Lippincott's* featured "Inside Japan," in which Griffis described an eight-day excursion to the Bōsō Peninsula (today's Chiba Prefecture). The appearance of this article under his name finally prompted the *Christian Intelligencer* to acknowledge that he was its correspondent Curio.[9] In 1874, his work first appeared in *Overland Monthly*, another high-profile monthly magazine. And in 1875, the prestigious quarterly *North American Review* published his essay on the Meiji Restoration, titled "The Recent Revolutions in Japan," which he revised and expanded to include as a chapter in *The Mikado's Empire* the following year.[10]

Griffis continued to write following his return to the United States in August 1874. From 1871 to the appearance of *The Mikado's Empire* in 1876, he published under the pseudonym Curio at least eleven articles on Japan in the *Christian Intelligencer* and *Home Journal*. In addition, he published under his name a total of more than forty articles in those two newspapers, as well as the *Independent*, *Philadelphia Evening Telegraph*, *Lippincott's Magazine*, *Appletons' Journal*, *Overland Monthly*, *North American Review*, and *Illustrated Christian Weekly*. Griffis thus quickly achieved significant levels of prominence and geographic range for his writing via a combination of newspapers and magazines reaching many audiences: *Lippincott's Magazine* was published in Philadelphia, *Appletons' Journal* and *Illustrated Christian Weekly* in New York City, *Overland Monthly* in San Francisco, and *North American Review* in Boston.[11] Furthermore, his essays were in good company: These magazines also featured writing by such talents as Mark Twain, Emma Lazarus, John Muir, and Henry James.

Griffis complemented this written work by traveling widely in the United States to deliver numerous public talks on Japan. Charging about thirty-five cents for admission, he spoke for nearly two hours without a script at churches, opera houses, and public halls. In March 1875, the *Chicago Daily Tribune* reported on one of these presentations to a full house and concluded that "through his writings and lectures, he may fairly be ranked as the interpreter of Japan to the great Christian world."[12] These efforts thus established his reputation as an American authority on Japan even before the debut of *The Mikado's Empire*, his single most important work.

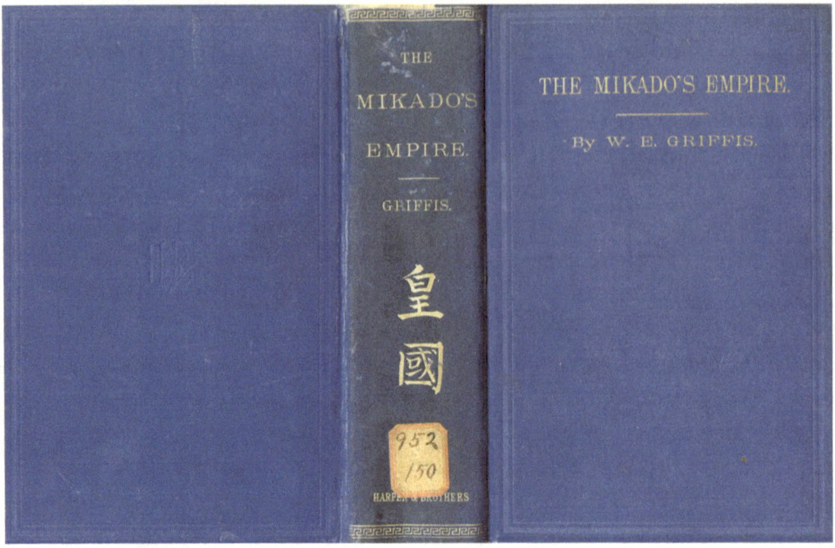

FIGURE 9.1. Griffis's first book, *The Mikado's Empire*. (Credit: William Elliot Griffis Collection, Rutgers University Libraries.)

Released by the eminent publisher Harper and Brothers in the summer of 1876, the book received widespread praise. In his native city, the *Philadelphia Press* described Griffis as "set apart by nature and circumstance as one most admirably fitted for the work of unfolding the secrets of Japan to the common as well as the cultivated mind."[13] The accolades continued as Griffis added supplementary chapters on recent events to later editions of the book. *The Mikado's Empire* was "by far the best American work on Japan," scholar Nitobe Inazō wrote in 1891: "No author has done more to present in attractive style the salient features of our tradition, history, manners, and customs." The book's "worn-out condition in many a public library," Nitobe claimed, "attests how diligently and deservedly it is perused."[14] With its tenth edition in 1903, Harper and Brothers began issuing the book in two separate volumes to accommodate its increasing length. Finally, in 1913, it reached its twelfth and last edition. For the rest of his life, Griffis's bylines frequently identified him as the "author of *The Mikado's Empire*," words that are also carved into the headstone at his grave in Schenectady, New York.

When the book first appeared, Griffis was studying at New York City's Union Theological Seminary. After his ordination in 1877, he began a twenty-six-year career in the ministry but never stopped publishing on Japan and East Asia. After he retired from the pulpit in 1903, he turned all of his attention to lecturing and writing, work that occupied him until his death in 1928. Over the course of nearly sixty years as an authority on Meiji and Taishō Japan, he delivered thousands of lectures while publishing some two dozen books and hundreds of articles in a wide range of journals and magazines.[15] He continued to contribute to the

Independent and *Christian Intelligencer* and regularly wrote religious essays for other church and missionary periodicals. He also frequently published articles on Japan in secular newspapers and popular magazines, including *Harper's Weekly*, *Harper's New Monthly Magazine*, *Scribner's Magazine*, *Century Magazine*, *Nation*, *Chautauquan*, *Outlook*, and *National Geographic Magazine*. And he wrote books on Japan and East Asia for prominent publishers such as Charles Scribner's Sons, Houghton Mifflin, Macmillan, and Princeton University Press.

While other Americans and Europeans writing for English-language readers spent more time in Japan than did Griffis, none had a career whose length and breadth matched his. Lafcadio Hearn, for example, who taught there from 1890 until his death in 1904, published many popular essays and books on Japanese culture and daily life. Because he arrived in Japan twenty years after Griffis, however, his work did not encompass the full sweep of the Meiji era. Basil Hall Chamberlain, another prominent writer, worked in Tokyo from 1873 to 1911 and published *Things Japanese* in 1890. An encyclopedic book, it went through multiple later editions (like *The Mikado's Empire*), but his other works on Japan were scholarly and focused on language and literature.[16] In contrast, Griffis and his more voluminous writing reached broader and much more varied audiences.

After Griffis's departure from Japan in 1874, he did not return until 1926. During these years, he corresponded regularly with an array of Japanese friends and acquaintances, foreign educators, and missionaries to update his knowledge of current events in Japan. Yet, as his years in Fukui and Tokyo receded into the past, his writing gradually became less original and insightful. He published his best work in the earlier years of his career, when he had an abundance of vivid firsthand observations and experiences to describe to readers.

Fukui in Griffis's Early Writing

In the 1870s, Griffis began several of his first published accounts of Fukui by focusing on what he saw and, as importantly, what he did *not* see there. Quoting from "Locksley Hall," Alfred Tennyson's poem acclaiming the progress of human civilization, Griffis pronounced himself to be an "heir of all the ages." Employing this perspective as a beneficiary of modern social and scientific development, he described his sensation of leaping in time from the present into the distant past when he arrived in Fukui.[17] Rather than describe the city's features, he wrote, it was more informative to list what was absent. As Griffis asked in the *Christian Intelligencer*, "Doesn't it seem a curious idea to live every day . . . where there are no railroads, nor snorting locomotive, nor telegraph wires, nor printing press, nor pavements, nor parks, nor milkman, nor newsboy? How *could* we do without gas, newspapers, glass windows and street cars? How *could* a nineteenth century New-Yorker live in the twelfth century?" Even after stepping indoors, he noted that "there was not a stove in any house. . . . No sofas, chairs, tables, bedsteads, or washstands." After one month in Fukui, when asked by a

Buddhist priest to identify what seemed strangest to a foreigner there, Griffis answered with another long inventory that included "houses without chimneys; hills without cattle; fields without fences; the wearing of loose clothes by men, and of tight ones by women."[18] To this metropolitan American, adjusting to life in Fukui was initially daunting: This "heir of all the ages" feared losing his modern inheritance.

Despite these material differences, however, Griffis observed that here "was a people civilized for centuries." From his first days in Fukui, his hosts were unfailing in their welcome, which he gratefully acknowledged. He regularly received small gifts for his home and table, and he also was "the recipient of hospitalities from prince, officer and merchant, and of kindness, honor and attention from all classes." In the following weeks and months, he traveled on horseback with samurai escorts into the surrounding countryside, where villagers were curious to see their first foreigner. They often kneeled and bowed their heads to the ground in respect not only to their domain's officers, but also to this teacher who was one of its employees. Griffis noted that, as an American, he did not relish the sight of so many on their hands and knees before him, but he announced humorously in *Overland Monthly* that "I now find out why the Japanese have no hair on their foreheads." The warmth of his reception in Fukui soon led him to begin referring to it as a "Well of Blessing," a literal translation of the characters that form its name. In an essay published in the Rutgers College newspaper, he also attempted to extend that welcome by inviting "Rutgersians" to visit him.[19]

Moreover, Griffis quickly learned that Fukui was not the twelfth-century anachronism that he had initially believed it to be. Instead, because of its progressive leadership, "evidences of the new civilization in Japan" were abundant there. In a letter published in *Scientific American*, Griffis wrote that several young men were already studying medicine and chemistry in Dutch and were practicing vaccination and dissection. He noted also that the city had a hospital, a gunpowder mill with a national reputation, and a factory producing high-quality breech and muzzle-loading rifles. Both the mill and factory utilized water-powered machinery. Griffis told his readers that "each mechanic seems desirous of trying his skill at something foreign, when said foreign thing is undoubtedly worth making." Although the Japanese welcomed foreign inventions and products, he wrote, they were protective of their independence and valued their ability to learn how to build such things themselves. He emphasized that these developments were taking place in a remote province, far from the eyes of foreigners in the treaty ports, where one was more likely to expect such scientific and technological advances.[20]

The single most momentous change that Griffis observed in Fukui occurred when its last daimyo and first governor, Matsudaira Mochiaki, bid farewell to his samurai and the city. In July 1869, daimyo throughout Japan had returned their lands to the imperial throne (*hanseki-hōkan*) and were named nonhereditary governors, the use of the title "daimyo" being eliminated. To further

FIGURE 9.2. Bridge leading to the interior of the castle, Fukui, 1871. (Credit: William Elliot Griffis Collection, Rutgers University Libraries.)

centralize authority, in August 1871, the new imperial government abolished the domains and replaced them with prefectures (*haihan-chiken*). At the same time, it ordered the governors into retirement and appointed prefectural governors to replace them.

Griffis immediately recognized the significance of this latter event, describing it soon thereafter for the *Independent* and the *Philadelphia Evening Telegraph*, then later for *North American Review* and in a chapter of *The Mikado's Empire* titled "The Last Year of Feudalism." His eyewitness accounts of Mochiaki's farewell ceremony remain valuable to historians today. On October 1, 1871, "a golden day in the golden autumn," the samurai of Fukui assembled in the castle hall and seated themselves by rank with their swords before them. Griffis wrote that "it was more than a farewell to their feudal lord. It was the solemn burial of the institutions under which their fathers had lived for seven hundred years. Each face seemed to wear a far-away expression, as if their eyes were looking into the past, or striving to probe an uncertain future." On the following day, the people of Fukui and nearby villages wore their best clothes and lined the streets to see their last daimyo for the last time as he departed for Tokyo. Griffis summarized the transition by writing in the *Independent* that "the day of loyalty has passed, the era of patriotism has begun." This, he believed, unmistakably signaled the imperial government's commitment to laying the foundations for modern, national improvement.[21]

Griffis also underscored the occasion's implications for Japan's position in the world. Chiding his fellow Americans for presuming that "we lead the world in the high-pressure lightning train of civilization," he urged them to understand this event as an important step for Japan toward becoming a peer of Western nations. By dismantling its centuries-old feudal system, Japan had effected a quiet revolution and united an empire. As Griffis wrote in the *Philadelphia Evening Telegraph*, "Japan astonishes the world by doing, in one day, what it took Europe centuries to do." Again quoting from Tennyson's "Locksley Hall," he linked the "increasing purpose" of Japan's new policies with the broader advance of civilization: Japan now had joined the inexorable march of human progress.[22]

After arriving in Tokyo in February 1872, Griffis at first shifted his attention as a writer away from Fukui and toward broader Japanese topics. As his audience grew, however, he realized how unique and valuable his experiences in Fukui had been in terms of geography and timing. One of few foreigners to have resided in a provincial city, he had immersed himself in the daily life of its people as they undertook momentous political, social, and material changes. Consequently, he recognized that his descriptions of its traditions and ongoing transformation were important components of his appeal to editors and readers.

While teaching in Tokyo, he returned to Fukui only once. In the summer of 1873, he and his sister Margaret, who had joined him in Japan in August 1872, embarked on a twenty-four-day sightseeing trip, much of it by rickshaw. Along the way, they visited other Rutgers alumni in the network: In Shizuoka, they stayed with their friend Edward Warren Clark; and in Fukui, Griffis met with Martin Wyckoff, who had replaced him as a teacher there (see chapters 7 and 8). The trip also included stops in Hakone, Kyoto, and Kanazawa. During their visit to Fukui, Griffis "took great pleasure in seeking all his old haunts," Margaret wrote in her diary. "Presents were coming in constantly & the house filled with friends, officers, to see Willie."[23]

Griffis's two-day return to Fukui gave him the opportunity to provide *Appletons' Journal* with an account of what he now classified as "a modernized Japanese city." Much had changed during his absence of only one and a half years. Mirroring his first accounts of Fukui in 1871 enumerating the material items that it was lacking, his piece now identified the elements of feudalism that had disappeared. As the national government centralized its power in Tokyo, officials in Fukui had closed the local gunpowder mill and rifle factory. They had also torn down the outer wall of the castle grounds, filled in the moat, and sold the gates for their stone, wood, and copper.[24]

Although Fukui had lost these structures of its past, it had gained important new features. Houses now stood on the site of the outer wall and moat. Griffis also pointed out the city's new lampposts, uniformed police officers, river steamboats, and scores of rickshaws. Hanging on the walls of the main street's "foreign store," he saw pictures of George Washington, Abraham Lincoln, Queen Victoria, and Emperor Wilhelm. Griffis's long list of the many items sold there included

"Connecticut clocks and thermometers, English bottled ale, Hennessy's brandy, Bordeaux claret, Borden's condensed milk, Pennsylvania petroleum and Yankee lamps with boxes of extra glass chimneys . . . neckties, gloves, suspenders, penknives, scissors, raw dry-goods material, traveling-bags, carpets, rugs, oil-cloth, window-glass, mirrors, stationery, etc." While the prospect of a railway line from Kyoto was still in the distant future, Griffis observed that the people of Fukui were waiting impatiently for the completion of a telegraph line from Tokyo. They were, he wrote, "stricken with the rage for 'civilization'—a word now in the mouth of every Japanese." From Griffis's American perspective and from his interpretation of the Japanese perspective, material goods and technologies constituted a significant part of modern civilization. Again, Griffis was careful to characterize Fukui as a provincial city, thus dispelling any Western misperception that Japan's transformation was like its famous lacquer: Modern change in Japan, he declared, was not merely a varnish that coated only the large cities and treaty ports.[25]

Fukui in Griffis's Later Writing

Although Griffis continued to write about Fukui and Japan after returning to the United States in the summer of 1874, he eventually exhausted his stock of experiences to recount. No longer an eyewitness, he instead pivoted to analyzing social, political, and military affairs from a distance. To compensate for this absence of firsthand observations and to maintain his status as an authority, he continued to highlight his time in Fukui. In later years, he did this in two ways: by reminding his readers that few foreigners had seen provincial Japan as he had and by pointing out the significance of Fukui's role in national events.

First, Griffis continually drew attention to his unusual position as a foreigner who had lived outside the treaty ports in the early Meiji era. Japan's treaties with the United States and European nations permitted the restriction of travel by foreigners to within a radius of ten *ri* (about twenty-four miles) from the ports. The Japanese government did not begin to issue interior travel passports to foreigners until 1874, the year when Griffis returned to the United States. While in Japan as a government employee, however, he was exempt from the travel restriction, which led him to identify himself in a *North American Review* article three decades later as "the one white man living who, at a daimio's capital, saw the working of the Japanese feudal system." Despite this assertion, he was relatively but not entirely unique: He overlooked the handful of other foreign employees, including his colleague Alfred Lucy in Fukui (see chapter 7), who had also lived outside the treaty ports. Nevertheless, to support his position as an expert, Griffis emphasized that he had seen firsthand not only a Japan without railroads, telegraphs, and newspapers, but also a provincial city in the throes of dramatic political and social change.[26]

Throughout the rest of his life, Griffis repeatedly reminded audiences that in Fukui he had attended the castle ceremony in which its last daimyo bid farewell to its samurai. Already in 1875 in *North American Review*, he identified it as "among the most impressive of all his life's experiences." Its spectacle and significance never ceased to resonate in the following years. In a *Current History* article in February 1928 (the month in which he died), he proudly recalled having witnessed "this moving scene . . . and felt the thrill of it." Complementing these descriptions, he frequently applauded the imperial government for its foresight in ending feudalism. By abolishing hereditary social classes and disarming the samurai, Griffis argued, "Japan set an example to the world."[27] He had lived and worked in Fukui for less than one year, but those months were pivotal in its history. Griffis was fortunate to have had this rare opportunity: a foreigner who had an insider's view of a feudal domain in its last days.

In addition, during his two years of teaching at Tokyo's Daigaku Nankō, he had a front-row seat for the transformations that were sweeping the new capital in this period of "civilization and enlightenment" (*bunmei kaika*), as the Japanese called it. Upon returning to Fukui to visit in 1873, Griffis certified that modern change was accelerating there as well. He recognized the importance of his experiences and observations in both Fukui and Tokyo, and years after leaving he encouraged his readers to do the same. Because he could write in the first person about provincial *and* urban, feudal *and* modern Japan, he claimed in 1905 that "My work has, I trust, what so many books on Japan have not,—perspective."[28]

Second, Griffis also publicly promoted his expertise by detailing Fukui's noteworthy role in the events of the Bakumatsu and early Meiji years. Again, he was fortunate because Fukui's leaders had introduced Western learning in their domain and advocated various local and national reforms (see chapter 2). Some leaders took part in the tumultuous politics of the 1850s and 1860s and continued to do so in the new imperial government. Writing about their accomplishments, Griffis noted that he became acquainted with their work during his time in Fukui and thus gained a close understanding of Japanese reform efforts and their recent history.

Griffis frequently praised Matsudaira Shungaku, Fukui's penultimate daimyo, for his commitment to innovation in his domain and the nation.[29] Beginning in the 1850s, Shungaku introduced Dutch medical studies and smallpox vaccination in Fukui, and he established its gunpowder mill and rifle factory. These achievements first attracted Griffis's attention in 1871 and never left his focus. Indeed, they prompted him to suggest in his 1907 book, *The Japanese Nation in Evolution*, that Fukui "may have led all the feudal fiefs in science." On the question of foreign relations, Shungaku shifted from initially opposing Japan's opening of relations with Western nations to supporting commercial treaties with them. He came to see exclusion of foreigners as unrealistic and foreign trade as a means to enrich and strengthen the country. Also, in 1862, he played an instrumental role in instituting political reforms, including a sharp reduction in the length of time that daimyo were required to reside in Edo under the alternate attendance system (*sankin-kōtai*), a modification that significantly eroded *bakufu* power. Griffis singled out these contributions to Bakumatsu politics in his later career, arguing that Shungaku had enabled Japan to take important first steps away from feudalism and toward national unity.[30]

Fukui's final daimyo and domain governor, Matsudaira Mochiaki, continued his predecessor's local efforts. The day after Griffis's arrival in Fukui, Mochiaki personally received him at the castle to welcome him. Seven months later, shortly after Mochiaki's farewell ceremony, he visited Griffis's house to thank him for his service. In the *Philadelphia Evening Telegraph* in 1871, Griffis commended Mochiaki as "a liberal-minded man, fully desirous of introducing Western civilization in his country." Because of the wisdom of its last two lords, Griffis argued, the domain was in the forefront of Japanese reform.[31]

To the end of his career, Griffis maintained his positive appraisal of Fukui. In 1923, he even employed an allusion to Jesus's Sermon on the Mount to describe Fukui as "a city which in eminence of intellectual and moral progress was set, as it were, upon a hill." Here Griffis also echoed Puritan leader John Winthrop's 1630 sermon depicting "a City upon a Hill" (a phrase that continues today to appear regularly in the rhetoric of American exceptionalism). Thus, Fukui not only stood as a model for other domains, it also constituted evidence that Griffis used to demonstrate to his audiences the admirable capacity of the Japanese to transform themselves successfully. In doing so, he emphasized that Japan was not a passive object being reshaped by its contact with the West; rather, it was actively engaged in determining its own modern development.[32]

In addition to its last two daimyo, Griffis pointed out, Fukui contributed other influential figures to national politics. Most notable were Yokoi Shōnan and Yuri Kimimasa. Yokoi, a Confucian scholar and reformer, was born in Kumamoto in the Higo domain but served Shungaku as an advisor in the Bakumatsu era.[33] Acting on Yokoi's guidance, Fukui established its domain school in 1855. Later, when he sent his two nephews to study in the United States, Griffis taught them at Rutgers Grammar School, thus forming early links in the network (see chapters 2 and 4). Yokoi, whom historian H. D. Harootunian described as "the most realistic and the most visionary of late Tokugawa thinkers," played an important part in the political discourse of the time. He criticized Japan's foreign policy of seclusion and the self-interest of the Tokugawa *bakufu*. Instead he favored foreign trade and insisted that civil education should complement military training to ensure good government for the benefit of all.[34]

Griffis never met Yokoi, who was assassinated by reactionaries in 1869, but reserved a prominent place for the scholar in his descriptions of Japanese reform efforts. In his later writing, he likened Yokoi's influence and role in the events leading to the Meiji Restoration to those of Benjamin Franklin and Alexander Hamilton in the founding years of the United States. (In an undated letter to Griffis, Yokoi's son suggested the parallel to Franklin because of Yokoi's age in comparison with younger statesmen in the early Meiji government.) Griffis's praise, however, did not end there. Engaging in wishful thinking, Griffis identified Yokoi as a "secret and unquailing [*sic*] follower" of Jesus and a "Christian martyr." Although Yokoi's assassins suspected him of being a Christian, his son, in correspondence with Griffis, specifically denied this claim.[35]

In addition, Griffis credited Yokoi as being an early advocate of elevating outcastes (*eta* and *hinin*) to citizenship, which prompted him to equate Yokoi also to Abraham Lincoln and abolitionist William Lloyd Garrison for their work toward ending slavery in the United States. While Yokoi's son wrote to Griffis describing hearsay accounts that his father had proposed the abolition of outcaste status, which the Meiji government effected by its Emancipation Edict of 1871, historians have found no evidence to support this.[36] Even without Griffis's mistaken claims, however, Yokoi deserves his prominent position among Japanese intellectuals of the 1850s and 1860s. Griffis, with his American readers in mind, linked Yokoi to familiar and esteemed figures in U.S. history in order to underscore the scholar's significance in Japanese history. Moreover, Griffis attempted to associate himself with Yokoi's eminence by noting their common ties to Fukui: The domain had employed both men as teachers.

One of Yokoi's students there, Yuri Kimimasa, also won Griffis's admiration.[37] Yuri successfully reformed the domain's finances and commerce, and then he served in the early Meiji government, where he helped to draft the Charter Oath of 1868. In recognition of this accomplishment, Griffis again reached back into U.S. history to identify Yuri as "the Thomas Jefferson of Japan," thereby drawing for his audience a parallel between the American Declaration of Independence and the Meiji Charter Oath as founding political documents. Later in Fukui, Yuri also proposed the recruitment of foreign teachers, which resulted in Shungaku's request to Guido F. Verbeck at the Daigaku Nankō for an American chemistry and physics instructor—a request that ultimately reached Griffis in New Brunswick in 1870 through the Rutgers network. After Griffis's arrival in Fukui, Yuri befriended him and gave him a signed copy of the Charter Oath. Griffis proudly recalled this gift in a 1912 *North American Review* essay commemorating the recently deceased Emperor Meiji and reflecting on Japan's achievements during his reign.[38]

Certainly, Fukui's leaders played significant parts in the late Tokugawa and early Meiji eras, which Griffis came to appreciate during his time teaching there. This development enabled him in his later writing to associate himself with Fukui's recent history. He had not only seen Japan's feudal system from the inside out, he had also worked in a domain notable for its commitment to progress and reform. Griffis purposefully praised Fukui's statesmen in part to share in their fame and to support his claim that his perspective was unrivaled by other foreign analysts. Living in Fukui and then Tokyo, he met and socialized with a wide range of Japanese officials as well as fellow foreign employees and missionaries. When he returned to the United States, he maintained these contacts to remain informed about ongoing developments in Japan. Now a distant observer, Griffis no longer had a supply of recent experiences to serve as material for his writing. Thus, to prevent his credentials as an expert from going stale, he frequently referred to his connections to Fukui and its notable leaders as a means of sustaining his status and career.

Conclusion

After leaving Japan in 1874, Griffis did not return until a lengthy visit there with his wife, Frances, in 1926–1927, during which they were continually celebrated as honored guests. At the start of the tour, the Japanese government decorated him with the Third Class of the Order of the Rising Sun; near its end, Emperor Shōwa granted him an audience at the imperial palace. Griffis also paid his respects to his former hosts. On December 25, 1926, in the cemetery of Kaianji Temple in Shinagawa, he laid flowers at the tombs of the last two Fukui daimyo: Shungaku, who had requested an American instructor for the domain; and Mochiaki, who had welcomed him.[39] Four months later, Griffis returned to visit Fukui for the first time in fifty-four years and reveled in his reception. Cheering crowds lined both sides of the street from the train station as a schoolboy choir sang "My Country, 'Tis of Thee." The following day, he recorded in his journal that he shared "chat, laughter, reminiscence" with one dozen of his former students. The visit also featured several speeches and a lantern procession along the river.[40]

The warm appreciation that Griffis received upon his return was tangible recognition that Fukui and Japan had benefited from employing him in 1870–1874. A product of, and contributor to, the Rutgers trans-Pacific network, he was an enthusiastic teacher to his Japanese students and a perceptive reporter to his American readers. He helped to extend the reach and effects of the network in the United States far beyond New Brunswick and into the twentieth century. Throughout his career as an experienced observer of Japan amid dramatic political and social change, he acted as a prominent advocate for its aspirations as it emerged from isolation and developed into a world power. He regularly extolled Japanese progress in an ever-flowing stream of articles and books until his death in 1928. No other American was so prolific or enduring as an analyst and friend of Meiji and Taishō Japan.

As significantly, Griffis benefited from his invitation to teach in Fukui. As he noted upon departing the city in January 1872, "Thou hast been a well of blessing; for in thee I have found some truth."[41] His hosts treated him with sincere hospitality and were always amiable and attentive. As he taught Fukui's students, its people also taught him: Some explained their heritage and traditions, and others shared their hopes for the future. The timing of his residence there, as feudalism slipped away, was opportune as well. Fukui changed before his eyes in these pivotal years of Japanese history. He saw first a feudal domain and then a modernized city. Finally, though Fukui was geographically remote, its leaders played significant roles in reshaping and transforming their nation as a whole. Griffis deliberately highlighted Fukui's contributions to Bakumatsu and early Meiji politics in order to demonstrate the importance of the domain where he had lived and worked. Such proximity to proponents of reform, he claimed, gave him valuable insight into Japan. On the foundation that Fukui provided to him, Griffis constructed a successful career that lasted nearly six decades. While Fukui indeed was fortunate to have employed him as a teacher, the greater beneficiary of those ten and a half months was William Elliot Griffis himself.

Notes

1 William Elliot Griffis, *The Mikado's Empire* (New York: Harper and Brothers, 1876).

2 At its peak circulation, the *Independent* (1848–1928) claimed in 1869 that its advertising revenue was more than triple that of any other religious newspaper and rivaled that of any secular newspaper. In 1916, Griffis claimed authorship of the 1870 *Independent* article. [Griffis], "The Japanese Students in America," *Independent* 22, no. 1131 (August 4, 1870): 6; Frank Luther Mott, *A History of American Magazines*, vol. 2, *1850–1865* (Cambridge, MA: Belknap Press of Harvard University Press, 1957), 368, 375–377; "The Publisher to the Public," *Independent* 21, no. 1096 (December 2, 1869): 1; Griffis, "The Japanese Students in America," *Japanese Student* 1, no. 1 (October 1916): 8.

3 William Hayes Ward to Griffis, September 9, 1872, scrapbook 5: Fukui scrapbook 1871, reel 42, part 3, in *Japan Through Western Eyes: Manuscript Records of Traders, Travellers, Missionaries and Diplomats, 1853–1941* (Marlborough, UK: Adam Matthew, 2000).

4 Griffis contributed his last article to the *Christian Intelligencer* (1830–1934) a few days before his death. Griffis, "Dr. Hartranft's Chief Triumph," *Christian Intelligencer and Mission Field* 99, no. 7 (February 15, 1928): 107; "William Elliot Griffis, D.D., L.H.D," *Christian Intelligencer and Mission Field* 99, no. 8 (February 22, 1928): 122.

5 Griffis [Curio, pseud.], "First Glimpses of Japan," *Christian Intelligencer* 42, no. 8 [9] (March 2, 1871): 2; Griffis [Curio, pseud.], "In the Heart of Japan," *Christian Intelligencer* 42, no. 16 [17] (April 27, 1871): 2.

6 The *Home Journal* (1846–1901) later identified Griffis as Curio. Griffis [Curio, pseud.], "Japanese Theatricals," *Home Journal*, n.d., item 129, scrapbook 5, reel 42, in *Japan Through Western Eyes*; Griffis, "A Japanese City," *Home Journal*, n.d., item 113, scrapbook 5, reel 42, in *Japan Through Western Eyes*; Griffis, "Americans in Japan," *Home Journal*, n.d., item 112, scrapbook 5, reel 42, in *Japan Through Western Eyes*; Mott, *A History of American Magazines*, 2:349–355; Alan Nourie and Barbara Nourie, eds., *American Mass-Market Magazines* (Westport, CT: Greenwood Press, 1990), 501–502.

7 Griffis, "A Philadelphian in Japan," *Philadelphia Evening Telegraph*, n.d., item 124, scrapbook 5, reel 42, in *Japan Through Western Eyes*; Griffis, "A Philadelphian in Japan," *Philadelphia Evening Telegraph*, n.d., item 114, scrapbook 5, reel 42, in *Japan Through Western Eyes*.

8 W. E. Griffis to Martha C. Griffis, April 4, 1873, box 132, folder 10, group 3, William Elliot Griffis Collection, Special Collections and University Archives, Rutgers University Libraries, New Brunswick, NJ.

9 Griffis, "Inside Japan," *Lippincott's Magazine* 12 (August 1873): 174–181; Griffis, "The Paper-Money of Japan," *Appletons' Journal* 10, no. 243 (November 15, 1873): 625–626; "Literary: *Lippincott's Magazine*," *Christian Intelligencer* 44, no. 31 (July 31, 1873): 7.

10 *North American Review*'s editor in 1875 was Harvard University historian Henry Adams, who was assisted by his former student and future U.S. senator Henry Cabot Lodge. In later years, Griffis contributed ten more articles on Japan to *North American Review*. Griffis, "A Japanese Merchant at Home," *Overland Monthly* 12, no. 1 (January 1874): 31–35; Griffis, "The Recent Revolutions in Japan," *North American Review* 120, no. 247 (April 1875): 281–315; Griffis, *The Mikado's Empire*, 291–324; Mott, *A History of American Magazines*, 2:247–248.

11 For brief histories of these magazines, see Mott, *A History of American Magazines*, 2:219–261; Mott, *A History of American Magazines*, vol. 3, *1865–1885* (Cambridge, MA: Belknap Press of Harvard University Press, 1957), 396–409, 417–421; Nourie and Nourie, *American Mass-Market Magazines*, 23–26, 213–217, 333–339.

12 "Lectures and Meetings: 'Inside Japan,'" *New York Daily Tribune*, November 12, 1874; "Lectures and Meetings: Street Life in Yedo (Japan)," *New York Daily Tribune*, December 21, 1874; "Philadelphia and Suburbs," *Philadelphia Inquirer*, January 27, 1875; "Special Notices: Prof. W. E. Griffis," *Philadelphia Inquirer*, January 11, 1876; "General News," *Chicago Daily Tribune*, March 25, 1875.

13 Griffis, *The Mikado's Empire*; "The Mikado's Empire," *Philadelphia Press*, August 17, 1876; "New Books: The Mikado's Empire," *Boston Daily Globe*, August 9, 1876; "Literary: The Mikado's Empire," *Christian Intelligencer* 47, no. 33 (August 17, 1876): 6; "Japan and the Japanese: Studies in the Mikado's Empire," *New York Times*, August 27, 1876; "New Publications: The Mikado's Empire," *Cincinnati Daily Gazette*, August 30, 1876; "The Mikado's Empire," *Nation* 23, no. 595 (November 23, 1876): 316–317.

14 Inazo (Ota) Nitobe, *The Intercourse between the United States and Japan: An Historical Sketch* (Baltimore: Johns Hopkins Press, 1891), 145–146.

15 For an anthology of his work, see Joseph M. Henning, ed., *Interpreting the Mikado's Empire: The Writings of William Elliot Griffis* (Lanham, MD: Lexington Books, 2021).

16 Basil Hall Chamberlain, *Things Japanese: Being Notes on Various Subjects Connected with Japan* (London: Kegan Paul, Trench, Trübner, 1890).

17 Griffis quoted from Tennyson's line: "I the heir of all the ages, in the foremost files of time." Griffis, "A Japanese City," *Appletons' Journal* 12, no. 280 (August 1, 1874): 140; Alfred Tennyson, "Locksley Hall," in *Poems*, vol. 2 (Boston: William D. Ticknor, 1846), 110; William Darby Templeman, "A Consideration of the Fame of 'Locksley Hall,'" *Victorian Poetry* 1, no. 2 (April 1963): 81–103.

18 Griffis [Curio, pseud.], "In the Heart of Japan," 2; Griffis, "A Japanese City," *Appletons' Journal*, 141; Griffis, "A Call on a Bonze," *Lippincott's Magazine* 13 (June 1874): 731.

19 Griffis cofounded the *Targum*, the Rutgers College student newspaper, in 1869. Griffis, "A Japanese City," *Appletons' Journal*, 141; Griffis, "A Call on a Bonze," 725; Griffis, "A Japanese Merchant at Home," *Overland Monthly* 12, no. 1 (January 1874): 31–33; Griffis, "A Japanese City," *Home Journal*; Griffis [Curio, pseud.], "The Rutgers Graduate in Japan," *Targum* 3, no. 7 (October 1871): 1–2.

20 Griffis, "A Philadelphian in Japan," item 124; Griffis, "Japan," *Scientific American* n.s., 26, no. 8 (February 17, 1872): 116.

21 Griffis, "The Sea Empire," *Independent* 24, no. 1207 (January 18, 1872): 2; Griffis, "A Philadelphian in Japan," item 114; Griffis, "The Recent Revolutions in Japan," 312; Griffis, *The Mikado's Empire*, 533–535.

22 Griffis quoted from Tennyson's lines: "Yet I doubt not thro' the ages one increasing purpose runs, And the thoughts of men are widen'd with the process of the suns." Griffis, "A Philadelphian in Japan," item 114; Griffis, "The Sea Empire," 2; Tennyson, "Locksley Hall," 106.

23 Griffis, July 18 to August 14, 1873, journal 11: Japan journal, reel 22, part 2, in *Japan Through Western Eyes*; Griffis, July 18 to August 11, 1873, journal 9: Fukui journal, reel 21, part 2, in *Japan Through Western Eyes*; Margaret Clark Griffis, August 13, 1873, diary, reel 58, part 4, in *Japan Through Western Eyes*.

24 Griffis, "A Modernized Japanese City," *Appletons' Journal* 13, no. 313 (March 20, 1875): 370.

25 Griffis, "A Modernized Japanese City," 369–370; Griffis, "Japan's Record of Progress in 1872," *Independent* 25, no. 1268 (March 20, 1873): 357.

26 Griffis, "The Development of Political Parties in Japan," *North American Review* 175, no. 552 (November 1902): 676; Joseph M. Henning, *Outposts of Civilization: Race, Religion, and the Formative Years of American-Japanese Relations* (New York: New York University Press, 2000), 117, 122; Griffis, "The Elder Statesmen of Japan: The Power Behind the Portsmouth Treaty," *North American Review* 182, no. 591 (February 1906): 219.

27 Griffis, "The Recent Revolutions in Japan," 312; Griffis, "Japan's Progress in Rebuilding an Empire," *Current History* 27, no. 5 (February 1928): 681–682; Griffis, *Dux Christus: An Outline Study of Japan* (New York: Macmillan, 1905), 88; Griffis, *The Japanese Nation in Evolution: Steps in the Progress of a Great People* (New York: Thomas Y. Crowell, 1907), 342–343; Griffis, "American Makers of the New Japan," *Century Magazine* 86, no. 4 (August 1913): 602; Griffis, *The Mikado: Institution and Person* (Princeton, NJ: Princeton University Press, 1915), 191.

28 Griffis, *Dux Christus*, viii–ix.

29 Griffis often referred to Matsudaira Shungaku, known earlier as Matsudaira Yoshinaga and Matsudaira Keiei, as the late or retired prince of Echizen. (Fukui was located in Echizen Province.)

30 Griffis, "Japan," 116; Griffis, *The Mikado's Empire*, 6th ed. (New York: Harper and Brothers, 1890), 609; Griffis, *The Japanese Nation in Evolution*, 288; Griffis, *The Mikado*, 68–76; Motoyama Yukihiko, "The Education Policy of Fukui and William Elliot Griffis," in *The Modernizers: Overseas Students, Foreign Employees, and Meiji Japan*, ed. Ardath W. Burks (Boulder, CO: Westview Press, 1985), 270, 272–273; Kanai Madoka, "Fukui, Domain of a Tokugawa Collateral *Daimyō*: Its Tradition and Transition," in Burks, *The Modernizers*, 57, 62.

31 Griffis, March 5 and October 1, 1871, journal 9, reel 21, part 2, in *Japan Through Western Eyes*; Griffis, *The Mikado's Empire*, 428–429, 535; Griffis, "A Philadelphian in Japan," item 124.

32 Jesus's Sermon on the Mount appears in Matthew 5:14 (King James Version): "Ye are the light of the world. A city that is set on a hill cannot be hid." Griffis, "Japan at the Time of Townsend Harris," in *Japan: A Comparison*, ed. William Elliot Griffis and Hugh Byas (New York: Japan Society, 1923), 14; John Winthrop, "A Model of Christian Charity," in *The Journal of John Winthrop, 1630–1649*, abridged ed., ed. Richard S. Dunn and Laetitia Yeandle (Cambridge, MA: Belknap Press of Harvard University Press, 1996), 10.

33 Yokoi was known also as Yokoi Heishirō.

34 Motoyama, "The Education Policy of Fukui and William Elliot Griffis," 267–272, 275–277, 286–287, 299n48; Kanai, "Fukui, Domain of a Tokugawa Collateral *Daimyō*," 57–60; William Elliot Griffis, *The Rutgers Graduates in Japan* (Albany, NY: Rutgers College Alumni Association, 1886), 21–22; H. D. Harootunian, *Toward Restoration: The Growth of Political Consciousness in Tokugawa Japan* (Berkeley: University of California Press, 1970), 325.

35 Griffis, letter to the editor, *The New York Times*, June 1, 1924; Griffis, *The Mikado*, 77; Griffis, *Dux Christus*, 138; J. T. Ise [Yokoi Tokiwo] to Griffis, n.d. [1889–1890?], reel 38, part 3, in *Japan Through Western Eyes*; Yokoi to Griffis, January 24, 1915, reel 38, part 3, in *Japan Through Western Eyes*; Judy Yoneoka, "Yokoi Shonan Through the Eyes of His Son: An Analysis of Three Letters by Yokoi Tokiwo and Their Influence on the Writings of William Elliot Griffis," *Kaigai jijō kenkyū* (Kumamoto Gakuen University) 41, no. 2 (March 2014): 41–64.

36 The 1871 edict abolished the class categories of *eta* and *hinin* and reclassified outcastes as commoners. Griffis, *The Mikado*, 77–78; Griffis, *Dux Christus*, 87–88, 138; Griffis, *The Japanese Nation in Evolution*, 110–113, 322; Griffis, "Japan in the World War," *North American Review* 208, no. 756 (November 1918): 723; Ise [Yokoi] to Griffis, n.d. [1889–1890?]; Yokoi to Griffis, May 26, 1904, reel 38, part 3, in *Japan Through Western Eyes*; Yoneoka, "Yokoi Shonan through the Eyes of His Son," 51–54, 57–58, 60–63; Ian Neary, *Political Protest and Social Control in Pre-War Japan: The Origins of Buraku Liberation* (Manchester, UK: Manchester University Press, 1989), 31; Noah Y. McCormack, *Japan's Outcaste Abolition: The Struggle for National Inclusion and the Making of the Modern State* (New York: Routledge, 2013), 62–64.

37 Yuri was known earlier as Mitsuoka Ishigorō and Mitsuoka Hachirō.

38 Motoyama, "The Education Policy of Fukui and William Elliot Griffis," 277–278, 280, 287; Griffis, *The Japanese Nation in Evolution*, 321–322, 334; Griffis, "Japan's Progress in Rebuilding an Empire," 681; Griffis, "Mutsuhito the Great," *North American Review* 196, no. 682 (September 1912): 331–332.

39 In 1908, the Japanese government had decorated Griffis in New York City with the Fourth Class of the Order of the Rising Sun. Griffis, December 22 and 25, 1926, and June 1, 1927, journal 30, reel 24, part 2, in *Japan Through Western Eyes*; "Decorated," *Japan Times and Mail* (Tokyo), December 24, 1926; "His Service Recognized," *Japan Times and Mail*, June 2, 1927; "Personals and Local Items," *Japan Times and Mail*, December 28, 1926; "The Order of the Rising Sun," *Ithaca (NY) Daily Journal*, May 6, 1908.

40 The United States did not adopt "The Star-Spangled Banner" as its national anthem until 1931. Griffis, April 25–29, 1927, journal 30, reel 24, part 2, in *Japan Through Western Eyes*.

41 Griffis, *The Mikado's Empire*, 540.

Part IV

The Rutgers-Japan Network in Action

The Iwakura Mission and Educational Reform in Japan

10

The Satsuma-Rutgers Connection During the Early Meiji Era

JOHN E. VAN SANT

> Knowledge shall be sought throughout the world so as to strengthen the foundations of imperial rule.
> —Charter Oath, Article Five, issued by Emperor Meiji, April 6, 1868

When U.S. Navy Commodore Matthew C. Perry and his fearsome "black ships" appeared in Uraga Bay, just off the coast of Edo in July 1853, Japan's government leaders—the Tokugawa *bakufu*—were forced to deal with a genuine threat from the West.[1] At the start of the Tokugawa era in the early seventeenth century, Japan had massive and powerful samurai armies that brushed off the then-major Western powers of Spain and Portugal and forced Dutch merchants to live and work on a small, heavily guarded island in Nagasaki Bay. The long Tokugawa era (1600–1868) advanced Japan's already impressive cultural and artistic achievements. It also witnessed the development of a sophisticated urban society—especially in Edo, the shogun's capital—which would be renamed Tokyo in 1868. Kyoto, the imperial capital since 794 and where the emperor resided until 1868, was a city full of Japanese traditions such as Buddhist temples, Shinto shrines, Noh and Kabuki theaters, and the finest kimonos made in Japan. Osaka, known as "the merchant capital" and the home of *bunraku* theater, was also among the finest of Japanese cities. On the southern island of Kyushu, Nagasaki and Kagoshima—the latter the capital of the Satsuma domain—were smaller but also culturally, commercially, and politically important urban areas during the Tokugawa era. This era also witnessed the development of a national transportation network of roads—the Tōkaidō Road being the most famous—and a commercial economy with a rising merchant class. Also, a handful of Japanese "Dutch studies" scholars, who needed approval from the Tokugawa government to study the foreign books that arrived in Nagasaki, contributed to Japan's scientific knowledge, especially in the area of medicine.[2]

By the mid-nineteenth century, however, Japan was no longer an economic or military match for even a middling power such as the United States. During this period, the Tokugawa *bakufu* was constantly confronted by serious internal problems affecting all classes of Japanese society. As the economy expanded and became increasingly commercialized, many merchants became wealthy. Many samurai—the elite of Japanese society—became poorer. Farmers were distressed by the rice tax they had to constantly pay (usually fifty percent of their harvest) to samurai who, in the opinion of farmers, contributed nothing in return. Prolonged famines during the 1830s in which hundreds of thousands died from starvation, malnutrition, and disease led to an upsurge in rebellions against rural elites and Tokugawa authorities, such as Ōshio Heihachirō's rebellion in Osaka in 1837. In other words, Japanese society was unraveling from within.[3]

At this vulnerable historical moment, the West knocked on Japan's door. Russian, British, and American ships began appearing off Japan's coasts with upsetting frequency. The China trade and North Pacific whaling had drawn most of these ships close to Japan's shores. Japan turned down their occasional requests for trade because it would have violated the centuries-old policy prohibiting contact between Japan and Western countries, except for the limited contact allowed with the Dutch.[4] After the Opium War of 1839–1841 between the British and the nearby Middle Kingdom of China, it became obvious to foresighted Japanese that someday the increasingly powerful and arrogant Westerners were not going to take Japan's "no" for a definitive answer to their requests for trade and contact. The government of Holland even sent the shogun a polite letter in 1844 with the message that the world was changing and that Japan would have to adapt to these changes.[5] While the shogun's reply to the letter was dismissive, there was no denying that more than two centuries of external peace resulted in deteriorated military strength in Japan, and large-scale industrialization had yet to begin.

The Tokugawa government reluctantly signed treaties on trade, extraterritoriality, and other matters with the United States, Russia, Britain, Holland, and France during the 1850s. Perry's intrusion and these "unequal treaties" (formally known as the Ansei Treaties) opened up a Pandora's box of long-simmering internal grievances in Japan. When Satsuma and Chōshū—large domains which were previously mutual enemies—joined together and rallied the divided anti-*bakufu* forces, they overthrew the Tokugawa *bakufu* in early 1868.

After Perry's expedition was completed in 1854, American officials in Washington, DC, paid relatively little attention to Japan because the crises over slavery, the Civil War, and Reconstruction diverted their attention from most foreign relations issues. On the other hand, Japanese officials paid significant attention to the United States from the 1850s to the 1870s. After all, it was a U.S. Navy officer who had "opened" Japan to the West and an American minister (ambassador)—Townsend Harris—who had negotiated the first comprehensive diplomatic treaties between Japan and the West. In 1860, the Tokugawa shogun sent a large delegation of high-ranking officials to ratify treaties between the two countries and meet with American officials, including President James Buchanan.[6]

From Satsuma to the West

Long before the mid-nineteenth century, the Shimazu family rulers of the Satsuma domain had economic and political interests outside of Japan's nominal boundaries, especially in the Ryukyu Islands. In 1609, ships and samurai from Satsuma invaded and conquered the Ryukyu Islands, forcing the king of the Ryukyu Islands to become a vassal of Satsuma. The already existing trade relationship between the Ryukyu Islands and China became a conduit for trade goods for Satsuma throughout the Tokugawa era.[7] Despite its seclusion policies of the 1630s, the Tokugawa *bakufu* sometimes encouraged, sometimes restricted, but nevertheless allowed Satsuma's trade with the Ryukyu Islands to continue throughout the Tokugawa era.

Earlier than probably any other daimyo, Shimazu Nariakira (1809–1858) of the Satsuma domain realized the "barbarians from the West" had significantly altered Japan's place in the world. Shimazu believed that if Satsuma could learn and utilize Western science and technology, the domain might be able to oust their Tokugawa overlords. He encouraged Satsuma's samurai to learn Western science and technology. After his death in 1858, his younger brother, Shimazu Hisamitsu (1817–1887), became the regent of the domain and continued these policies.[8]

Satsuma's leadership became even more motivated to learn Western science and technology following an altercation with a group of British nationals in September 1862 known as the Namamugi Incident. An entourage of Satsuma samurai were escorting Regent Shimazu Hisamitsu on the Tōkaidō Road near Yokohama when one of the British merchants, Charles Richardson, did not dismount from his horse as the entourage passed by. Such recognition of daimyo status was expected by all Japanese and foreigners. Outraged at what was perceived as a lack of respect for the daimyo regent, one of the samurai slashed

Richardson. Other samurai then slashed Richardson to death and injured two other members of the British party. The British immediately requested reparations and for the samurai who had killed Richardson to be brought to justice. Unsatisfied with subsequent negotiations with the Satsuma domain and with the Tokugawa *bakufu*'s response, British Royal Navy ships bombarded Kagoshima in August 1863. Five Japanese were killed, and hundreds of houses and three of Satsuma's ships were destroyed before the British departed.[9] While understandably upset at this "gunboat diplomacy," Satsuma's leaders were, on the other hand, impressed with the power and accuracy of British ship cannons. After paying reparations for the death of Richardson, Satsuma began a trade relationship with Britain.[10]

Godai Tomoatsu (1836–1885), a young samurai from Kagoshima, originally approached daimyo Shimazu Nariakira with a plan to send Satsuma samurai as students to the West in 1857.[11] Subsequent events in Japan, including Nariakira's untimely death one year later, treaty negotiations and agreements between the Tokugawa government and Western countries, the shogun's embassy to the United States, the assassination of the shogun's regent Ii Naosuke, and the Namamugi Incident rendered such a plan all but forgotten. After the British bombardment of Kagoshima, however, Godai approached Thomas Glover (1836–1911), a Scottish merchant based in Nagasaki, requesting help for a plan to send samurai as students to Britain. Glover, who had assisted a group of five samurai students from the Chōshū domain to journey to England one year earlier, agreed to assist.[12] Godai was then able to obtain approval from Shimazu Hisamitsu for this audacious and dangerous plan in December 1864.[13] Fifteen students were selected from the Kaiseijo, an academy for samurai from elite families of Satsuma who studied Western sciences and languages.[14] In April 1865, the students, accompanied by Godai and three others, secretly departed on the two-month journey to Britain.[15] Because traveling outside of Japan was against the law, unless granted special permission from the Tokugawa government, the students were given false names to use while away from Japan. All nineteen survived the journey and arrived at Southampton Harbor on June 21, 1865.

Most of these Satsuma students took courses at University College London for more than one year and spent some time traveling on the European continent. Mori Arinori (1847–1889) spent some of his time in St. Petersburg, Russia, where he learned about Peter the Great, who had transformed Russia more than a hundred years earlier by adopting reforms based on Western methods. Nagasawa Kanaye (1852–1934), being the youngest of the Satsuma students at thirteen years of age, was sent to Aberdeen, Scotland, and lived with Thomas Glover's relatives while attending a grammar school. In early 1867, Sameshima Naonobu (1845–1880) and Yoshida Kiyonari (1845–1891) visited New York, where they met and were impressed by the charismatic Thomas Lake Harris (1823–1906) of the Brotherhood of the New Life, a quasi-Christian and utopian colony in Brocton, in upstate New York. By the spring of 1867, lack of money was becoming a major problem for the Japanese students because Satsuma was concentrating all of its resources on the intensifying battle against the Tokugawa government.

Most of the students decided to return home. However, six journeyed to the United States to join the Brotherhood of the New Life.[16] Lawrence Oliphant (1829–1888), a mentor and sponsor of the Japanese students and formerly a member of the British legation in Edo, and Thomas Lake Harris, the leader of the Brotherhood of the New Life, were on a visit to England in the spring of 1867. Harris and Oliphant offered free passage, room, board, and education to any of the Satsuma students who would go and live at the colony in New York. In addition to Yoshida and Sameshima, Hatakeyama Yoshinari (1842–1876), Matsumura Junzō (1842–1919), Mori Arinori, and Nagasawa Kanaye accepted the offer and journeyed to Brocton, New York. Five additional young Japanese men, all from Satsuma, made their way to the Brotherhood of the New Life in Brocton by November 1867, becoming the largest group of Japanese living in the United States at the time.[17]

It is doubtful that the Japanese who agreed to go to New York and join the Brotherhood of the New Life community clearly understood Harris's theology, a theology loosely based on the ideas and visions of eighteenth-century Swedish scientist, theologian, and mystic Emanuel Swedenborg. They were impressed (and made impressionable) by Harris's mystically charismatic persona. And their studies of Western science had expanded into the realm of Western cultural values, which were still new to the young Japanese samurai. They were eager to explore and learn about the United States, which was then a Western country on the rise. Thomas Lake Harris was their ticket to do just that.

The Brotherhood of the New Life

The Brotherhood of the New Life colony had just moved to Brocton, New York, when Matsumura, Yoshida, Hatakeyama, Mori, Sameshima, and Nagasawa arrived in August 1867. The two-thousand-acre Brocton Colony was located on the shores of Lake Erie. The principal profit-making business of the colony was its winery. Hundreds of acres were planted with Salem grapes. The colony's massive, arched-stone wine cellar could hold up to fifty thousand gallons of wine. The colony also had a dairy farm, a steam grist mill, a restaurant, a general store, a nursery, a hotel, and a printing shop.[18] At its height, the Brocton Colony had nearly two hundred resident adherents, with perhaps two thousand nonresident supporters in the United States, Scotland, and England.[19]

The Japanese did not live together at the Brocton Colony. Soon after their arrival, Nagasawa was placed in Harris's mansion while Yoshida and Sameshima lived in a house with Oliphant and at least three other members of the Brotherhood of the New Life.[20] Hatakeyama, Matsumura, and Mori appear to have lived in a house near Harris's mansion. Their daily routine was to rise early and attend to the tasks assigned to them by Harris. All the Japanese worked in the grape orchards at least part of the time. After a schoolhouse was constructed on the grounds in November 1867, the Japanese spent half the day working and the other half studying English and the Bible. One month after the arrival of the six students from Satsuma, Oliphant wrote that they were "every day hard at work with their countenances beaming with delight.... They say they never knew what happiness was before."[21] While there is no clear indication that the students from Satsuma who came from England became disillusioned during their sojourn at Brocton, all except Nagasawa began to leave in the late spring of 1868.[22]

According to Oliphant, they desired to return to Japan "on patriotic grounds" to assist Satsuma in the domain's leading role in toppling the Tokugawa government.[23] Sameshima and Mori left on June 8, 1868. They wrote to their remaining comrades that they left "simply to discharge our duty to our country" and additionally wanted them to know that their departure did not indicate a loss of faith.[24]

For Hatakeyama Yoshinari, Yoshida Kiyonari, and Matsumura Junzō, another reason for departure was the lack of educational opportunities at the Brocton Colony.[25] They studied languages and Western technology in Kagoshima, Nagasaki, and London, and Brocton's hastily constructed schoolhouse was hardly the place to advance their secular education. With the Charter Oath released a few months earlier by the newly enthroned Emperor Meiji, Japanese were encouraged to seek knowledge "throughout the world so as to strengthen the foundations of imperial rule."[26] While these Japanese students were originally sent abroad to study Western science, technology, and culture in order to enhance the knowledge and power of their home domain of Satsuma, they were now seeking this knowledge to strengthen a new Japan led by a new leader with a new government largely controlled by samurai from the Satsuma and Chōshū domains.[27]

To New Brunswick and Rutgers College

Matsumura Junzō left the Brocton Colony shortly before Sameshima and Mori returned to Japan. Matsumura first traveled to Monson Academy in Wilbraham, Massachusetts, where he stayed for several months. While at Monson Academy, Matsumura learned of three Japanese students at Rutgers College and decided to join them in New Brunswick, New Jersey. The brothers Yokoi Saheita (1845–1877) and Yokoi Daihei (1850–1870) from Kumamoto, and Kusakabe Taro (1845–1870) from Fukui, were already studying at the Rutgers Grammar School and Rutgers College in 1868. They were guided from Japan to New Brunswick by Guido F. Verbeck (1830–1898), then a missionary for the Dutch Reformed Church teaching Western studies in Nagasaki. The Yokoi brothers and Kusakabe were among the first Japanese to study in the United States.[28]

Hatakeyama Yoshinari and Yoshida Kiyonari left Brocton shortly after Sameshima and Mori's departure and went straight to New Brunswick to join Matsumura and the others. William Elliot Griffis (1843–1928), a graduate of Rutgers College hired by the Japanese government to work as an educator in Fukui and Tokyo during the early 1870s, wrote that Rutgers saved Hatakeyama, Yoshida, and Matsumura from "the hands of some socialist fanatics," meaning from the Brotherhood of the New Life.[29]

Matsumura, Hatakeyama, and Yoshida began their studies at Rutgers in the fall of 1868. David Murray, professor of mathematics and natural sciences, soon became their mentor and friend. Hatakeyama was so enamored of Dr. Murray and his wife, Martha, that he was baptized as a Christian in December 1868 at the Second Reformed Church in New Brunswick, where David and Martha Murray held leadership positions.[30] Murray soon realized that the three students from Satsuma were more advanced in their English-language skills and general knowledge of the world than other Japanese students who were already in New Brunswick or who arrived shortly afterward. In his biography of David Murray, Benjamin Duke perceptively discusses how the Satsuma students had already spent three years in the West: two years in London including trips to the European continent, plus one year in upstate New York. Meanwhile, Japanese students who came with the assistance of Guido F. Verbeck in the 1860s came directly from Japan to New Brunswick. The Satsuma students had spent much more time in the West learning science and culture and communicating with people who only spoke English.[31]

Matsumura, Hatakeyama, and Yoshida enrolled in the Scientific School at Rutgers College. Matsumura's interest in naval affairs had been a reason for his selection by Satsuma's leadership as one of the students to send to London in 1865. Nearing completion of his second semester at Rutgers, he learned that the U.S. Naval Academy would allow Japanese students to apply.[32] Matsumura and Yokoi Saheita applied for and were accepted into the U.S. Naval Academy. Although Yokoi was academically unable to complete the course of studies, Matsumura completed the regular course of studies in 1873 and was commissioned as a captain in the Imperial Navy upon his return to Japan. After serving as captain of two ships and then as a squadron commander, he became the chief instructor of the Japanese Naval Academy in 1875. He was promoted to the rank of rear admiral in 1882 and then vice admiral in 1891.[33] With his promotion to vice admiral, he was placed on the reserve list, and he officially retired from the Imperial Navy in 1910. Matsumura's overseas studies and experiences in Britain and then in the United States with the Brotherhood of the New Life, at Rutgers College, and at the U.S. Naval Academy had prepared him for an important role in a Japan strengthening itself in a world of industrialization and imperialism. He died in 1919.

Yoshida Kiyonari, like Matsumura and Hatakeyama, began his courses at the Rutgers Scientific School. Yoshida took courses during the fall semester in 1868.

FIGURE 10.1. Matsumura Junzō (Zun Zow Matsmulla), 1871. (Credit: William Elliot Griffis Collection, Rutgers University Libraries. Photo by N. S. Bowdish.)

It is unclear whether he took courses during the spring semester in 1869 as well. In July 1869, he registered as a student at Wilbraham Academy in Massachusetts and studied political economy.[34] Returning to Japan in late 1870, he was assigned to the new Finance Ministry. He was soon able to raise a foreign loan that was used to pay the final samurai stipends. In 1874, he was appointed as Japanese minister to the United States and served in that position for nearly eight years. During his time in Washington, DC, as Japan's top diplomat, he continued discussions with the Grant, Hayes, and Garfield administrations over treaty

FIGURE 10.2. Mori Arinori. (Credit: William Elliot Griffis Collection, Rutgers University Libraries.)

revisions. Yoshida also arranged many of the details of former President Grant and his wife Julia's two-month visit to Japan in 1879.[35] Yoshida was appointed to the position of vice minister of foreign affairs in 1884, but he was soon in disagreement over policy issues with his boss, Foreign Minister Inoue Kaoru, and was transferred to the position of vice minister of agricultural and commercial affairs despite his expertise in foreign affairs and finance. After leaving the ministry two years later, Yoshida served in honorary positions until his death from illness in August 1891.

Hatakeyama Yoshinari was often referred to by his alias, Sugiura Kōzō, during his years at Rutgers. As mentioned previously, he became especially fond of David and Martha Murray, a fondness that was mutual.[36] As he was completing his studies with David Murray at Rutgers Scientific School, he was hastily appointed to join the Iwakura Mission as it arrived in Washington, DC, in late February 1872. He was formally appointed as part of the secretariat, in which capacity he served as interpreter and occasional advisor. Although Vice Ambassador Kido Takayoshi (1833–1877) made the appointment, Hatakeyama was clearly recommended for the position by his childhood friend from Kagoshima, Mori Arinori, who was now the chargé d'affaires for the Meiji government in Washington, DC.[37]

The Iwakura Mission, Mori Arinori, and Hatakeyama Yoshinari

The major reason Mori was dispatched by the Japanese government to Washington, DC, was to prepare for and assist the Iwakura Mission, which stayed in Washington from February 29 to July 27, 1872. Led by Prince Iwakura Tomomi (1825–1883), this embassy included many of the Meiji government's top officials, including Ōkubo Toshimichi (1830–1878), Itō Hirobumi (1841–1909), and Kido Takayoshi, along with many lower-level officials and assistants. Starting in the United States, the Iwakura Mission then traveled to several European countries. The political objective of this diplomatic mission was to renegotiate the "unequal treaties" between Japan and several Western countries signed in the wake of Perry's mission of 1853–1854. Unfortunately for Japan, the United States and all European countries refused to renegotiate the treaties during the Iwakura Mission, primarily because they felt that Japan's legal system did not yet measure up to "Western" standards. A second objective for this Japanese embassy was to study the West. Japanese officials carefully observed American and European science, business methods, education systems, government systems, and many other aspects of Western society and culture during the nearly two-year duration of the embassy. They also brought fifty-eight Japanese students to study at American and European educational institutions, and several American and European teachers and scientists were hired to work in Japan as *oyatoi* ("foreign experts") for one or more years.[38] Despite the failure to renegotiate the "unequal treaties," much of the "intellectual technology" acquired during the Iwakura Mission of 1871–1873 was both directly and indirectly utilized in Japan and significantly contributed to the country's industrialization in the remainder of the nineteenth century.

Mori arranged meetings between Japanese officials and their American counterparts. He arranged visits to nearby schools, factories, military bases, prisons, and libraries. He and Hatakeyama were often included in meetings as both interpreters and participants. In the official record of the Iwakura Mission, however, Mori is barely mentioned.[39] According to Kido Takayoshi's diary, Mori and his assistants from Japan's Washington legation were too willing to openly criticize Japan and Japanese society in conversations with Americans.[40] It does not appear that Kido included Hatakeyama when criticizing Mori and his assistants because, as demonstrated by Haruko Wakabayashi (see chapter 11 in this volume), Kido and Hatakeyama seemed to have a good relationship while the Iwakura Mission was in Washington.

In addition to assisting Kido and other leaders of the Iwakura Mission, Hatakeyama translated the U.S. Constitution into Japanese.[41] And, although credited solely to Mori, Hatakeyama possibly assisted with Mori's essay on "Religious Freedom in Japan," completed and distributed to Japan's government officials in November 1872. The religious beliefs of the West, particularly Christianity, were of intense interest and political debate in Japan during the 1860s and 1870s.

Japanese had been prohibited from converting to Christianity since the early seventeenth century, and this prohibition was reemphasized soon after the new Meiji government was established in 1868. Mori's experiences in London and with the Brotherhood of the New Life had given him some exposure to Christianity. Hatakeyama took it one step further and converted to Christianity in New Brunswick, something of which members of the Iwakura Mission must have been aware. According to Marlene Mayo, Kido trusted Hatakeyama "in spite of his conversion to Christianity and exposure to Western learning."[42] Japanese officials decided to repeal the laws against Christianity four months after the publication of "Religious Freedom in Japan." Official publications credit Mori, the Iwakura Mission, and Nakamura Masanao (1832–1891), discussed in chapter 8 eight by A. Hamish Ion, as being responsible for the repeal of the anti-Christian edicts.[43] The repeal of the anti-Christian edicts removed a major source of contention between Japan and the West during Japan's journey to becoming a major industrialized nation.

One of the planned tasks of the Iwakura Mission while it was in Washington, DC, was to interview and select an American educator to work with Tanaka Fujimaro (1845–1909), who would be in charge of the new Ministry of Education in Japan. Before the embassy arrived in Washington, DC, Mori had written to several prominent Americans involved in education requesting them to respond to questions about the structure of educational institutions and how education could strengthen the people and country of Japan. These letters were sent to the presidents of Harvard, Amherst, Williams College, the former president of Yale, and others. Mori and his staff were impressed with the response from Birdsley G. Northrop, the secretary of the Connecticut State Board of Education, and with the response from Dr. David Murray of Rutgers College. Northrup was a graduate of Yale and a Christian minister who, having established a strong system of public schools in Connecticut, had the experience to take on a similar task in Japan.[44] Mori initially favored Northrop and advised his seniors at the Iwakura Mission to offer him the position. However, after interviewing Northrop and David Murray, Tanaka Fujimaro and Kido Takayoshi chose to hire the latter. Based on Kido's diary, he was increasingly upset with Mori's failure to consult with Kido and senior members of the Iwakura Mission. Meanwhile, Hatakeyama got along well with Kido and, as Benjamin Duke writes, "The presence of Hatakeyama with the mission had to have a positive influence on the reaction of the leading figures of the Japanese delegation toward Murray."[45] Haruko Wakabayashi (see chapter 11) also clearly demonstrates that Hatakeyama strongly lobbied for the selection of David Murray. Murray and his wife traveled to Tokyo, where he held the position of superintendent of education from 1873 to 1879. He would play a key role in forming education policies in Japan during these early Meiji years (see chapter 12). Although the higher-ranking Tanaka and Kido chose the person for this important position, it is clear that Hatakeyama put the Rutgers professor into strong contention.[46]

Both Hatakeyama Yoshinari and Mori Arinori returned to Japan in 1873. Despite their disagreement over the selection of David Murray, they remained friends. Hatekeyama even joined the Meirokusha Society, a society of intellectuals founded by Fukuzawa Yukichi (1835–1901) and Mori to discuss liberal ideas and Western studies. William Elliot Griffis, who knew Hatakeyama from when they were both students at Rutgers College, was a foreign member of Meirokusha. Hatakeyama was appointed to several positions, often simultaneously, in the Ministry of Education over the next few years. He became the first director of Tokyo Kaisei Gakkō, later to become the University of Tokyo. He also served as curator of the Tokyo Library and the Tokyo Museum.[47] During all of these years, he closely worked with David Murray, who held the number-two position in the Ministry of Education. In April 1876, he joined Vice Minister of Education Tanaka Fujimaro to visit and inspect the Centennial International Exhibition in Philadelphia, Pennsylvania. However, Hatakeyama, who most likely suffered from tuberculosis, died on the return journey to Japan at thirty-four years of age. Marlene Mayo observed that Hatakeyama's death "cut short a promising career and has obscured his enormous contribution to the [Iwakura] Embassy."[48] One could slightly rephrase this observation to state that despite his passing at a relatively early age, Hatakeyama made enormous contributions to Japan during the early Meiji era.

Mori Arinori, a friend of the Satsuma students who studied at Rutgers College (Hatakeyama Yoshinari, Matsumura Junzō, and Yoshida Kiyonari), served in diplomatic posts in Britain and China beginning in 1875. He was then appointed education minister by Prime Minister Itō Hirobumi in 1885. Perhaps ironically, the nation-directed, uniform education policies for Japan he promoted in the late 1880s were similar to those advocated by David Murray in the 1870s. Mori was assassinated in 1889 by a right-wing extremist who believed the education minister had disrespected the Shinto gods during a visit to the Grand Shrines of Ise.[49]

Another connection between Satsuma and New Brunswick during this era was Matsukata Kōjirō (1865–1950), who began his studies at the Rutgers Grammar School in 1885 and later attended Rutgers College. He even played on the football team while at Rutgers. From Kagoshima, in the Satsuma domain, his father was Matsukata Masayoshi, who served as finance minister and then as prime minister (1891–1892, 1896–1898). After his studies in New Brunswick, Matsukata went on to earn a law degree from Yale University. Upon his return to Japan, Matsukata Kojirō worked in shipbuilding and became president of Kawasaki Shipbuilding Company. He expanded the company's business and became president of Kawasaki Dockyards. Unfortunately, economic problems in the post–World War I era significantly hurt Matsukata's shipping business. During the late nineteenth and early twentieth centuries, however, he had amassed a significant collection of artwork, including thousands of traditional Japanese woodblock prints, which are now housed in the Tokyo National

FIGURE 10.3. Matsukata Kōjirō with the Rutgers freshman football team, ca. 1885. (Credit: William Elliot Griffis Collection, Rutgers University Libraries.)

Museum. Especially fond of Western art, he also collected works by Van Gogh, Monet, Gauguin, and Rodin, now housed in the Matsukata Collection at the National Museum of Western Art in Tokyo.[50] It is unclear whether Matsukata's interest in Western art began during his years at Rutgers, but he could have easily visited great art museums in nearby New York City and in not-so-far-away Boston. His legacy continues, because his collections are viewed by more than one million visitors each year to both the Tokyo National Museum and the National Museum of Western Art. In 1988, a major exhibition of the Matsukata Collection was held at the Zimmerli Art Museum at Rutgers University.[51]

Conclusion

After the Meiji Restoration, the province of Satsuma transitioned from a proud principality to the western half of Kagoshima prefecture. Satsuma was well represented, however, in the leadership of the new government. Similarly, the Satsuma students who studied at Rutgers in the nineteenth century—Matsumura Junzō, Yoshida Kiyonari, Hatakeyama Yoshinari, and Matsukata Kōjirō—significantly influenced foreign affairs, the founding of educational institutions, the military, business, and the cultural sphere. Their experiences living and studying in the West, including at Rutgers College in New Brunswick, New Jersey, contributed to internally and externally strengthening Japan in a world being transformed by imperialism and industrialization.

Notes

1 Perry's ships were referred to by Japanese at the time as *kurofune*, literally "black ships," because their hulls were dark and two of the four ships spewed dark smoke from coal-fired steam engines. The color black can also symbolize death, as it does in Japan and much of East Asia. The official account of the Perry expedition is Francis L. Hawks, *Narrative of the Expedition of an American Squadron to the China Seas and Japan* (New York: D. Appleton &, 1857), which was republished as Commodore M. C. Perry, *Narrative of the Expedition to the China Seas and Japan, 1882–1854* (Garden City, NY: Dover, 2000).

2 Known as Rangaku (literally "Dutch studies"), these books arrived by way of the Dutch East India Company merchants in Nagasaki. While these books were usually in the Dutch language, many were translations from other languages, such as German, French, and English.

3 There are several excellent articles on nineteenth-century Japan in Marius Jansen, ed., *The Cambridge History of Japan*, vol. 5, *The Nineteenth Century* (Cambridge: Cambridge University Press, 1989).

4 A series of regulations restricting contact between Japan and Western countries was adopted by the Tokugawa government in the 1630s. These regulations became collectively known as the *sakoku* (closed country) policy. Documents containing these regulations can be found in David J. Lu, *Japan: A Documentary History*, vol. 1 (Armonk, NY: M. E. Sharpe, 1997), 220–223.

5 D. C. Greene, "Correspondence Between William II of Holland and the Shogun of Japan," *Transactions of the Asiatic Society of Japan*, first series, 34 (June 1907). This source contains the original Dutch text of the letter from William II, King of Holland, to the shogun; an English translation; a Japanese translation; and the "Reply of the Shogun's Government to the Government of Holland."

6 Awaji-no-kami Muragaki, *Kōkai Nikki: The Diary of the First Japanese Embassy to the United States*, trans. Helen M. Uno (Tokyo: Foreign Affairs Association of Japan, 1958); Masao Miyoshi, *As We Saw Them: The First Japanese Embassy to the United States* (Berkeley: University of California Press, 1979). James Buchanan was president of the United States from March 4, 1857, to March 4, 1861. He first met with the Japanese delegation on May 17, 1860.

7 Robert K. Sakai, "The Satsuma-Ryukyu Trade and Tokugawa Seclusion Policy," *Journal of Asian Studies* 23, no. 3 (May 1964): 391.

8 Shimazu Tadayoshi was the son of Nariakira and officially the daimyo of Satsuma after his father's death, but Shimazu Hisamitsu was appointed as regent to rule Satsuma on behalf of the youthful Tadayoshi.

9 This bombardment of Kagoshima by the British Royal Navy is sometimes referred to as the Anglo-Satsuma War.

10 Many works on late Tokugawa-era Japan include mention of the Namamugi Incident, with different versions of exactly what happened. William De Lange, *The Namamugi Incident: The Murder That Sparked a War* (Ehime, Japan: Toyo Press, 2020), is an excellent source for this controversial event.

11 Andrew Cobbing, *The Satsuma Students in Britain: Japan's Early Search for the Essence of the West* (London: Japan Library, Curzon Press, 2000), 16. Although it has been cataloged with Andrew Cobbing as the author, *The Satsuma Students in Britain* is actually Cobbing's translation and revision of Takaaki Inuzuka, *Satsuma-han Eikoku Ryūgakusei* (Tokyo: Chūō Kōronsha, 1974).

12 These Chōshū samurai students included Itō Hirobumi, who would later become a prime minister during the Meiji era, and Inoue Kaoru, who would become a foreign minister during the Meiji era. Both Itō and Inoue had returned to Japan before the samurai students from Satsuma arrived in England.

13 Cobbing, *The Satsuma Students in Britain*, 22–23.

14 Ten of the nineteen had leadership positions in addition to being students.

15 They stopped at several British-controlled ports for fuel and provisions along the journey, including Hong Kong, Singapore, Bombay, Crete, and Gibraltar, before arriving at Southampton Harbor.

16 The most extensive collection of materials on the Brotherhood of the New Life is Jack T. Ericsom, ed., *Thomas Lake Harris and the Brotherhood of the New Life: Books, Pamphlets, Serials, and Manuscripts* (Glen Rock, NJ: Microfilming Corporation of America, 1974). For a study, though dated, see Herbert Schneider and George Lawton, *A Prophet and a Pilgrim* (New York: Columbia University Press, 1942).

17 Hayashi Takeji, *Mori Arinori* (Tokyo: Chikuma Shobō, 1986), 238–239. U.S. Bureau of the Census, *Historical Statistics of the United States, Colonial Times to 1957* (Washington, DC: U.S. Department of Commerce, Bureau of the Census, 1960), 59, reveals that sixty-seven Japanese entered the United States in 1867. Most of them were diplomats, businessmen, and a group of acrobats who remained in the country for a short period of time.

18 Joseph Slade, "Historical Sketch of Thomas Lake Harris, Laurence Oliphant, and the Brotherhood of the New Life," in Ericsom, *Thomas Lake Harris*, 15–16.

19 Slade, "Historical Sketch of Thomas Lake Harris," 11.

20 Laurence Oliphant to William Cowper, 1 December 1867, in Hayashi, *Mori Arinori*, 226. Laurence Oliphant regularly corresponded with William and Georgianna Cowper of England during his residence at the Brocton Colony.

21 Laurence Oliphant to William Cowper, September 1867, in Hayashi, *Mori Arinori*, 242.

22 Nagasawa Kanaye would remain with the Brotherhood of the New Life and with Thomas Lake Harris for the rest of his life. He would become one of the most successful Japanese farmers in America with the Fountaingrove Winery in Santa Rosa, California. See Paul Akira Kadota and Terry Earl Jones, *Kanaye Nagasawa: A Biography of a Satsuma Student* (Kagoshima, Japan: Kagoshima Prefectural Junior College, 1990), for a biography of Nagasawa's extraordinary life.

23 Laurence Oliphant to Georgianna Cowper, 6 November 1868, in Hayashi, *Mori Arinori*, 242.

24 Noda (Sameshima) and Sawai (Mori) to "Our dear Brethren," 17 June 1868, in Ericsom, *Thomas Lake Harris*, reel 13, frame 302. This letter is also reproduced in Cobbing, *The Satsuma Students in Britain*, 176–177.

25 Hatekeyama was using the name Sugiura Kōzō; Yoshida was using the name Nagai Iosuke; and Matsumura, whose original name was Ichiki Kanjūrō, continued to use the name Matsumura Junzō for the rest of his life.

26 Ryusuke Tsunoda, Theodore De Bary, and Donald Keene, eds., *Sources of Japanese Tradition*, vol. 2 (New York: Columbia University Press, 1964), 136–137.

27 Leaders from the Tosa and Hizen domains were also part of the new imperial government, though leaders from Satsuma and Chōshū held most of the top positions for much of the Meiji era (1868–1912).

28 Nakahama Manjirō and Hamada Hikozō attended primary schools in the United States in the 1850s, and Niijima Jō began his studies at Amherst College in Massachusetts at the same time as Kusakabe Tarō.

29 *Scarlet Letter* (Rutgers College yearbook, 1873), 37; and *Scarlet Letter* (1874), 33, Special Collections and University Archives, Rutgers University Libraries, New Brunswick, NJ. For a discussion of William Elliot Griffis and other Rutgers alumni in Japan, see Fernanda Perrone, "The Rutgers Network in Early Modern Japan," *Rikkyo American Studies* 39 (March 2017): 79–101.

30 Benjamin Duke, *Dr. David Murray: Superintendent of Education in the Empire of Japan, 1873–1879* (New Brunswick, NJ: Rutgers University Press, 2019), 64.

31 Duke, *Dr. David Murray*, 62–64.

32 Robert Van Valkenberg to Date Chuinguong [*sic*], 19 July 1869, and Date Chuinguong [*sic*] to Japanese Students, 8 July 1869, both in U.S. Department of State, *Despatches from U.S. Ministers to Japan, 1855–1906* (Washington DC: National Archives Microfilm, 1949), reel 12. The U.S. government permitted twelve Japanese to enroll at the Naval Academy from 1869 to 1906, four of whom graduated from the regular course of study.

33 Cobbing, *The Satsuma Students in Britain*, 144.

34 Cobbing, 142. Wilbraham Academy merged with Monson Academy in 1971.

35 Japan Foreign Ministry, *Nihon Gaikō bunshō*, 45 vols. (Tokyo: Gaimushō, 1936–1963), 15:127–158; U.S. Department of State, *Foreign Relations of the United States*, vol. 1, *1879–1880* (Washington, DC: U.S. Government Printing Office, n.d.), 643–649. For a first-person account of Grant's visit to Japan, see James D. McCabe, ed., *A Tour Around the World by General Grant* (Philadelphia: National, 1880).

36 Numerous letters to friends, family, and colleagues by both David Murray and Martha Murray cited in Duke, *Dr. David Murray*, attest to this mutual respect and fondness.

37 Meanwhile, Sameshima Naonobu—Hatakeyama and Mori's compatriot from Satsuma and fellow student in London and at the Brotherhood of the New Life colony in New York—was appointed Japan's chargé d'affaires in London, with simultaneous responsibilities in Paris and Berlin.

38 Five of the Japanese students were young girls and three would eventually graduate from American colleges (two from Vassar College and one from Bryn Mawr).

39 Kume Kunitake, comp., *The Iwakura Embassy, 1871–73*, vol. 1, *The United States of America*, trans. Martin Colcutt (Richmond, Surrey, UK: The Japan Documents, Curzon Press, 2002).

40 Takayoshi Kido, *The Diary of Kido Takayoshi*, vol. 1, trans. Sidney D. Brown and Akiko Hirota (Tokyo: University of Tokyo Press, 1985), 142, 147, 154, 167, 181.

41 Kido, 153.

42 Marlene J. Mayo, "The Western Education of Kume Kunitake, 1871–76," *Monumenta Nipponica* 28, no. 1 (Spring 1973): 11.

43 *Japanese Religion* (Tokyo: Kodansha International, 1972), 83. This book was published under the direction of the Japanese government's Agency for Cultural Affairs. Nakamura Masanao (also known as Nakamura Keiu) was a member of a Tokugawa government group of students in Britain from 1866 to 1868. He

translated and published Samuel Smiles's *Self Help* and John Stuart Mill's *On Liberty*, which were widely read in Japan in the 1870s. See chapter 8.

44 Duke, *Dr. David Murray*, 106.

45 Duke, 121.

46 See chapter 4 in Duke, *Dr. David Murray*, for a detailed discussion of Murray's selection for this position.

47 Cobbing, *The Satsuma Students in Britain*, 141.

48 Mayo, 12. See also chapter 11 for an account of Hatakeyama's influence on early Meiji Japan.

49 Mori was assassinated on February 11, 1889, the same day Emperor Meiji formally announced the Meiji Constitution.

50 See chapter 4 in David M. Challis, *Foreign Currency Volatility and the Market for French Modernist Art* (Leiden: Brill, 2021), for an examination of Matsukata's interest in Western art.

51 Julia Meech, *The Matsukata Collection of Ukiyo-e Prints: Masterpieces from the Tokyo National Museum (Jane Voorhees Zimmerli Art Museum)* (New Brunswick, NJ: Rutgers University Press, 1989). See also William Zimmer, "Prints from Tokyo at Rutgers Zimmerli," *New York Times*, April 17, 1988.

11

The Rutgers Network and the Iwakura Mission

Guido F. Verbeck and Hatakeyama Yoshinari

HARUKO WAKABAYASHI

> May 5th. . . . Daybreak came in New Brunswick of the New Jersey state. This is the city where the famous school is [located].[1]

The above lines appear in the official record of the Iwakura Mission, a diplomatic embassy headed by Iwakura Tomomi (1825–1883) sent by Japan to the United States and Europe. On December 23, 1871, the mission left Yokohama with several aims: to gain recognition for the new Meiji state by presenting a message from the Japanese emperor to the heads of treaty nations, to start renegotiations of the "unequal" treaties detrimental to Japan's interests, and to investigate the institutions of advanced Western nations.[2] It arrived at San Francisco in January 1872, and after four months in Washington, DC, its delegates passed by New Brunswick while heading to New York by rail via Jersey City. The "famous school" (*yūmei naru gakkō*) referred to is undoubtedly Rutgers College. As discussed in earlier chapters, Rutgers and its preparatory Rutgers Grammar School had become home to dozens of Japanese students by 1872, including Iwakura's two sons, Tomosada (Tatsu, 1852–1910) and Tomotsune (Asahi, 1853–1890).[3] Like many of their compatriots at Rutgers, the Iwakura brothers had studied in Nagasaki under Guido F. Verbeck (1830–1898). They left for New Brunswick in 1870, accompanied by Orita Hikoichi, Hattori Ichizō, and Yamamoto Jūsuke;[4] Katsu Kaishū's son, Koroku, accompanied by Tomita Tetsunosuke and Takaki Saburō, had arrived ahead of them. They were joined in New Brunswick by three students from the Satsuma domain—Hatakeyama Yoshinari, Matsumura Junzō, and Yoshida Kiyonari.

Although the mission's official itinerary included neither Rutgers nor New Brunswick, the Rutgers network was indispensable in its planning and implementation. First and foremost, Guido F. Verbeck shared his vision for such a mission with his former student Ōkuma Shigenobu (1838–1922), who forwarded it to Iwakura, a senior counselor in the Meiji government.[5] Verbeck advised that the embassy's main goal should be to observe and learn rather than to seek treaty revision. He further proposed a structure that would best serve this purpose and suggested ways to disseminate the knowledge acquired to the general public. As William E. Griffis asserted in 1900, "It may be said without any exaggeration whatever, that Guido F. Verbeck was the originator and organizer [of the Iwakura Mission]."[6]

Lesser known, yet equally important, were the Japanese students and alumni of Rutgers College and Rutgers Grammar School whose knowledge, experience, and linguistic skills contributed to the mission's success, most notably Hatakeyama Yoshinari (1842–1876), who attended Rutgers from 1868 to 1871. Upon the arrival of the mission to the United States, he was appointed as third secretary and was "ordered always to be in attendance on the ambassador wherever he went, to ask questions and to make a complete record of each event."[7] Equally important was his leading role in the commission for overseas students, organized by the mission's members, which determined the regulations that governed Japanese students studying abroad. Furthermore, he was instrumental in the appointment of David Murray, who subsequently spearheaded Japan's educational reform, as the superintendent of the Ministry of Education. Upon his return to Japan in 1873, Hatakeyama joined the Ministry of Education and later became the first president of the Kaisei Gakkō (present-day University of Tokyo). This chapter focuses on the critical roles played by Verbeck, Hatakeyama, and the Rutgers network in facilitating Meiji Japan's most important diplomatic mission and laying the foundations of modern education in Japan.

Guido Verbeck and His "Brief Sketch"

From the outset, the primary diplomatic agenda of the new Meiji government was the revision of "unequal treaties" that granted extraterritorial privileges to foreign residents and fixed low tariffs.[8] The timing was critical, as Article XIII of the Treaty of Amity and Commerce—signed in July 1858 between Japan and the United States and also called the "Harris Treaty"—stated that the treaty would be subject to revision as desired by either government after July 4, 1872, with one year's notice.[9] As early as the first month of Meiji 1 (1868), the newly established government announced that Japan would continue to respect the treaties signed during the Tokugawa regime while intending to revise them. In the second month of Meiji 2 (1869), Senior Counselor Iwakura Tomomi submitted a proposal for Japan to "send an Imperial envoy to pay his respects to the monarchs and presidents of other countries and to discuss the problem of revising the treaties."[10] In response to this proposal, Verbeck sent an opinion paper known as the "Brief Sketch" to Ōkuma, now in charge of foreign affairs.[11] Ōkuma had put the paper aside, judging that it was too early to discuss the matter, but in October 1871, Iwakura Tomomi abruptly called on Verbeck, whom he knew not only as an advisor to the government but also as the teacher of his sons, who were now studying at Rutgers. This connection, as well as Verbeck's reputation as an educator and a political advisor, would have added to Iwakura's trust in Verbeck. Iwakura had the paper translated for him and requested several interviews with Verbeck to go over his ideas. Verbeck noted in his letter to John Ferris that "[a]t the end he told me it was the *very* and the *only* thing for them to do, and that my program should be carried out to the letter."[12]

The "Brief Sketch" attests to Verbeck's critical role in designing and defining the goals of the Iwakura Mission. While supporting the idea of a mission, Verbeck proposed that treaty revision not be its main purpose; instead, it should focus on communicating to America and European countries Japan's undertaking of major reforms and its wish to maintain peaceful ties while improving relationships with treaty nations. He further suggested that it would be most appropriate to inquire of these nations what measures the government of Japan should take to implement its desired reforms and to investigate and learn from them. More importantly, he stated that "personal experience is necessary to understand the theory of civilization so thoroughly as to enable one to introduce it into other parts" and that "there is no evidence so convincing as that of the eyes." To fully understand the conditions of the West, he wrote, Japan had "not only to know the underlying reasons, but also to observe the practical operations."[13]

According to Verbeck, the merits of such a mission were twofold. First, the knowledge acquired in the West would help create a new Japan; second, by going and speaking to the governments of the treaty nations, Japanese officials would be able to determine what they would need to do to be treated as equals. Only after "raising the country to a perfect political equality with the States of the West" could Japan begin its negotiations for treaty revisions.[14] He further noted that Europe and America had experimented with every imaginable system of government, finance, and education over the centuries, and therefore, "there may be seen, in the greatest variety, excellences to be studied and imitated, as well as defects to

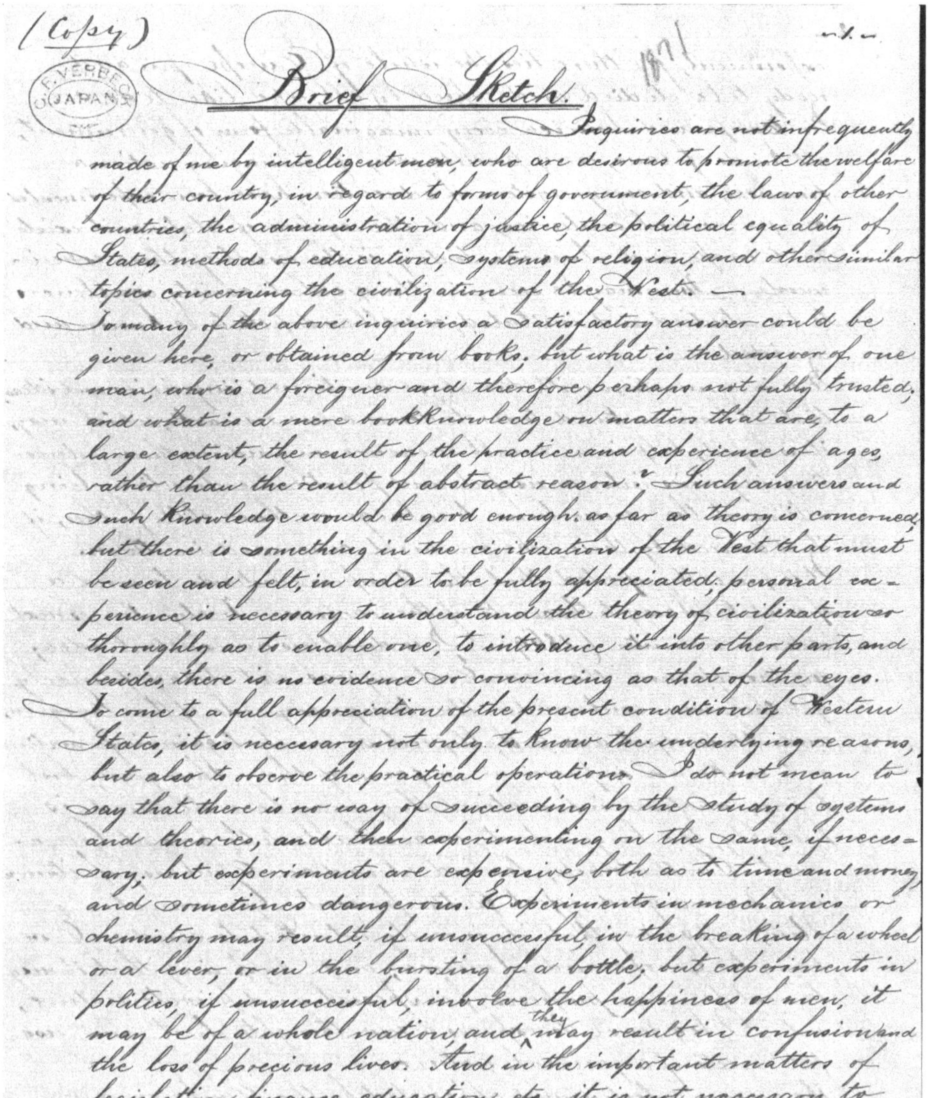

FIGURE 11.1. First page of the "Brief Sketch" by Guido F. Verbeck. (Credit: Archives of the Reformed Church in America.)

be known and avoided."[15] For him, the countries whose institutions deserved thorough study were France, England, Prussia, Holland, and the United States—namely, the theories and applications of their constitutions and laws, financial regulations and institutions, as well as education, military, and religious systems.[16]

In his "Brief Sketch," Verbeck also offered counsel on who should constitute the mission, advising that "the person selected and appointed by the Emperor and Government to the important office of Chief Ambassador ought to be a man of high position, in whom the Emperor and the nation have full confidence on account of his intelligence, vigor, and high character."[17] As he explained, "Such a man's advice . . . will be very valuable, and likely to be followed for the promotion of the welfare of the nation" on his return. He further suggested that the mission's other officers should all be men of intellect and character—perhaps "a Kuge [aristocrat] and a Daimio [domain lord]."[18]

Scholars have analyzed the complex political factors behind the selection of Iwakura as chief ambassador and the mission's other members.[19] The new Meiji government at the time was split between the faction led by Iwakura and the former leaders of Satsuma and Chōshū (Ōkubo Toshimichi, Itō Hirobumi, Kido Takayoshi) and that led by the courtier Sanjō Sanetomi and the former leaders of Tosa and Hizen (Ōkuma, Itagaki Taisuke, Etō Shinpei). According to Tanaka Akira, the mission, which Ōkuma had proposed, was initially planned for Ōkuma to serve as its ambassador. However, Iwakura and Ōkubo feared that giving Ōkuma and his allies leadership in foreign policy would inevitably allow them to dominate the government.[20] In the fall of 1871, Iwakura successfully convinced Kido, Saigō Takamori, Itagaki, and even Sanjō Sanetomi to appoint him as chief ambassador;[21] it was also around this time that he met with Verbeck to discuss the mission. Verbeck's advice to send "a man of high position" certainly aligned with the appointment of Iwakura over Ōkuma. Iwakura, aged forty-six, was a courtier from a prestigious aristocratic family, a close advisor to the emperor, and a central figure in the new Meiji government. Ōkuma, while a prominent member of the government, was a relatively young man of thirty-three. In terms of age and career, Iwakura was undeniably the candidate "in whom the Emperor and the nation [would] have full confidence."

In addition to leading officials, Verbeck specified that special commissions, each consisting of three officers and a secretary, must be appointed "with a special view to their abilities for the commission on which they are respectively to serve." These would consist of four commissions: one to examine constitutions and laws, one to examine financial regulations and institutions, one to examine schools and educational systems, and one to examine armies and navies.[22] Accordingly, the respective commissioners (*rijikan*), accompanied by one to six officers, were appointed from each of the following departments: the Bureau of Census and the Treasury Department (Tanaka Mitsuaki), the Imperial Court (Higashikuze Michitomi), the Imperial Army (Yamada Akiyoshi), the Department of Education (Tanaka Fujimaro), the Public Works Department (Hida Tameyoshi), and the Judicial Department (Sasaki Takayuki).[23]

Last but not least, Verbeck advised that the above secretaries compile detailed reports of all they saw and heard and obtain all possible information to publish the mission's results "for the general benefit and enlightenment of the nation."[24] Another paper he submitted detailed in ten points how the mission's experiences should be written,[25] including the recommendation that the government appoint

FIGURE 11.2. Members of the Extraordinary and Plenipotentiary Iwakura Mission. (Credit: Yamaguchi Prefectural Archives.)

a veteran historiographer to compile its records. The prose was to be elegantly but simply written and the published work to be sold at a price low enough for even poor people to afford.[26] The year 1878 saw the creation of the *Tokumei zenken taishi Beiō kairan jikki* (A True Account of the Ambassador Extraordinary and Plenipotentiary's Journey of Observation of America and Europe), a five-volume diary account of the journey compiled by Kume Kunitake and issued by the Daijōkan (Great Council of State).[27] This text embodied the realization of Verbeck's plan—a publication to benefit and enlighten the public—and it had a lasting impact on the people of the Meiji era, driving them to transform Japan into a modern nation.

On the eighth day of the tenth month of Meiji 4 (1871), the appointment of Iwakura Tomomi as the mission's ambassador extraordinary and plenipotentiary was announced. Kido Takayoshi and Ōkubo Toshimichi were appointed its vice ambassadors, to be assisted by Deputy Ambassadors Yamaguchi Naoyoshi and Itō Hirobumi. In addition, clerks and commissioners were assigned to prepare reports of their investigations, making a total of forty-six official members. With additional junior officials, students, and the five young girls sent to stay and study in the United States, the group totaled 107 people. It included Kume, who was tasked with recording and compiling the embassy's observations.

The Iwakura Mission left Yokohama for San Francisco on the twelfth day of the eleventh month of Meiji 4 (1871). It traveled to twelve nations—the United

States, Britain, France, Belgium, the Netherlands, Germany, Russia, Denmark, Sweden, Italy, Austria, and Switzerland—before returning to Yokohama on the thirteenth day of the ninth month of Meiji 6 (1873). While it did not completely follow Verbeck's "Brief Sketch," as Griffis noted, the document was instrumental in the planning of what Tanaka Akira assesses as the mission of the largest and highest quality among those sent during the Bakumatsu and Meiji periods.[28]

Hatakeyama at Rutgers

The Iwakura Mission arrived at its first destination, San Francisco, on January 15, 1872. It then traveled through Sacramento, Salt Lake City, and Chicago, and it reached Washington, DC, on February 29. In Washington, it was met by Mori Arinori, Japan's chargé d'affaires to the United States, and Hatakeyama Yoshinari, a former Rutgers student who had been recruited to assist the mission.[29] As discussed in chapter 10, Mori and Hatakeyama, known as "Kozo Soogiwoora" at Rutgers, were two of the first fifteen students secretly sent by the Satsuma domain to study in England in 1865.[30] After attending University College London for a year, they left for Brocton, New York, together with Sameshima Naonobu, Yoshida Kiyonari, Matsumura Junzō, and Nagasawa Kanaye, to join the Brotherhood of the New Life, Thomas Lake Harris's Christian spiritualist community. In 1868, Mori and Sameshima returned to Japan following the Meiji Restoration; Hatakeyama, Matsumura, and Yoshida went to New Brunswick in search of further opportunities for Western education, and they entered Rutgers College that fall.[31] Matsumura and Yoshida moved on to the Naval Academy in Annapolis and Wilbraham Academy in Massachusetts, respectively, and Hatakeyama chose to stay at Rutgers.[32] Hatakeyama's experiences as a *ryūgakusei* and the wide network of friends and acquaintances he established while at Rutgers helped him accomplish some of the mission's most critical tasks.

As mentioned in chapter 4, New Brunswick had become a hub of Japanese students on the East Coast around this time, and Hatakeyama soon assumed a leadership role among them. He is interviewed in the article, "The Japanese in College," published on June 23, 1870, in the New York newspaper *The Sun*, as a representative of the fourteen Japanese students studying in New Brunswick and the only one who could speak English well enough.[33] According to his mentor, David Murray, "His experience and knowledge of the language were always at [the Japanese students'] disposal"; subsequently, the Japanese government, "realizing the value of his services to his fellow students in America appointed him as their guardian and superintendent."[34] Multiple letters that Hatakeyama wrote to Ferris, the transcriptions of which can be found in the William E. Griffis Collection at Rutgers University, attest to his care and management of his compatriots, including oversight of their finances. His letter dated December 31, 1869, for example, thanked Ferris for sending a fifty-dollar check for a student named Kodama and reported that "Shimats" and three other students "do study pretty hard now so that they are getting on nicely in their studies of English,"[35] adding a mention that his "time is considerably occupied in teaching them."[36] Another letter, dated May 14, 1870, suggested that he managed his friend Kusakabe Tarō's death in the previous month. "This morning," he wrote, "I received yours of yesterday in which you enclosed check for two hundred & ninety-five Dollars ($295) the remainder of the amount we wished on account of Kusakabe. I am very much obliged to you for your kindness and K. talking of pain so much for our request while you are very busy in your work."[37]

In 1871, while still a senior at Rutgers "expecting to graduate with high honors," Hatakeyama received orders from the new Meiji government to return home and examine Europe's educational systems on his way back.[38] A farewell party held at the St. Nicholas Hotel in New York on August 14 was attended by twenty-six Japanese students, including Prince Kachōnomiya Hirotsune and his attendants, who had been studying in Brooklyn; those from New Brunswick, including Shiramine Shunme, Takaki Saburō, and Hattori Ichizō; and others from as far as Boston, Connecticut, and Philadelphia.[39] The list attests to the extensive network of Japanese students on the East Coast to which Hatakeyama belonged.

Hatakeyama's American friends and teachers at Rutgers held him in equally high regard. David Murray writes that "his diligence, capacity and amiable character endeared him to his associates and instructors."[40] A letter written by Professor D. T. Reiley to "Their Excellencies the Ministers of Education of the Japanese Empire," dated September 27, 1871, underscores how Hatakeyama established himself as the caretaker of the Japanese students in New Brunswick. Reiley further expresses regret that "Mr. Soogiwoora" had been recalled home and hopes that he will be permitted to return soon, continuing:

> No person either Japanese or American so well understands all the necessities of the Japanese students in this country. His experience, [*sic*] is so great, his studies have been so varied, his judgement [*sic*] is so discriminating and his manner is so pleasant that he best of all can understand and obviate all the difficulties that surround your students here. There must be some such person to direct them else their education will be full of mistakes & failures by which at last their country must suffer. A great hope of Japan is in education & especially in those students receiving this education abroad. While we know that Mr. Soogiwoora will be very useful to his country everywhere, we hope that you will not consider it an interference if we say that Mr. Soogiwoora will be of the greatest service to his country in directing to education of his

FIGURE 11.3. Hatakeyama Yoshinari in Western dress, ca. 1868. Photo by D. Clark Studio. (Credit: William Elliot Griffis Collection, Rutgers University Libraries.)

> countrymen abroad. He has gained the esteem of every one [*sic*] for his character & high principles.[41]

Reiley's letter shows that the professors at Rutgers also acknowledged and appreciated Hatakeyama's leadership of the Japanese students and saw him as someone who would be missed. Ironically, Hatakeyama returned to the United States not long after he left, because he was called back from Europe to join the Iwakura Mission. He was appointed third secretary, and the network he had created in New Brunswick would prove useful for achieving the tasks assigned to him in this capacity.

Hatakeyama, the Iwakura Mission, and the Commission for Overseas Students

One of the Iwakura Mission's main purposes was to observe educational institutions in the West.[42] This plan was clearly spelled out in the emperor's proclamation of the mission's goals, which stated the aim of investigating "various rules of education in each country, in other words researching the methods of education, establishment of public and private schools, methods of collecting funds, order of courses taken (curriculum), rules and formats of certificates awarded to the various ranks; examine closely the institutions and workings of public and private schools, schools of commerce, art schools, hospitals, nursery schools—with the goal of finding the methods by which we may adopt and establish the same in our country."[43]

Six Ministry of Education officials, headed by commissioner and Deputy Minister Tanaka Fujimaro (1845–1909), were appointed to the mission. Vice-Ambassador Kido Takayoshi (1833–1877) was deeply interested in Western educational systems and worked closely with Tanaka throughout the trip, visiting schools, universities, museums, and other institutions of public education; he was appointed minister of education upon his return.[44] Verbeck in his "Brief Sketch" identified the United States as a country particularly instructive to observe in the area of education,[45] and the detailed reports on American educational institutions in the mission's official record indicate that the delegates heeded his advice.[46] However, the mission had two other key education-related assignments: reviewing the status and regulations of the government-sponsored Japanese students in Western countries and appointing a Ministry of Education superintendent who would spearhead the modernization of Japan's educational system.[47] The Rutgers network, and Hatakeyama in particular, played a key role in achieving these tasks.

One of the first duties assigned to Hatakeyama as a member of the mission was to serve on the committee to review the state of the Japanese students studying overseas.[48] Since the Meiji era's inception, the leaders of Japan's new government had been enthusiastic about sending students to the West to acquire knowledge. Article Five of the Charter Oath, drafted by Yuri Kimimasa, a former retainer of Matsudaira Shungaku, and promulgated by Emperor Meiji on April 6, 1868, famously proclaimed, "Knowledge shall be sought throughout the world in order to promote the welfare of the empire." Accordingly, Ōkubo Toshimichi, among others, had proposed to Iwakura as early as the twelfth month of Meiji 1 that the government establish policies to send promising members of aristocratic and samurai families overseas, which would nurture a new group of leaders who would speed up Japan's modernization. During its first years, the Meiji government encouraged the domains and the newly established Daigaku Nankō to recruit students eager to, and capable of, studying abroad. Ishizuki Minoru shows that a total of 586 Japanese students were sent to Europe and the

United States between 1868 and 1874, many of whom were sponsored either by individual domains or the government. Of these students, 223 went to the United States, with 86 already there when the Iwakura Mission arrived in 1872.[49]

In fact, almost half of the students who studied abroad chose to go to the United States for several possible reasons. First, the United States was the Western nation geographically and diplomatically closest to Japan, because it had been the first country with which Japan had signed a treaty. Second, American missionaries were already active in the field of education by training Japanese youths in Western languages and sciences, sending students to schools in the United States and inviting American teachers and advisors to Japan. Third, America as a young nation was viewed as a model for a newly rising Japan.[50] With the rapid increase in the number of students sent abroad, however, issues inevitably emerged. Many students were academically unprepared to study at Western institutions, and there was a growing sense of inequity in the selection process. Furthermore, the abolition of the domain system (*haihan chiken*) and the return of shogunal authority to the emperor in 1871 meant that the central government was now responsible for funding the educational and living expenses of students who had been initially sponsored by their respective former domains; this support was increasingly straining government finances. One of the nine articles in the imperial rescript issued on February 29, 1872, outlining the mission's goals, tasked the Iwakura Mission with reviewing the status of overseas students: "Examine and ascertain the subjects and training being received by students sent to study abroad using government funds to various countries. Order those not performing well or engaging in misconduct to return home. Furthermore, reevaluate expenses for students studying abroad and verify the laws [to which they are subject]."[51]

Accordingly, on March 8, 1872, twelve men were summoned to Washington, DC, to serve on the committee headed by Mori and Tanaka to ascertain the status of overseas Japanese students. Its members' names, shown in the order listed, are as in table 11.1.[52] All of them, except Hiraga Yoshinari, an official member of the Iwakura Mission, and Niijima Jō were natives of Satsuma and Chōshū or students of Katsu Kaishū. However, rather than tying this group to these respective networks, we could see it as a product of the Rutgers network that was linked to Satsuma, Chōshū, and Katsu. Of the twelve members listed above, seven (marked by an asterisk before their names) had studied in New Brunswick: two were from Satsuma, three had accompanied Katsu's son, and two had accompanied Iwakura's sons. Furthermore, Hatakeyama's name is listed second, after Hiraga's; he is then followed by Yoshihara Shigetoshi, another Satsuma student also officially appointed to the mission, and Toyama Masakazu, Mori's secretary.[53] This list strongly suggests that Hatakeyama played a leading role in the committee and may even have been responsible for selecting its members.

Hatakeyama would certainly have been an ideal leader of this committee. As mentioned earlier, he had taken charge of the Japanese students while at

Table 11.1
Members of the Commission on Overseas Students

Name (dates)	Pre-Meiji affiliation	Role in the United States and overseas study experience
Hiraga Yoshinari (Yoshimoto, 1826–1882)	Fukuoka	Official member of the Iwakura Mission; studied in Boston, 1867–1870
* Soogiwoora Kōzō (Hatakeyama Yoshinari)	Satsuma	Member of the first group of Satsuma students; studied at Rutgers College, 1868–1871
Ōhara Reinosuke (Yoshihara Shigetoshi, 1845–1887)	Satsuma	Member of the second group of Satsuma students; studied at Monson Academy, 1866, and then at Yale College, 1869–1870
Toyama Sutehachi (Masakazu, 1848–1900)	Former Tokugawa retainer	Secretary of Mori Arinori; studied in England, 1866–1868, through a recommendation from Katsu Kaishū
*Tomita Tetsunosuke	Sendai	Student of Katsu Kaishū and accompanied Koroku to New Brunswick; studied at Bryant, Stratton, and Whitney's Business College in Newark, 1870–1871; appointed acting consul of the Consulate of Japan in New York in March 1872
*Yamamoto Jūsuke	Chōshū	Accompanied the Iwakura brothers to New Brunswick; studied at Rutgers Grammar School and then at Rensselaer Polytechnic Institute in Troy, New York, 1870–1872
*Hattori Ichizō (1851–1929)	Chōshū	Accompanied the Iwakura brothers to New Brunswick; studied at Rutgers Grammar School and Rutgers College, 1870–1875
*Takaki Saburō	Shōnai	Student of Katsu Kaishū; accompanied Koroku to New Brunswick and studied at Rutgers Grammar School, 1869–1871; appointed secretary to Mori Arinori in Washington, DC, in 1871
Niijima Shimeta (Jō, 1843–1890)[1]	Annaka	Stowaway to the United States in 1864; studied at Amherst College, 1867–1870
* Matsumura Junzō	Satsuma	Member of the first group of Satsuma students; studied at Rutgers College and transferred to the U.S. Naval Academy in 1869
Nawa Yurumu (?)	Chōshū	Accompanied Mori Arinori to the United States in 1871
* Shiramine Shunme (1847–1909)	Nagaoka	Student of Katsu Kaishū; studied at Rutgers College for one term in 1871

[1] Niijima was the first Japanese student to graduate from an American college. He wrote in a letter that he met two Japanese students attending Monson Academy in 1867, most likely from the second group of Satsuma students that included Yoshihara Shigetoshi. See John Van Sant, *Pacific Pioneers: Japanese Journeys to America and Hawaii, 1850–80* (Urbana: University of Illinois Press, 2000), 64–78.

Rutgers, and he had stayed abroad long enough to observe their financial difficulties, academic challenges, and health issues. He himself had experienced hardships as a student in a foreign land. According to Inuzuka Takaaki, Hatakeyama had initially hoped to study military science and aspired to enter the United States Military Academy West Point; however, the stakes were too high for a Japanese student to be allowed entrance.[54] Furthermore, as Japan was experiencing political upheaval when he arrived, the necessary funds did not reach him and his fellow Satsuma students in time, leaving them in constant financial difficulties that forced them to borrow from Ferris and others. And Hatakeyama had also witnessed the death of his friend, Kusakabe Tarō.

A copy of an opinion paper that Hatakeyama wrote while in England, dated December 18, 1871, attests to his concerns regarding these issues prior to joining the committee.[55] He begins by stating that students lacking proper supervision and guidance cannot accomplish their academic goals in either normal or specialized studies.[56] He next offers detailed and constructive proposals for the Japanese government to appoint a supervisor in England who would ensure an environment that facilitated students' learning; such a supervisor, he emphasized, would need to know every student's background—name, age, family, education received, length of stay and stipend while in England, health history, and whether they had previously studied Western languages or subjects. This overseer would also report on students' progress every six months and listen to their concerns and complaints.[57] Hatakeyama further included instructions on what to do when a student fell sick, and one easily imagines that his ideas were shared at the committee meeting held in Washington, DC, in March of the following year.

Niijima Jō recounts this meeting in two letters to his benefactors in Boston, Mr. and Mrs. Hardy, dated March 8 and 10, 1872, reproduced as follows:

> The object of our meeting is to make statutes for the Japanese students who are supported by the government in the foreign countries. . . . Several topics for discussion were given out by Mr. Mori. The parties divided the topics and met in different rooms to discuss their own topics. This morning we met together and brought our separately discussed topics into the general assembly. The commissioner was appointed our chairman, but he did not appear this morning. I rather suspect that he is somewhat afraid of us, because we, the students in this country, are the true democratic. We do not hesitate to say anything. Last Saturday we made a petition to the chief ambassador to grant us a power to make a statute by the vote of majority, and when it is passed we may order it even to the Commissioner of the Educational Department. So we have more power of making statutes pertaining to students in the foreign countries than the minister himself.[58]

Niijima does not delve into the topics discussed at this meeting, but his letter provides a vivid picture of how the committee was run. Hatakeyama's record of the meeting in his notebook attests to its democratic nature and structure as described by Niijima. Hatakeyama also indicated that the committee broke into smaller groups to discuss individual topics, and he recorded the agenda covered during the session as follows:

- Regulating students sponsored by the government choose a specific subject to study
- Investigating students currently abroad and not upholding conduct as expected, academically insufficient, or sick
- Selecting students who have requested government sponsorship from among those currently on private sponsorship
- Handling of school expenses
- Determining school expenses depending on academic progress
- Investigating procedures to submit students' progress and health conditions to the embassy in timely fashion
- Examining how to handle the death of a student

The death of Kusakabe Tarō in 1870 had likely prompted discussion of the final agenda item.

In September 1872, the statutes for government-funded students studying abroad were revised. Details were also added to the First National Plan for Education, which was again supplemented in April 1873. The new regulations brought all overseas government-sponsored students under the supervision of the Ministry of Education through Japan's ambassadors in each country; they also stipulated the annual number of students sent, the number of years they could stay, and the fair selection of students through examinations. Furthermore, in December 1873, after the Iwakura Mission had returned, the government issued an order that all government-sponsored overseas students should return to Japan within sixty days for review and reapproval.[59] How many of the committee's proposals were adopted is difficult to ascertain, but it is evident that their suggestions helped the government to comprehend the conditions and needs of overseas students.

Hatakeyama and David Murray

In addition to surveying the state of overseas Japanese students, the Iwakura Mission was responsible for finding a Western advisor for the newly established Ministry of Education. In February 1872, prior to the mission's arrival in Washington, DC, Mori Arinori sent letters to American educators seeking advice on how to develop a modern educational system in Japan.[60] William H. Campbell, president of Rutgers College, passed this letter on to David Murray (1830–1905), professor of mathematics at Rutgers from 1863 to 1873.[61] Murray had been instrumental in creating Rutgers's science curriculum and successfully lobbying for the school to become the New Jersey land-grant college in 1864. He was a teacher and friend to many Japanese students at Rutgers, and according to a local newspaper issued in 1910, "[t]hese young men referred to Dr. Murray's residence as their 'American Home' and spent much of their leisure time there."[62]

Murray's response, which spans more than twenty pages, offers a comprehensive and detailed analysis of education and its impacts on modern society. His advice, addressed specifically to the needs of Japan and its people, included the establishment of universal education and education for women.[63] Most notably, and owing perhaps to the knowledge of Japan and its people that he had acquired through his acquaintance with the Japanese students at Rutgers, he expressed confidence in the prospects of education in Japan and suggested reforms to retain its native traditions and spirit. While Mori's first choice for the position is known to have been Birdsey Northrop, an educator and a member of Connecticut's Board of Education, Northrop ultimately declined the offer, leading to Murray being deemed an ideal candidate for three reasons: First, he produced the most thoughtful and knowledgeable response to Mori's inquiries; second, he was a professor of natural sciences who would not clash with those concerned about Christian proselytizing and the hiring of too many Westerners with religious affiliations in Japan; and third, he had demonstrated his administrative skills through establishing the Scientific School at Rutgers.[64] Most importantly, Murray had taught many of the Japanese students at Rutgers, including Iwakura's two sons and Hatakeyama, and the latter had now become a trusted member of the mission.

Sources attest to the key role the Rutgers network played in Murray's appointment, including a copy of an 1872 letter sent to Hatakeyama from D. T. Reiley, the same professor who had written to express his regret over Hatakeyama's departure from Rutgers:[65]

> New Brunswick, March 18th
>
> Mr. Soogiwoora
>
> I would desire to present the name of Prof. David Murray of New Brunswick as a suitable person for the position of superintendent of education. You & many of the Japanese students know personally of his high character [*sic*] entire trustworthiness. He has had a lifelong experience in education in school & college. He is a scholar & learned especially in scientific studies. He has shown his ability in organization since he has been in New Brunswick & especially in the formation of the scientific school of Rutgers College. While he is familiar with all branches of education & learning he would be especially valuable in establishing scientific & technological schools & colleges which I believe are the first great need of Japan.

Prof. Murray is a valuable man here & we should regret very much to lose him but if he should be selected for this responsible position we should congratulate him on his wider sphere of usefulness. Judge Bradley of the Supreme Court at Washington & senator Frelinghuysen are graduates & trustees of Rutgers College & you may refer to them for such information as you desire.

Yours truly
D. T. Reiley

The letter suggests that Hatakeyama consulted Reiley, his former professor, on how he could lobby for Murray. Both Joseph P. Bradley (1813–1892) and Frederick T. Frelinghuysen (1817–1885), whom Reiley mentions, were Rutgers alumni from the class of 1836 and influential political figures at the time. It seems that Rutgers's American network helped secure an impressive list of supporters within a few months. A copy of another letter included in Hatakeyama's memo, addressed to the embassy and dated June 24, 1872, reads as follows:[66]

To the Honorable, the Japanese Embassy

Having learned that among other duties in this country your Honorable Embassy has been charged with that of examining the Educational Institutions of the United States, with a view to the introduction of modifications into the system of education in Japan and as friends of education and well-wishers of your great and progressive Empire being anxious that whatever changes are introduced in your system may be such as the best experience of this country can suggest.

We earnestly recommend to your Honorable Embassy Professor David Murray at Rutgers College in New Jersey as a competent and suitable person to give such counsel and assistance in the work of educational reform in Japan as your Government may require. Professor Murray's experience in matters connected with the organization and management of Higher Institutions of learning and the special attention he has given to scientific and technical education, together with his enthusiasm [*sic*] interest in the progress of Japan, render him peculiarly qualified for so responsible a task.

Wm. H. Campbell
President of Rutgers College

Frank T. Frelinghuysen
US Senator

Joseph Henry[67]
Secy. Smithsonian Institution

Isaac Ferris[68]
Enr: Chancellor of University of N.Y.C.

Joseph P. Bradley
Judge of Supreme Court U.S.
Howard Crosby[69]
Chancellor of University of N.Y.C.
Geo. H. Cook[70]
V. Prest. Rutgers College & State Geologist N.J.
I.W. Jackson[71]
Senior Prof. of Univ. C.
Elipht N. Potter[72]
President of Univer. C.
M.B. Anderson[73]
Presit. University of Rochester
Johnt. L. Pruyn[74]
Chancellor of the Univer. of New York
S.B. Woolworth[75]
Secretary of Regents of the University
Chas. H. Bell[76]
Rear admiral US Navy

Kido Takayoshi, as vice-ambassador in charge of educational affairs, and Tanaka Fujimaro, as commissioner from the Ministry of Education, were charged with making the selection. Kido's frequent references to Hatakeyama in his diary suggest that the latter had become a trusted companion who would have had ample opportunities to promote Murray, his former professor. Kido began visiting Hatakeyama from April 22, 1872, when he went to Hatakeyama's place "to look over a newly translated version of the [U.S.] Constitution."[77] He visited him again on April 24 to "examine the Constitution of the United States" and again on May 1, 2, and 3. On May 11, he "studied the American system of government all day at Sugiura's," visited him again on May 12, and studied the *Science of Government* together with him on May 13.[78] From time to time, the two also went on leisurely walks.[79] On June 4, at Hatakeyama's residence, they were joined by Matsumura Junzō, whom Kido describes in his diary as "a man of strong character, one on whom we may rely in the future."[80]

These regular visits with Hatakeyama, often in the evenings, continued through May and June while Kido was in Washington, DC. Meanwhile, he exchanged letters with Tanaka, who was on excursions visiting educational institutions accompanied by Niijima Jō.[81] On July 13, Kido wrote a note with a red circle next to it in his diary: "At Sugiura's request, I sent a letter to Tanaka Fujimaro."[82] It is likely that by this time, Hatakeyama had convinced Kido that Murray would best fit the position.[83] Records indicate that Murray met with Kido and the Iwakura Mission at least twice—once in Washington and again in

Boston in August 1872, just before the latter sailed for England. Murray's letter to Griffis, dated August 14, 1872, mentions that he had "seen a good deal of Kido and Itō and something of Iwakura and they go home with my high ideas I think of American institutions."[84] Although he said nothing of his potential appointment in Japan, he shared his views of Japan's progress, recognizing the highly "advanced" members of its people and asserting that the mission's members were "certainly men of great intelligence and have a perfectly clear insight into the wants of their country and the challenges encountered in regard to them." He further stated that their goals must be accomplished by "agencies working from within and not without" and that "foreigners can do very little to help them," points he had "tried very hard to impress upon those of the Embassy I have met."[85] Such views resonate with his response to Mori's letter regarding education and reveal Murray's deep understanding and appreciation of the Japanese leaders he met.

Kido mentions in his diary that in September he received a letter from Hattori Ichizō, another Rutgers student from his home province of Chōshū. It is likely that this missive, too, included recommendations for Murray; a letter from Kido to Shinagawa Yajirō on October 9, 1872 (dated the seventh day of the ninth month) contains a note marked "confidential" (*naimitsu*), which mentions the employment of one American and Kido's receipt of a message from Hattori that would be later sent in another note.[86] The "American" mentioned here is, without doubt, David Murray. As such, the network of influential Rutgers alumni and Murray's Japanese students successfully won Murray his new position. Kido met with Tanaka in London on November 25, and on January 10, 1873, Mori drew up a formal offer of employment to make Murray the superintendent of education in the Ministry of Education.[87]

Murray left for Japan with his wife, Martha, in June 1873. Hatakeyama, who joined the Ministry of Education in September of the same year upon returning from the Iwakura Mission, briefly served as Murray's interpreter. In December, he was appointed the first president of Tokyo Kaisei Gakkō and continued to work closely with Murray, devoting his short life to building a foundation for the school as a modern institute of higher education. Murray served the Ministry of Education until December 1878 and is remembered today as one of the most pivotal figures in the history of modern Japanese education.

Conclusion

The contributions of Guido F. Verbeck and Hatakeyama Yoshinari to the Iwakura Mission demonstrate the crucial role that the Rutgers network played in key events during modern Japan's formative years, especially in the field of education. Verbeck, as a teacher and mentor to many young men in Nagasaki, had formed ties with leading figures of Meiji Japan, some of whom had gone to Rutgers with his assistance. Such connections inevitably drew him deeper into politics, and his "Brief Sketch" demonstrates his acute awareness of Japan's political and diplomatic situation in the wake of the Meiji Restoration. However, his text would not have had such an impact without the trust he had earned from his former students and their fathers, particularly from Iwakura Tomomi, who also happened to be one of the era's most powerful figures.

Hatakeyama's network, predominantly Satsuma-centered on his leaving for the United States, expanded once he arrived in New Brunswick. It grew to encompass Japanese students of diverse backgrounds and abilities, Rutgers professors and classmates, and members of the local community, even extending to Rutgers alumni and their respective connections. This vast network, established over the years, was key to his accomplishing the tasks assigned to him as a member of the Iwakura Mission.

Ironically, the appointment of David Murray marked the waning of Verbeck's influence in the Meiji government. When Verbeck returned in 1874 from a much-deserved six-month vacation in Europe and the United States, Murray and Hatakeyama had already assumed their new positions. In a major shift in its educational policy, the Japanese government had hired a prominent educator and a Japanese official trained at an American higher institution, whereas it had earlier relied heavily on Verbeck, a missionary. Verbeck resigned as the head teacher of Daigaku Nankō, now renamed Kaisei Gakkō and headed by Hatakeyama; he continued to work as a translator and advisor to the government but gradually focused on missionary work. He remained in Japan and devoted the rest of his life to proselytizing, Christian education, and translation until his death in 1898.

As for Hatakeyama, he traveled to the United States in 1876 with Murray and Tanaka Fujimaro, now the Minister of Education, to study American educational institutions, attend conferences, and attend the Centennial Exhibition in Philadelphia. During this time, he was awarded an honorary master's degree from Rutgers University.[88] His health, however, had deteriorated over many years of hard work, and he died on board the *City of Peking* on the way home.[89] Murray, who learned of Hatakeyama's death in San Francisco, wrote an eight-page obituary expressing deep respect and remorse for the loss of his friend and colleague. Its final words summarize well Hatakeyama's contributions to Japan's educational reform:

> His intimate knowledge of the traditions and institutions of his country fitted him in an eminent degree to aid in the reorganization of her educational system. He knew not only her present aspirations and wants, but also her past history to which her new career must be joined and adapted. He was familiar both with the resources and advantages of foreign science and arts and with the peculiar genius and capabilities of his own countrymen.
>
> His loss at this time is not only a serious one to his personal friends and to his family who looked to him with pride and hope but a calamity to the cause of education and civilization in this country. . . . Many have been educated in

foreign lands and have returned to render valuable services to their country but I know of none who can take the place and do the work of Hatakeyama Yoshinari.[90]

Notes

1 This is from a passage in *A True Account*, as the mission passed New Brunswick on a train ride from Washington, DC, to Jersey City. Kume Kunitake, ed., *Tokumei zenken taishi Beiō kairan jikki*, 5 vols. (Tokyo: Hakubunsha, 1878), 1:259, National Diet Library Digital Collection, https://dl.ndl.go.jp/info:ndljp/pid/1151920. For an English translation of *A True Account*, see Kume Kunitake, *The Iwakura Embassy, 1871–1873*, vol. 1, *The United States of America: A True Account of the Ambassador Extraordinary & Plenipotentiary's Journey of Observation Through the United States of America and Europe*, ed. Graham Healey and Chushichi Tsuzuki, trans. Martin Collcutt (Matsudo, Chiba, Japan: The Japan Documents, 2002).

2 Tanaka Akira, *Iwakura Shisetsudan no rekishiteki kenkyū* (Tokyo: Iwanami Shoten, 2002), 19–25.

3 Charles Lanman (1819–1895), secretary of the Japanese Legation in Washington, DC, at the time, mentions that upon arrival in the United States, Iwakura sent a telegram to his sons, and "an answer was received just as he had concluded his first address to the American people. It announced the good health of his sons, and their joy at his safe arrival in this country. The contents and the occasion combined to render him exceedingly happy." Charles Lanman, *The Japanese in America* (London: Longmans, Green, Reader, and Dyer, 1872), 12.

4 Griffis and Lanman mention a third son, "Minami," who was also in New Brunswick at the time. William E. Griffis, *The Rutgers Graduates in Japan, Revised and Enlarged and Republished at the 150th Anniversary of the College* (New Brunswick, NJ: Rutgers College, 1916), 13; Lanman, *The Japanese in America*, 12. On the Japanese students in New Brunswick, see Fernanda Perrone, "Invisible Network: Japanese Students at Rutgers During the Early Meiji Period," *Kindai Nihon kenkyū* 34 (2017): 3–20; Takagi Fuji, *Bakumatsu ishinki no Beikoku ryūgaku: Yokoi Saheita no kaigun shūgaku* (Tokyo: Keio University Press, 2015); Takahashi Shūetsu, *Kaishū nikki ni miru bakumatsu ishin no Amerika ryūgaku: Nichigin sōsai Tomita Tetsunosuke no Amerika taiken* (Tokyo: Nihon Hyōronsha, 2018).

5 Albert Altman, "Guido Verbeck and the Iwakura Embassy," *Japan Quarterly* 13, no. 1 (1966): 54–62.

6 William Elliot Griffis, *Verbeck of Japan; a Citizen of No Country; a Life Story of Foundation Work Inaugurated by Guido Fridolin Verbeck* (New York: Fleming H. Revell, 1900), 255.

7 Kume, *The Iwakura Embassy*, 5; Kume, *Tokumei zenken taishi Beiō kairan jikki*, 3. Although Hatakeyama did not take part in the actual compilation of *A True Account* due to his appointments after his return to Japan, Kume notes in the preface that he "really made a great effort to include everything faithfully." Kume, *The Iwakura Embassy*, 8; Kume, *Tokumei zenken taishi Beiō kairan jikki*, 8–9. On Hatakeyama's involvement in the compilation of *The True Account*, see Ōkubo Toshiaki, ed., *Iwakura Shisetsu no kenkyū* (Tokyo: Sōkō Shobō, 1976), 144–154.

8 On the Meiji government's early foreign relations and moves toward treaty revision, see Michael R. Auslin, *Negotiating with Imperialism: The Unequal Treaties and the Culture of Japanese Diplomacy* (Cambridge, MA: Harvard University Press, 2004), 146–175, https://doi.org/10.4159/9780674020313.

9 "ARTICLE XIII. After the (4th of July, 1872.) fourth day of July, one thousand eight hundred and seventy-two, upon the desire of either the American or Japanese Government, and on one year's notice given by either party, this treaty, and such portions of the treaty of Kanagawa, as remain unrevoked by this treaty, together with the regulations of trade hereunto annexed, or those that may be hereafter introduced, shall be subject to revision, by commissioners, appointed on both sides, for this purpose, who will be empowered to decide on, and insert therein, such amendments as experience shall prove to be desirable." Treaty of Amity and Commerce between the United States of America and the Empire of Japan (Treaty of Amity and Commerce, Harris Treaty; Edo, July 29, 1858), "The World and Japan" database in *Database of Japanese Politics and International Relations*, National Graduate Institute for Policy Studies, Institute for Advanced Studies on Asia, University of Tokyo, accessed May 5, 2022, worldjpn.grips.ac.jp/documents/texts/pw/18580729.T1E.html.

10 Altman, "Guido Verbeck and the Iwakura Embassy," 55.

11 A copy of this document, known as the "Brief Sketch," is currently held at the Reformed Church in America Archives in the Gardner A. Sage Library of the New Brunswick Theological Seminary of the Reformed Church. The upper-left corner of the first page shows the handwritten word "copy" and Verbeck's seal beneath it; a note at the end says: "Sent to Okuma 11 June, 1869. Revives 26 and 29 Oct. 1871." The "Brief Sketch" was rediscovered and published by Altman, "Guido Verbeck and the Iwakura Embassy," 54–62.

12 Altman, "Guido Verbeck and the Iwakura Embassy," 58. The mission selectively adopted Verbeck's proposals; however, as I argue below, their influence on its planning and design cannot be overestimated.

13 Altman, 58.

14 Altman, 59.

15 Altman, 59.

16 Altman, 60–61.

17 Altman, 59.

18 Altman, 59.

19 See, for example, Ōkubo Toshiaki, "Iwakura Shisetsu haken no kenkyū," in *Iwakura Shisetsu no kenkyū*, ed. Ōkubo Toshiaki (Tokyo: Sōkō Shobō, 1976), 7–154; Tanaka, *Iwakura Shisetsudan no rekishiteki kenkyū*, 19–25.

20 This factionalism surged upon the mission's return to Japan and led to crises for the government in the mid- to late 1870s, including the famous debate over the Korean invasion and the samurai uprising led by Saigō Takamori in 1877.

21 Tanaka, *Iwakura Shisetsudan no rekishiteki kenkyū*, 19–25.

22 Altman, "Guido Verbeck and the Iwakura Embassy," 60–61. Interestingly, Verbeck did not recommend a special commission to study religious institutions; he explained that no treaty or other public document needed to mention religion and that religious tolerance would suffice. The mission's members, he thought, could observe through European and American life the influence of Western religion on public morality.

23 For a list of members of the Iwakura Mission, see "Appendix," in Kume, *The Iwakura Embassy*, 401–404. For a complete list, see Tanaka, *Iwakura Shisetsudan no rekishiteki kenkyū*, 329–342. Charles Lanman also provides a list in *The Japanese in America*, 6–8.

24 Altman, "Guido Verbeck and the Iwakura Embassy," 60–61.

25 Shigekazu Kondō, "Kume Kunitake as a Historiographer," 18–182. The original paper in Japanese is published as "Furubekki yori nainai sashidashi sōrōsho," in *Kaikoku: Nihon kindai shisō taikei*, vol. 1, ed. Tanaka Akira (Tokyo: Iwanami Shoten, 1991), 371–380.

26 Kondō, "Kume Kunitake as a Historiographer," 181.

27 Kume, *Tokumei zenken taishi Beiō kairan jikki*. The abridged edition is published as Kume Kunitake, *Japan Rising: The Iwakura Embassy to the USA and Europe 1871–1873*, ed. Chūshichi Tsuzuki and R. Jules Young (Cambridge: Cambridge University Press, 2009).

28 Tanaka, *Iwakura Shisetsudan no rekishiteki kenkyū*, 25–26.

29 Kido Takayoshi, *The Diary of Kido Takayoshi*, vol. 2, *1871–1874*, trans. Sidney D. Brown and Akiko Hirota (Tokyo: University of Tokyo Press, 1983), 133 (29 February 1872). In Washington, DC, the mission recruited two other overseas students. Yoshihara Shigetoshi (1845–1887), a member of the second group of Satsuma students, had studied at Monson Academy and briefly attended Yale University before leaving for Europe. He was one of the students that Hatakeyama and others visited at Monson immediately after leaving Brocton, the other being Niijima Jō (1843–1890), known in the United States as Joseph Hardy Neesima, who had smuggled himself out of Japan in 1864 at the age of twenty-one. He arrived in Andover, Massachusetts, attended Phillips Academy, and moved to Amherst College in 1867, graduating in 1870 and subsequently attending Andover Theological Seminary to become a missionary. Mori played a decisive role in appointing Yoshihara, Niijima, and Hatakeyama as secretaries of the Iwakura Mission upon its arrival in Washington; he knew Yoshihara and Hatakeyama as his Satsuma comrades and had previously asked Niijima to serve the Japanese government, having most likely met him through Yoshihara or another of the Satsuma students at Monson. Niijima declined, but Mori still provided him with a Japanese passport and official permission to finish his studies in the United States. See also John Van Sant, *Pacific Pioneers: Japanese Journeys to America and Hawaii, 1850–80* (Urbana: University of Illinois Press, 2000), 64–78.

30 On Hatakeyama, see chapter 5, "Sappan ryūgakusei Hatakeyama Yoshinari no Seiō taiken: Kokka ishiki no keisei to Kirisutokyō," in Inuzuka Takaaki, *Meiji ishin taigai kankeishi kenkyū* (Tokyo: Yoshikawa Kōbunkan, 1987), 193–341.

31 They had learned about Rutgers from their fellow Satsuma students then studying at Monson Academy in Massachusetts—the so-called second [group of] Satsuma students who left secretly in 1866 for the United States. Monson Academy was the alma mater of Dutch Reformed Church missionary Samuel Brown, who taught in Yokohama. The trio borrowed money for three months of tuition and living costs and also went to John M. Ferris for assistance.

32 On the Satsuma students, see chapter 10. See also Van Sant, *Pacific Pioneers*, 79–96.

33 "The Japanese in College: The Yellow-Faced Students in Rutgers College," *The Sun*, June 23, 1870.

34 David Murray, "Hatakeyama Yoshinari of Japan. Died on board the Steamship 'City of Peking' October 20th, 1876," William Elliot Griffis Collection, Special Collections and University Archives, Rutgers University Libraries, New Brunswick, NJ (hereafter Griffis Collection), 5.

35 Hatakeyama to J. M. Ferris, 31 December 1869, box 159, folder 2, Griffis Collection. "Shimats" refers to Shimazu Matanoshin, son of the lord of the Sadowara domain in Kyushu, who arrived in the United States in 1869.

36 Hatakeyama to J. M. Ferris, 31 December 1869.

37 Letter to J. M. Ferris, 14 May 1870, box 159, folder 2, Griffis Collection.

38 "Hatakeyama Yoshinari," obituary in Japan Scrapbook, section 3, p. 61, box 112H, Griffis Collection. This text also recounts the moment of his departure: "We well remember how with his eyes full of tears and a voice quivering with emotion he told us of his sore disappointment in not being allowed to take his degree; but, with that

loyalty to his country which was one of his chief characteristics, he obeyed promptly."

39 Inuzuka Takaaki, "Honkoku: Sugiura Kōzō memo" (Transcription of the Sugiura Kōzō memo), *Kagoshima Kenritsu Tanki Daigaku Kiyō* 18 (1990): 43.

40 Murray, "Hatakeyama Yoshinari of Japan," 4.

41 Four notebooks dated from Hatakeyama's days in the United States, which include diary entries, copies of letters and documents, and memos, are housed at Shōko Shūseikan in Kagoshima Prefecture. They were transcribed and published by Inuzuka Takaaki as "Sugiura Kōzō notes" and "Sugiura Kōzō memo." See Inuzuka Takaaki, "Honkoku: Sugiura Kōzō memo," *Kagoshima Kenritsu Tanki Daigaku Chiiki Kenkyūjo kenkyū kenpō* 18 (1990): 31–54; "Honkoku: Sugiura Kōzō nōto," *Kagoshima Kenritsu Tanki Daigaku Chiiki Kenkyūjo kenkyū kenpō* 15 (1987): 95–129. A copy of this letter is included in his "memo." Inuzuka, "Honkoku: Sugiura Kōzō memo," 49–50.

42 On the Japanese students' involvement with the Iwakura Mission, see also Haruko Wakabayashi, "Iwakura Mission and the Network of Japanese Students in the United States," *Journal of American-East Asian Relations* 31 (2024): 278–307. On observing educational institutions in the West, see Martin Collcutt, "Education for a New Japan: Kume Kunitake's Observations on Education in 1872 America," in *Japan and Its Worlds: Marius B. Jansen and the Internationalization of Japanese Studies*, ed. Martin Collcutt, Mikio Katō, and Ronald P. Toby (Tokyo: I-House Press, 2007), 188–189.

43 Ōkubo, *Iwakura Shisetsu no kenkyū*, 162.

44 Collcutt, "Education for a New Japan," 188–189.

45 Altman, "Guido Verbeck and the Iwakura Embassy," 61.

46 Collcutt, "Education for a New Japan," 187–208.

47 "Ryūgakusei kankei monjo," in Ōkubo, *Iwakura Shisetsu no kenkyū*, 248–251.

48 Inuzuka, "Honkoku: Sugiura Kōzō nōto," 128–129.

49 Ishizuki Minoru, *Kindai Nihon no kaigai ryūgakushi* (Tokyo: Chūō Kōronsha, 1992), 204–205.

50 Ishizuki, *Kindai Nihon no kaigai ryūgakushi*, 207–209.

51 "Tokumei zenken taishi no shimei ni kansuru chokushi," in Ōkubo, *Iwakura Shisetsu no kenkyū*, 180–181.

52 Inuzuka, "Honkoku: Sugiura Kōzō nōto," 128–129.

53 The same list of names appears in *Taishi zensho*, a compiled record of the Iwakura Mission. This work lists Hatakeyama's name fourth, after Niijima Shimeta and Tomita Tetsunosuke, but otherwise follows the same order as in Hatakeyama's note. *Taishi zensho tankōsho/taishi shorui genkō zaibei zatsumu shorui* (1871–1872), *Taishi zensho*, https://www.digital.archives.go.jp/img/644252.

54 Inuzuka, *Meiji ishin taigai kankeishi kenkyū*, 228–229.

55 "Eikoku ryūgakusei torishimari ikensho (1872.12.18)," in Inuzuka, "Honkoku: Sugiura Kōzō memo," 45–47.

56 "Eikoku ryūgakusei torishimari ikensho (1872.12.18)," 45.

57 "Eikoku ryūgakusei torishimari ikensho (1872.12.18)," 46–47.

58 "No. 84, Letter to Mr. & Mrs. Hardy, Georgetown, D.C., 10 March 1872," in *The Complete Works of Joseph Hardy Neesima 6: Letters in English*, ed. The Complete Works of Joseph Hardy Neesima Editorial Committee (Kyoto: Dōhōsha Shuppan, 1985), 98. Another letter dated March 8 also mentions that "twelve Japanese students in the States were summoned to meet the Minister of Educational Bureau [i.e., Tanaka Fujimaro] to give him some advice. The power was granted them to make any motions or give any advice to him, and the motions would be carried by

the vote of the majority." See "No. 83, Letter to Mr. & Mrs. Hardy, Georgetown, D.C., 8 March 1872," in The Complete Works of Joseph Hardy Neesima Editorial Committee, *The Complete Works of Joseph Hardy Neesima 6*, 96.

59 Ishizuki, *Kindai Nihon no kaigai ryūgakushi*, 218–224.

60 Mori compiled and published his letters and the responses he received as *Education in Japan: A Series of Letters Addressed by Prominent Americans to Arinori Mori* (New York: Appleton, 1873).

61 On David Murray, see Benjamin Duke, *Dr. David Murray: Superintendent of Education in the Empire of Japan, 1873–1879* (New Brunswick, NJ: Rutgers University Press, 2019).

62 "Japan to Honor a Brunswick Grave," *New Brunswick Home News*, February 18, 1910, Historical New Brunswick Newspapers & Board of Health Records, http://newbrunswick.archivalweb.com/imageViewer.php?i=692218&q=David%20Murray&s=q%3DDavid%2BMurray%26p%3D2%26r%3D0. On Murray's relationship with the Japanese students, see Duke, *Dr. David Murray*, chapters 1–3.

63 Mori, *Education in Japan*, 87–109.

64 Duke, *Dr. David Murray*, 97–134; Gotō Sumio, "Gakkan Morurē koyō no keii (II)," *Kyōikugaku zasshi* 20 (1986): 1–15.

65 Inuzuka, "Sugiura Kōzō memo," 50–51.

66 Inuzuka, 52–53.

67 Joseph Henry (1797–1878) was the first secretary of the Smithsonian Institution and a professor at the College of New Jersey (present-day Princeton University).

68 Isaac Ferris (1798–1873) was the third chancellor of New York University, having succeeded Theodore Frelinghuysen, the adoptive father of Senator Frank T. Frelinghuysen.

69 Howard Crosby (1826–1891) was the chancellor of New York University and previously a professor of Greek at Rutgers College from 1859 to 1863.

70 George Cook (1818–1889) was a professor of chemistry and natural sciences and later vice president of Rutgers College. In 1864, he was appointed state geologist of New Jersey.

71 Isaac W. Jackson (1804–1877) was a professor of mathematics and natural philosophy at Union College from 1831 to 1877.

72 Eliphalet Nott Potter (1836–1901) was president of Union College from 1871 to 1884.

73 Martin Brewer Anderson (1815–1890) was the first president of the University of Rochester.

74 John V. L. Pruyn (1811–1877) was a member of the U.S. Senate and the House of Representatives in the 1860s. From 1862 to 1877, he served as chancellor of the Board of Regents of the University of the State of New York. He was the cousin of Robert H. Pruyn, the second U.S. minister resident to Japan (1862–1865; Rutgers College class of 1933 and MA 1936) and father of Robert C. Pruyn (1847–1934; Rutgers College class of 1969), a classmate of Griffis who encouraged him to go to Japan.

75 Samuel B. Woolworth was president of the New York State Teachers' Association in 1847 and later secretary of the State Board of Regents of the University of the State of New York.

76 Charles H. Bell (1798–1875) was a rear admiral in the U.S. Navy who had retired in 1868.

77 Kido, *The Diary of Kido Takayoshi*, 143 (22 April 1872).

78 Kido, 163n3. This refers to Joseph Alden's *The Science of Government: In Connection with American Institutions* (Hungerford, UK: Legare Street Press, 1867).

79 Kido, *The Diary of Kido Takayoshi*, 155–181.

80 Kido, 171 (4 June 1872).
81 A letter received from Tanaka and Niijima on May 6 (161), sent to Tanaka and Niijima on May 8 (162).
82 Kido, *The Diary of Kido Takayoshi*, 184 (13 July 1872).
83 Gotō, "Gakkan Morurē koyō no keii (II)," 5–6.
84 David Murray to William E. Griffis, 14 August 1872, Griffis Collection.
85 David Murray to William E. Griffis, 14 August 1872, 2–3.
86 Gotō, "Gakkan Morurē koyō no keii (II)," 5–6. Kido had also received a letter from Hattori Ichizō, a fellow native of Chōshū, regarding Murray. Nihon Shiseki Kyōkai, ed., *Kido Takayoshi nikki*, vol. 2 (Tokyo: Tokyo Daigaku Shuppankai, 1967), 227 (4 August 1872); Tsumaki Chūta, ed., *Kido Kōin monjo*, vol. 4 (Tokyo: Nihon Shiseki Kyōkai, 1930), 395–396.
87 Gotō, "Gakkan Morurē koyō no keii (II)," 7.
88 *Hatakeyama Chūtokugaku Beikoku nite gakushi no shōgō jushū todoke* (Report on School Inspector Hatakeyama Yoshinari's receiving of an academic degree in the United States) (August Meiji 9), National Archives of Japan Digital Archive, accessed January 7, 2023, https://www.digital.archives.go.jp/img/3069407.
89 With him on the ship was Orita Hikoichi, another Satsuma student who initially came to the United States with the Iwakura brothers and with whom Hatakeyama had spent his years in New Brunswick. Orita had just graduated from the College of New Jersey (present-day Princeton University); his diary recounts the moment of Hatakeyama's death.
90 Murray, "Hatakeyama Yoshinari of Japan," 8–9.

12

David Murray's Influence on Japanese Education

BENJAMIN DUKE

Edited by Fernanda Perrone

In the histories of early U.S.-Japan relations, the roles of Dr. David Murray, professor of mathematics at Rutgers College, and of Rutgers College itself have not been appropriately recognized. Murray, appointed by the Japanese as superintendent of education in the empire of Japan in 1873, served as a senior officer in the Ministry of Education for over five years when the first public school system in Japan, the *Gakusei*, was launched. The significance of the *Gakusei* is that it marks the beginning of modern education in Japan following the end of several hundred years of feudal Tokugawa government. The monumental goal of the restored Meiji government was to launch the nation's first modern public school system to accommodate all children of elementary school age, a standard that no nation in the world had achieved at that time. As superintendent of education in the Ministry of Education responsible for implementing the *Gakusei*, Murray displayed an unwavering commitment to its success, rendering him a pioneer of modern Japanese education.

Background and Early Life

David Murray was born in the tiny hamlet of Bovina in Delaware County, New York, on October 15, 1830. He attended district public school for two years and

FIGURE 12.1. David Murray, ca. 1868. (Credit: William Elliot Griffis Collection, Rutgers University Libraries. Photo by D. Clark Studio.)

then moved on to the private Delaware Academy and later to Fergusonville Academy.[1] Upon completing his college preparatory course at Fergusonville, Murray attained an academic standard that enabled him to enter Union College in Schenectady, New York, as a sophomore in 1849. After graduation three years later, Murray was qualified to join the faculty of Albany Academy, one of the leading preparatory schools in America, to teach mathematics. He was appointed principal of Albany Academy in 1857.[2] In 1863, he was awarded a PhD from the University of the State of New York. This accolade was not an earned doctorate from a university but rather an honorary degree awarded by a state education office in recognition of outstanding academic achievements.[3] In the same year, he was offered a professorship in mathematics and natural philosophy at Rutgers College.

David Murray and His Japanese Students

Murray became interested in Japan during his tenure as a professor at Rutgers College. He first encountered the young samurai from Japan who had found their way to this small college in his mathematics class. Knowing that the Japanese students were thousands of miles from home in a foreign country strange to them in every way, David and his wife, Martha Murray,[4] made a special effort to provide a home setting for them. On a fateful evening during this period, the Murrays invited the Japanese students into their living room for a social evening, surely with American-style refreshments prepared by Mrs. Murray. It marked the first of many such open house evenings for the young samurai at the Murray

FIGURE 12.2. Japanese students at Rutgers, 1870, given as a gift to David Murray. (Credit: William Elliot Griffis Collection, Rutgers University Libraries.)

home, with Martha as the gracious hostess. The students were always welcomed with great kindness. The Murray home was described in a local newspaper as "a social center for the Japanese students" and "a symbol of hospitality."[5]

The Murrays were profoundly impressed not only by the manners and politeness of the Japanese students, but by the experiences of their upbringing in a feudal society. Among the topics most frequently discussed was the state of Japanese education as the boys knew it from their experiences in the domain schools for the ruling class of samurai in feudal Japan.[6] These conversations piqued Murray's interest in education in Japan. It was, however, the very personal relationships that emerged between the Murrays and Hatakeyama Yoshinari (1842–1876), Iwakura Asahi (1853–1890), and Katsu Koroku (1852–1892) that most deeply motivated Murray's commitment to the future of Japan. As Murray recalled many years later, "Hatakeyama [who initially took the name Soogiura Kōzō upon coming to the West] was a native of Kagoshima, in the province of Satsuma. Before the abolition of the feudal system in Japan, his family belonged to the landed nobility, owing allegiance to the ancient Daimiate of Satsuma. . . . The College in Kagoshima [Zōshikan] where he was educated was one of the most celebrated of those institutions which lent a luster to the best age of Japanese learning."[7] Iwakura Asahi, whose original name was Iwakura Tomosada, and his brother Tatsu were the sons of Junior Minister of State Iwakura Tomomi. Iwakura was not a samurai but a senior chamberlain in the imperial household confined in the city of Kyoto during the Tokugawa period. Among the brightest students in Murray's mathematics class was Katsu Koroku, son of the vice minister, later minister of the Japanese Navy, Katsu Kaishū, who had served as a ranking official of the Tokugawa shogunate before the Meiji Restoration. It was through these students and their families that David Murray would make important connections in Japan.

David Murray Is Invited to Japan

The *New York Times* carried a front-page article in the December 18, 1871, edition from its San Francisco reporter entitled "The New Japanese Embassy."[8] It was the first newspaper report in America announcing the impending arrival of a fifty-member diplomatic delegation of ranking Japanese political leaders to San Francisco on their way to Washington, DC. "The Embassy which sails from Yokohama today, which is due here [San Francisco] January 18, will be the most important that has ever left an Oriental nation for America or Europe. It is sent out by order of the Japanese Parliament and the Mikado, that the ruling classes must study for themselves Western civilization and not depend upon the reports of informers, as hitherto."[9] The leader of the mission was Iwakura Tomomi, father of David Murray's students Asahi and Tatsu. Among the diplomats and government administrators on the mission was an official appointed to the Iwakura Embassy from the Ministry of Education, Tanaka Fujimaro (1845–1909), a mid-level samurai from the Owari *han* in central Japan, who held the title of *mombu daijō* (ministry secretariat). Also traveling with the mission was Hatakeyama Yoshinari, who had been recalled from Rutgers by the Japanese government to first study the education system in Europe and then to serve as a translator and secretary for the mission. One of the mission's assignments was to search for an appropriate Western educational system to serve as a model for modern Japan. During that process, a qualified Westerner was also to be found to serve in the Ministry of Education as an advisor to the head of the ministry.

There were four Japanese officials, three with the Iwakura Embassy, who participated in the search for a Western educational advisor. It was intended that Tanaka Fujimaro, from the Ministry of Education, would be most directly involved. The second figure to play an important role was one of the leaders of the embassy, Vice Ambassador Kido Takayoshi (1833–1877), although his primary concern was diplomatic. The third member of the embassy to become involved directly, indirectly, or both in the search was Hatakeyema Yoshinari. The fourth Japanese official involved, Mori Arinori (1847–1889), played a controversial role in the selection of a Western educational advisor by independently initiating the search process. Mori, at that time Japanese ambassador to the United States was, like Hatakeyama, from Satsuma, and was with him at

University College London and at the Thomas Lake Harris religious colony in Brocton, New York.[10]

While the Iwakura Mission was in the American West, Mori sent out a letter of inquiry to a curious mixture of Americans including several presidents of colleges and universities seeking their advice on education for Japan. William Campbell, president of Rutgers, who received a letter, passed it on to David Murray. In his 1872 reply, Murray prepared a comprehensive and detailed analysis of the effects of education in modern societies—precisely what Mori was seeking. In his letter, Murray addressed the conditions in Japan about which he had learned from his students. "There are traditional customs which it would be unwise to undertake to subvert. There are institutions already founded which are revered for their local and national associations, which without material change may be made the best elements of a new system." After meeting with members of the Iwakura Embassy in Washington and Boston, Murray was offered the position in January 1873.

David Murray, accompanied by his wife, Martha, arrived at the Port of Yokohama on June 30, 1873. Once in Japan, Murray was reunited with his former students at Rutgers. On September 2, over two months after the Murrays arrived at Yokohama, their Western-style house in Tokyo was finally ready for them. Since their furniture from America that had been stored in Yokohama did not reach Tokyo until a day or so after they moved, the Murrays spent their first night in Tokyo at the home of William Elliot Griffis, another of David's former students, who had transferred from Fukui to Nankō (the major national college that later became Kaisei Gakkō and then the University of Tokyo). Their new house was situated on a former daimyo estate, years later to become the campus of Tokyo University, noted to this day for a red gate (*akamon*) at the entrance that has survived since the days when the Murrays lived within the compound. Asahi came to see them in their new home with a gift of "an old writing case, which has been a long time in their family. It is a lacquer box . . . raised and very eloquent."[11] The gift was all part of the appreciation extended to the Murrays by the Iwakura family for their kindness in befriending the two Iwakura sons in New Brunswick.

Murray, according to the autobiography of his first translator and assistant, Takahashi Korekiyo, also made sure to meet Katsu Kaishū shortly after he arrived in Japan.[12] The Murrays wanted the opportunity to personally report to the parents on their son's positive experiences as a student at Rutgers College. It was a gesture of goodwill by Murray that was greatly appreciated by both the father and mother of Koroku. By that time, Koroku had transferred from Rutgers College to the U.S. Naval Academy in Annapolis, Maryland, from where he would graduate and return to Japan to serve in the Japanese Navy, as had his father.

The informal reception that the Murrays hosted for the new American minister to Japan in early November 1873 best illustrates how the connections that Murray had formed in America had an impact on his social and professional life in Japan. In addition to the "Americans of Yedo," they "added a sprinkling of very high Japanese": "Mr. Iwakura, the Prime Minister and his son Asahi; Mr. Katz Awa [Katsu Kaishū], a Privy Councilor and Minister of Naval Affairs; Mr. Ōkubo [Toshimichi], a Privy Councilor and one of the [Iwakura] Embassy; Mr. Mori, late Minister to the U.S., Mr. Soogiwoora [Hatakeyama]; and Mr. Tanaka [Fujimaro], the Minister of Education with wife . . . Mr. Kido could not come because of sickness [nor could] Yoshida [Kiyonari] who used to be in America under the name of Nagai and who is now the Assistant Minister of Finance."[13] The reception not only reflected the connections the Murrays had with the most powerful figures in the government but also showed Martha Murray's thoughtfulness toward the couple's Japanese acquaintances by including them in the festive occasion. It was reminiscent of Martha hosting the Japanese students at Rutgers College in the Murrays' home for social events.

Notably, present at the reception was Hatakeyama Yoshinari, who had just arrived home from Europe with the Iwakura Embassy. Taking advantage of the close personal relationship that he and his wife had developed with Hatakeyama, Murray invited him to join the Ministry of Education, where he would become Murray's "most confidential friend and adviser."[14] In that capacity he served as Murray's language interpreter on special occasions. But of greater importance to Murray, Hatakeyama became an interpreter of his educational recommendations to his Japanese superior, Tanaka Fujimaro. With Hatakeyama playing a key role, Murray was much better prepared for his challenging assignment at the Ministry of Education. David Murray recognized the accomplishments of Hatakeyama with multiple assignments: "It is safe to say that no man had come back with sounder or more useful qualifications in education, in experience of the world, and in a knowledge of foreign institutions and affairs. Withal he had not lost his patriotic sentiments, but longed and was ready to labor with all the forces of his character for the good of his country."[15]

Upon Hatakeyama's appointment to head Kaisei Gakkō in Tokyo in late 1873, he was joined by another former student from Rutgers College: Edward Warren Clark (1849–1907), whose "warmest Japanese friend" from their time together as classmates at Rutgers College happened to be Hatakeyama, had been teaching science for two years at a government school in Shizuoka, south of Tokyo. Described previously, the school was under the direction of Katsu Kaishū, whose son Katsu Koroku was also a good friend of Clark's. When the school in Shizuoka was cut back in 1873, many of the staff were assigned to Tokyo, with Clark assigned to Kaisei Gakkō to teach chemistry. This move brought Clark together with two of his dearest friends from Rutgers College, Hatakeyama and Griffis.[16]

David Murray's Initial Efforts at Educational Reform in Japan

In Tokugawa Japan, education was based on the clan schools or *hankō*, one in each castle town of the feudal *hans*, which resembled a national school system restricted for samurai, which consisted of about six to eight percent of the population, although with widely varying facilities and standards according to local conditions.[17] By the middle of the nineteenth century, the *han* schools for the ruling hereditary samurai class had undergone many changes since their beginning. What were originally designed as institutions for military training to teach the arts of archery, swordsmanship, and horsemanship during the era of civil war in the sixteenth century had gradually become absorbed into centers of academic learning dominated by the teachings of Confucius from China.[18] The primary educational opportunity for the commoners took the form of the *terakoya*, or "temple schools," a name attached to a variety of private schools for boys—and to a much lesser extent, girls—who could afford them. The name originated from the site where the earliest ones were located when Buddhist priests taught local children the moral beliefs that were influential in the community. By the time of the Meiji Restoration of 1868, an estimated forty percent of Japanese boys and ten percent of girls attended some form of formal schooling outside the home.[19] The *terakoya* formed the mainstay of education for both rural families and commoners in the towns as private elementary schools. The other category of schools primarily for non-samurai youth were the *shijuku*, an amorphous category of private schools beyond the elementary level where subjects ranging from the practical to the classical Chinese to Western studies were offered to meet the growing needs of an increasingly complex society.[20]

In July 1871, the *han* schools of feudal Japan, where the samurai statesmen and students who awakened Murray's interest in Japan were educated in the ways of the warrior, had been closed by governmental decree following the abolition of *han* and the establishment of prefectures.[21] Murray was unaware of the existence of a historic ordinance promulgated by the new Japanese Ministry of Education (founded 1871) several months before he signed his contract. Titled the *Gakusei*, literally the "school system," or the Fundamental Code of Education of 1872, it was intended to replace the clan schools of feudal Japan and the *terakoya* temple schools, among others, which appealed to many non-samurai parents with their moral teachings. The most critical provision of the Code of Education compelled each community of six hundred residents to establish and maintain an elementary school to accommodate every child of school age with a curriculum of studies set by the Ministry of Education. David Murray's primary assignment as superintendent in the ministry was to provide advice and counsel to Tanaka Fujimaro on the implementation and administration of the nation's first public school system.

The first major assignment for Murray at the Ministry of Education in the fall of 1873 was to prepare a written report for Tanaka recommending reforms of Japanese education under the newly promulgated Code of Education as he knew it. Murray recommended the establishment of normal schools as "the most rapid means for reforming the system of education in Japan." In response, the Ministry decided to establish a teacher training school in each district patterned after the Tokyo Teacher Training School, which had opened in August 1872. In order to implement the Code of Education, the country had already been divided into seven grand districts to administer the new national school system. By February 1874, teacher training colleges had been established in each district.[22] Murray played a prominent role in the development of this plan because it was his responsibility to make arrangements for the student scholarships at appropriate teacher training colleges in America.

One of Murray's most important recommendations related to the education of girls and women. "I come now to a branch of my subject which I am well aware has already received from this department very earnest consideration. . . . I mean female education. The importance of the education of the women of the country cannot be overrated. To them are necessarily entrusted the care and training of children in their earliest and most impressible years."[23] As he had for men, Murray advocated for the establishment of teacher training schools for women. His recommendation hastened the procedure to establish the first normal school for women, with formal government approval received on January 20, 1874—three weeks after Murray's report, extraordinarily rapid for bureaucratic action. The facilities and the selection of the first class of twelve girls to enter the Tokyo Teacher Training School for Women (Tokyo Joshi Shihan Gakkō) were completed for the grand opening on November 29, 1875.[24]

Murray became familiar with the problems involved in setting up a nationwide system of elementary schools through translated reports by inspectors in the field from the Ministry of Education. The next step called for Murray to visit the new elementary schools under the code in several distant prefectures—Nagasaki, Hyōgo, Osaka, and Kyoto—in 1874. It would be his first opportunity as a Western advisor to personally observe the effects of the Code of Education in order to recommend appropriate revisions in his second official report to Vice Minister Tanaka.

Murray's primary criticism of the schools throughout the four sites was the comparatively low rate of attendance of girls in the elementary schools. Depending on the prefecture, he felt that the public education of boys had developed satisfactorily in contrast to the limited progress of education for girls. He noted that private schools had been founded to accommodate girls, but they often emphasized subjects such as needlework and embroidery. Murray summarized his recommendations from his trip to southern Japan under four categories:

1. Progress at the elementary school level has reached a stage where the development of middle or secondary schools should be planned. . . .
2. In order to recruit qualified teachers for the new middle or secondary schools, there are two tracks. . . . The first are the national foreign language schools whose graduates would make good middle school teachers. The second is to develop the curriculum for the new schools at

the government teacher training schools . . . where the student can be prepared to teach the new courses. . . .

3. In order to improve the teaching of the Japanese Language, better textbooks are needed. Improved textbooks for other subjects such as geography and mathematics are also urgently required. . . .
4. English language schools under the control of the Ministry of Education should be made more effective utilizing oral methods for foreign language teaching modeled on Western methods.[25]

By the time of Murray's inspection trip to the south in late 1874, a division between him and Tanaka on the course of educational reform was emerging slowly and almost imperceptibly. In contrast to Murray's recommendation to "push forward" the modern educational reforms, Tanaka was increasingly concerned about local opposition to them.[26]

The Japanese Educational Exhibit at the American Centennial

In 1875, the Japanese government was invited by the American government to participate in the 1876 Centennial International Exhibition. The event celebrating the one-hundredth anniversary of American independence was scheduled to run from May through November in Philadelphia, Pennsylvania. Japan, along with governments from all over the world, was invited to enter exhibits in a huge display of national progress. Among the exhibits was a special area set aside for education. In an extraordinarily daring decision, Tanaka Fujimaro proposed that the Ministry of Education assume sole responsibility for entering an educational exhibit from Japan independent of the national exhibit.[27] Since the plans called for David Murray to spend over half a year in the United States prior to the opening of the centennial, the ministry signaled that it was placing a heavy responsibility on its senior American official. It was also indicative of Tanaka's increasing interest in American education.

Among the officials in the Ministry of Education delegation, Hatakeyama Yoshinari stands out as the one member with the broadest experiences in the West and the closest relationship with the Murrays. By the time of the centennial, he had become a confidant as well as a trusted colleague of Murray. Moreover, he served as the Murrays' translator on official trips within the country and explained David Murray's ideas to ministry officials, most of whom could not understand English. All these duties assisting Murray took place while Hatakeyama simultaneously served as president of Kaisei Gakkō. He had recovered sufficiently from an earlier illness when the Murrays took care of him in their Tokyo home to make the long journey to Philadelphia in May 1876. The trip was most likely at Murray's request.

In preparation for the exhibit, Tanaka decided to have the Ministry of Education prepare a publication in English on the history of Japanese education. Titled

An Outline History of Japanese Education, it was to be published by an American company and made ready for display at the centennial. An indication of his confidence in Murray, Tanaka appointed his American advisor to carry out the project. Moreover, Tanaka commissioned Murray to write the first chapter covering the modern period that was initiated with the *Gakusei*. The book, published by Appleton, marks the first publication in any language on the history of Japanese education. The fact that an American who had known little about Japanese education a few years previously was the editor and author of the introductory chapter on modern Japanese education is without precedence.

Murray was given several major assignments to carry out while in America. They demonstrated the breadth of his contacts and the contributions to modern Japanese education that he made during his tenure with the Ministry of Education. First of all, he was authorized to purchase up to $20,000 worth of materials for an educational museum and a library under consideration by Tanaka. Murray purchased the materials in America and had them sent to Japan, where they formed the nucleus of the exhibits for Japan's first educational museum in Ueno, Tokyo. Murray was also entrusted with $5,000 by the Kaisei Gakkō to purchase educational materials, primarily books for the library.[28] The fact that this leading Japanese institution entrusted Murray with its funds reveals the close ties he had developed with the school then under the presidency of Hatekayama Yoshinari. The task also fell within the terms of his contract, which stipulated that he would "use all diligence to advance knowledge and science" in Japan.

The centennial provided the first opportunity for Murray to meet educators from Europe and the United States who were directly involved in forming educational policy in their respective countries as Murray was in Japan. He took advantage of the opportunity, reporting that he "gave much time . . . to the conferences with the representatives from different countries."[29] Murray's ideas on the critical issue of the administrative control and supervision of education in Japan were crystallized during the centennial. For the first time, his writings and speeches included references to the topic with conviction. Ironically, they would provoke an inevitable division between him and Tanaka concerning the reform of Japanese education.

Murray's *Report on the Educational Exhibits at the Philadelphia Exhibition of 1876* was in part intended as a means to advance his growing convictions on the best system of administration for Japanese education:

> In a country like Japan where the people have been accustomed and rely much upon the guidance and assistance of government, more will be required of the governmental administration than in a country where the communities had been more accustomed to rely upon themselves. The deficiencies in the old system of education in the additions that have been required to the subjects of

> study have made the interference and assistance of the government much more necessary. It is evident that at least for the present not only elementary schools be encouraged and direction given to their organization and management but even higher education must receive help and direction from the Department. In doing this something may be done indirectly by encouragement and systems of careful inspection and supervision.[30]

Murray's report reveals for the first time his bias toward the central control and administration of education as practiced in Europe—notably Germany—in contrast to the American system as he understood it. His unequivocal conclusion that "it has always been found necessary for an enlightened government to take direct control of the education of the masses of the people" henceforth set the tone of his recommendations to Tanaka for Japanese education.

Murray was influenced by leading educators who participated in the conferences, such as James Wickersham, who, as Pennsylvania superintendent of education, was responsible for the education exhibition at the centennial because it was held in Pennsylvania. Wickersham's report is, not coincidentally, similar to Murray's. For example, in the section on European schools, Wickersham contrasted the locally elected lay school board system in Pennsylvania with that of Prussia, by then part of Germany, indirectly criticizing the system in his own state.[31] Concurring, Murray wrote, "In more recent times experience has shown that the system of leaving education in the care of the local communities produces uncertain and unsatisfactory results. The poor and ignorant neighborhoods retain their ignorance, because of their inability or unwillingness to support the necessary schools."[32]

The centennial exhibition closed on November 10, 1876, after a successful six-month run. The delegation from the Japanese Ministry of Education took the opportunity before departing for Japan to visit schools in several southern states, including Virginia and North Carolina. At one stop Tanaka was able to arrange a visit to a public school for African American children.[33] The Murrays' departure for Japan was, however, overshadowed by sorrow. Hatakeyama had fallen ill again with tuberculosis in the midst of the centennial and had decided to return home. While waiting to depart for Japan themselves, the Murrays received word that Hatakeyama had died on October 20, 1876, on board his ship as it neared Japan. It was devastating news for the Murrays. David wrote a passionate and heartwarming memorial of his dearest Japanese friend and colleague during the long voyage home: "In the particular work in which it has been my lot to be engaged, Mr. Hatakeyama has been not only my most confidential friend and advisor but my most efficient ally and colaborer [*sic*]. . . . His loss at this time is not only a serious one to his personal friends and to his family who looked to him with pride and hope but a calamity to the cause of education and civilization in his country."[34]

David Murray's Later Career in Japan

Upon Murray's return to Japan from the American centennial, he became immersed in a concentrated effort by Tanaka to overhaul the 1872–1873 Code of Education. Murray was given the assignment to recommend revisions of the code by Tanaka, who had returned to Japan highly motivated by his experiences during the six months in America. Tanaka was determined to bring about a major reform in Japanese education based more firmly than ever on the American model. Using a collection of laws and regulations gathered during his trip and published in Japanese by the Ministry of Education as reference, he launched a campaign to replace the Code of Education with a new law on education.[35] Tanaka's experiences in America and Europe led him to conclude that the school system under the Code of Education proved too rigid in applying its key provision: compelling each community of six hundred residents to establish and maintain an elementary school with its curriculum set by the Ministry of Education.

Since the new system of public elementary schools had provoked widespread opposition among the peasant class virtually from the moment of its inception, Tanaka, being the progressive that he was, had become deeply concerned about the opposition that was expressed through acts of violence in many rural areas. In response, he had come to the conclusion that a modern society was an outgrowth of a people who have freedom of thought (*jiyū shisō*). The American system of education, with its control of education under locally elected lay school boards reflecting the will of the community in its policies, was the epitome of freedom of thought to Tanaka. Accordingly, he set out to develop an educational reform plan that was patterned loosely on the American model in order to decentralize the control of education to the maximum extent possible.[36] David Murray and his staff were given the assignment to draw up a proposal from an American perspective for the revision of the code. The two reports were then to serve as reference materials for Tanaka himself to oversee the final version of the educational reform plan for government approval and ultimate implementation.

By 1877, the challenging task of educational reform had become embroiled in controversy, dividing the senior Japanese officials within the ministry and, for the first time, provoking a split between Tanaka and Murray. The fundamental question was, in simple terms, at what level—the local, the prefectural, or the national—should the authority be vested to regulate the nation's public elementary schools? The answer would influence what courses should be prescribed for all students; how many years of schooling should be required; how schools, teachers' salaries, textbooks, and so on should be financed; and of great import, who would determine the course content.

Murray's recommendations can be characterized as adhering to the basic principles outlined in the Code of Education of 1872. His advice to Japan was to primarily follow the German system by investing strong powers at the central level of government. The sentiments expressed in Murray's 1877 recommendations bear a close resemblance to those in Wickersham's 1876 report from the Philadelphia centennial. Wickersham's report was intended as a critique of the decentralized administrative structure of Pennsylvania schools, which prevented him from properly addressing the academic imbalances and vastly divergent standards according to wealth and civic commitment among local school districts.

By the end of 1877, Tanaka had prepared a new code of education for approval by the ruling body of the government, the Genrōin. It was intended to replace the Code of Education of 1872 with the second plan for a public school system titled simply the School Law (*Kyōiku Rei*). In the process, however, it set off a provocative dispute concerning the direction of Japanese education in the modern era, which presented an unprecedented challenge to David Murray as superintendent of Japanese education.

Although Tanaka's proposed law stipulated that the Ministry of Education was responsible for the educational affairs of the country in principle, it introduced into Japan the *gakumuin*, the locally elected school board system on the American pattern. Local school boards were empowered to supervise (*kanri*) the local curriculum. Officially, the ministry was granted the authority to approve curriculums. Tanaka, however, intended it to be liberally applied. Private schools were given considerable freedom, since prefectural offices had little authority to compel curriculum revisions. The following articles were among the critical and most controversial provisions of Tanaka's proposed School Law: "Each community shall be responsible for organizing a public elementary school administered by a committee elected by the citizens of the community. Each local public school will design its own curriculum subject to the approval of the Ministry of Education."[37] Tanaka ignored Murray's primary recommendations as well as those of the senior Japanese officials who supported the same position. Tanaka staked not only his reputation but his future and that of Japanese education on the American model of education. Critics within the ministry characterized Tanaka as "*America kabure*"—that is, obsessed with America.[38]

By the time Tanaka formally submitted his Education Law proposal to the government for approval on May 14, 1878, a second controversial issue had emerged. It related to Article 3 in Tanaka's bill: The basic curriculum of the public elementary schools will include reading, calligraphy, mathematics, geography, history, and morals (*shūshin*).[39] The contentious issue over this particular provision concerned the morals course. Some critics of the modern school system based on Western models, particularly the American model as envisioned by Tanaka, decried the absence of moral direction for the youth of Japan since the Meiji Restoration. They became increasingly alarmed at the imbalances in the subjects listed in the required curriculum of the new public elementary schools. The issue was focused initially on what should be taught in the required morals course during the new era of enlightenment championed by the Meiji government. During the several hundred years of the Tokugawa regime, Confucian morality from China teaching respect for parents, elders, and those in authority through ethical lessons in the *terakoya* schools perpetuated a moral foundation of the society that was generally accepted by all social levels, including the peasant class. The call for traditional moral teachings to be included in the national curriculum provoked further controversy when the proponents demanded that the Ministry of Education rebalance the curriculum between Eastern morality and Western science. They advocated reversing the order of required subjects in the public schools of Japan, elevating the course on morals from the bottom to the top. Significantly, David Murray did not involve himself in the morals debate, contending that morality was determined by the Bible. Since Japan was not a Christian country, Murray did not attempt to impose his views on moral education.

In spring 1878, David Murray found himself marginalized at the Ministry of Education. The ministry, mired in controversy over Tanaka Fujimaro's Education Law, had essentially bypassed Murray. Searching for another role for himself, in March 1878, Murray "proposed to the Senior Vice Minister Tanaka to make a systematic inspection of the Public Schools of the city of Tokio."[40] As it turned out, Murray's proposal resulted in one of his major contributions to modern Japanese education. It was the most systematic research since the implementation of a universal system of education five years prior ushered in a social transformation from feudalism to modernism. For the first time, Murray confronted the reality of the problems of the *Gakusei* from a firsthand perspective as it was enforced at the local level. When the Ministry of Education had drawn up the first "Plan of Study" in 1872–1873, it had proved impossible to implement in the capital city. Perhaps grudgingly, Murray recognized that "It has been found a matter of no little difficulty to contrive an elementary school course which could be used in common for the education of all classes of the community." Although Murray did not refer to this challenge, it was one of the results of the *Gakusei* that motivated Tanaka to recommend that it be replaced with a new code of education.

In his report to Tanaka on the Tokyo schools, Murray listed the colleagues from his office at the Ministry of Education who joined him in his research: "Mr. Orita from the *Mombusho* (Ministry) was my associate in nearly the whole time the visits were made, his place being taken on various occasions by Messrs Egi and Hirayama." Orita Hikoichi (1849–1920) had met Murray in New Brunswick as a samurai youth and was one of the first Japanese to graduate from Princeton University.[41] Hirayama Tarō (1849–1891) was one of Murray's samurai students at Rutgers College. Murray's other assistant, Egi Kazuyuki (1853–1932), stood out from both Orita and Hirayama in that he had no prior relationship to Murray. In contrast to the other two assistants, Egi was politically oriented and highly motivated by his aspirations to attain a leadership position. He would become the Minister of Education after Murray left Japan, becoming one of the most powerful figures to assume that position.

Tanaka's Education Law was approved on September 29, 1879. Intended by Tanaka as a means for local communities to adapt the new public schools to the needs of each community, the new school boards were ill-equipped to design a curriculum for their community schools, nor did they know how to go about choosing textbooks for each course. There was an immediate and sharp decrease in the enrollment of female students. In some communities, public schools were closed due to inadequate funding. At the same time, in many communities the morals course in the public elementary schools was simply dropped because the purpose of the course had never been clearly defined by the Ministry of Education under Tanaka.

Although the progressive positions of Tanaka's Education Law went into effect in the 1879 academic year, opposition to local control of education and to the lack of concern for traditional morals education in the public school system had by then solidified into a powerful movement that brought about the great reverse course of modern Japanese education in 1880. The imperial advisor and Confucian scholar Motoda Eifu (1818–1891) led the movement from the imperial household, providing the theoretical and compelling foundation for the reverse course through his Imperial Will on Education. In effect, Tanaka found himself pitted against the "will" of the Emperor Meiji himself. Leading the opposition camp from within the Ministry of Education and forging an alliance with the imperial household was a coterie of strong-minded officials who had opposed Tanaka's progressive ideas from the beginning. Among them, the most influential turned out to be Murray's assistant Egi Kazuyuki. Egi, by then more knowledgeable about Murray's ideas than any other ministry officer, was confident in his understanding and appreciation of the American's thoughtful recommendations, which were carefully designed for the future of Japan in the modern world. Egi attributed his own position on the central control of education for Japan to what he had learned from Murray while working with him on his report for Tanaka.

Egi interpreted Murray's ideas on education in his own way. According to Egi, contrary to what many people assumed—that Murray held liberal educational ideas—his convictions on educational administration were the opposite. Egi believed Murray advocated strict government control over education, with the Ministry of Education "intervening" in local education to maintain a proper national standard. Moreover, Egi was impressed with Murray's understanding of and appreciation for German education, with its strict central control. He claimed that based on Murray's convictions, Murray advocated strong centralization of education for Japan in his recommendations as senior advisor to Tanaka. Based on Egi's interpretation of Murray's position, he concluded that Murray's educational plan for Japan was correct.

The first official step in the reverse course of modern Japanese education was the temporary appointment of Terashima Munenori (1832–1893) as Minister of Education on September 10, 1879.[42] Tanaka Fujimaro, having served as head of the ministry since 1873, although without the title, was not replaced. Nevertheless, Tanaka was aware of the precariousness of his position. With the selection of Kōno Togama (1844–1895) as Minister of Education on February 28, 1880, replacing Terashima, the reverse course was finally set in motion.[43] Two weeks later, Tanaka was transferred to the Ministry of Justice, surprisingly as minister, on March 13, 1880.[44] Thus ended the long reign of Tanaka as the top official in the Ministry of Education.

In August 1880, Education Minister Kōno appointed an extraordinary (*rinji*) committee for the revision of Tanaka's Education Law. Egi, one of three members appointed to the committee, was given the responsibility to write the draft.[45] Four months later, on December 28, 1880, the Education Law (*Kyōiku Rei*) was promulgated by the government.[46] It replaced Tanaka's Education Law, which had only been in place for fifteen months. Egi played a major role in its formation and wrote the law in an impressively short period. The primary purpose of the Revised Education Law of 1880 and its guidelines was to set a national curriculum for the country's public schools. By doing this, Egi returned the nation's school system to the centralized control of education under the Ministry of Education as it was under the 1872 code, but with increased powers. This change was based on one of Murray's major recommendations—that "the Department of Education should be distinctly authorized to issue all necessary measures to carry into full effect the provisions of the Code"—which Tanaka had rejected in his 1879 Education Law.

The second issue of great historical significance concerned the repositioning of moral education from the bottom of the list of subjects to the top of the required curriculum. In the process of elevating morals education, one of the important moments in Japanese educational history transpired. Through the morals course, Egi was instrumental in introducing a new and ultimately highly provocative theme—imperial ideology and loyalty to the country—into the curriculum of the nation's public schools. In the first section of the Guidelines for Elementary School Teachers, Egi instructed teachers that their students must be taught loyalty to the imperial family and their homeland of Japan—that is, "Revere the emperor—love our country (*sonnō aikoku*)."[47]

Egi's Education Law of 1880 and its guidelines for implementation consequently set the direction of modern education in Japan for the twentieth century from a nationalistic perspective. It conformed to the convictions of both his mentors. At the same time, it represented Egi's great divergence from Murray's recommendations to the ministry by stipulating precisely the official attitude toward the imperial institution and its integral position in the nation's cultural history that each child should learn in school. One possible critique of Murray that deserves consideration concerns the negative consequences of the strongest recommendation he made to Tanaka Fujimaro for modern Japanese education: It could be argued that by advocating centralization, Murray's recommendation provided the opportunity for ultranationalists to gain control of the government in the twentieth century, which provoked the rise of militarism in the name of the emperor. This course ultimately led to disaster for Japan in World War II. Although his purpose in enabling the government to determine what was taught in the public schools of Japan had nothing to do with militarism and emperor worship, it nevertheless could be contended that Murray's passion for the centralized control of Japanese education in 1877 contributed to a dictatorial form of government in Japan in the twentieth century.

As superintendent of Japanese education, however, Murray's assertion that a highly centralized school system was best for Japan reflected the unconditional commitment he felt for the well-being of Japan and its future. Murray's commitment to the future of Japan was dependent upon his confidence that Japanese government leaders were capable of carrying out his most demanding recommendation. Regardless of the complexities of administering a public school system, Murray had no doubt that the officials charged with that responsibility would conduct themselves in a manner beneficial to the country.

Conclusion

After the expiration of Murray's second contract with the Ministry of Education in 1878, David and Martha prepared to leave Japan. On December 12, 1878, Martha wrote, "We leave our house two weeks from today. . . . We go to some entertainment almost every afternoon or event."[48] Ten days later, she wrote, "Last week Wednesday David had his farewell audience with the Mikado who bestowed upon him the 'Order of Rising Sun,' a beautiful decoration with writing signed with his own handwriting."[49] Due to delays in the departure of their ship, the Murrays left Japan on January 21, 1878, headed for a trip through Europe on the way home to their beloved New Brunswick. Back in New Jersey, Murray did not resume teaching but instead became a trustee of Rutgers College. He also devoted himself to writing—publishing *Japan*, part of the "Story of the Nations" series, which first appeared in 1894 and went through six editions. He also wrote *History of Education in New Jersey* (1899). David Murray died on March 6, 1905, and is buried at Elmwood Cemetery in New Brunswick. After his death, Martha Murray donated his portrait wearing the Order of the Rising Sun to the Rutgers Kirkpatrick Chapel, where it hangs to this day.

Notes

This chapter consists of excerpts from Benjamin Duke's *Dr. David Murray: Superintendent of Education of the Empire of Japan, 1873–1879* (New Brunswick, NJ: Rutgers University Press, 2019). I thank Suchisman Gangopadhyay for help with editing the earlier version of this chapter.

1 See David Murray, ed., *Delaware County, New York: History of the Century, 1797–1897* (Delhi, NY: William Clark, 1898), 121–131.
2 See William Chamberlain, ed., *In Memoriam* (self-published, 1915), 2.
3 See Chamberlain, 20.
4 Martha Neilson Murray of New York (born 1833) and David Murray met in New Brunswick, where she had relatives, and were married in 1867.
5 *Daily Home News*, January 19, 1929.
6 Chamberlain, *In Memoriam*, 3.
7 David Murray, "Hatakeyama Yoshinari of Japan," *The Japanese Student* 1, no. 3 (February 1917): 108–109.
8 See chapter 11 on the Iwakura Mission.
9 *New York Times*, December 18, 1871.
10 See chapter 10 on the Satsuma-Rutgers connection.
11 Martha Murray to Lucy Carpender, 9 September 1873, box 1, David Murray Papers, 1866–1930 (Washington, DC: U.S. Library of Congress, 2023) (hereafter David Murray Papers, 1866–1930).
12 Since Murray could not speak or read Japanese, Tanaka Fujimaro assigned Takahashi Korekiyo, a twenty-year-old ex-samurai who had spent a short period in America, as Murray's first translator and assistant. Takahashi Korekiyo eventually became the president of the Bank of Japan, the minister of finance on several occasions, and the prime minister of Japan. See Takahashi Korekiyo, *Takahashi Korekiyo jiden* (Tokyo: Chūō Kōronsha, 1996), 146.
13 David Murray to Lucy Carpender, 16 November 1873, box 1, David Murray Papers, 1866–1930.
14 David Murray to Lucy Carpender, 21 September 1873, box 1, David Murray Papers, 1866–1930.
15 Murray, "Hatakeyama Yoshinari of Japan," 112.
16 E. Warren Clark, *Life and Adventures in Japan* (New York: American Tract Society, 1878), 131–132.
17 Richard Rubinger, *Private Academies of Tokugawa Japan* (Princeton, NJ: Princeton University Press, 1982), 6.
18 Ronald Dore, *Education in Tokugawa Japan* (Oakland: University of California Press, 1965), 254.
19 Dore, *Education in Tokugawa Japan*, 11.
20 Rubinger, *Private Academies*, 193–199.
21 Kaigo Tokiomi, *Nihon kindai kyōiku shi jiten* (Tokyo: Heibonsha, 1971), 781.
22 Mizuhara Katsutoshi, *Kindai Nihon kyōin yōseishi kenkyū* (Tokyo: Kazama Shobō, 1990), 56.
23 David Murray, *Copy of the Official Report of the Honorable Superintendent of Schools and Colleges in Japan to the Vice Minister of Education, in Circulars of Information, United States Bureau of Education*, no. 2 (Washington, DC: U.S. Government Printing Office, 1875), 2.
24 Tsuchiya Tadao, *Meiji zenki: Kyōiku seisaku shi no kenkyū* (Tokyo: Kōdansha, 1962), 187.
25 Meiji Bunka Kenkyū Kai, *Meiji bunka zenshū, kyōiku hen*, vol 11, *Kyōiku hen* (1928; reprint, Tokyo: Nihon Hyōronsha, 1992), 124–136.
26 Murray, *Copy of the Official Report*, 141–151.
27 Ishizuki Minoru, "Firaderufia Hakurankai to Nihon no kyōiku," in *Jūkyū seiki Nihon no jōhō to shakai hendō*, ed. Yoshida Mitsukuni (Kyoto: Kyoto Daigaku Jinbun Kagaku Kenkyūjō, 1985), 431–432.
28 Ishizuki, "Hiraderufia Hakurankai to Nihon no kyōiku," 434.

29 David Murray, *Report on the Educational Exhibits at the Philadelphia Exhibition of 1876*, n.p., David Murray Papers, 1866–1930.
30 Murray, *Report on the Educational Exhibits.*
31 See James Wickersham, *A History of Education in Pennsylvania* (Lancaster, PA: The Inquirer, 1882).
32 Murray, *Report on the Educational Exhibits.*
33 *Abe Taizō den* (Tokyo: Meiji Seimei Hoken Sōgō Kaisha, 1971), 53.
34 Murray, "Hatakeyama Yoshinari of Japan," 113.
35 David Murray, *Report upon a Draft Revision of the Code of Education in Japan*, David Murray Papers, 1866–1930.
36 Tanaka Akihiro, *Monbu jihō* (Tokyo: Ministry of Education, 1941), 109.
37 Kyōikushi Hensankai, ed., *Meiji ikō: Kyōiku seido hattatsu shi*, vol. 1 (Tokyo: Ryūginsha, 1938), 141–165.
38 Tsuchiya, *Meiji zenki*, 184.
39 Ministry of Education, *Meiji ikō*, 162.
40 David Murray, "Public Schools of Tokio, 1877," David Murray Papers, 1866–1930.
41 On Orita, see chapter 6 in this volume.
42 Inuzaka Takaaki, *Terashima Munenori* (Tokyo: Yoshikawa Kōbunkan, 1990), 299–300.
43 Kaigo, *Nihon kindai kyōiku shi jiten*, 778.
44 Yamazumi Masami, *Nihon kindai shisō: Kyōiku taisei* (Tokyo: Iwanami Shoten, 1990), 106–107.
45 Egi Kazuyuki-Ō Keireki Dan Kankōkai, ed., *Egi Kazuyuki-ō keireki dan* (Tokyo: Ōzorasha, 1933), 46–47.
46 Kaigo, *Nihon kindai kyōiku shi jiten*, 777.
47 Egi, *Egi Kazuyuki-ō keireki dan*, 67.
48 Martha Murray to Lucy Carpender, 12 December 1878, box 1, David Murray Papers, 1866–1930.
49 Martha Murray to Lucy Carpender, 23 December 1878, box 1 David Murray Papers, 1866–1930.

Part V

Reformed Church Missionaries and Early Christian Education

13

James H. Ballagh

The First Rutgers Graduate in Japan

KOJI NAKAJIMA

The first American who built a bridge between Rutgers College and Japan was Samuel Robbins Brown (1810–1880), a missionary of the Reformed Church in America (RCA).[1] At the request of his church's Board of Foreign Missions, in the spring of 1859, just before leaving for Japan, Brown visited the New Brunswick Theological Seminary (NBTS) to encourage its students' interest in Japan as a newly opened mission field. There, in response to an anxious question from a prospective missionary, he replied, "You need not feel badly about it; I will go and prepare the way for you."[2]

It is not clear whether the student who asked the question was James Hamilton Ballagh (1832–1920), a graduate of Rutgers College, but when Ballagh was about to complete his seminary studies the following year, he submitted a letter of application to the RCA Board of Foreign Missions. Since the slots for Japan were already filled, he requested and got approval to go to Amoy (Xiamen) in China. However, a physical examination revealed that Ballagh had a suspected lung disease, and his departure was postponed for one year. During this time, he tried to learn the Fujian dialect of the Xiamen region but found it too difficult, so he withdrew his application and put in a new request to be sent to Japan. His wish was granted at

FIGURE 13.1. James H. Ballagh, 1860. (Credit: Archives of the Reformed Church in America.)

the end of 1860, and in June 1861, accompanied by his new wife, Margaret, Ballagh left New York Harbor with great ambitions for his future service in Asia.[3]

Thus, Ballagh crossed the bridge that Brown had built, becoming the fourth missionary of the RCA and the first Rutgers College graduate to go to Japan. This chapter traces his life as a missionary for fifty-eight years in Japan who contributed greatly to the development of the Protestant Church during the critical period of Japan's modernization.

Early Life and Awakening to Faith

James H. Ballagh was born on September 7, 1832, in Odell's Lake (Hobart), Delaware County, New York, to John Hamilton Ballagh (1800–1888) and Ann Prudencia Craig Ballagh (1807–1887). He was the second of five sons and five daughters. The Ballagh family adhered to the traditional Scotch-Irish Presbyterian faith and belonged to the Associate Reformed Presbyterian Church in North Kortright, New York, where James was baptized as an infant. His mother, Ann, was a devout believer who, as a young woman, had been asked by a female friend to accompany her to India as a missionary. Ann replied, "No, you go. I'll stay at home and raise up missionaries!"[4] As promised, once she had a family of her own, she raised and sent four missionaries out into the world from among her ten children, three of whom devoted their lives to Japan.[5]

The large Ballagh family was never wealthy, but under his parents' influence, James developed the habits of religious life in early childhood. His exposure at a young age to diverse environments also helped shape his religious attitudes. At the age of six he was sent for some time to live with a relative who owned a household goods store in Brooklyn, New York, where he attended parochial school and experienced city life. When his younger brother John was born, their father took on a businessman acquaintance's debt as a guarantor, after which he had to give up his land and began renting farmland from a relative in neighboring Davenport, New York. On Sundays, James attended the Associate Reformed Presbyterian Church to which his parents belonged, eight miles from their village. At this time, he began to think about his future options, first as a storekeeper, second as a schoolteacher, and third as a pastor. He came to believe that a pastor would be the best choice, because this vocation would enable shopkeepers and schoolteachers to come and hear the teachings of God.[6]

In 1844, when James was twelve years old, the Ballagh family left Davenport and moved to New York City due to hardship. James and his older siblings worked part-time at a drugstore to help make ends meet. However, the family's finances became increasingly difficult, and they soon moved to Rockland County, where they again rented a relative's farmland and started anew. While helping on the farm, James had the opportunity to attend the local county school for a year, but after a while he had to stop and work in his uncle's store about ten miles from home. Instead, he attended Sunday school at a local church whose simple but faithful teachers inspired him spiritually.[7]

At the age of sixteen, James experienced two life-changing incidents that confirmed his faith. The first incident occurred in March 1848, when his mother fell critically ill after giving birth to her tenth child, Robert. His father told him to gather their relatives in town, so he walked several miles alone in the dark to reach the railroad station at dawn, praying to God to spare his mother's life along the way. He took the train to town and told his relatives about his mother's condition, upon which they encouraged and reassured him that she would be all right. When he returned home that night, he found his mother had recovered. For the first time, James felt the power of prayer.[8]

That same year, James left his parents and went to New York City to work in a general store. The mother of its owner was a devout Methodist, and her attitude toward religious life taught him devotion to God and warmth of heart. In May 1849, when the owner's three-year-old daughter, Libby, died of an illness, James was so saddened that he exclaimed, "What a dark world was this! . . . I sincerely wished to die."[9] This event was the catalyst for his awakening to faith.

It was at this store, which also served as a post office and carried various religious newspapers, that James learned of the death of Samuel D. Scudder, who had been preparing to go to India as a missionary. He was greatly moved by an article in the *Christian Intelligencer* in November of that year reporting the death of the twenty-two-year-old Scudder, who had graduated from Rutgers College and then studied at NBTS. His father, John Scudder, was a famous physician affiliated with the RCA who had carried out medical missions in India, and Samuel had been born in Ceylon (now Sri Lanka), his father's assigned site. Ballagh is said to have instinctively and instantly thought that he would be the one to continue Samuel's legacy and responded, "Here am I Lord, send me."[10] This experience led James to think seriously about confessing his faith, and he spent the next year reading through the entire Bible.[11]

Around this time, his parents purchased and moved to a small plot of farmland in Tenafly, Bergen County, New Jersey. James Ballagh went instead from New York City to Haverstraw, Rockland County, west of the Hudson River, where he found employment in a large household goods store. There he interacted with his fellow clerks like a family, his devotion to God growing ever stronger as he attended services at the Central Presbyterian Church (CPC) and made the acquaintance of the young Reverend Amasa S. Freeman. Speaking with Freeman day and night, he found that the minister's words provided a home for his soul, though his sense of sin continued to torment him.[12]

One day, he finally found the Savior and the impetus for his conversion. Ballagh came across a tract entitled "The Harvest Perishing for Lack of Laborers." The author was John Scudder, the father of Samuel Scudder, whose death Ballagh had found so moving. Ballagh was so taken by its contents that he said, "Here am I, Lord, send me!" and vowed to work in pagan lands.[13] His decision, however, raised one concern: Ballagh's parents belonged to the Presbyterian Church of the Old School, whereas the CPC he attended belonged to the New School.[14] Ballagh went to his parents' home in Tenafly and confided in his mother about his decision to become a pastor of the New School. To his surprise, she consented and told him that she and his father would soon be transferring to the RCA, which also belonged to the New School, so Ballagh told Reverend Freeman of his mother's consent and officially joined the CPC.[15]

Ballagh attended the RCA whenever he returned home to his parents in Tenafly and came to know many of its members. Through such interactions, at the age of nineteen in 1851, after a struggle between loyalty to the CPC's Reverend Freeman and the encouragement of his parents, friends, pastors, and theologians from the RCA, Ballagh finally decided to transfer to the RCA in Tenafly and to become a pastor and undertake an overseas mission.[16]

Rutgers College, the New Brunswick Theological Seminary, and Departure for Japan

Although James Ballagh was determined to become an RCA missionary, this required a general college education and specialized training at a seminary. The best way to achieve this goal was to study at the RCA-affiliated Rutgers College and the denomination's seminary, the NBTS. However, because he lacked basic academic skills—he had been constantly working and changing schools—he moved to Tenafly so that he could study for college entrance exams while helping his parents with the farm, and he also applied for a scholarship loan for aspiring pastors. After a year and a half of diligent study, in the fall of 1852, Ballagh enrolled in Rutgers Grammar School at the age of twenty and soon moved on to Rutgers College. In his autobiography, he casually states that "Of College life four, busy, happy years I need not recount much," but he must have struggled with his studies due to his family's financial situation.[17]

In 1857, Ballagh attended his Rutgers College graduation ceremony at the First Reformed Church of New Brunswick, where he saw his spiritual mentor, Reverend Freeman, who came to congratulate him. Ballagh enrolled that year at NBTS, which was located on the college campus. He spent two summers on a mission trip that included the selling of bibles. During his time at the seminary, he also attended lectures by senior missionaries about to embark on overseas missions and was actively mentored by a professor at Princeton Theological Seminary, which the Presbyterian Church ran.[18]

A post opened in Japan just as Ballagh was about to graduate from the seminary. In May 1859, three missionaries of the RCA—Samuel R. Brown, Guido F. Verbeck (1830–1898), and Duane B. Simmons (1832–1889)—had left for Japan. Brown and Simmons arrived in Kanagawa and Verbeck in Nagasaki in November of the same year. However, Simmons resigned as a missionary less than a year later, and Brown requested that the Board of Foreign Missions dispatch Ballagh, who had been asking to go to Japan for some time. In the spring of 1860, Ballagh graduated from the seminary and received a master of arts degree from Rutgers College. At the same time, he was ordained at the RCA's Bergen Classis. After qualifying as a pastor, he applied to the board to conduct a mission in Japan.[19]

Ballagh was surprised and delighted when the board informed him at the end of December 1860 that he would soon receive a letter of appointment to go to Japan, and he immediately told his family and relatives the news. His aunt, Jane Ballagh Kinnier, advised him to bring a wife on an overseas mission and introduced him to a distant relative, Margaret Tate Kinnear (1840–1911).[20] Born on November 23, 1840, in Rockbridge County, Virginia, Margaret had been raised by her paternal aunt after her parents had died when she was very young. She was an extremely intelligent woman who had graduated in 1857 at the top of her class from a girls' school in Norristown, Pennsylvania. Ballagh was pleased that she was a religious woman who had considered evangelizing abroad, and Margaret trusted in his character.[21] Aunt Jane arranged for the couple to be married on May 15, 1861, at a church in Brownsburg, Virginia, where Margaret lived. Before leaving the United States, they stopped by Ballagh's parents' house to pray together, and on June 1 they left New York Harbor for Shanghai aboard the *Cathay*. Although Confederate troops had opened fire in South Carolina on

April 12, plunging America into civil war, Ballagh's sense of duty was already focused on his mission in Japan.[22]

Margaret later wrote a memoir titled *Glimpses of Old Japan*, which begins with their departure from the port of New York.[23] The *Cathay* sailed southward across the Atlantic, but Margaret, seasick from the first day of the voyage, had little appetite until June 16, and she could only sit down to dine on June 18. The newlyweds subsequently enjoyed the Equator Festival on June 27, passed the Cape of Good Hope on July 24, and started across the Indian Ocean on August 12. On August 25, they arrived in Anjir, Java, where the governor-general of the Netherlands welcomed them. They entered Xiamen on September 11 and sailed for Shanghai the next day, but the sea was rough, and they finally arrived on September 27, 122 days after leaving New York. After spending about a month in Shanghai, they left for Japan on October 23 aboard the *Aida D. Rogers*, a small boat of 196 tons. The seas remained calm, and the sailing ship made slow progress, and on November 7, they approached the Kumano coast. At this point, a sudden storm almost sank the ship and threw the captain into despair. Ballagh prayed, "God spare this ship, and if she makes it to shore safely, I will spare none of my life, but will be faithful to my duty and complete this mission."[24] Margaret clung to her bed and prayed for the storm to pass. On November 10, the sea calmed down and the beautiful snowcap of Mount Fuji appeared. The next day, they finally anchored off Kanagawa. James would later write in his memoir that "God saved me in the Kishu Sea to fulfill my vow."[25]

Arrival in Japan and Baptizing the First Japanese Protestant

The Ballaghs joined a group of American missionaries who had already settled in Kanagawa, a small seaport just inside Tokyo Bay, about three miles from what was to become the city of Yokohama.[26] They were assigned a residence at Jōbutsuji, a Pure Land Buddhist temple where the Brown family had lived before them. Jōbutsuji also housed James Curtis Hepburn (1815–1911), a Presbyterian physician who lived with his wife, Clara, in the main building. The Brown family and Caroline Adriance, a self-supporting missionary, lived in the head priest's quarters, and Jonathan Goble and his family, missionaries of the Free Baptist Church, occupied a small house within the temple grounds that then served as the only Protestant mission house in Japan. With Samuel Brown away in Shanghai printing his book, *Colloquial Japanese*, his wife warmly welcomed the Ballaghs. Hepburn, who lived alone in the spacious main building as Clara had temporarily returned home, gladly received his young colleague and invited him and his wife to stay at the main building. Thus began the Ballaghs' mission to Japan.[27]

The couple arrived in Japan when the country was in the midst of the *sonnō jōi*, or "revere the emperor, expel the barbarian," exclusionist movement. In January of that year, Henry C. J. Heusken, an interpreter for Townsend Harris, the U.S. minister to Japan, had been killed by extremist samurai, and in July, a similar attack had targeted the British legation and its minister, Sir Rutherford Alcock, at Tōzenji in Edo; Alcock survived, but several staff members were wounded. Many agitators who sought to expel Westerners also frequented Kanagawa, where foreign diplomatic offices were located. Meanwhile, the Edo shogunate, which had opened the country to the Western powers, still prohibited Christianity and strictly controlled the religion's domestic propagation. It sent spies to Jōbutsuji to monitor the missionaries' activities and stationed shogunal officials at the temple gate in shifts as guards to protect the foreigners from *jōi* activists.[28]

Since the ban on Christianity prevented the missionaries from direct evangelism, their first task was to learn the Japanese language and culture in preparation for the proscription's lifting. Ballagh began receiving the tutelage of Yano Ryūzan (1815–1865), an acupuncture and moxibustion doctor attached to Jōbutsuji. Yano, who was about fifty years old, had previously taught Japanese to Brown and later also tutored Caroline Adriance.[29]

On Sundays, Brown officiated at a service held at the British Consulate in the Yokohama settlement attended by the British minister, the American consul, the Dutch consul, and others, for which his eldest daughter, Julia, played the harmonium. The congregations of the Anglican, Reformed, and Presbyterian churches held joint services in this location. Ballagh gave his first sermon in Japan at the December 1 meeting, and in the afternoon, he returned to Kanagawa to administer Holy Communion to the missionary families at Jōbutsuji.[30]

In late April 1862, Robert Hewson Pruyn (1815–1882) succeeded Harris as the second U.S. minister to Japan, arriving at Zenpukuji in Edo. Pruyn, a deeply religious member of the RCA, soon began attending Sunday services after his arrival in Japan. As the second Rutgers College graduate to go to Japan, he became a close friend of Ballagh. Pruyn listened to his wishes, negotiated with the shogunate to acquire land at 167 Yokohama Foreign Settlement for the RCA mission in Japan, and donated $500 for the construction of a church building. But this stalwart supporter left Japan midway through his term of office in May 1865, citing illness.[31]

Meanwhile, the exclusionist movement in Japan intensified, and the Namamugi Incident, which had occurred in mid-September of the same year, caused unrest among the residents of the foreign settlement. The Goble family, who had been living at Jōbutsuji, built a house in Yokohama the following spring, and Hepburn secured land in the foreign settlement to build a missionary residence and sanatorium, where he moved at the end of 1862. The Brown and Ballagh families remained at Jōbutsuji, but before dawn on June 1, 1863, rising tensions between the British and the shogunate over the Namamugi Incident made Kanagawa unsafe.[32] Ballagh, Margaret, and their newly born daughter, Carrie Elizabeth (1862–1936),[33] along with David Thompson (1835–1915), an American Presbyterian missionary who had just arrived on May 18, took refuge at house number 39 in the foreign settlement in Yokohama, where the Hepburns resided.[34] The Browns rented a small house in the settlement as a temporary home, and the Ballaghs soon moved to a Japanese-style house within the precincts of the U.S. Consulate. On May 23,

1864, the Ballaghs welcomed a second baby girl, naming her Anna Hepburn (1864–1946) in gratitude to the Hepburns for assisting Margaret with her birth.

After settling down in their new home, Ballagh began translating the Chinese Bible into Japanese under the guidance of Yano, with whom he had aims to share the Gospel. According to Hepburn's diagnosis, Yano had pulmonary tuberculosis and his health was slowly declining, but he still commuted daily from his home in Kanagawa to the settlement to see Ballagh. Eventually, Yano's understanding of the Bible improved, and he came to be inspired by Ballagh's passion and personality. When his illness worsened, Ballagh often went to Kanagawa to visit him and comforted him by reading from the Bible they had translated together. Finally, Yano begged Ballagh to baptize him, and on November 5, 1865, this ceremony occurred in the presence of Hepburn and his family, producing Japan's first Protestant.[35] The baptism was a life-threatening event not only for Yano but also for his family because Christianity remained prohibited.

Ballagh and his wife, Margaret, visited Yano at his sickbed the next day during the Harvest Thanksgiving celebration. When Yano saw them, he raised his weak body and, according to Ballagh, "He thanked us each in turn, saying he could never repay us for favors rendered, but he was going to Jesus and he would make mention to Him of our names."[36] With these words, Ballagh and Margaret felt they had received their first reward after coming to Japan. Shortly thereafter, Yano died in the early morning hours of December 5, and the monks of Jōbutsuji buried him in a Buddhist ceremony. He had contributed to Brown and Ballagh's translation of the Gospels of Mark and John, Genesis, and Exodus.[37]

Teaching at the Yokohama Academy and the Construction of the "Sacred Dog Kennel"

By the early 1860s, Yokohama had begun to develop as a trading port, and at Hepburn's suggestion the Kanagawa Magistrate's Office opened the Yokohama Academy (Eigakusho) in July 1864, with the approval of the shogunate, as a language school for customs officials and their children. Brown, Ballagh, and Thompson were assisted by two Japanese—Ōta Genzaburō Sukemasa, a Chinese interpreter, and Ishibashi Sukujūrō Masakata, a Dutch interpreter—as they began teaching twenty-five students. Despite the considerable risk of this endeavor under the prohibition, they prioritized the benefits of acquiring new Western knowledge from highly educated missionaries with trustworthy identities and personalities. The missionaries, on the other hand, volunteered without pay, seeing their teaching as an opportunity to secretly sow the seeds of Christianity among young people in Japan.

Brown was also teaching six students at home at the time, but in November 1865 he passed these duties over to his oldest son, Robert Morrison Brown (1842–1900), who had graduated from Rutgers College in the spring and become the school's third alumnus to work in Japan. Brown subsequently reported to the Board of Foreign Missions that he now had time to translate the Bible,[38] whereas Ballagh sent the board a letter dated November 14, 1865, expressing his joy at the unexpected arrival of a fellow Rutgers alumnus in Japan after Minister Pruyn's departure: "He [Brown] will doubtless inform you of his happiness in his son's arrival a few days since. It is a great pleasure to me also to have a friend from old Brunswick. It carries me quite back in memory to its very old scenes."[39] Notwithstanding this pleasure, Ballagh deemed Robert's abilities somewhat questionable after the latter temporarily took over his father's accounting work for the mission in Japan. Nevertheless, Robert went on to pursue a career in business and politics. According to the *Japan Directory*,[40] he lived in Yokohama until 1879, but his whereabouts after that are unknown. The Rutgers College Alumni Association records indicate that he died in Girard, Pennsylvania, on February 18, 1900.[41]

In the meantime, Margaret became ill in March 1866 and had to return to her native Virginia with her two young daughters for her convalescence. Ballagh accompanied her to San Francisco, where they remained for a while before he returned to Yokohama in August. Margaret gave birth in October to their first son, James Curtis (1866–1944), but her health did not improve afterward, and her stay in the United States was prolonged. Ballagh, after returning to Japan, began holding worship services and Bible classes in Japanese at his home in the U.S. Consulate on the first Sunday of the month.

On November 26 of that year, the Great Fire of Yokohama, commonly known as the "piggery fire" (*butaya kaji*), occurred. It destroyed three-fifths of the town, consumed one-third of the settlement area, and razed the buildings of the Yokohama Academy and James's consular residence. Ballagh reported the crisis to the Board of Foreign Missions as follows:

> I wrote a long reply to your letter received in November, but that letter and my reply were both destroyed by fire on the 26th that month. My house was completely burned . . . and I lost all my furniture, clothes, and books except for a collection of Robert Hale's sermons; the manuscripts of my translations of the four Gospels, Acts of the Apostles, and Genesis were all lost as well. It is a great pity that these manuscripts were destroyed by fire. Two years of work gone in an instant. But I hope to start over in a few months.[42]

Ballagh moved in with Thompson at the sanatorium in the Hepburn residence, which had withstood the fire. While Brown's house had survived, a few months later, on April 26, 1867, another fire—a suspected arson attack—demolished one of its two buildings and destroyed most of the household goods and manuscripts of the Bible translation. Fortunately, it spared the manuscripts of the Gospels of Matthew and Mark, which were on loan, but Brown was devastated and soon left Japan with his wife and their daughter, Harriet. James eventually decided to build a house far from these fire-prone areas and purchased a plot uptown at Yamate number 48.[43]

After settling down in the sanatorium, Thompson and James immediately began to offer English classes and Sunday services in both English and Japanese, and it was around this time that Seki Shinpachi, Ishikawa Kyōan, and Tsuda Sen came to receive English instruction from them. The shogunate had decided to dispatch a delegation led by Ono Tomogorō to the United States to purchase surplus warships from the Civil War, and it had selected Seki and the others to participate as interpreters. They presumably came for lessons to quickly improve their English skills before leaving for the United States. The Ono Mission left on March 28, 1867, with Fukuzawa Yukichi among its members. Ogasawara Kenzō and Iwata Heisaku, who served as naval officers, had also studied English under Ballagh.[44]

In a letter dated February 26 to John M. Ferris of the Board of Foreign Missions, Ballagh requested that the Ono Mission arrange a meeting with his father, visit the Bible Society, the College of the City of New York, and welfare schools, and attend church services.[45] Unlike Verbeck's letter to Ferris in June of the previous year, in which he had personally arranged for Saheita and Daihei to study in the United States, Ballagh aimed to deepen the relationship between the shogunate and the RCA and, by extension, to end the former's ban on Christianity.

The collaboration between Thompson and Ballagh continued, and in this regard, Hepburn wrote, "Mr. Thompson in conjunction with Mr. Ballagh of the Dutch Mission, has commenced and kept up through the year Christian services regularly on the Sabbath for the Japanese. The attendance has been small, averaging some 12 persons, but it is an encouraging beginning of the great work of preaching the Gospel which we regard as the great object of our mission."[46] Eventually, the time came for these meetings to bear fruit. Ajiki Keijirō (later renamed Awazu Takaaki) and Suzuki Kan'ichi confessed their faith and were baptized by Ballagh in May 1868. The following February, three men—Ogawa Yoshiyasu, Suzuki Kōjirō and Toriya Dai—were baptized by Thompson.[47] Although the shogunate had since given way to the new Meiji government, the latter maintained and strengthened the Christian prohibition policy. Under these circumstances, baptisms continued to be matters of life and death.

While Ballagh's evangelism gradually bore fruit, he was troubled by Margaret's medical expenses and the extreme poverty of his family back home. His missionary remunerations provided inadequate support for them, and his parents sent letters asking him to help and return home as soon as possible. However, Ballagh kept pursuing his mission. He took a brief leave to see his wife, children, and parents after completing a small stone church building in December 1868, which he called the "Sacred Dog Kennel"; it stood at number 167, a lot owned by the RCA. In the United States, Ballagh continued to work hard and reap rewards. He raised $3,000 to build a church in Japan before returning to his mission. He also appealed for help for poor mixed-race children and girls' education, which was much needed in the opened port area, and secured an appointment in Japan for Mrs. Mary Putnam Pruyn, a member of the First Reformed Church of Albany.[48] Fortunately, Margaret's health recovered and Ballagh was able to return to Japan with his family, although his parents' plight remained unchanged.

The First Japanese Protestant Church and the Founding of the United Church of Christ in Japan

On November 25, 1870, Ballagh and his family arrived in Yokohama. It was the first visit to Japan in four and a half years for Margaret, their eldest daughter Carrie, and their second daughter Anna, and the first ever for their eldest son James. While Ballagh was away, his house in Yamate had been completed, but he had been renting it, so he temporarily moved his family into a newly built nearby residence at number 75A owned by Goble and recommenced his evangelistic work.[49]

At that time, many young samurai who were aiming for success through Western studies were gathering in Yokohama to learn English from foreign teachers. The government-run Shūbunkan and Takashima Kaemon's Ranshadō employed missionaries as teachers; Brown was invited to teach at the former and Ballagh at the latter. Ranshadō's three hundred students reflected the period's fervor for English learning. In 1871, James opened a school in the small stone hall, where young people attending Sunday meetings studied English and the Bible. Because of Ballagh's enthusiasm and the free English lessons, it was well received and soon attracted over forty students. When Ballagh could no longer conduct classes, he invited his younger brother, John, to Japan as a substitute teacher and devoted himself to teaching at the Ranshadō.[50]

During the New Year's celebrations of 1872, the students saw the first weekly prayer meeting held by foreigners in the small stone church and asked Ballagh if they could hold a similar assembly. Ballagh described the circumstances during this time as follows: "Shinozaki Keinosuke, a kind and loving young man, came to me and asked me to lend him a room (in the small meeting hall) for a time. When I asked him what he was going to do, he said he would hold a prayer meeting, so I agreed. On the second day of the Lunar New Year, the meeting was held, and I joined. We read Isaiah 32:13–15. Mr. Ogawa (Yoshiyasu) prayed. On March 10, nine people were baptized."[51] Thus was the first Japanese Protestant church in Japan founded on March 10, 1872, by nine baptized members and eleven others, including Ogawa and Nimura Morizō, who were baptized by G. Ensor, an Anglican missionary in Nagasaki. It was named the Yaso Kōkai (later renamed the Yokohama Kaigan Church), and Ballagh became its first acting pastor.

Around the time of the Yaso Kōkai's founding, Ballagh's Bible class was attended by future Japanese Christian leaders: Oshikawa Masayoshi (president

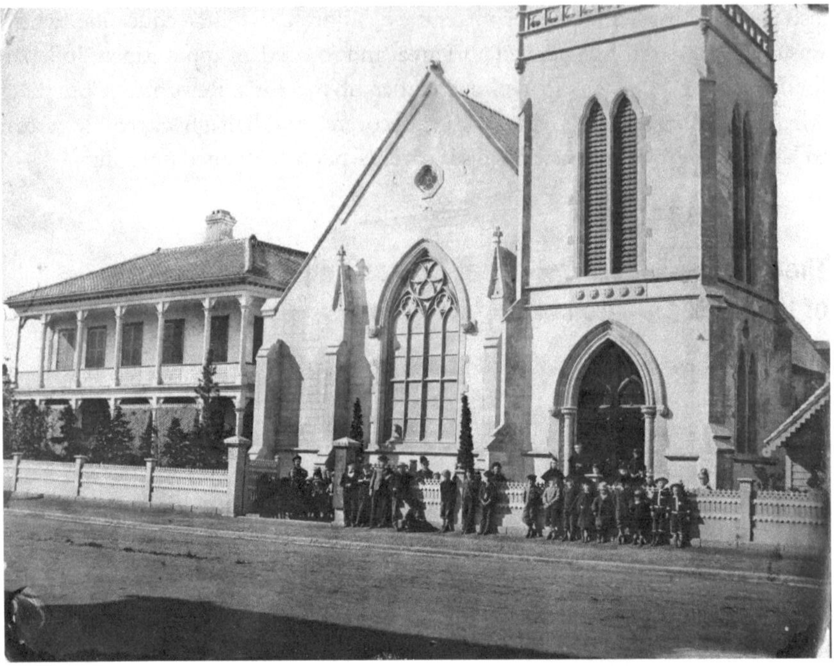

FIGURE 13.2. Kaigan Church, Yokohama, undated. (Credit: William Elliot Griffis Collection, Rutgers University Libraries.)

of Tōhoku Gakuin), Honda Yōitsu (president of Aoyama Gakuin and director of the Japan Methodist Church), Kumano Yūshichi (secretary of Meiji Gakuin), Uemura Masahisa (pastor of Fujimichō Church), and Yamamoto Hideteru (pastor of Yokohama Shiro Church and professor at Meiji Gakuin) were all initiated into the church, confessed their faith, were baptized by Ballagh, and became Protestants. Honda Yōitsu later wrote, "Mr. Ballagh was full of the spirit of evangelism. I was not moved by his words, but I was impressed by his spirit. I was moved by his tears of passion. He treated us as samurai,"[52] testifying that Ballagh's passion for evangelism led these young men to faith. Ibuka Kajinosuke (later president of Meiji Gakuin), who was also taught by Ballagh and baptized by Brown, reminisced, "While teaching English to more than a dozen young men, he explained the Bible to them with a fervor that almost burned, and even though he was not proficient in the language, he prayed and evangelized for them with an ardent sincerity that could be heard in both voice and tears. If not for this, the first Protestant Church in Japan would probably not have been established in March 1872."[53]

The Japanese congregations at that time had little understanding of denominational adherence, and they drew up rules for Yaso Kōkai with pride in its independence from foreign denominations. However, to reduce the burden of overhead costs, Ballagh registered the church as the Japanese branch of the RCA.

He made this decision while Hepburn was in Shanghai and Thompson in Europe and the United States as a mission interpreter, and it is unclear whether or not Ballagh had their consent. In any case, Ballagh became ill from overworking and entrusted Yaso Kōkai to Thompson, who returned to Yokohama in July, and devoted himself to recuperation.[54]

A movement toward establishing an interdenominational church in Japan emerged around this time. From September 20 to 25, 1872, thirteen Protestant missionaries in Japan and their affiliates gathered at the Hepburn residence to hold the first conference on future missionary policies in Japan. At this meeting, they decided to jointly translate the Bible, establish a seminary for all denominations, and found a church based on interdenominationalism. In response, the Yaso Kōkai held its first general meeting on March 1, 1873, and drafted an ordinance that officially named the church the Church of Christ in Japan (otherwise known as the Yokohama Church) and declared interdenominationalism as its principle.[55] Later, in the fall of 1873, Samuel R. Brown opened a theological school in his home at Yamate number 211, which many of the aspiring theologians among Ballagh's students entered to study theology in earnest.[56] It is important to remember that James Ballagh was the starting point for these future leaders of Christianity in Japan.

Thus did Ballagh lead the establishment of the interdenominational Church of Christ in Japan. Ironically, the removal of the ban on Christianity on February 24, 1873, brought a surge of missionaries from European and American churches to Japan who formed denominational institutions in rapid succession and hampered the realization of an interdenominational church as espoused by James, Brown, and Thompson. The Congregational Church–affiliated American Board and the Mission of the Presbyterian Church in the United States of America (PCUSA,[57] founded in 1789; not to be confused with the Presbyterian church founded in 1983 that uses the same acronym), which had been sympathetic to the formation of interdenominational churches, changed their policy and began to establish their own denominations under the direction of the U.S. Board of Foreign Missions. Under these circumstances, Thompson, who had founded the interdenominational Tokyo Church of Christ (later the Shin-Sakae Church) in the Tsukiji Foreign Settlement on September 20, 1874, found himself isolated from the PCUSA's mission in Japan. He became an interpreter for the United States legation in Japan, declined PCUSA compensation, and became a self-supporting missionary who pursued the formation of an ideal interdenominational church.[58]

Meanwhile, as Ballagh continued his pastoral ministry at Yokohama Church, he became interested in rural evangelism and visited mountain villages in places including Gotenba, Mishima, Ueda, and Kamiyama in Kanagawa Prefecture, where he preached the Gospel and baptized converts. In Ueda, he oversaw thirty-six laymen in founding the interdenominational Ueda Christian Church on October 8, 1876. However, this congregation struggled as Baptist, Methodist, and Anglican churches from the United States, Canada, and the United Kingdom came to Japan one after another. Led by the American Presbyterian William Imbrie (1845–1928), and with the support of Ballagh and Thompson, a union was formed among the RCA, the PCUSA, and the United Presbyterian Church of Scotland. In response, nine Japanese churches under the leadership of the above three missions held their first meeting on October 3, 1877, at Yokohama Kaigan Church (the former Yaso Kōkai) and founded the United Church of Christ (renamed the Church of Christ in Japan in 1890), which adopted Presbyterianism and followed denominational governance. At the same time, the church established the Tokyo Union Theological School (TUTS) in Tsukiji with missionary teachers. The school opened on October 7 with thirty-two students, seven of whom were students of Ballagh, including Uemura Masahisa, Kitahara Yoshimichi, and Yamamoto Hideteru.[59] The RCA mission in Japan opened the Senshi School as a preparatory school for TUTS on the grounds of Ballagh's house at Yamate number 48; Ballagh served as principal, Harriet Winn, the niece of Samuel R. Brown, as a full-time teacher, and Amenomori Nobushige as prefect. However, because Margaret was about to give birth, the Ballaghs took a furlough in April 1879, and the school closed after the final examinations at the end of June. At the same time, Ballagh resigned as the acting minister of Yokohama Kaigan Church. By this time, he had baptized 171 people since his arrival in Japan.

A Life Dedicated to Pioneer Evangelism

In April 1874, Ballagh family temporarily returned to United States, and in late November, the family returned to Japan. Ballagh immediately resumed teaching at the Senshi School, but with about twenty students, half of whom were boys between the ages of eight and twelve, it was far from being a preparatory school for TUTS. Ballagh therefore decided to give up teaching after about a year to concentrate on direct evangelism, and he asked the Board of Foreign Missions to dispatch a faithful education specialist who could oversee Senshi in his stead. They eventually chose Martin Nevius Wyckoff, an 1872 graduate of Rutgers College who had previously taught in Fukui after William E. Griffis had left. Wyckoff arrived with his family on September 25, 1881.

Around the same time, Ballagh's eldest daughter, Carrie, became a teacher of English and music at Ferris Girls' School and accompanied Ballagh on his summer mission trip to Nagoya. In April 1885, she married Francis Woodley Harrell (1859–1904), an American Anglican missionary doctor, and resigned from Ferris. The Harrells returned to the United States in 1887 and later lived in Mexico. Anna, the second daughter, replaced her sister at Ferris in 1884. Three years later, in October 1887, she married Robert Eugenius McAlpine (1862–1950), an American Southern Presbyterian Church missionary, and like her parents, she devoted her life to evangelism in Japan.

FIGURE 13.3. Ballagh preaching at the Kaigan Church, 1911. (Credit: Archives of the Reformed Church in America.)

Despite these familial changes, Ballagh was able to devote himself to the local missionary work for which he had longed. He first traveled around Kanagawa Prefecture, and in 1884 and 1886, he went as far as Kōchi in Shikoku. Later, the RCA in Japan divided its mission field into northern and southern regions, and Ballagh took charge of the former. In areas where trains and boats were unavailable, he rode in palanquins or on horses, and in others he made his rounds on foot. Wearing frayed clothes and carrying a worn-out umbrella at his waist, he traveled in a style that became known as "evangelism in straw sandals." His pioneering efforts gradually bore fruit as churches were built in Nagano, Matsumoto, Iida, Suwa, Mishima, and Gotenba. By 1903, when Ballagh was over seventy years old, he had conducted a total of 250 baptisms.[60]

In 1906, Ballagh and Margaret returned to the United States for a furlough. During that time, Ballagh's many years of evangelism in Japan were recognized with a doctor of divinity degree from his alma mater, Rutgers College. The following year the couple returned to Japan, but Margaret left alone for the United States soon after due to failing health. Although she eventually returned to Yokohama, she died suddenly on March 16, 1909, after forty-eight years of hard work in Japan. A funeral service was held at Ferris Girls' School on March 18, and her remains were buried in the Yokohama Foreign Cemetery. The bereft Ballagh continued to reside in Yokohama, comforted by the close proximity of his second daughter's large family of eleven. He was already seventy-seven, and although his trips to distant missions were less frequent, he actively attended events at the Church of Christ and other churches in Yokohama and Tokyo, served on the boards of Meiji Gakuin and Ferris Girls' School representing the RCA, and continued to be engaged in education.[61]

On November 11, 1911, a "Celebration of the 50th Anniversary of Dr. James H. Ballagh's Arrival" was held at Yokohama Kaigan Church from 2:00 P.M. Over three hundred people, including his colleagues and students, attended the event and delivered congratulatory speeches one after another. In his speech, Ballagh spoke in dignified Japanese that listeners found difficult to understand, emphasizing that the present evangelistic achievements were the work of Japanese Christians rather than his own efforts, and then finally, in English, he spoke of the power of prayer and the need for unity through God's Holy Spirit.[62]

James Ballagh spent a total of fifty-eight years in Japan. In June 1919, he returned to his homeland accompanied by his son-in-law, McAlpine, harboring hopes of setting foot on Japanese soil again. He died at the home of his eldest son, James, in Richmond, Virginia, on January 29, 1920, at the age of eighty-eight, and he was buried at Hollywood Cemetery in the city.[63]

Conclusion

In Japan, James H. Ballagh devoted his life to evangelism, baptized the first Japanese Protestant, and founded the first Japanese Protestant church. These achievements are widely acknowledged in the history of Christianity in Japan. He also translated the Bible and edited hymns together with Hepburn and Thompson in the early days of the Japanese mission. He was a teacher at the Yokohama Academy, Ranshadō, and Senshi School who recognized the importance of education as part of evangelism. He took part in the campaign against the prohibition of Christianity. In later years, he served as a trustee of Meiji Gakuin and Ferris Girls' School and participated in their administration. In light of these activities, it is incorrect to evaluate Ballagh only on his direct evangelism, which he saw as his personal mission; his single-minded dedication to converting the Japanese only made his work more remarkable than that of any other missionary. Ibuka Kajinosuke described Ballagh as "a man of heavenly resources, fervent in prayer, a lover of the Bible, a man of action rather than thought, and a man of deep friendship and sympathy."[64] These words befit the first Rutgers College graduate who dedicated his life to Japan.

Notes

Original essay written in Japanese; translated and edited by Haruko Wakabayashi.

1 The church was called The Reformed Protestant Dutch Church from 1819 to 1867, and in 1867 it was renamed the Reformed Church in America (RCA). This chapter uses the latter name.

2 James H. Ballagh, "Grandpa's Romance of the Missions," box 135, folder 1, William Elliot Griffis Collection, Special Collections and University Archives, Rutgers University Libraries, New Brunswick, NJ; James H. Ballagh, *Jēmusu Bara no wakaki hi no kaisō*, trans. Hida Taeko (Tokyo: Kirisuto Shinbunsha, 2018), 113.

3 Ballagh, *Jēmusu Bara*, 134; Ballagh, "Grandpa's Romance of the Missions," 158.

4 Inoue Heizaburō, *Hama no tomoshibi* (Tokyo: Kirisuto Shinbunsha, 1983), 60.

5 In addition to James, his younger brother, John Craig Ballagh (1842–1920), went to Japan from 1872 to 1920 as a missionary of the Presbyterian Church in the United States of America (PCUSA), and Ballagh's younger sister, Annie Prudencia Ballagh (1844–1925), was also in Japan from 1884 to 1904 as a missionary of the PCUSA.

6 Ballagh, *Jēmusu Bara*, 21; Ballagh, "Grandpa's Romance of the Missions," 10–11.

7 Ballagh, *Jēmusu Bara*, 34; Ballagh, "Grandpa's Romance of the Missions," 29.

8 Ballagh, *Jēmusu Bara*, 37; Ballagh, "Grandpa's Romance of the Missions," 33.

9 Ballagh, *Jēmusu Bara*, 40; Ballagh, "Grandpa's Romance of the Missions," 39.

10 Ballagh, *Jēmusu Bara*, 42; Ballagh, "Grandpa's Romance of the Missions," 42.

11 In the Presbyterian Church, infant baptism alone does not qualify a person as a Christian, only a confession of faith does. Ballagh was baptized as an infant in the Presbyterian Church, but at this point he had not yet made a confession of faith.

12 Ballagh, *Jēmusu Bara*, 62; Ballagh, "Grandpa's Romance of the Missions," 72.

13 Ballagh, *Jēmusu Bara*, 61; Ballagh, "Grandpa's Romance of the Missions," 71.

14 The Presbyterian Church split into the Old School and the New School in 1837 and was reunited as the PCUSA in 1869. See Walter L. Lingle and John W. Kuykendall, *Presbyterians: Their History and Beliefs* (Atlanta: John Knox Press, 1978), 73.

15 Ballagh, *Jēmusu Bara*, 65; Ballagh, "Grandpa's Romance of the Missions," 76.

16 Ballagh, *Jēmusu Bara*, 81; Ballagh, "Grandpa's Romance of the Missions," 94.

17 Ballagh, *Jēmusu Bara*, 89; Ballagh, "Grandpa's Romance of the Missions," 104.

18 Ballagh, *Jēmusu Bara*, 89; Ballagh, "Grandpa's Romance of the Missions," 109.

19 James H. Ballagh, ed. and trans. Enomoto Yoshiko, "Jēmusu Bara no tegami 1," *Ayumi*, no. 13 (1984): 13; Ballagh's letter, 20 February 1861, Reformed Church in America Archives, New Brunswick, NJ (hereafter RCA Archives).

20 The Kinnier family name is found written on tombstones and in records as Kinnier, Kinneir, and Kinnear.

21 Ballagh, *Jēmusu Bara*, 126; Ballagh, "Grandpa's Romance of the Missions," 152.

22 Ballagh, *Jēmusu Bara*, 129; Ballagh, "Grandpa's Romance of the Missions," 156.

23 Margaret Tate Ballagh, trans. Kawakubo Tokuo, *Furuki Nihon no bekken* (Yokohama: Yūrindō, 1992), originally published as *Glimpses of Old Japan* (Tokyo: Methodist Publishing House, 1908).

24 Translated from Ballagh's speech in Japanese given at the fortieth-anniversary celebration of his arrival in Japan. Cited *Uemura Masahisa to sono jidai*, 2 vols., ed. Saba Wataru (reprint, Tokyo: Kyōbunkan, 1966), 1:356.

25 Saba, *Uemura Masahisa to sono jidai*, 1:356.

26 Gordon D. Laman, *Pioneers to Partners: The Reformed Church in America and the Christian Mission with the Japanese* (Grand Rapids, MI: William B. Eerdmans, 2012), 44.

27 Ballagh, *Jēmusu Bara*, 143; Ballagh, "Grandpa's Romance of the Missions," 169.

28 William E. Griffis, trans. Sasaki Akira, *Hebon: Dōjidaijin no mita* (Tokyo: Kyōbunkan, 1991), originally published as *Hepburn of Japan and His Wife and Helpmates: A Life Story of Toil for Christ* (Philadelphia: Westminster Press, 1913), 92.

29 Ballagh, *Jēmusu Bara*, p. 142; Ballagh, "Grandpa's Romance of the Missions," 168.
30 Ballagh, "Jēmusu Bara no tegami 1," 19; Ballagh's letter, 9 December 1861, RCA Archives.
31 Susanna Fessler, "The Letters of Robert Hewson Pruyn," East Asian Studies Faculty Scholarship, 2022, 19, https://scholarsarchive.library.albany.edu/eas_fac_scholar/19.
32 The Namamugi Incident, which occurred on September 14, 1862, refers to the killing of a British merchant, Charles Lennox Richardson, by the retainers of Shimazu Hisamitsu, regent of the Satsuma domain (present-day Kagoshima Prefecture), on a road in Namamugi, near Yokohama, for not dismounting from his horse upon encountering Shimazu's procession. It became a major political crisis and resulted in the bombardment of Kagoshima by the British Royal Navy squadron.
33 Dr. Hepburn handled Carrie's birth on June 26, 1862, seven months after the Ballaghs arrived in Japan. See Margaret Tate Ballagh, letter dated July 1862, in Ballagh, *Glimpses of Old Japan*, 75–76.
34 David Thompson was a native of Ohio, where his maternal grandfather, John Rea, was a prominent Presbyterian minister. His mother church was the First United Presbyterian Church of Cadiz, which was established in the late 1850s through the efforts of his grandfather and father by merging the Associate Reformed Presbyterian Church and the Associate Presbyterian Church. Coming from a church with such a history of denominational unification, Thompson agreed with the idea of forming one Christian church across denominational lines in Japan and joined Ballagh and Brown in advocating for this in later years. Despite their denominational differences, James and Thompson were close in age and soon became friends. See Nakajima Kōji, "Tamuson" (Thompson), in *Chōrō, Kaikaku Kyōkai rainichi senkyōshi jiten* (Tokyo: Shinkyō Shuppansha, 2003), 33–38.
35 James H. Ballagh, *SHINONOME: Day-Dawn, or the Beginnings of the Kingdom of God in Japan*, 6, in Hope College Archives, Holland, Michigan.
36 Ballagh, *SHINONOME*, 9.
37 Ballagh, *Jēmusu Bara*, 143–144; Ballagh, "Grandpa's Romance of the Missions," 170.
38 Samuel R. Brown, *S. R. Brown shokanshū*, trans. Takaya Michio (reprint, Tokyo: Nihon Kirisutokyōdan Shuppankyoku, 1980), 167.
39 James H. Ballagh's letter to Philip Peltz, 14 November 1865, Japan Mission Files, box 6, "North Japan-1865-/Ballagh," RCA Archives; Ballagh, "Jēmusu Bara no tegami 1," 1.
40 *Japan Directory* (Yokohama: Japan Gazette, 1879).
41 Robert worked for Walsh, Hall & Co., the largest of the American trading companies in Japan, where he remained until 1872 as head of the camphor trade. He then became consul general of the Kingdom of Hawaii in 1873, and in 1874 he was appointed consul general and chargé d'affaires. At the same time, he became a comanager of Edward Fischer & Co., which connected him with the business world. In 1875, he returned as consul general, but it is not clear how long he served in this position since some records from this period also refer to Van Reed as consul general of the Kingdom of Hawaii. See *Class of 1865, Robert Morrison Brown, Secretary, Chinese Engineering and Mining Co.; deceased Feb. 18, 1900*, Rutgers University Biographical Files: Alumni, box 32, Special Collections and University Archives, Rutgers University Libraries. (This information has been provided by Fernanda H. Perrone, archivist of the William E. Griffis Collection, Rutgers University Libraries.)

42 Ballagh, "Jēmusu Bara no tegami 8," *Ayumi*, no. 21 (1988): 11; Ballagh's letter, 28 January 1867, RCA Archives.
43 Bought in October 1867. See Ballagh's letter, 23 October 1867, in Enomoto Yoshiko, "Jēmusu Bara no tegami 11," *Ayumi*, no. 30 (1992): 40.
44 James H. Ballagh, letter, 26 February 1867, in Ballagh, "Jēmusu Bara no tegami 8," 16.
45 Ballagh, letter, 26 February 1867, 16.
46 See Hepburn's letter, 22 October 1867, in *Hebon shokanshū*, ed. and trans. Takaya Michio (Tokyo: Iwanami Shoten, 1959), 188.
47 See Thompson's letter, 30 March 1869, in *Tamuson shokanshū*, ed. Nakajima Kōji (Tokyo: Kyōbunkan, 2022), 72.
48 Mary P. Pruyn, *Yokohama no josei senkyōshi Mearī P. Purain to "Guranmama no tegami,"* ed. and trans. Abe Sumiko (Tokyo: EXP, 2000), 161–163, originally published as *Grandmamma's Letters from Japan* (Boston: James H. Earle, 1877).
49 Kawashima Daijirō, *Jonasan Gōburu kenkyū* (Tokyo: Shinkyō Shuppansha, 1988), 129.
50 William Imbrie, "John Craig Ballagh," *The Japan Evangelist*, December 1920, 349.
51 James H. Ballagh, translated from an original interview in Japanese with *Fukuin Shinpō* (a Christian journal); Saba, *Uemura Masahisa to sono jidai*, 2:206–207.
52 Saba, *Uemura Masahisa to sono jidai*, 1:578.
53 Bara/Makarupin senkyō kinenshi hakkan henshū iinkai, *Nihon dendō hyakunenshi* (Nagoya: Tsunobuesha, 1878), 48.
54 See Thompson's letter, 19 July 1872, in Kōji, *Tamuson shokanshū*, 105–106.
55 Saba, *Uemura Masahisa to sono jidai*, 2:125.
56 See Brown's letter, 19 July 1872, in *S. R. Buraun shokanshū*, ed. and trans. Takaya Michio (Tokyo: Nihon Kirisutokyōdan Shuppankyoku, 1965), 105–106.
57 Founded in 1789; not to be confused with the Presbyterian church founded in 1983 that uses the same acronym.
58 See Thompson's letter, 7 April 1875, in Kōji, *Tamuson shokanshū*, 160.
59 *Meiji Gakuin hyakugojūnenshi* (Tokyo: Meiji Gakuin, 2013), 99–101.
60 Bara/Makarupin senkyō kinenshi hakkan henshū iinkai, *Nihon dendō hyakunenshi*, 53.
61 His name appears as a board member in the minutes of the board of directors' meetings at Meiji Gakuin (Meiji Gakuin Zaidan Hōjin rijikai ketsugiroku, 1906–1912) and as a member of the examination committee in a Ferris Girls' School brochure (*Ferisu Eiwa Jogakkō ichiran*, 1887–1888). He had also signed the diplomas for Ferris until 1911, which confirms that he was involved with the school until nearly the end of his life.
62 Bara/Makarupin senkyō kinenshi hakkan henshū iinkai, *Nihon dendō hyakunenshi*, 124.
63 The date of burial was January 31, 1920, according to the Hollywood Cemetery records.
64 Bara/Makarupin senkyō kinenshi hakkan henshū iinkai, *Nihon dendō hyakunenshi*, 48–49.

14

Rutgers Missionaries and Meiji Gakuin

NAOTO TSUJI

There was once a school in Japan with an anthem called "On the Banks of the Old Sumida": the Tokyo Union College (TUC; Tokyo Icchi Eiwa Gakkō), established in 1883 and a predecessor school of Meiji Gakuin University (Meiji Gakuin). TUC's song drew on "On the Banks of the Old Raritan," the Rutgers College anthem, changing the river's name to that of the Sumida, which ran through the center of Tokyo, while keeping the melody.[1] This interesting fact gestures to the deep relationship with Rutgers that Meiji Gakuin has had since its earliest days.

Meiji Gakuin emerged from TUC's 1886 merger in Tsukiji with the Tokyo Union Theological School (TUTS; Tokyo Icchi Shingakkō) and the Eiwa Preparatory School (Eiwa Yobikō). Like Rutgers, Meiji Gakuin was founded by the Reformed Church in America (RCA), but in this case the RCA embarked on a joint endeavor with the Presbyterian Church in the United States of America (PCUSA, founded in 1789; not to be confused with the Presbyterian church founded in 1983 that uses the same acronym) and the United Presbyterian Church of Scotland (UPC).

The *Meiji Gakuin 150-nen shi* (150 years of Meiji Gakuin), an official institutional history published in 2013, notes that the school's origins are currently thought to be a private academy founded in 1863 at the home of James Curtis Hepburn (1815–1911), a missionary doctor with the PCUSA. Meiji Gakuin thereby

FIGURE 14.1. Meiji Gakuin, 2024, showing Memorial Hall and chapel. (Credit: Tsuji Naoto.)

claims to be the oldest Protestant school in Japan, but it has long emphasized its original founding as a collaboration of the PCUSA, RCA, and UPC churches in Japan. In fact, up until the publication of the *Meiji Gakuin 100-nen shi* (The centennial history of Meiji Gakuin) in 1977, Meiji Gakuin traced the first year of its founding to the beginning of TUTS, an interdenominational institution established in 1877.[2] It is no exaggeration to say that its development would not have been possible without the work of RCA missionaries from Rutgers College. This chapter aims to clarify how Rutgers affiliates contributed to establishing and developing Meiji Gakuin by examining their activities related to the school.

The Origins of Meiji Gakuin: The Hepburn School and Brown School

Among Meiji Gakuin's multiple origins, the oldest is a private English school started in 1863 by Clara Maria Leete Hepburn (1818–1906), the wife of Dr. James Curtis Hepburn, at their home and sanatorium in Yokohama. This school, now known as the Hepburn School, was originally called Mrs. Hepburn's School; it enrolled girls along with boys and taught medicine and English, producing many future leaders of Japan, including Prime Minister Takahashi Korekiyo, Minister of Foreign Affairs Hayashi Tadasu, and Miyake Hiizu, professor of medicine at the University of Tokyo.[3]

Meiji Gakuin's other predecessor was the Brown School, also in Yokohama, which started in 1873 at number 211 in the foreign settlement. This address was the home of Samuel Robbins Brown (1810–1880), one of the first RCA missionaries sent to Japan who arrived in Yokohama in 1859, a little later than Hepburn. The RCA sent two other missionaries: Duane B. Simmons, also a doctor, and

Guido F. Verbeck, who spent his early missionary years in Nagasaki. Brown briefly lived with Hepburn at Jōbutsuji Temple when he first arrived and later taught at government-run English schools in Niigata and Yokohama, but he felt it was his mission to translate the Bible into Japanese and devoted much of his time to this task. However, at the request of Japanese students who admired him, he decided to offer his home as a space to teach theology and English.

In a February 1874 letter to John M. Ferris of the RCA Board of Foreign Missions, Brown reported that his school had eight capable theological students.[4] In 1876, the church sent James Lansing Amerman (1943–1928), a New Brunswick Theological Seminary (NBTS) graduate from the class of 1868, to help teach at the school and allow Brown to devote more time to his Bible translation. The Brown School had been primarily an English-language school, but Amerman's efforts in theological pedagogy made it begin to resemble a seminary.[5] In fact, the Brown School produced a number of individuals who later became teachers at Meiji Gakuin and other missionary schools like Tōhoku Gakuin and Aoyama Gakuin, or who became pastors of Christian churches, including Uemura Masahisa, Yamamoto Hideteru, Ibuka Kajinosuke, Honda Yōitsu, Kumano Yūshichi, Oshikawa Masayoshi, and Amenomori Nobushige.

Amerman oversaw theological education (lay and ministry training), and later, when the Brown School merged with a Presbyterian seminary and became TUTS, he built a new seminary curriculum together with the PCUSA missionary William Imbrie (1845–1928). After the seminary developed into the Meiji Gakuin School of Theology, Amerman continued to lecture to train Japanese ministers, assisted by Ibuka Kajinosuke, a theologian in training. While in Japan Amerman struggled with illness, but he continued writing numerous textbooks on theology for his students at Meiji Gakuin.[6] He also endeavored to make notes in roman characters in order to speak to his students in Japanese, and he devoted himself to theological education until his return to the United States in 1892 while actively engaging in missionary work at the churches in Ueda, Kōjimachi, and Shitaya.

The Union Church and the Theological School

The establishment of a full-fledged theological school—the Meiji Gakuin—stemmed from the desire of PCUSA and RCA missionaries to jointly form an interdenominational church. Brown and James H. Ballagh (discussed in chapter 13), an RCA missionary who came to Japan in 1861, believed that denominational differences should not restrict local missionary work and that the Japanese should organize their own churches. The RCA, which had fewer resources than other denominations, was more willing to form interdenominational churches.[7] In response to the efforts of these missionaries, it attempted to establish four such churches in Yokohama and Tokyo, along with two more in the Osaka and Kobe areas in October 1874, which it planned to operate under a common ecclesiastical ordinance. But Niijima Jō, who had returned to Japan as an associate missionary from the congregational American Board of Commissioners for Foreign Missions in 1874, opposed the union based on his belief in denominationalism, which resulted in the Kobe and Osaka churches withdrawing.[8]

In 1876, the RCA mission in Japan asked its PCUSA counterpart to collaborate in founding educational institutions and joint churches. In September 1877, the PCUSA, RCA, and UPC churches in Japan, and their affiliated missions, decided to set up a union church based on Presbyterianism. In addition to the nine churches already established,[9] the Kōjimachi, Asakusa, and Ushigome churches were added to form the United Church of Christ in Japan. TUTS emerged in 1877 as a joint effort of the three denominations to establish a seminary for training ministers and laypeople to serve these churches. The Brown School became the fountainhead of TUTS, and it collaborated with the PCUSA's Tsukiji Rokuban Seminary and the Thompson School, and UPC's Waddell and Davidson theological schools. In October 1877, TUTS held its first class, with about thirty students, at the Tsukiji Rokuban Seminary's small chapel.

The Enhancement of Preparatory and General Education

The missionaries also felt the need to improve secondary-level general education to increase the number of seminary students in Japan. John Craig Ballagh of the PCUSA (James Ballagh's younger brother) took over the boys at the Hepburn School and began teaching English and the Bible to about thirty students; the school became known as the Ballagh School in 1876. Meanwhile, Mary Kidder of the RCA taught the female students, and in 1870, the school was opened as the Ferris Seminary and continued to grow. The Ballagh School moved to Tsukiji to serve as a channel for sending students to TUTS and offered general education after it became Tsukiji College in 1880.

The RCA also saw the need to provide its own preparatory education for aspiring theologians. James Ballagh initially opened a preparatory school, the Senshi School (Senshi Gakkō), at his home at Yamate number 48, Yokohama; however, it temporarily closed when he returned to the United States. Amerman, concerned about this situation, recommended to the Board of Foreign Missions that a general education institution be opened, and in 1881, the RCA sent Martin Nevius Wyckoff (1850–1911) to be the new principal of the Senshi School. In 1872, Wyckoff had taught at a junior high school (a former domain school) in Fukui after graduating from Rutgers College; he replaced William E. Griffis, his senior Rutgers alumnus, hired earlier by the Fukui domain.[10] After his contract in Fukui expired, Wyckoff taught English and other subjects at the Niigata Foreign Language School from 1874 to 1875, at the request of the Ministry of Education, and at the Tokyo Kaisei Gakkō for about a year in 1876. He returned to the United States in 1877 and did graduate study in chemistry at Rutgers College; a year later, he opened a grammar school in Somerville.[11]

In 1881, Wyckoff returned to Japan, this time as a missionary of the RCA. However, his assigned task was not theological education or missionary activity, but to serve as the principal of the Senshi School that was to be reopened in Yokohama. Missionaries not only preached the Bible or trained pastors; some had come to Japan to teach general education based on Christianity. Wyckoff single-handedly took charge of both education and administration at the Senshi School. During the first year of his principalship, it had twenty-eight students, fifteen of whom lived in boarding houses. In addition, many worked during the day, so classes were often held in the evenings.[12] With the merger with John Ballagh's Tsukiji College in 1883, the school moved to Tsukiji and became TUC. Like Amerman, Wyckoff became a professor and board member of Meiji Gakuin upon its establishment in 1886, and he supported its early efforts in general education.

Amerman and Wyckoff both went to Japan as RCA missionaries but worked in different fields. Wyckoff was not a theologian and instead taught a wide variety of subjects, including chemistry, physics, geology, English conversation, Japanese-English translation, translation methods, English literature, English studies, Latin, and German, for thirty-two hours a week. He and his wife also taught English hymn-singing in the chapel every Saturday. In addition, he served on the board of directors of the Ihaien, a sanatorium for sufferers of Hansen's disease, and actively took part in comfort and relief activities for the patients housed there.[13] In an era of intense discrimination, missionaries strove to aid the vulnerable. Wyckoff died suddenly of a heart attack at Meiji Gakuin in January 1911 at the age of sixty.

Preparatory and General Education at TUC

As mentioned above, as cooperation between the RCA and PCUSA progressed, the Tsukiji College merged with Senshi, and in September 1883, the new institution in Tsukiji started a regular education program that later became TUC. Howard Harris, another Rutgers graduate from the class of 1873, joined the faculty of the newly founded TUC. He, together with Wyckoff, is likely to have introduced the anthem mentioned at the beginning of this chapter. The Sumida River, which flowed by the Tsukiji settlement, may have reminded them of the Raritan River at their alma mater. Harris, the eleventh male missionary sent to Japan by the RCA, engaged in missionary and educational work there for twenty-one years from 1884 to 1905. Born in July 1848 in Belleville, New Jersey, he had served in the Civil War as a flag bearer. After leaving Rutgers, he immediately entered the NBTS and graduated in 1876. He was then admitted to the RCA's Newark classis and served as pastor of the Hawthorne Church in New York State from 1876 to 1884. On April 21, 1884, Harris arrived in Japan with his wife, Lizzie, to assist Henry Stout in Nagasaki, but after about a year, they were transferred to Yokohama.

FIGURE 14.2. Union Theological School, Tsukiji, 1886. (Credit: Unidentified artist. Hand-colored albumen print on paper mounted on paper. Sheet: 10 × 14 cm (3 15/16 × 5 1/2 in.). Collection Zimmerli Art Museum at Rutgers University, 1989.0286.009. Gift of Lee Knox Trent. Photo by Peter Jacobs.)

After moving to Tokyo, Harris became a professor at TUC, where he taught English literature. In 1885, he was hired as a teacher at the TUC-affiliated Eiwa Preparatory School (established in Awaji-chō, Kanda, in 1884), along with Mrs. Geny C. Macaulay, Annie P. Ballagh (John Ballagh's younger sister), Sugimori Konoma, Muraoka Motoichirō, and others. Eiwa Preparatory School had already hired Wyckoff, James M. Macaulay, John C. Ballagh, Orly N. Benton, Hattori Ayao, and Ishimoto Sanjūrō as teachers, but it increased its teaching staff after moving to Kōjimachi Fujimi-chō in 1885; it made sense for teachers to hold joint positions in the two affiliated schools. After TUC and Eiwa Preparatory School merged into Meiji Gakuin, Harris became a professor at the School of General Studies and served as treasurer. Although Harris came to Japan as a missionary, he was deeply involved in general educational activities during his time there. Like Wyckoff, he served as a teacher, and although a former military man, he is said to have had a gentle disposition.[14]

Early Rutgers Missionaries: The RCA South Japan Mission and the Kyushu Schools

As noted earlier, Meiji Gakuin relied on the work of RCA missionaries who were also Rutgers alumni. Two such men were tangentially involved with the school:

James H. Ballagh and Henry Stout. The former brought his brother, John C. Ballagh, to Japan. John Ballagh took over the Hepburn School, which became the earliest antecedent of Meiji Gakuin. Many of James Ballagh's students also studied at the Brown School, another early predecessor of Meiji Gakuin. Meanwhile, the RCA missionaries of the South Japan Mission contributed by establishing schools in Kyushu and sending students to Tokyo. Henry Stout (1838–1912), an important figure in the Kyushu mission, graduated from Rutgers in 1865 and was Amerman's classmate at NBTS. Stout came to Japan in 1869 and succeeded Guido Verbeck, focusing on missionary work in Kyushu, particularly in Nagasaki. When he first arrived, he took over Verbeck's instructorship at Kōunkan (the former shogunal English language school, Saibikan), but he resigned in 1872 to start an evening Bible school that tutored students in English. Segawa Asashi, who studied under Stout, was baptized in 1873, and when TUTS opened in 1877, he was immediately dispatched to be its first student and graduated as a qualified teacher. Following Segawa, Tomekawa Ichiro studied under Stout and entered TUTS in 1879, and after being ordained in 1882, he and Segawa devoted themselves to developing Kagoshima Church; they also subsequently served as pastors of Nagasaki Church and other churches. Stout's missionary work in Kyushu gradually bore fruit and grew into the Western Central Association of the United Church of Christ in Japan and the Reformed Church South Japan Mission.[15]

In 1881, with a donation from William H. Steele, a director of the RCA's overseas mission bureau, Steele Memorial Academy (Tōzan Gakuin after 1892) opened in Nagasaki City as a boys' school consisting of a theology department and a general education department, like Meiji Gakuin. The missionaries involved in the school were Howard Harris, Eugene Booth, Albert Oltmans, and others from Rutgers, as well as Willis G. Hoekje from the RCA-affiliated Hope College. The theological department had its largest enrollment of twenty-seven students in 1894, but numbers declined sharply after 1895 and it was forced to shut down in 1897. Later, the School of General Studies and the missionary teaching staff were absorbed into Meiji Gakuin in October 1930 due to financial difficulties. Stout's work was also indirectly related to Meiji Gakuin in that he encouraged church formation in Kyushu, sent students to TUTS, and supported the growth of Steele Memorial Academy.

The Opening of Meiji Gakuin and the RCA Missionaries

With the modernization of Japan its educational system also developed rapidly, and the various missions there felt the need to organize a public educational institution that adhered to the Japanese legal system. By this time Eiwa Preparatory School, which had been founded in Awaji-chō, Kanda, had been moved to Fujimi-chō in Kōjimachi. As the number of students at TUC and Eiwa Preparatory School increased, the schools began to seek a more spacious location than the small lot in Tsukiji.

FIGURE 14.3. Theological school students, 1886. (Credit: Unidentified artist. Albumen print on paper mounted on paper. Sheet: 20.4 × 26.4 cm (8 1/16 × 10 3/8 in.). Collection Zimmerli Art Museum at Rutgers University, 1989.0286.015. Gift of Lee Knox Trent. Photo by Peter Jacobs.)

The PCUSA planned to merge TUTS and TUC into "a large Christian-based college that in the future should be known as 'Japan's Princeton University.'"[16] After receiving approval from the RCA the plan was proposed to the UPC, and in April 1886 a joint missionary council of the three missions adopted the proposal to establish a new school. Amerman wrote that "the aim of Meiji Gakuin is to provide for its students a thorough education under Christian influences, and especially to train young men for the Christian Ministry."[17]

Meiji Gakuin was established by reorganizing TUTS into the Department of Japanese Theology and TUC into the Department of General Studies. It was initially opened while still using the school building in Tsukiji, but in October 1886 its leadership acquired a large plot of land in Shirokane Village, and in September 1887 the first 280 students in the Department of General Studies attended the new campus. Faculty appointments at the time of Meiji Gakuin's opening were carried over from the system of the previous school, and Wyckoff and Harris were both appointed as professors in the Department of General Studies. Meanwhile, the Department of Japanese Theology briefly used the TUTS building in Tsukiji but moved to Shirokane in 1890 when its departmental library was completed. According to an 1889 report by Amerman, there were 42 students enrolled in the Department of Japanese Theology and 258 students enrolled in the Department of General Studies in the same year.[18] Three missionaries from Rutgers—Luman James Shafer, Albert Oltmans, and Eugene C. Duryee—arrived in Japan after the opening of Meiji Gakuin and played key roles in its development.

Luman James Shafer

Luman James Shafer (1887–1958), born in Richmondville, New York, entered Rutgers College in September 1905 and graduated in 1909; he went on to NBTS, graduating in 1912 and leaving for Japan as a missionary in October of the same year at the age of twenty-five. In March 1915, he engaged in missionary work in Aomori, but due to his wife's illness, he returned to Tokyo in September where he was assigned to the School of Theology and Advanced Studies at Meiji Gakuin. He was then sent to Nagasaki and taught at Tōzan Gakuin, which had been associated with the RCA since Stout's time, and in 1919 he was appointed the school's acting rector.[19]

Shafer returned to the United States in 1935 and became a director of the RCA Board of Foreign Missions. He was one of the first church officials to return to Japan at the end of World War II, and in April 1946, along with Douglas Horton, James Baker, and Walter Van Kirk, he headed a delegation of the Christian churches in America to Japan, where they met with Christian school officials and inspected devastated churches and schools. After returning home, he reported to the Japan Committee of the North American Council on Foreign Missions that "the Japanese are longing for a first-class Christian university,"[20] and he became the chairman of a standing committee for the establishment of a Christian university in Japan. He came to Japan once more in July 1949 and became president of Ferris University in April 1952, but his health failed and he returned to the United States in June of the same year, dying of a cerebral hemorrhage at his Florida home in January 1958. His efforts to restore Christian schools razed by the Great Kanto Earthquake and the Pacific War are considered a great achievement in the history of Japanese Christianity.

Albert Oltmans

Albert Oltmans was born on November 19, 1854, in Groningen, the Netherlands, and immigrated to Grand Rapids, Michigan, in 1873. After graduating from Hope College in 1883, he went to NBTS and upon graduation went to Japan as an RCA missionary in September 1886. Oltmans was the first Hope College alumnus in Japan; most RCA missionaries in Japan until then had been Rutgers graduates, but after 1886, Hope College sent many more to join them, including A. Pieters, H.V.S. Peeke, and W. G. Hoekje. After Oltmans, most such missionaries went on to Western Theological Seminary on the same campus. This trajectory became the predominant pattern for missionaries sent to Japan, whereas the number of NBTS missionaries decreased.[21]

The purpose of Oltmans's mission to Japan, at Stout's request, was to head a boys' school in Nagasaki. He became the first principal of the Steele Memorial Academy, which opened one year after his arrival in Nagasaki, in September 1887.

He served in this role for three years, and after resigning from his principalship he resided in Saga and actively evangelized in various parts of Kyushu. In 1902, Meiji Gakuin offered him a position as a professor of theology, an appointment he held until 1925. The theology department had been led by Verbeck and Amerman since the school's inception. Amerman left Japan in 1892 and Verbeck died in 1898, leaving a void in the department, so Oltmans took charge of teaching the Old Testament through theology, history, and exegesis. In 1920, Ibuka Kajinosuke resigned as the second president of Meiji Gakuin after Hepburn, as well as chairman of the school's board of trustees. Oltmans was subsequently appointed as secretary to the new president, a post he held for eight months. He was thus involved not only as a teacher and missionary but also in the practical management of the school.

While he contributed greatly to Meiji Gakuin's development in the early twentieth century, Oltmans is especially remembered for his leadership of Ferris Seminary after its building was destroyed in the Great Kanto Earthquake of September 1, 1923. One of the school's most tragic losses was that of its principal, Jennie M. Kuyper, who had assumed her post months before, in October 1922, as the successor to Eugene Booth. During the quake, the school building collapsed on her; her secretary, Nakamura Teiji, and others in the new building who escaped confirmed that Kuyper was alive under the rubble, but a fire that broke out soon after engulfed her before she could be rescued.

In Ferris's dire straits, Oltmans took over as its interim principal. Although he was already sixty-eight years old at the time, he devoted himself to rebuilding the school, which had been established by Mary Kidder and developed by Booth. After an initial attempt to build a temporary school building with about 2,300 yen from the alumnae association, Oltmans approached the RCA's American headquarters, and after several rounds of negotiations, he succeeded in getting them to invest $9,000 (about 20,000 yen at the time) to subsidize the reconstruction. In April of the following year, he resigned due to his increased official duties at Meiji Gakuin, and Shafer succeeded him. Until then, he commuted almost daily from his home in Tokyo to Yokohama to work on the school's reconstruction.

Another of Oltmans's outstanding achievements in missionary work was his commitment to helping people affected by leprosy. He began this work after Wyckoff's sudden death in 1911, when he took over the latter's position as director of Kōzensha, a home for lepers, whose office had moved to Meiji Gakuin during Wyckoff's directorship, and he devoted his efforts to leprosy relief. Thus, Oltmans developed the work of Rutgers missionaries in Japan, such as Stout, Booth, and Wyckoff, and then he passed the baton at Ferris to Shafer, who was also from Rutgers.[22]

Eugene C. Duryee

The last Rutgers missionary to Japan discussed in this chapter is Eugene C. Duryee (1901–1981). Born in Cherry Hill, New Jersey, in September 1901, his father was the Reverend Abraham Duryee, and his grandfather was a teacher. Duryee graduated from Rutgers in 1923 and then from Hartford Seminary in Connecticut in 1926. He was later appointed a missionary by the General Synod of Hope College and assigned to Meiji Gakuin at the age of twenty-five, where he helped write *Useful English: A Textbook of English Conversation*, prepared by his PCUSA colleague, Willis Church Lamott.

After returning to the United States in 1931, Duryee assisted the youth education program at the Middle Collegiate Church in New York while earning a master's degree in Christian education from Union Theological Seminary and Columbia University, which he completed in 1933. In 1943, he became pastor of Blue Mountain Reformed Church, in Saugerties, New York, a position he held until his retirement in 1968, and in 1981 he was called to be pastor emeritus of Cornwall Presbyterian Church, in Cornwall, New York, at the age of seventy-nine.

While in Japan, Duryee contributed an article to the *Christian Intelligencer* on the Meiji Gakuin Junior High School, which consisted of five grades and had about one thousand students at the time, with about sixty students in the classrooms for most subjects. Boys in round-cropped hair lining up by classes as they entered the classroom, the class standing and making a bow at the beginning and end of class—such were some of the alien customs that amused him.[23] He reported seeing students playing with a toy lizard stuck to the wall during class. Club activities included tennis, baseball, table tennis, judo, soccer, English conversation, and harmonica; baseball and tennis were especially popular. He also held extracurricular Bible study sessions. And while riding the bus, a Japanese gentleman who saw how Duryee's head was hitting the ceiling because of his height gave up his seat to him. These anecdotes offer glimpses of how much Duryee enjoyed his sojourn in Japan.

Conclusion

This chapter has examined the activities in Japan undertaken by missionaries from Rutgers, including NBTS graduates, which were linked to Meiji Gakuin. As we have seen, these men laid the foundation for the school, and it is clear that Rutgers alumni played direct and major roles in the development of Meiji Gakuin and other schools established by the RCA, which may be summarized as follows.

James H. Ballagh brought his brother, John, who took over the Hepburn School, to Japan; this institution subsequently developed into the Ballagh School, Tsukiji College, TUC, and the Meiji Gakuin School of General Education. In addition, the Ballagh brothers' students later continued their studies at the Brown School and served as teachers and pastors at Meiji Gakuin and churches around Japan. In this sense, Meiji Gakuin might not have survived without the work of James H. Ballagh.

Guido F. Verbeck, though only briefly discussed in this chapter (he is discussed more thoroughly in chapter 1), enabled the opening of Meiji Gakuin in the sense that he broke ground for establishing modern schools in Japan. Verbeck, the vice-principal of Daigaku Nankō, brought Rutgers alumnus Griffis from Fukui to join the school, and he helped to appoint Rutgers professor David Murray as an advisor to the Ministry of Education, thereby solidifying the relationship between Japan and Rutgers. He also sent many Japanese students to Rutgers and later lectured at TUTS and Meiji Gakuin's School of Theology. In other words, he was a missionary who was involved with both Rutgers and Meiji Gakuin.

After graduating from Rutgers, Wyckoff succeeded Griffis in the latter's position at a junior high school in Fukui and later taught at the Tokyo Kaisei Gakkō. After a brief return to the United States, he came back to Japan to become the principal of Senshi School, a preparatory school proposed by Amerman. Wyckoff became a professor when TUC merged with Tsukiji College and moved on to a faculty post at Meiji Gakuin's School of General Education, which Harris and Duryee later took over.

Amerman, a NBTS graduate, became the president of TUTS and laid the foundation of theological education in Japan by writing numerous textbooks and lecturing. Oltmans, his fellow NBTS alumnus, supported Stout's missionary and educational activities in Nagasaki; he also taught at Meiji Gakuin's School of Theology, took over Wyckoff's leprosy-relief work, and played a major role in helping to restore Ferris Girls' School after the Great Kanto Earthquake before passing his work on to Shafer.

In addition to the above missionaries, there were a few others who have not been discussed in this chapter: Frank Seymour Scudder (1862–1956) was involved in missionary work in the Shinshū region from 1898 to 1906, and after teaching English at a police department in Nagano for two years, he taught English at Meiji Gakuin's Schools of General Education and Theology from 1906 to 1907. From 1907 to 1936, he conducted missionary work for the Japanese in Hawaii. Harold William Schenck (1892–1960) served as the pastor of Yokohama Union Church from 1930 to 1937, and Garret Hondelink was a missionary who focused on evangelism in Kyushu (mainly in Kumamoto and Kagoshima). Many of the early missionaries had graduated from Rutgers and attended NBTS before arriving in Japan.[24]

In this way, affiliates of Rutgers University and NBTS played major roles in the foundation of Meiji Gakuin. They undertook not only theological education and ministry training but also general and congregational education. A new anthem, composed in 1907 by Shimazaki Tōson, a renowned writer and Meiji Gakuin alumnus, replaced the school song mentioned at the beginning of this chapter. Nevertheless, the base of Christian education that these Rutgers graduates established continues to flourish in both Meiji Gakuin and, as discussed in chapter 15, Ferris University for Women.

Appendix 14A: Genealogy of Meiji Gakuin

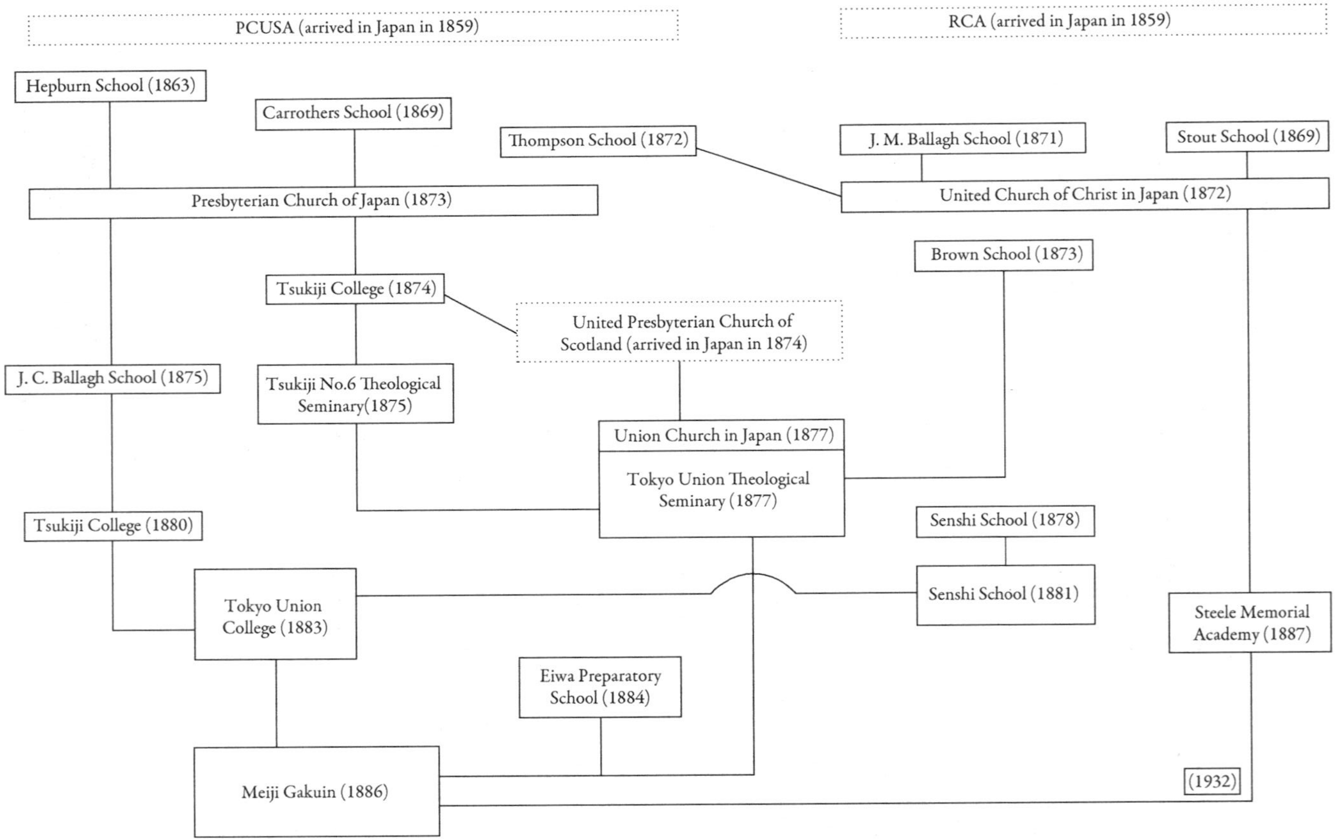

FIGURE 14.4. Lineage Chart of Meiji Gakuin. CPUSA = Presbyterian Church in the United States of America; RCA = Reformed Church in America. The Carrothers School was founded by missionary Christopher Carrothers.

Appendix 14B: Missionaries from Rutgers College and the New Brunswick Theological Seminary

Following is a list of twelve missionaries associated with Meiji Gakuin comprising ten from Rutgers and two from NBTS. As discussed in the chapter, Wyckoff, Harris, and Amerman were deeply involved in Meiji Gakuin's early establishment.

Rutgers graduate missionaries to Japan		
Year of graduation	Name	Years in Japan
1857	James Hamilton Ballagh	1861–1920
1865	Henry Nelson Stout	1869–1904
1876	Eugene Samuel Booth	1879–1922
1872	Martin Nevius Wyckoff	1881–1911
1880	Nathan Henry Demarest	1883–1890
1873	Howard Harris	1884–1905
1885	Frank Seymour Scudder	1897–1907
1912	Luman James Shafer	1912–1935, 1946, 1949–1952
1913	Harold W. Schenck	1930–1937
1923	Eugene Clarke Duyree	1926–1931
NBTS graduate missionaries to Japan		
1868	James Lansing Amerman	1876–1892
1886	Albert Oltmans	1886–1939

Notes

Original essay written in Japanese; translated and edited by Haruko Wakabayashi.

1 Meiji Gakuin, ed., *Meiji Gakuin Dōsōkai hyakunenshi* (Tokyo: Meiji Gakuin Dōsōkai, 2008), 194–199.
2 See preface of Meiji, *Meiji Gakuin hyakunenshi.*
3 Okabe Kazuoki, *Hebon den* (Yokohama: Yūrindō, 2023); Takaya Michio, *Hebon* (Tokyo: Yoshikawa Kōbunkan, 1986); William Elliot Griffis, *Hepburn of Japan and His Wife and Helpmates: A Life Story of Toil for Christ* (Philadelphia: Westminster Press, 1913).
4 Gordon D. Laman, *Pioneers to Partners: The Reformed Church in America and Christian Mission with the Japanese* (Grand Rapids, MI: William B. Eerdmans, 2012), 131.
5 Nakajima Kōji, Tsuji Naoto, and Ōnishi Haruki, *Chōrō Kaikaku Kyōkai rainichi senkyōshi jiten* (Tokyo: Shinkyō Shuppansha, 2003), 176.
6 These include *Yūshinron* [An argument for the being of God, 1888], *Shin'yaku Seisho shingaku* [The theology of the New Testament on the basis of Van Oosterzee, 1888], *Shinseiron* [The attributes of God and the trinity, 1888], *Kami no sadameshi mune* [The decrees of God, 1888], *Jinseiron* [Anthropology, 1886], *Soshiki shingaku*

[Systematic theology, 1887], *Kyōkai seiji* [Church government, 1888], and *Kyūjōgaku* [Soteriology, 1888].

7 Laman, *Pioneers to Partners*, 172–174; Nakajima et al., *Chōrō Kaikaku Kyōkai*, 174, 202.

8 Laman, *Pioneers to Partners*, 174; Nakajima et al., *Chōrō Kaikaku Kyōkai*, 174, 202.

9 Namely, Yokohama Kaigan Church (Yokohama Kōkai), Tokyo Shinsakaebashi Church (Tokyo Kōkai), Ueda Church, Nagasaki Church, Yokohama Sumiyoshi-chō Church (Yokohama First Presbyterian Church, now Yokohama Shiloh Church), Tokyo Shiba Rogetsuchō Church (Tokyo First Presbyterian Church, now Shiba Church), Shimousa Hōden Church, Tokyo Shinagawa Church (now Ōimachi Church), and Shimousa Ōmori Church.

10 His time in Fukui is described in more detail by Fernanda Perrone in chapter 7 of this volume.

11 A. Oltmans, "Prof. Martin Nevius Wyckoff, Sc.D.," *The Christian Intelligencer*, March 15, 1911.

12 James Lansing Amerman, *Sketch of the Japan Mission* (New York: The Board of Foreign Missions of the Reformed Church in America, 1889), 9.

13 Nakajima et al., *Chōrō Kaikaku Kyōkai*, 248–249.

14 About Howard Harris, see Laman, *Pioneers to Partners*, 197, 229, 231; Nakajima et al., *Chōrō Kaikaku Kyōkai*, 251–253.

15 About Stout, see Laman, *Pioneers to Partners*, 95–97, 121–124; Nakajima et al., *Chōrō Kaikaku Kyōkai*, 208–217.

16 Meiji Gakuin Hyakugojunenshi Henshu Iinkai, eds., *Meiji Gakuin 150-nen shi* (Tokyo: Meiji Gakuin, 2013), 105.

17 Amerman, *Sketch of the Japan Mission*, 10.

18 Amerman, 94–95.

19 About Shafer, see Laman, *Pioneers to Partners*, 433, 436, 456–457.

20 *Kokusai Kirisutokyō Daigaku sōsetsushi—ashita no daigaku e no bijon* (Tokyo: International Christian University, 1990), 30, translated from C. W. Iglehart, *International Christian University: An Adventure in Christian Higher Education in Japan* (1964).

21 Laman, *Pioneers to Partners*, 232; Nakajima et al., *Chōrō Kaikaku Kyōkai*, 254.

22 Nakajima et al., *Chōrō Kaikaku Kyōkai*, 259–260; "And Now Again—Japan!," *The Church Herald*, March 25, 1949, 12–13.

23 Eugene C. Duryee, "A Middle School in Japan," *Christian Intelligencer and Mission Field*, June 12, 1929.

24 This trend, however, shifted from 1886 onward. Hope College, with its graduates moving on to the Western Theological Seminary, located within its campus, produced most missionaries who were sent to Japan thereafter.

15

The Contributions of Rutgers and the Reformed Church in America to Women's Education in Modern Japan

RUI KOHIYAMA

It might be hard to imagine that the nineteenth-century faculty and alumni networks of Rutgers College, which all consisted of men, impacted the education of women in Japan. In those days, reformers in the United States generally considered this field part of the women's sphere, especially in the world of foreign missionary efforts, where "woman's work for woman" was the slogan of female activism. In a curious turn of events, however, the men affiliated with Rutgers and its close associate, the Reformed Church in America (RCA), exerted a reverberating influence on women's education in modern Japan.

The first section of this chapter outlines Rutgers and RCA sojourners' engagement in the public education of Japanese women at the beginning of the Meiji period. It explains how they helped the Meiji government plan and execute basic educational programs for women.

The next section focuses on Eugene S. Booth (1850–1931), an RCA missionary who graduated from Rutgers and the New Brunswick Theological Seminary. In 1882, Booth succeeded Mary E. Kidder (1834–1910), a missionary sent to Japan by the RCA in 1869. Kidder, the first unmarried female missionary to reside in Japan, started the Ferris Seminary in Yokohama in 1870, which became the RCA's most important women's mission school in Japan, and Booth served as its principal for about forty years until 1922. His objectives for educating girls and young women at Ferris included his firm belief in the importance of instilling in students the concept of "home" based on monogamous marriage. The analysis here will explain traditional Japanese womanhood and gender relationships in the premodern period and show their variance from Booth's ideals.

The final section deals with Kimura Kumaji (1845–1927), who graduated from Hope College in Michigan and the New Brunswick Theological Seminary. Kimura was sent back to Japan by the RCA as an ordained preacher in 1882 and started the Meiji Jo Gakkō (MJG) in 1885 with no financial support from the RCA mission in Japan. The MJG quickly grew into a leading women's school and flourished until 1896, when a fire burned down its buildings in the center of Tokyo. The discussion here compares Kimura's initial plan for female education at MJG to the Ferris catalog in 1882 and examines the women's school in Komoro briefly run by his third wife, a graduate of MJG and Ferris. Kimura and other Japanese Christians started MJG as a critique of missionary endeavors in educating Japanese women. The school in Komoro attempted to propagate what had been tried out at MJG and Ferris. By introducing the MJG and the school in Komoro into our view, we can trace the process and extent to which the changes introduced by RCA missionaries and Japanese Christians spread in Japanese society by the beginning of the twentieth century.

The Meiji Government's Interest in Women's Education and the Rutgers Network

In 1860, the Tokugawa shogunate sent a group of delegates to the United States to exchange instruments of ratification for the U.S.-Japan commercial treaty concluded in the previous year. This official government delegation was the first of its kind sent overseas since Japan's opening to the West in 1854. The samurai participants in the mission who observed the United States at first hand listed the status and behavior of American women among the numerous shocks they experienced during their travels. They could not help but note the differences between how Japan and the United States treated and positioned women. For example, Vice-Envoy Muragaki Norimasa was puzzled by women's presence at a public ceremony as important as a treaty ratification, and he wrote in his diary on May 26, 1860, that a niece of President James Buchanan (1791–1868) who acted as the first lady "was the host. . . . She had power like a queen and the president looked like a chancellor."[1]

Fukuzawa Yukichi, who had accompanied the delegates to San Francisco on a different vessel, took a photo with an American girl who happened to be at a local photo shop he visited. He bragged about this incident to his fellow samurai, who wondered if the girl was a kind of geisha.[2] Japanese men of the time could not imagine how an innocent female teenager not in the sex trade would consent to be photographed alongside a male stranger in a kimono and topknot. Their confusion made the photo a worthy souvenir for a keen observer like Fukuzawa to bring home, together with a Webster's dictionary, to show his compatriots the unique features of American society he had found.

The early Meiji government's tendency to look to the United States for guidance on educating Japanese women seems to have originated in experiences like Fukuzawa's—namely, those of a few elites who had the rare chance to visit the United States toward the end of the Tokugawa era. More concrete influence came from Guido F. Verbeck, an RCA missionary who came to Japan in 1859. He stayed in Nagasaki, a mecca of Western knowledge that had long been the only port of call for Dutch traders before Japan's partial opening to other Western countries in 1854. Verbeck was first employed by the Tokugawa shogunate and later by the Saga domain to teach in Nagasaki schools in the 1860s, and he was acquainted with many promising young men. Some of his students, like Ōkuma Shigenobu (1838–1922), became influential in the Meiji government, which invited Verbeck in 1869 to Edo (later Tokyo) to advise the new government and to oversee its higher education program for men at the Kaisei Gakkō (later Nankō), one of the original schools that became the current University of Tokyo.[3]

As explained in other chapters, Verbeck helped send Japanese male students to Rutgers in the latter half of the 1860s and early 1870s via J. M. Ferris, the secretary of the RCA's Board of Foreign Missions. Through Verbeck's good offices, Rutgers graduates came to teach in Japan—for instance, William Elliot Griffis (1843–1928), who also shaped the Meiji government's early endeavors to educate women, albeit indirectly.

In 1869, Verbeck wrote the "Brief Sketch" for sending a Meiji government mission to America and Europe and conveyed it to Ōkuma Shigenobu. The Meiji government took notice of this proposal in 1871 and summoned Verbeck in October to discuss the objectives, organization, and route of the mission, which was dispatched at the end of the same year. Although Verbeck's "Brief Sketch" did not mention women's education, it is possible that he advised on this matter through urgent discussions with Iwakura Tomomi, the mission's ambassador extraordinary and plenipotentiary.[4] We can infer this from a letter Verbeck wrote to J. M. Ferris including a letter of introduction to Sarah Platt Doremus, an RCA associate and a leading advocate of women's foreign missionary enterprise, so that Iwakura could meet her in New York and ask for her advice on the objectives of women's education.[5]

On November 17, Kuroda Kiyotaka of the Hokkaidō Development Commission formally proposed to send five girls to the United States for ten years of education. Kuroda, another Japanese man impressed by American women while visiting the United States, independently made his proposal in consultation not with Verbeck but with Mori Arinori, then the Japanese chargé d'affaires to the United States. Iwakura's quick acceptance of Kuroda's proposal to have the five girls accompany his mission suggests that he acknowledged the importance of women's education, an acknowledgement that must have at least partially come from his discussions with Verbeck.

In January 1872, the Ministry of Education announced the opening of a women's school in Tokyo, the Kanritsu Tokyo Jo Gakkō (KTJG). Although there are no records of this school's initial establishment, Verbeck may have been involved, as he was the deputy head of Nankō, its male counterpart. The KTJG's first teacher was Amelia Woodruff Jacks Veeder (1841–1888), the wife of the Reverend Dr. Peter Vrooman Veeder, a descendant of the New York Knickerbockers and a graduate of Union College, a school near Albany backed by Dutch descendants in the region. Veeder was well known in the RCA's foreign mission circle in the United States as president of the City College in San Francisco.[6] Verbeck recommended Veeder for a position at Nankō, although he did so with hesitation because he thought Veeder overqualified. Nevertheless, Veeder came to Japan in 1871, and Amelia was asked, probably by Verbeck, to teach the English curriculum at KTJG from its beginning in 1872.[7] In August 1872, Margaret Clark Griffis (1838–1913) came to Japan from the United States to stay with her younger brother, William Elliot Griffis, a Rutgers graduate whom Verbeck had brought in from Fukui to teach at Nankō earlier that year. Verbeck asked Margaret, an experienced teacher, to help at KTJG on February 17, 1873, probably because Veeder had become pregnant, and she took over the latter's position from September 1873 until July 1874.[8]

Meanwhile, David Murray (1830–1905), a Rutgers professor of mathematics and astronomy, came to Japan in June 1873 to serve at the Ministry of Education as the superintendent of education. Murray was of Scottish descent and, like Veeder, a graduate of Union College. In July 1873 he visited KTJG with Iwakura Tomomi, and in November of the same year his wife did the same with Julia N. Crosby (1833–1918), the daughter of a Rutgers professor of Latin and Greek who had been sent to Japan as a missionary in 1871 by the Woman's Union Missionary Society (WUMS), an interdenominational organization in New York City led by RCA women. Martha Murray, David Murray's wife, and Julia Crosby probably felt kinship with Margaret Griffis, who had visited the Doremus School (Kyōritsu Jo Gakkō) in Yokohama, which Crosby had run since 1871 together with Louise Pierson (1832–1899) and Mary P. Pruyn (1820–1885), the latter another RCA woman from Albany. This school, originally the American Mission Home, changed its English name to honor Sarah Platt Doremus, who chaired the WUMS and belonged to an RCA church in New York City. Margaret Griffis had exchanges with the three women missionaries throughout her tenure in Japan.[9]

In his 1873 report to the Ministry of Education, David Murray advised the establishment of a normal school for women in Tokyo to produce model teachers for the public elementary schools that the ministry wanted to establish across the nation. Tanaka Fujimaro, a higher official of the ministry close to Murray, submitted the proposal to the Minister of Education on January 4, 1874. As a result, the school was formally opened in November 1875 with Nakamura Masanao as its principal, a Christian and Confucian scholar widely known for his translation of Samuel Smiles's *Self-Help*. When the KTJG closed in 1877 due to financial difficulties resulting from the Satsuma Rebellion in Kyūshū that same year, its students were transferred to the new English department at the Normal School for Women.[10]

In summary, the Meiji government initiated efforts to promote women's education from approximately 1870 to 1877, under the guidance of Rutgers and RCA affiliates. Guido Verbeck sent men in his network to teach at Nankō, and their female relatives taught at KTJG. After Verbeck left Nankō in 1873, David Murray effectively stepped in to maintain the influence of the Rutgers and RCA network in the field of education in Meiji Japan, including women's education.[11]

E. S. Booth and the Ferris Seminary

North American women missionaries made significant contributions to private education for girls and women from the beginning of the Meiji period. The RCA women missionaries, in particular, were pioneers in the field. As mentioned above, Mary Kidder became the first single woman to settle in Japan and founded the Ferris Seminary in Yokohama. In 1871 the American Mission Home, later known as the Doremus School, was also established in the same city. Both schools still exist on the hills of Yokohama, overlooking the port.

The RCA missionaries undertook another endeavor to educate women in Nagasaki. Henry Stout (1838–1912), a Rutgers graduate who arrived in Nagasaki in 1869, began to teach Japanese students at home in 1872, and his wife started a women's class a little later.[12] This project was promoted in the United States soon after the Woman's Foreign Mission Society (WFMS) was formally organized among RCA women in 1875: A special fundraising campaign was launched in 1876, and two women missionaries were sent to Nagasaki in 1878, but they became sick and returned in 1879. The Nagasaki women's school, named Jonathan Sturges Seminary in honor of its benefactor, businessman Jonathan Sturges, whose wife Mary was the WFMS president in the RCA, did not become a stable institution until 1890. In 1914, it moved to Shimonoseki and merged with a Presbyterian women's school to form the Baikō Jo Gakkō, which still exists as a coeducational institution.[13]

Of the three institutions for women's education that involved RCA missionaries, this section focuses on Ferris and the work of its second principal, E. S. Booth, because it was the only institution to which the RCA singularly committed itself. An examination of Booth's major objectives in educating girls and

FIGURE 15.1. Ferris Seminary, Yokohama, undated. (Credit: William Elliot Griffis Collection, Rutgers University Libraries.)

women helps clarify the contributions of Rutgers and the RCA to the reinvention of womanhood and gender relationships in Meiji Japan.

Booth graduated from Rutgers College in 1876 and New Brunswick Theological Seminary in 1879. Immediately afterward, he married Emily Steele (1855–1917) of North Brunswick, was ordained, and was sent to Japan by the RCA Board of Foreign Missions, arriving in Yokohama in October 1879. He stayed in Nagasaki for two years and visited Yokohama at the end of 1881 to improve his health. There he joined Ferris, which had declined in the absence of its principal Mary Miller (Kidder), who was on furlough with her husband, missionary E. Rothesay Miller, from 1879.[14]

In January 1882, Booth issued a catalog for Ferris, the first of its kind to be published since the school's inception in 1870. In its introduction, he explained some benefits of female education. First, he pointed out that it would increase domestic comfort and happiness because educated women would become good helpmeets for their husbands and be relied upon to manage their homes. Second, he insisted that it would make their lives more enjoyable. Education would strengthen women's minds, increase their dignity, and heighten their purity, and consequently, purify society and uplift the pleasantness of women's and men's companionship. Third, he claimed that women's education mattered to a nation because mothers would raise and educate the children who would build its future, making women's education an issue of national importance. This last idea was a corollary of Republican motherhood, an ideology promoted in the post-Revolutionary period in the United States.[15]

Booth seems to have maintained his belief in these benefits of female education throughout his tenure. In February 1917, when he was conferred with the Order of the Blue Ribbon, he said the following in an interview with a newspaper reporter:

> With the promotion of education among the women of this country, the Japanese men will have less occasion to seek their clubs and tea houses or associate with geisha than is the case today . . . with a wide gulf separating the companionship, intelligence and interests of men and women in Japan, home is not all that the name should imply. . . . It is highly imperative therefore, that education be advanced among Japanese women in order to produce wives who can truly sympathize with their husbands. Although the geisha have cultivated for centuries their special methods of appealing to the spirits and minds of the men, they are only playthings. . . . When the women of the country are further advanced in education, the men will feel ashamed of their vicious conduct and they will come to sincerely love their wives and more highly respect them. As a result, their homes will be purified and will become their real headquarters for retreat and comfort.

The article that carried this interview was titled "WERE WIVES BETTER EDUCATED CHARMS OF GEISHA WOULD WANE."[16]

To our eyes, Booth's explanation may appear banal and old-fashioned in how it prioritizes men's satisfaction and pleasure in marriage and "home." However, in his day it was still novel and modern to place an educated woman in a "house" as a wife of dignity and quality, whom her husband would respect. His ideal of companionship between a husband and a wife did not define marriage in the Japan of that time, where monogamy had yet to be established. A man could be entertained by professional women and buy their sexual services or keep concubines if he had the means, whereas marital companionship was secondary. In Japan, the most important quality for an ordinary wife was obedience; an old saying decreed that "a woman when young must obey her father, when married her husband, and when old her son. She has no house (*ie*) of her own in the whole world."[17]

To elaborate on this point, in the Tokugawa or Edo period (ca. 1603–1868), marriage was basically for maintaining the *ie*, in the sense of *oikos*, or a household, as an economic unit in which obtaining the means for living took prime importance. This was especially the case for the warrior class because the *karoku*, the pension given initially to the founder of an *ie* for distinguished military service, was secured for his family—the members of his household—as long as the *ie* was maintained through a male heir, without which it would be discontinued. This practice made it crucial for a family to produce a male heir through marriage, and divorce or adoption was common when a marriage did not do so. Also, as the *ie* relied on a kinship network based on marriage and adoption, marriage necessitated permission from this network and the domain (*han*) in the case of samurai. By the end of the era, the mindset of the need to maintain the *ie* had permeated society beyond the warrior class excepting the poor, who could not afford to have the *ie*.[18]

On the other hand, many Japanese at that time understood the mutual attraction between women and men as a fickle phenomenon. In general, people did not distinguish the spiritual or the platonic from the carnal in love until they began encountering Western customs after more than two hundred years of Japan's near-complete isolation.[19] Most people understood the spiritual and the carnal to unite when men and women experienced *koi*, or yearning, for each other. But *koi* did not last long, however intense it might be; its mutability made it too unstable as the basis for marriage and the foundation of *ie*. Thus, emotions and passion for marital partners were not primary. Parents took the initiative to make marital arrangements early for the *ie* to continue, and children had to obey. A bride and a bridegroom often met for the first time on their wedding day.[20]

To satisfy their *koigokoro*, or yearning hearts, therefore, men and women had to seek relationships outside marriage, which, as mentioned above, were openly available for men. In Edo, the Yoshiwara pleasure quarters served as a place of licensed prostitution where men could enjoy pseudoromantic affairs following intricate rules peculiar to the space, which contained the tragedies and suffering that are part and parcel of sex work and human trafficking.[21] Poverty was the major propeller of prostitution. Yoshiwara was also a cultural center; unlike Christian countries, Japanese cultural tradition did not highly value women's chastity. Rather, sexual experiences were prized as an essential part of *koi*. Top-ranking prostitutes were adored not only for their beauty and sophistication but also for their literary flair and worldliness, and they were often taken as models for *ukiyo-e* woodblock prints.[22]

Yoshiwara had cultivated a culture of *iro* (color) that defined the fleeting sentiments of *koi* as *uwaki*, or capriciousness. If a man entered an illicit relationship, he had to do so on the presumption of *uwaki* and never lose his head over the woman involved. This attitude was known as *iki*, or sophistication, and it was highly regarded in *iro* culture. On the other hand, wallowing in such a relationship was referred to as *yabo*, or boorishness. In this culture, women were generally divided into two categories: *yūjo*, women for play, and *jionna*, or "earthly" or ordinary women. The latter was described by the author Ihara Saikaku in the seventeenth century as charmless women who were "unimaginative, irritatingly repetitive when they speak, somewhat mean, write letters differently, drink saké awkwardly, unable to sing, gawky in outfits, unstable in manners, totter, talk about miso and salt when sleeping together and are stingy enough to use toilet paper piece by piece."[23] In the *iro* formulation, *jionna* were thus denied sexuality and put in charge of everyday life to maintain the *ie* as obedient wives and mothers, whereas *yūjo* were denied motherhood and consigned to the world of pleasure.

And yet, the divide between *yūjo* and *jionna* was unclear: A woman might be in either stage of life depending on her economic situation. Prostitutes in Yoshiwara or other places offering sexual services went out of business around the age of twenty-eight, after which they could marry and live as *jionna* or become concubines. According to the historian Yokoyama Yuriko, no great stigma was attached to them for previously selling sex.[24] Furthermore, there were not a few young housemaids on the spectrum between *jionna* and *yūjo*, because women could seek employment as domestic helpers of several kinds to various ranks of daimyo (feudal lords). This type of position might equip them with opportunities that included learning manners, letters, and sophistication, which would prepare them for a good marital arrangement or allow them to be chosen by their masters for concubinage. They could also perform lifelong service as maids in their masters' households.[25] In this context, people at the time probably recognized and accepted the sheer fact that women's sexuality or beauty, particularly when young, was an asset that allowed them to survive or advance in society.

Yūjo were ubiquitous in Tokugawa-era Japanese society, whether they were licensed or unlicensed, or geishas who sold sex as an extension of their artistry, or those who aspired to the profession. In general, the culture of *iro* nurtured in Yoshiwara and other such places seems to have thoroughly "colored" social norms. Popular literature and *ukiyo-e* effectively enhanced the influence of the *iro* culture to define people's sentiments and attitudes toward women and their relationships with men.[26]

The objectives of women's education and the ideal of educated womanhood that E. S. Booth upheld at the Ferris Seminary from the 1880s onward must be understood in light of the Tokugawa period's construction of womanhood and norms around heterosexual relationships, which retained influence in Japan at least until World War II. The women who Booth envisioned cultivating in his school followed the American Christian model: They were moral and chaste, educated enough to teach their children, and capable of understanding, helping, and entertaining their husbands as equal and lovable partners. They were angels and makers of "home" as an important institution that provided not only care and moral guidance but also warmth and enjoyment to its members and guests.[27]

Described in terms of the Japanese construction of womanhood in the Edo period, this ideal simultaneously embraced the identities of *jionna* and *yūjo*. A woman had to be a good housewife and mother and "equipped" with sexuality at the same time. But the last characteristic was ultimately only accessible to her husband: She could flirt when single, but sexual intercourse was allowed only after marriage and only with her husband. She should be "pure," and sexual experiences with multiple men debased and deprived her of true womanhood. Homemaking was her paramount responsibility; unlike her traditional counterpart, she was no mere addition to her husband's family who could be replaced easily. The "home" she ran exemplified her character and represented her capability and worth.

From early on, Mary Kidder, Booth's predecessor, sensed the gulf between the American and the Japanese constructions of womanhood. In 1873, she invited all Ferris students to her wedding ceremony to impress upon them the Christian spirit of lifelong commitment. Kidder also tried to intervene in the marriages of her students because she perceived Japanese marital customs to be terribly opposed to Christian teachings. She inspired her students to prioritize loving their prospective husbands and criticized the marriages arranged by their parents, regardless of how favorable the terms were.[28] For Kidder, the introduction of love-based marriages was crucial to change Japanese womanhood and establish Christian "homes" as idealized in the United States.

When Booth initially took over as principal of Ferris, some of its first students had reached marriageable age. As Western knowledge and customs were enthusiastically sought in Japan during the mid-1880s, the girls' mission schools in the Yokohama and Tokyo areas held social events to which suitable Christian young Japanese men were invited with the aim of matchmaking, or at least of allowing young women and men to meet and understand each other. Uchimura Kanzō, later a leading Japanese Christian, exclaimed as a young man of twenty-two in 1883, "I received an invitation from the Methodist girls' school!!!!!! [*sic*] A fair chance for hunting."[29] Ferris also held evening gatherings in 1886 and 1887 for about two hundred guests comprising the parents, relatives, or guardians of students and suitable youths. Young teachers' and students' performances included playing the organ or koto, reciting English verses, singing together, and presenting skits and tableaux vivants. Iwamoto Yoshiharu, the future husband of Shimada Kashi, also known as Wakamoto Shizuko (1864–1896)—Ferris's first graduate and also its Japanese teacher—reported in 1887 in the *Jogaku zasshi* (The Woman's Magazine) that the recitation of King Lear in which Shimada had participated was very well done. Iwamoto was editor-in-chief of this popular magazine on women's education, which was widely read among men and women of the intellectual persuasion from the latter half of the 1880s through the 1890s. Aside from this performance at Ferris, Iwamoto and Shimada had other interactions at similar meetings as well as others, and they married in 1889.[30]

In 1888 and 1889, an association for literary studies composed of affiliates from four boys' mission schools in Tokyo held gatherings to which they invited the teachers and students of girls' mission schools in the Tokyo and Yokohama areas, including Ferris.[31] Around that time, Shimazaki Tōson, who would become one of the era's greatest writers, was a student at Meiji Gakuin, one of the boys' mission schools cosponsored by the RCA and the North American Presbyterian Church. He later described such gatherings as follows:

> Soon he learned the culture of the sons of good families . . . wearing a soft hat, short pants and woolen knee socks, he went by invitation, together with other

> young boys whose faces radiated joy, to literary meetings where many girls gathered. . . . He forgot almost everything when listening to English recitations and songs issuing from their lips . . . he visited places and gatherings where young men and women would meet, as well as the homes of church elders, and he sought a young, pretty partner who would make him feel happy.[32]

Uchimura Kanzō participated in this Christian circle in Tokyo in 1883 and fell in love with Asada Take, who had been educated at mission schools in Kyoto and Yokohama. He married her immediately against his parents' will and divorced in seven months. Wounded deeply by this failure, Uchimura left for America to recover and later wrote about the experience:

> Fresh from my country church, with childish innocence and credulity, I plunged myself into the society of metropolitan Christianity, like a Turkish bath, to be lulled and shampooed with hymns sung by maidens and sermons that offended nobody. God's kingdom was imagined to be one of perfect repose and constant free exchange of good wishes, where tea parties and lovemaking could be indulged in with the sanction of the religion of free communion and free love.[33]

Uchimura further criticized American missionaries as follows:

> Mainly, American missionaries taught Japanese people how to make such happy homes. They . . . tried to have Japanese whom they had converted to Christianity make happy homes and thus to create happy people. Many Japanese Christians so taught by American missionaries tried to make happy homes that ended in total disappointment. Some of them even came to doubt the efficacy of Christianity. . . . Happy homes! Christ does not promise such things to those who believe him.[34]

E. S. Booth was one of the missionaries "who taught Japanese how to make such happy homes." Despite criticisms from Japanese observers like Uchimura, the education at mission schools in general produced women different from those of premodern Japan. Uchida Roan (1868–1928), a critic, translator, and novelist, wrote about the girls' mission schools and their students in Tsukiji, the foreign concession in Tokyo, and raised the following points:

> [In those days, there were three girls' mission schools in Tsukiji, namely, the Presbyterian, Methodist, and Episcopal schools.] As they [the girls] went to church schools . . . their clothes were like those of nuns. Some of them . . . had totally lost the femininity of young women, but they modeled themselves on the language and gestures of Western people and therefore were lively like their models in spite of their quiet clothes. They dealt with everything energetically

> and spread the atmosphere of something new. Further, their responses had a decency and dignity that the lascivious girls in town could never possess. They were familiar with the Western lifestyle, and their taste was Western. . . . In those days, mission school graduates were among the most stylish women and possessed the highest culture.[35]

Kaburaki Kiyotaka (1878–1972), an artist who specialized in *ukiyo-e* and Japanese painting, released his *Tsukiji Akashi-chō* in 1927, one of his representative works that received the Japan Fine Arts Academy Award in the same year. When Kaburaki was young, he lived for about fifteen years (1885–1895 and 1901–1906) in the Kobiki-chō area close to the foreign concession that was colloquially called Tsukiji, specifically in the Akashi-chō district. He vividly remembered his old home as a peculiar space of foreign presence. The painting was one of a trilogy that depicted three women representing three towns with which he was familiar: Tsukiji or Akashi-chō, Shintomi-chō, and Hamachō Kashi. Kaburaki produced these works as reminiscences of the towns circa 1890, before they were completely destroyed in the Great Kanto Earthquake of 1923.[36]

When interpreting *Tsukiji Akashi-chō*, it is essential to consider that, since its establishment in 1869, the majority of residents in the concession were missionaries from various denominations and countries rather than traders, as the port in Tokyo Bay was unable to handle commercial deliveries. Akashi-chō was thus known for churches and mission schools.[37] It had at least four such girls' schools between 1885 and 1895 and two between 1901 and 1906, when Kaburaki lived in the area. Thus, the Japanese women he saw there in the mid-Meiji period were most likely affiliated with girls' mission schools.

The image of the woman in *Tsukiji Akashi-chō*, therefore, might be best interpreted as that of a mission-school graduate who once lived in a mission-school dormitory. She poses against a scene set in the early morning at the start of autumn, the season indicated by fog and withering morning glories, clad in a summer kimono without underrobes and geta (clogs) without *tabi* (socks). As an overgarment, she has on a long black *haori* with family crests. The way she wears her kimono, *haori* and geta is suggestive of geisha fashion, or more specifically, the style of Fukagawa or Tatsumi geishas, reputed for their pride and manlike vigor.[38] When the painting became widely known, some commented that the woman was a *rashamen*, or foreigner's mistress.[39]

But Kaburaki denied this identification, saying that "in Tsukiji in those days, there were not a few well-educated families from or above the middle class. The sea coast of Akashi-chō was probably most suitable for their walks."[40] The gold ring on the woman's left hand implies that she is married; the Western custom of ring-wearing, including wedding rings, was introduced to Japan toward the end of the Tokugawa period and quickly gained popularity.[41] According to Kaburaki, the woman's hairstyle, a "*yakaimusubi* or English twist, was popular for a time in the Meiji era among the educated class."[42] From this description,

FIGURE 15.2. Kaburaki Kiyokata, *Woman at Akashi-chō, Tsukiji, Tokyo,* woodblock print, 1931. (Credit: Harvard Art Museums/Arthur M. Sackler Museum. Bequest of C. Adrian Rübel. Photo © President and Fellows of Harvard College, 1978.233.)

FIGURE 15.3. Portrait of Wakamatsu Shizuko. (Credit: Ferris Archives of History.)

he obviously had in mind an educated woman familiar with Western knowledge and customs.[43] Even her geisha-like style of kimono might be interpreted as her casualness about the rules and meanings attached to the ways of wearing kimono, geta, and *haori*: She does not wear underrobes and *tabi* because of the warm weather in early autumn, yet she casually puts on a *haori*, whose family crests denote a garment normally worn on formal occasions, for walking in the chilly morning. Educated in a mission school, she is not overly particular about Japanese rules. Such a carefree attitude gives her the air of a geisha and puts her on the border between *jionna* and *yūjo*. Her facial expression shows the strength of will, self-esteem, and dignity that Uchida Roan associated with mission-school graduates.

In other words, the woman that Kaburaki created to represent Tsukiji Akashi-chō was a middle-class married woman with the sexuality and charm of a geisha. This image aligns with the concept of the educated woman that E. S. Booth mentioned in 1917, which he sought to create at his school in the Yokohama concession throughout his career. In fact, the image of Wakamatsu Shizuko (Shimada Kashi), Booth's favorite student, somewhat resembles the woman in *Tsukiji Akashi-chō*, given the similarities in their hairstyles and dignified auras. According to Shimazaki Tōson, Wakamatsu was "like a woman who wore a red rosebud in her hair in foreign style."[44] She had also worn a ring even before she got married.[45]

Kimura Kumaji, the Meiji Jo Gakkō, and Beyond

Kimura Kumaji graduated from Hope College in 1879 and studied at New Brunswick Theological Seminary to be ordained in the classis of New Brunswick in 1882. Although he was not a Rutgers graduate, he had been educated for about twelve years in the RCA network and was sent back to Japan in 1882 as a pastor by the RCA Board of Foreign Missions.[46]

Kimura and his wife, Tōko, started MJG in 1885 in the center of Tokyo. The women's school was in a sense the antithesis of women's mission schools, particularly Eugene Booth's Ferris Seminary, which Kimura criticized in 1883 when he visited it: "Foreign teachers do not know the details of Japanese tradition and yet boast [of their schools], which is laughable and deplorable."[47] On the other hand, when studying in the United States, Kimura wrote to his wife in Japan in 1872 that he was "very sorry for Japanese women, for they are ignorant compared to the women here," and later explained that he had decided to start a school due to being "shocked by the lack of education among women in our country after coming back."[48] It is clear that the American ideal of educated womanhood had long inspired Kimura.

The RCA mission in Japan, however, opposed Kimura's plans. It requested that he go to Nagoya to set up a mission station and run a school for either boys or girls. Kimura rebelled, declined a salary from the RCA mission, and continued with his school in Tokyo. Although Tōko died in the summer of 1886, MJG quickly expanded and became one of the most popular women's schools in Japan, albeit for a short period. Kimura had been the principal of the school, at least in name, until 1892, when Iwamoto Yoshiharu—who had actually run the school after Tōko's untimely death—took over the position.[49] Despite Kimura's half-hearted involvement in the school, his admiration of American women combined with his criticism of Western-run mission schools like Ferris seems to have set the basic tone of MJG.

The RCA missionaries Howard Harris (1848–1916), Martin N. Wycoff (1850–1911), and their wives taught or held meetings in MJG at least until Kimura withdrew as principal.[50] The school thus maintained a cooperative relationship with the RCA Japan mission through Kimura, through which it sought to incorporate American influences, knowledge, and English.

In fact, according to the school's application to the Tokyo local government seeking permission for its establishment in 1885, most of the subjects that Kimura planned to teach at MJG resembled those in the regular four-year course at Ferris in 1884: English, geography, history, zoology, botany, mineralogy, physiology, physics, chemistry, mathematics, Chinese literature, and ethics. Many of the texts listed in the 1885 application were written by Westerners.[51] And in 1889, as mentioned above, Iwamoto Yoshiharu, the second principal of MJG, married Wakamatsu Shizuko, Ferris's first graduate and Japanese teacher. Although Wakamatsu could not teach at MJG due to tuberculosis and consecutive pregnancies, mission-school education must have influenced the school through her presence even after Western missionaries stopped coming after 1892.[52]

On the other hand, the obvious difference between the two schools was that singing, music, watercolor painting, and sewing in the curriculum at Ferris were not listed at MJG, which means that the former put more emphasis on education in the arts of feminine ornamentation than the latter. This difference corresponded to the introduction of Ferris' 1884 catalog, which explained the importance of women's education in terms of homemaking, whereas MJG's 1885 call for applications simply stated the kind of knowledge the school would provide. The absence of a clear vision of "home" in the latter's framing suggests that Kimura did not envision reforming the *ie* as strongly as did his missionary counterparts. The second difference was that MJG's call for applications made no mention of Christianity, whereas Ferris's catalog wrote that the Bible "was to be read and applied to daily ethics throughout the entire educational program"—a stipulation added in very small print because of concerns over anti-Christian sentiment in Japanese society at that time.[53]

In contrast, the MJG application only explained that ethics and morals lessons would teach "good language and good manners" using Henry Calderwood's (1839–1897) *A Handbook of Moral Philosophy* and Herbert Spencer's (1820–1903) *The Principle of Ethics*. The former book was known for balancing science with religion and the latter for social Darwinism.[54] The MJG under Kimura Kumaji made Christianity an elective subject, although in actuality, the school promoted the religion, and many students went to church on Sundays.[55] In its 1885 application to the Tokyo government, all the teachers were Japanese: one man (Kimura) and three women. In the 1890s, the school introduced lessons in *naginata* (pole swords used by female warriors from the nobility) combat and on female etiquette, sewing, painting, and music to its curriculum. These additions implied an increased emphasis on Japanese tradition as well as the practical and ornamental aspects of femininity.[56]

Although this chapter does not discuss MJG's later development, it is obvious that Kimura Kumaji was a standard-bearer of the indigenization of women's education started and developed at Ferris, and that Iwamoto Yoshiharu further publicized and popularized educated womanhood under Christian influence through his work with the *Jogaku zasshi*.

In 1892, Kimura left Tokyo to engage in missionary activities in the northwestern region of Shinshū, where he settled in the village of Komoro and established a school for young men, known as the Komoro Gijuku. In 1896, he married Tōgi Taka, a graduate of MJG and the higher school of Ferris, who was working as a Bible woman helping RCA women missionaries in Ueda, north of Komoro. Kimura Taka held Sunday school and a class for women in Komoro and began a women's school named Gakushūsha in 1901, where her husband served as principal.[57]

Gakushūsha taught morality, the Bible, translation of English into Japanese, Chinese characters, Chinese literature, and world history. In the first year of its founding, Uchimura Kanzō came to give a lecture. Gakushūsha students played tennis, and in the summer Taka took them to the Tazawa hot springs, where they stayed for seven days and used the kitchen of a Japanese inn to learn cooking. Taka's school plan was undoubtedly based on her experiences at MJG and Ferris as well as her work as a Bible woman. Her students came from wealthy families in the town, and the school was severely criticized for its "flamboyance" and Christian influence. Such criticisms formed a significant part of the censure of Komoro Gijuku, whose finances were partly maintained by subsidies from the town. It lasted only two years and closed in the summer of 1903.[58]

Kimura Kumaji and his wife thus tried to transfer the modern womanhood nurtured in MJG and Ferris to rural areas. Education that promoted this ideal, however, remained too urban for rural societies at the beginning of the twentieth century. Nonetheless, the Kimuras' efforts suggest how far-reaching the influence of Rutgers and RCA agents on women's education had become in Japan by that time.

Notes

1 Nichibei Kyōkai, ed., *Man'en gannen dai'ichi kenbei shisetsu nikki* (Tokyo: Nichibei Kyōkai, 1918), 136. Translation mine.

2 Nishizawa Naoko, *Fukuzawa Yukichi to josei* (Tokyo: Keiō Gijuku Daigaku Shuppankai, 2011), 4–5.

3 Inoue Atsuo, *Furubekki den* (Tokyo: Kokusho Kankōkai, 2022), 124–132.

4 See Inoue, *Furubekki den*, chapter 3, for details.

5 Takaya Michio, ed. and trans., *Furubekki shokanshū* (Tokyo: Shinkyō Shuppansha, 1978), 207.

6 As for Veeder's biography, see Watanabe Masao, *Zōtei*: *Oyatoi Beikokujin kagaku kyōshi* (Tokyo: Hakusensha, 1996), 49–50.

7 Takaya, *Furubekki shokanshū*, 194–195; *Daijō ruiten dai 2 hen* 70 (1871–1877): 97–100, https://www.digital.archives.go.jp/DAS/meta/listPhoto?LANG=default&BID=F0000000000000000417&ID=&TYPE=dljpeg.

8 Usui Chizuko, *Joshi kyōiku no kindai to gendai* (Nagano: Kindai Bungeisha, 1994), 138–139. Amelia gave birth to a son on October 20, 1873. See "Howard Potter Veeder," Find a Grave, accessed November 3, 2022, https://www.findagrave.com/memorial/134473591/howard-potter-veeder.

9 Usui, *Joshi kyōiku*, 41. As for Doremus School, see chapters 1 and 2 of *Yokohama Kyōritsu Gakuen 120-nen no ayumi* Henshū Iinkai, ed., *Yokohama Kyōritsu Gakuen 120-nen no ayumi* (Yokohama: Yokohama Kyōritsu Gakuen, 1991). On its relationship with the RCA, see Ferris Jogakuin 150 Nenshi Hensan Iinkai, ed., *Ferris Jogakuin 150-nen shi jōkan* (Yokohama: Ferris Jogakuin, 2022), 54–56.

10 "Ochanomizu University," Archives of Ochanomizu Women's University, accessed November 4, 2022, https://www.lib.ocha.ac.jp/archives/chrono1874.html#1874. On

Murray's involvement in the establishment of the Normal School for Women, see Benjamin Duke, *Dr. David Murray* (New Brunswick, NJ: Rutgers University Press, 2019), 202–205.

11 The Rutgers and RCA network had nothing to do with the women's education sponsored by the Hokkaidō Development Commission, except its indirect influence in sending the five girls to the United States with the Iwakura Mission in 1871 as explained herein. In the autumn of 1872, the Hokkaidō Development Commission opened a women's school in Shiba, Tokyo, to educate women to contribute to the development of Hokkaidō. Almost nothing is known about the faculty at this institution, which consisted of two Dutch women outside of the Rutgers and RCA network. The Ministry of Education, to which the network was connected, seems to have competed, rather than cooperated, with the Hokkaidō Development Commission in the matter of women's education, at least in the beginning of the Meiji period. Mori Arinori of the Satsuma domain was closer to the women's school of the Hokkaidō Development Commission, which was led by Kuroda Kiyotaka, also from Satsuma. Mori's first wife was a student at the girls' school sponsored by the Commission, which was abruptly shut down in 1876 due to an internal scandal. See Arie Mikio, *Hokudai hyakunen shi: Tsūsetsu* (Sapporo: Hokkaido University, 1982), 25–27, https://eprints.lib.hokudai.ac.jp/dspace/bitstream/2115/30012/1/tsusetu_p1-28.pdf.

12 Nakajima Kōji, Tsuji Naoto, and Ōnishi Haruki, *Chōrō Kaikaku Kyōkai rainichi senkyōshi jiten* (Tokyo: Shinkyō Shuppansha, 2003), 211.

13 Ferris Jogakuin 150 Nenshi Hensan Iinkai, *Ferris Jogakuin 150-nen shi jōkan*, 56–57, 156.

14 Ferris Jogakuin 150 Nenshi Hensan Iinkai, *Ferris Jogakuin 150-nen shi jōkan*, 64–70.

15 Ferris Jogakuin 150 Nenshi Hensan Iinkai, ed., *Kindai joshi kyōiku shin gakusei madeno kiseki* (Yokohama: Ferris Jogakuin, 2012), 9. On Republican motherhood, see Linda Kerber, *Women of the Republic* (Chapel Hill: University of North Carolina Press, 1980).

16 News clipping in the file of Eugene Samuel Booth in the Reformed Church in America Archives, New Brunswick, NJ. The clipping is undated.

17 On marriages and divorce in the Meiji period, see Yuzawa Yasuhiko, *Meiji no kekkon, Meiji no rikon* (Tokyo: Kadokawa Shoten, 2005).

18 There is a vast array of research on the *ie* in Japan. Here I have consulted the Joseishi Sōgō Kenkyūkai, ed., *Nihon joseishi, dai 3 kan (kinsei)* (Tokyo: Tōkyō Daigaku Shuppankai, 1982); Yonemura Chiyo, *"Ie" no sonzoku senryaku* (Bunkyo: Keisō Shobō, 1999); Shimazu Ryōko, "Kinsei kōki ni okeru buke no ie sonzoku senryaku," *Hikaku kazokushi kenkyū* 27 (March 2013): 76–102.

19 "*Sakoku*" was not a blanket policy with regard to the "four windows" of trade/foreign relations, especially with China, Korea, and the Netherlands, that remained on Nagasaki, Tsushima, Satsuma, and Matsumae.

20 In view of class and regional differences, this claim requires some qualification. Among rural peasants, young people had more autonomy in their selection of partners, whereas the children of merchants were given chances to meet potential spouses and were asked about their willingness before the final decision of marriage. In fact, customs varied according to class and region. Yet, the supremacy of the *ie*'s survival over the sentiments of the parties involved held as a rule. For details, see Sekiguchi Yūko, Hattori Sanae, Nagashima Junko, Hayakawa Noriyo, and Asano Tomie, *Kazoku to kekkon no rekishi* (Tokyo: Shinwasha, 2000), 97–108. See also Yuzawa, *Meiji no kekkon*.

21 On Yoshiwara, see Watanabe Kenji, *Edo 300-nen Yoshiwara no shikitari* (Tokyo: Seishun Shuppansha, 2004).

22 On the spread of prostitution in the premodern period, see Sone Hiromi, *Shōfu to kinsei shakai* (Tokyo: Yoshikawa Kōbunkan, 2003); Saga Ashita and Yoshida Nobuyuki, eds., *Yūkaku shakai*, vol. 1 (Tokyo: Yoshikawa Kōbunkan, 2013); Sawayama Mikako, *Sei kara yomu Edo jidai* (Tokyo: Iwanami Shoten, 2020). On Yoshiwara as a cultural center, see Tanaka Yūko, *Yūkaku to Nihonjin* (Tokyo: Kōdansha, 2021).

23 Ihara Saikaku, *Seken munasan'yō*, as quoted in Tanaka Yūko, *Edo no koi* (Tokyo: Shūeisha, 2002), 94.

24 Yokoyama Yuriko, "Bakumatsu ishinki no shakai to seibaibai no hen'yō," in *Meiji ishin to josei*, ed. Meijiishinshi Gakkai (Tokyo: Yūshisha, 2015), 159–163. We must also note that many did not survive their indentureship as *yūjo*.

25 On housemaids, see Shinoda Kōzō, *Onna hyakuwa, jō* (Tokyo: Iwanami Shoten, 1997), 36–41, 54–61, 159–163; Shinoda Kōzō, *Onna hyakuwa, ge* (Tokyo: Iwanami Shoten, 1997), 14–20, 69–73, 240.

26 Tanaka, *Yūkaku to Nihonjin*, chapter 4.

27 See Steven Seidman, *Romantic Longings* (New York: Routledge, 1991), part 1; Caren Lystra, *Searching the Heart* (New York: Oxford University Press, 1989); Colleen McDannell, *The Christian Home in Victorian America, 1840–1900* (Bloomington: Indiana University Press, 1986).

28 Ferris Jogakuin 150 Nenshi Hensan Iinkai, *Ferris Jogakuin 150-nen shi jōkan*, 28–32, 42–43.

29 Uchimura Kanzō, *Uchimura Kanzō zenshū*, vol. 36 (Tokyo: Iwanami Shoten, 1983), 63.

30 Ferris Jogakuin 150 Nenshi Hensan Iinkai, *Ferris Jogakuin 150-nen shi jōkan*, 93–95.

31 Ibuka Kajinosuke to Sono Jidai Kankō Iinkai, ed., *Ibuka Kajinosuke to sono jidai*, vol. 2 (Tokyo: Meiji Gakuin, 1970), 99.

32 Shimazaki Tōson, *Sakuranomi no jukusuru toki* (Tokyo: Shinchō Bunko, 1955), 10–11. Translation mine.

33 Uchimura Kanzō, "How I Became a Christian," in *Uchimura Kanzō zenshū*, vol. 3 (Tokyo: Iwanami Shoten, 1982), 72.

34 Uchimura Kanzō, *Uchimura Kanzō shinkō chosaku zenshū*, vol. 20 (Tokyo: Kyōbunkan, 1962), 34.

35 Uchida Roan, *Dokusho hōrō* (Tokyo: Heibonsha, 1996), 40.

36 Yamada Hajime, "Kōki," in *Meiji no Tokyo*, ed. Kaburaki Kiyokata (Tokyo: Iwanami Shoten, 1989), 219–223; Shimizu Masao, *Tokyo Tsukiji kyoryūchi hyakuwa* (Tokyo: Toseisha, 2007), 82; Kaburaki Kiyotaka, Kamakura-shi Kaburaki Kiyokata Kinen Bijutsukan, and Kamakurashi Geijutsu Bunka Shinkō Zaidan, *Kamakura-shi Kaburaki Kiyokata Kinen Bijutsukan shūzōhin zuroku* (Kamakura, Kanagawa: Kamakura-shi Kaburaki Kiyokata Kinen Bijutsukan, 2014), 72.

37 Shimizu, *Tokyo Tsukiji kyoryūchi hyakuwa*, 2.

38 Iwashita Hisafumi, *Geisha ron*, rev. ed. (Tokyo: Yūzankaku, 2008), 82–90; Kishii Yoshie, *Onna geisha no jidai* (Tokyo: Seiabō, 1974), 142, 420. The red-light district of Fukagawa was suppressed in the Tenpō Reformation from 1841 to 1843, and many of its geishas moved to Yanagibashi, partially maintaining the style of Fukagawa geishas into the Meiji period. See Iwashita, *Geisha ron*, 92, 96–100; Kishii, *Onna geisha no jidai*, 41–44, 196–226.

39 Kiyotaka, Kiyokata Kinen Bijutsukan, and Geijutsu Bunka Shinkō Zaidan, *Kamakura-shi Kaburaki Kiyokata Kinen Bijutsukan shūzōhin zuroku*, 72; Shimizu, *Tokyo Tsukiji kyoryūchi hyakuwa*, 199–200.

40 Kaburaki Kiyokata, "Jisaku jikai," in *Kiyokata gashū* (Tokyo: Bijutsu Shuppan, 1957), 19.

41 Hamamoto Takashi, *Yubiwa no bunka-shi* (Tokyo: Kawade Shobō Shinsha, 2018), 104–106.

42 "Jisaku wo kataru," in *Kaburaki Kiyokata bunshū*, vol. 1, as quoted in Kiyotaka, Kiyokata Kinen Bijutsukan, and Geijutsu Bunka Shinkō Zaidan, *Kamakura-shi Kaburaki Kiyokata Kinen Bijutsukan shūzōhin zuroku*, 73.

43 The model for the woman's face was Maseko Egi, the wife of a government official whose family operated famous photo shops in Tokyo. She was a friend of Kaburaki's wife, with whom she had attended the girls' school attached to the Tokyo Normal School for Women. The model for the woman's figure was Kaburaki's daughter. See Kaburaki Kiyokata, *Zoku Koshikata no ki* (Tokyo: Chūō Kōron Bijutsu Shuppan, 1967), 166–169.

44 Shimazaki, *Sakuranomi no jukusuru toki*, 130. Roses were imported from the United States and other countries in the Meiji era and spread rapidly. See Chiba Kenritsu Chūō Hakubutsukan, "Bara no Subete," accessed November 27, 2022, http://www.chiba-muse.or.jp/NATURAL/special/all_about_roses_audio_guide/06.htm.

45 Iwamoto Yoshiharu, "Ramabai sudeni Nihon wo hatsu," *Jogaku zasshi* 143 (January 5, 1889): 27.

46 As for Kimura, see Takatsuka Satoru, *Komoro Gijuku no kenkyū* (Tokyo: San'ichi Shobō, 1989), 17–60.

47 Kimura Kumaji, *Kōtei zōho Kimura Kumaji nikki* (Tokyo: Tokyō Joshi Daigaku Hikaku Bunka Kenkyūjo, 2008), 48.

48 Aoyama Nao, *Meiji Jogakkō no kenkyū* (Tokyo: Keiō Tsūshin, 1970), 435.

49 Kohiyama Rui, "Oranda Kaikaku-ha to Kimura Kumaji," *Ayumi* (*Ferris Jogakuin Rekushi Shiryōkan kiyō*) 75 (2023): 16–19; on the history of MJG, see "Nenpyō," in Aoyama, *Meiji Jogakkō no kenkyū*, 819–838.

50 Kohiyama, "Oranda Kaikaku-ha," 19.

51 Aoyama, *Meiji Jogakkō no kenkyū*, 783–786; Ferris Jogakuin 150 Nenshi Hensan Iinkai, *Kindai joshi kyōiku*, 16–17. At Ferris, geology and psychology were offered instead of mineralogy and zoology.

52 Kohiyama, "Oranda Kaikaku-ha," 19

53 Aoyama, *Meiji Jogakkō no kenkyū*, 783–786; Ferris Jogakuin 150 Nenshi Hensan Iinkai, *Kindai joshi kyōiku*, 15.

54 On Calderwood, see the profile page on the Institute for the Study of Philosophy, University of Sioux Falls, accessed December 6, 2022, http://www.scottishphilosophy.org/philosophers/henry-calderwood/. It must be taken into account that in the application to the government, Kimura and others might have been hesitant about explicitly stating the school's involvement with Christianity.

55 The diary of Satō Sukeko, an MJG student, recorded that she went to church every Sunday and that the school was full of Christian instructions and atmosphere. See Oikawa Kazuo, ed., *Satō Sukeko no nikki* (Kiso, Nagano: Tōson Kinenkan, 2003).

56 Aoyama, *Meiji Jogakkō*, 828–827.

57 Kohiyama, "Oranda Kaikaku-ha," 25–26.

58 Kohiyama, "Oranda Kaikaku-ha," 26–27.

Epilogue

Griffis's Legacies: Rutgers and Fukui

RYUHEI HOSOYA

Overview of the Network

The chapters in this book each shed new light on William Griffis, Kusakabe Tarō, and other key figures, both American and Japanese, who played their respective parts in the trans-Pacific network of the time. Together they present a panoramic view of the network, which gives us pause for thought on such questions as: What were their impacts, individually and collectively, on Japan and on U.S.-Japan relations in the context of geopolitics, economics, society, and culture? And were those impacts felt—and if so, to what extent—beyond the timeline of this project, the late nineteenth century? It is obviously not for this epilogue to attempt a coherent synthesis of the rich and varied findings of the volume; instead, it offers a few general observations.

The nature of the network lay essentially in its supporting role in the building of the new post-feudal Japan. The Japanese students, driven by their aspiration to take in Western ways, ventured out to the United States, within which Rutgers was for a while the hub owing in large part to its connection with the Dutch Reformed Church. That thrust of learning would not be confined to the students, as famously attested to by the U.S. leg of the Iwakura Mission.[1] The *oyatoi* teachers, technocrats, and missionaries who came to Japan on invitation—many of them through the network—completed the other side of the coin in the singular project of "modernizing Japan." They did so by way of direct interventions drawing on their knowledge and skills, but perhaps, in a more lasting way, through capacity-building. To what extent the ecclesiastical mission of faith-building bore fruit in the event is a matter for further discussion. By and large, the consequence of this network was an influx of knowledge of the ways of the West. The Japanese students would return to Japan—although not all of them, because some stayed in the United States and some, like Kusakabe, fell to illness—to play a pivotal role in their respective areas of expertise and authority throughout the Meiji period. Indeed, some became political leaders and diplomats of the highest rank, representing the nation to the United States. The overall magnitude of the network's impact cannot be measured independently from the myriad of other factors that lay behind Japan's modernization or its international dealings, not least with the United States. We may at least be justified in saying that it was considerable.

A by-product of the network was the discovery by the Americans of the ways of Japan. Influence certainly flowed both ways. First, the Japanese students presumably played a certain role in introducing Japan to the Americans with whom they came into contact. Griffis records in *The Mikado's Empire* how impressed he was with the diligence, intellectual acumen, polite demeanor, sense of honor, and aspiration of the Japanese students he knew at Rutgers, among them Kusakabe Tarō. He does not record so much about learning of Japan per se from those students as he did, for example, from his American classmate Robert "Bob" Pruyn, who had been in Tokyo with his father, Robert H. Pruyn, who served as the second Minister Resident to Japan of the United States. In any case, the exchanges accomplished through these personal connections must have been limited compared with the major effort made by the *bakufu* and later by the Meiji government to introduce Japan, particularly its culture, to the United States. Insofar as the network was concerned, the introduction of the "real" Japan to the United States on a historically significant level had to wait for those *oyatoi* who took in the ways of the Japanese on the ground and who took it upon themselves to disseminate that knowledge broadly among the American public. In this respect, William Griffis stands out as having no equal in the network.

All in all, given the geostrategic climate in the Far East at the time, one hardly needs to be reminded that the network's impact on the bilateral relationship across the Pacific was perforce skewed in favor of the United States' influence upon Japan, not the other way around. What should be noted in this regard, however, is that the nature of the influence was constrained in one important respect. It has to do with the very meaning of the term *oyatoi* (i.e., a foreign employee hired to *assist* the Japanese authorities with their knowledge and skills). James Hommes in chapter 1 and Haruko Wakabayashi in chapter 11 take up Guido F. Verbeck, who was the central figure among the *oyatoi*. Held in high esteem and confidence by the Meiji government, Verbeck held leading positions in institutions of higher learning, and his influence extended as far as the successful proposal and design of the Iwakura Mission. To Griffis, who wrote

Verbeck's biography, this was a remarkable display of Verbeck's *servant* attitude, which came in part from his humility, but more importantly reflected his firm understanding of the role of *oyatoi*, which was in essence that of an advisor. Another case in point was David Murray's appointment as superintendent of education. The Japanese would be guided and enlightened but would always preserve the driver's seat for themselves.

Griffis as a Unique Figure in the Network

William E. Griffis—the man, his college life at Rutgers, his Fukui days, and his lifelong mission as the leading authority on Japan of the era—is amply and eminently covered by Fernanda Perrone in chapters 5 and 7, and by Joseph M. Henning in chapter 9. Suffice it to say here that Griffis was a true renaissance man, if ever one was called for at the time in Japan, and in whose lap the opportunity happened to fall to unleash that potential to the full.

By a stroke of providence, his letter dated September 26, 1870, to his sister Maggie expressed his inclination to accept an invitation to teach in Fukui, which he had earlier declined because of his attachment to Ellen Johnson, his fiancée and "femme fatale." In the event, she became the very reason for his resignation to accept the call because they broke up for an unknown reason. Be that as it may, five months later, he arrived in Fukui, which would become his *ville fatale* as it were. There he resided for eleven months, which turned out to be a critical period of transformation both for Fukui and for Griffis himself. For Fukui, 1871 was a momentous year when *haihan-chiken* (abolition of the feudal domain and establishment of the prefecture) took place, ending not just the Fukui-*han* (domain) that had existed under the 260-year rule by the Tokugawa *bakufu*, but also the seven-hundred-year tradition of feudalism since the Kamakura shogunate. Griffis was the only foreigner to witness firsthand this political transition in a domain at an actual ceremony marking the occasion. He thus went through two politico-cultural metamorphoses within a few months, first in his transition from liberal East Coast United States to feudal Fukui, and then from there to a newborn modern Japan.

To emphasize only that side of his experience would, however, be to blur the more profound awakening that he underwent. What distinguishes Griffis from many other Japan hands at the time is the fact that he placed equal importance on both the transformation of Japan into a modern nation and the preservation of its traditional ways. He was passionate for both and would spare no effort in exploring a creative synthesis, a new true way to reconcile the ways of the East and the West and of the old and the new. That was the defining nature of his experience in Fukui. Not long after his arrival in Fukui he noted the following: "I had come hither to be a builder of knowledge, to help bring the new civilization that must destroy the old. Yet it was hard to be an iconoclast. I often ask myself the question—Why not leave these people alone? They seem to be happy enough; and he that increaseth knowledge increaseth sorrow."[2] On the eve of his departure from Fukui, he made the following remark: "Farewell, Fukui, thou hast been a well of blessing; for in thee I have found some truth."[3] What he meant by that "truth" is a matter for speculation. A standard interpretation is that of "common humanity," which is to say that there are many different cultures in this world and yet there is only one *true* culture: that of humankind. He explains:

> During my life in a feudal city in Japan far away from foreigners, I have seen the Japanese at home. It has sometimes seemed to me, in my walks through the old castle, or along the moats, or upon the ramparts, in the cemeteries, in the houses of the people, on the mountains, in my rides through the villages, that I was in fairy-land or in a dream. Yet these people are just like ourselves, their hearts the same as ours. Their emotions and traits, both noble and despicable, are twin to those which belong to mankind between the Alleghanies [*sic*] and the Atlantic. This is a trite truism. Yet in its truth consists of its novelty. When men of differing climes and nations see behind each other's mail of codes, manners, education, and systems their common humanity, the hope of their dwelling in peace as children of one Father is no longer a chimera.[4]

How these words ring true today—perhaps even more so! That was Griffis's spiritual awakening after his eleven months in Fukui as a young man of twenty-seven.

One event that marked this transition of his heart toward the end of his days in Fukui was, at face value, a rather mundane one. In December 1871, he decided to hold a Christmas party at his house for his students and servants, also inviting the teachers and staff of the domain school where he taught. This plan materialized after some soul-searching as he was suffering from acute homesickness, missing his family back in Philadelphia, and lovesickness, still not over his loss of Ellen. He overcame his depression somehow, coming to recognize the students and servants who shared his abode as his "Fukui family," and saw the Christmas party as a secular ritual that carried a universal appeal transcending cultural or religious divides. He went so far as to play Santa Claus, stuffing with presents the "Tabi" socks that he had asked his "family" to hang on the fireplace. As far as the present author's research to date shows, this event was most probably the first Christmas party held in Japan with many Japanese invited publicly. It was thus of historical and sociocultural significance in its own right.

Griffis's impact in Fukui in his formal role (i.e., as a teacher) was notable. One may say that he laid the foundations of modern education in Fukui. He was also instrumental in proposing that a network of polytechnic schools for teacher training be set up nationwide. This message reached the Ministry of Education through the auspices of Yuri Kimimasa, the influential Fukui clansman whom Griffis befriended while Yuri was back in Fukui before he was summoned to Tokyo to become the first governor of the capital. The ministry took up the

FIGURE E.1. Artist's impression of William Griffis's Christmas Party in Fukui, December 25, 1871. (Credit: © Hayashi Yukari.)

proposal. In the event, that scheme led to Griffis's departure from Fukui to Tokyo to teach at Kaisei Gakkō (later Tokyo University) under Guido Verbeck. Although his influence in Tokyo was relatively short-lived because he would return to the United States after two years, Griffis's impact as an educator there should also be noted because his class included a number of students who would become leading figures of Meiji Japan.

Griffis's most important contribution came thereafter and throughout his long career as a prolific writer and advocate for Japan through his many books, articles, and lectures. That side of Griffis is well portrayed in chapter 9 by Joseph M. Henning and at more length in his recent book.[5] In terms of his influence on Japan, Griffis was one among several peers, most notably Guido Verbeck. What put Griffis in a league of his own was his towering and enduring influence over U.S. public opinion as the undisputedly most read and heard authority on Japan throughout the Meiji and Taishō eras.

Griffis's Legacy in Fukui

In examining how the network connects to the present, we may as a case study look into the legacy of William Griffis in Fukui. But how are we to assess the legacy of someone from 150 years ago? There is no telling in any measurable way what lasting impact he still has in present-day Fukui. The teachings he gave to his students, some of whom went on to make names for themselves, were significant, yet their total impact on the region, let alone on the whole nation, can only be described, at best, as fragmentary. The footprint he left on the system of education was perhaps more important but is hardly visible today because so many others have since been involved in the construction of the school system of Fukui, which has a complex history of its own. We may be contented by the thought that there must have been a butterfly effect—that is, whatever small innovations Griffis initiated in the system, such as the chemistry laboratory at the domain school Meishinkan, resulted in a significant change years later (e.g., when any direct trace of that lab would have been long lost).

That said, there is one *measurable* indicator of Griffis's legacy: how much he is remembered in Fukui. That measure has waxed and waned remarkably during the intervening century and a half. Here it should be kept in mind that this period represents roughly the entirety of the history of U.S.-Japan relations. We may note in this regard that in 1850, Griffis as a boy of seven witnessed the launching from the dockyard of the USS *Susquehanna*, which was to become the flagship of Commodore Perry's expedition to Japan.

Whether by pure coincidence or by certain underlying forces at work, Griffis's popularity in Fukui has followed a distinct pattern of a fairly stable fifty-year cycle. The point of departure is 1871, the year in which he first arrived in Fukui and established his reputation. That was to be expected given the special status he was offered. Greatness was thrust upon him, so to speak. He left Fukui in 1872 with much fanfare, and he was missed dearly. Griffis revisited Fukui with his sister, Maggie, in 1873 for a short holiday, but he would not return for another fifty-four years. As the years went by, people's memory gradually but surely faded, except among the few who remembered him in person.

To the present author's knowledge, no organized initiative was taken at the time to celebrate Griffis nor Kusakabe Tarō as historical figures associated with the region. That development had to wait until 1927, when Griffis was invited back to Japan for a six-month tour around the nation, including four days in Fukui. He was by then a much-revered authority and supporter of Japan making a triumphal return. This time he had achieved greatness. The welcome by the people of Fukui, who turned out in the thousands to greet him on the street and hear his lectures, was as enthusiastic as it was warm. However, by that time the United States and Japan were on the way to becoming the worst of adversaries in an era where imperialism still held sway in international relations. As much as Griffis lamented that trend and did everything in his capacity to put a stop to it, the overwhelming forces of realpolitik were at work relentlessly and far beyond his power—or that of practically anyone else at the time. Thus, it was inevitable that the revival of Griffis's fame in 1927 would be short-lived.

Another feature of the 1927 visit was that Fukui came to realize in earnest the legacy of Kusakabe Tarō. That he achieved academic brilliance at Rutgers College and, in the bargain, died young on foreign soil—never to return to Japan—struck a strong emotional chord locally. In the prewar environment steeped in Confucianism as a guide for education, Kusakabe was a fitting figure to be idolized. In turn, Griffis was welcomed as the teacher who befriended Kusakabe and who accepted the invitation to teach in Fukui out of their personal amity—or so people were led to believe. This story, which was not entirely unfounded but largely romanticized, persists to this day. In other words, Griffis was given an honorable local standing in large part as second fiddle to Kusakabe Tarō.

Not surprisingly, the next two decades of Shōwa swept away any visible remnant of this invaluable regional legacy connecting Fukui to the United States. The local ignorance of the historical tie extended into the mid-1970s, when a delegation of the Fukui chapter of Junior Chamber International paid a visit to Kusakabe's grave in New Brunswick. It was dilapidated. Out of dismay and with youthful energy, they managed to mobilize the local community within a few years to stage a wholesale revival of the story. This time the local authorities and the University of Fukui were fully involved. The Kusakabe-Griffis Foundation[6] was set up in 1980 with public and private funds to support international student exchange and projects to promote the two legendary figures. Soon afterward, the University of Fukui formed a partnership with Rutgers University. Fukui and New Brunswick signed a sister city agreement, which was followed later by a similar arrangement between Fukui Prefecture and the State of New Jersey. That flurry of institutional arrangements was expected to nail down and finally cast in stone the local legend of the two men. To perpetuate the myth, a statue of a sitting Griffis with Kusakabe standing beside him was erected along the banks of the Asuwa River, which flows through the city center. More recently, in 2015, the city managed to reconstruct Griffis's house, not far from where the original house once stood, to honor him in the form of a museum. The first display that strikes the visitor upon entry there is a digital avatar of Kusakabe and Griffis recounting their amity.

To a certain extent, the institutions, memorials, and the Kusakabe-Griffis story itself have together contrived to render it a local folklore. By its very nature and owing to the paucity of supporting evidence, the main audience of the story has been primary school pupils and the accompanying tales necessarily fictive. There is no shortage of history buffs in Fukui, because the region rightly prides itself on its outstanding array of famous figures from its long history as the powerful Echizen domain. As far as the attention of Fukui's general public is concerned, the Meiji restoration period alone features Matsudaira Shungaku, Yokoi Shōnan, Yuri Kimimasa, Hashimoto Sanai, and others, all of whom are prominent enough by domestic standards, thereby receiving premium limelight but at the expense of those who follow not far behind, such as Kusakabe and Griffis.

FIGURE E.2. The Fukui City Griffis Museum, designed after the house in which William Griffis lived. (Credit: © ASA Corporation, https://asa-fukui.co.jp/works/detail.php?id=2.)

Clearly a differentiation from the others is required if we are to do real justice to Griffis and install him in his rightful place in history.

Now we come to the latest cycle. As already noted, the revival of Griffis's name in tandem with Kusakabe from the mid-1970s onward did see some significant developments. One culmination of this came in 1984 when the University of Fukui organized a major international conference on the theme of *oyatoi*, attracting prominent academics in the field from around the world. Exchange of students between Fukui and Rutgers continued for about a decade, albeit sporadically. The mayors, or their representatives, of Fukui and New Brunswick have continued to make mutual visits every five years. Yet, the underlying structure of all these activities has suffered a want of support and drive to preserve, if not augment, the momentum in the long run. With interest rates having fallen to de facto zero amid a profound shift in monetary policy, the foundation has lost its main source of revenue. Short of a game-changing lift in Griffis's fame, it is expected to slowly but steadily grind to a halt. The name of the root cause is frailty of public memory. When the present author was asked to take over the direction of the foundation in 2018, he started his round of lectures asking the audience how many knew the name Griffis. It was roughly one in twenty.

At the time of writing, Griffis is facing a moment of truth in Fukui and beyond in Japan. Whether he connects to the present at a popular level and becomes a household name, or will be retained only in an academic niche, is still to be seen.

This question holds a practical implication for the promotion of Fukui as a place to be visited by tourists now that the Shinkansen's bullet train service finally reached its doors in March 2024.

Meanwhile, 2020–2021 marked the 150th anniversary of Griffis's arrival in Japan and in Fukui. Celebrating this occasion, the foundation launched a public relations campaign centering around the reproduction of the first public Christmas party in Japan, and through it Griffis, the person who hosted it. This effort was joined by the City of Fukui, the Griffis House, and other partners, including the private sector, and the Fukui City History Museum, which commemorated the anniversary with a special exhibition on Griffis. According to a survey conducted at Fukui station in January 2023, the name recognition of Griffis had risen to over one out of two persons having heard the name, with half of them actually knowing who he was. In the same year, the foundation published a nonfiction novel[7] featuring Griffis as the protagonist.[8]

Together, these activities are designed to elicit public interest in Griffis by connecting him to a topic of universal appeal (i.e., Christmas). It remains to be seen if this populist approach to promoting Griffis will prove to have a real impact and be mutually reinforcing with the more academic treatment of him, or for that matter, of the other figures in the Rutgers-Japan network.

Conclusion

This epilogue has covered the project to revive Griffis's name in Fukui and hopefully throughout Japan. It is recalled that when Griffis was back in Japan in 1927, looking forward to his return to Fukui after over half a century, he sent this message to its people: "Love me little, love me long."[9] He was indeed welcomed there with much reverence and enthusiasm, for which he was most grateful. Whether the city has remained unflagging in its commemoration of Griffis over the ensuing century is at best debatable. Still, there is a glimmer of hope now that the Prefecture and City of Fukui, in their official Grand Design for Revitalization, have designated the Griffis House and its surrounding area as one of the key spots to be promoted for tourism. This plan is with specific reference to Christmas.

The reader may wonder if there is anything to be said to relate this matter to the main subject of this book, namely, the late nineteenth-century trans-Pacific network. One might approach that theme through the lens of the "true ways" of modernization that the network's constituent members sought. There may be next to no common ground, because the true ways that each *oyatoi* or student sought were surely individual. Moreover, how those true ways may have been passed on to today is at best an exploratory question. Insofar as Griffis was picked out for this epilogue as one of the key figures of the network, it falls on the present author to try to offer a viewpoint.

The turbulence of history over the past 150 years has been such that whatever true ways might have been attained then would have since been reset or overwritten several times over. To be sure, some true ways could hold universal value that transcends space and time. The present author submits that one such experience was that of Griffis. The "truth" that he said he had found in Fukui is subject to as many interpretations as there are interpreters. The simple, lasting truth that holds synchronic *and* diachronic value is the message of the *common humanity* referred to earlier. That trite truth is manifested nowhere else more than in the ubiquitous celebration of Christmas in Japan, which is a supremely secular nation. That Griffis heralded that tradition would have been lost to the tides of history, but now it seems that it may survive by the skin of its teeth.

Notes

1 Its link to the network is detailed in chapter 11.

2 William E. Griffis, *The Mikado's Empire* (New York: Harper & Brothers, 1876), 439–440.

3 Griffis, *The Mikado's Empire*, 540.

4 Griffis, 539.

5 *Interpreting the Mikado's Empire: The Writings of William Elliot Griffis* (Lanham, MD: Lexington Books, 2021).

6 The present author headed the board from 2018 through 2024.

7 Ryuhei Hosoya, *The Tabi of Happiness: A Tale of Christmas in Fukui* (originally published in Japanese by the author) was published in 2022 by URALA Communications in Fukui. A free translation in English is available at https://drive.google.com/file/d/1z4XzoYjwNJEQolJIvobMv8M-9ITfJup8/view.

8 The 150th anniversary of Griffis's first arrival in Fukui (2021) was also marked by virtual symposia held in Fukui and at Rutgers in 2021 and 2022, and joint online classes of the two universities during the COVID-19 pandemic. There have been ongoing exchanges of students on a one-to-two semester program and mutual short-term visits between the two universities in 2022 and 2024. At the time of writing, plans are being made for events in 2027 to celebrate the centennial of Griffis's revisit to Fukui.

9 From an anonymous poem, the first four lines of which read, *Love me little, love me long, is the burden of my song. Love that is too hot and strong, burneth soon to waste.* Griffis jotted down the first line "Love me little, love me long" as a message for Fukui in a note dated 28 January 1927.

Acknowledgments

William E. Griffis, Rutgers class of 1869 and a key figure in the Rutgers-Japan connection, was a man of networks. At Rutgers he became acquainted with the Japanese students, the first of whom was Kusakabe Tarō, who arrived in 1867 and tragically died in New Brunswick in 1870. When Griffis landed in Japan in 1870, he quickly connected with the Meiji leaders who sent their sons and retainers to Rutgers, as well as with the missionaries already working there. For decades after his return to the United States in 1874, he maintained connections with his students, friends, and acquaintances in Japan, and with Westerners involved in Japan, Asia, and U.S.-Japan relations. One hundred fifty years later, as we traced his trans-Pacific connections, we found ourselves forming a network of scholars, local communities, organizations, and institutions that have explored, cherished, and maintained the history of the Rutgers-Japan connection. This book owes much to these networks, past and present, that intertwined and expanded, often in the most unexpected ways, enriching our knowledge and understanding of this history.

A multiyear international research project was initiated in 2020 in response to the revival of the academic partnership between Rutgers University and the University of Fukui in 2017, as well as preparations for the sesquicentennial celebration of the friendship between Rutgers and Japan. While many planned events were canceled or postponed due to the COVID-19 pandemic, the first international conference, "Rutgers Meets Japan: Foreign Teachers, Missionaries, and Overseas Students in the Early Meiji Era," was hosted by Rutgers University and convened by Haruko Wakabayashi online in March 2021. This conference was made possible by funding from the Japan-U.S. Friendship Commission (JUSFC), the Northeast Asia Council of the Association for Asian Studies (NEAC), Rutgers University's School of Arts and Sciences (SAS), the Department of Asian Languages and Cultures (ALC), and Rutgers Global. With the help of Rui Kohiyama, a second workshop was held in August 2021 at Ferris Jogakuin Historical Archives. This workshop received generous support from the Toshiba International Foundation (TIFO). In Fukui, Ryuhei Hosoya organized multiple symposiums and events with supports from the Kusakabe-Griffis Foundation, the City of Fukui, and the University of Fukui. The scholars from the United States, Japan, and Canada who participated in the above events became the core members of the research project.

With additional funding from TIFO, an International Collaborative Research Grant from Rutgers Global, and a grant from the New Jersey Historical Commission, together with support from the Rutgers SAS, ALC, the University Libraries, Rutgers Global, and the Global Asias Initiative, a series of conferences and workshops were held at Rutgers and Tokyo to explore the early Rutgers-Japan network. The project members also organized panels at the annual meetings of the Mid-Atlantic Regional Association for Asian Studies (2022) and the Society for Historians of American Foreign Relations in Washington, DC (2023).

These endeavors were intimately intertwined with a wider community beyond academia, including the cities of New Brunswick and Fukui, which celebrated their sesquicentennial year of friendship; Ferris, founded in 1872 by a Reformed Church missionary and initially led by a Rutgers graduate; the Japanese community in New York, who commemorated the 150th anniversary of the arrival of the Iwakura Mission, the first diplomatic embassy to the United States and Europe sent by Emperor Meiji of Japan, in which several Rutgers students were involved. Our network has since continued to expand, encompassing the following organizations: the New Brunswick Sister Cities Association; the Reformed Church in America (RCA); the New Brunswick Theological Seminary; the New York Buddhist Church; the American Buddhist Study Center; the Japanese American Associations of New York and Princeton, New Jersey; the Japan History Council of New York; and numerous museums and archives that house materials related to the Rutgers-Japan history, including the RCA Archives, Zimmerli Art Museum, Cornell University Library (the home of the "other" Griffis Collection), Edo-Tokyo Museum and Katsu Kaishū Memorial Museum in Tokyo, the Fukui City History Museum and the Griffis Museum in Fukui, and the Ferris Jogakuin Historical Archives. We extend our gratitude to Michael Tublin, Nicole Simpson, Elizabeth Pallitto, Daniel J. McKee, Suzuki Keiko, Hoshikawa Reo, and Yamada Hiroki for their support at various stages of our research.

We must also acknowledge that this volume would not have been possible without the works of our predecessors: Ardath Burks, a Rutgers University administrator and professor of Asian Studies, who organized the first conferences and publications in the 1960s that focused on the relationship between Rutgers and Japan; Abe Juri, professor of American Studies at Rikkyō University in Tokyo with whom Fernanda Perrone began collaborating on a book project but sadly did not live to see it come to fruition; and scholars from Japan and the United States who contributed to the publications that emerged from the international conferences in 1967 and 1985. All have laid the foundations for this project.

Lastly, we express our sincere gratitude to our reviewers, Andrew Cobbing and Steven Ericson, who offered invaluable comments, to Shi-Lin Lo and Penny Yeung for their editorial assistance, and to Peter Mickulas for guiding us through the publication process of this book from the very beginning.

Notes on Contributors

BENJAMIN DUKE is professor emeritus at International Christian University in Tokyo, Japan, where he was chairman of the graduate faculty of education. His research focuses on the history of education in Japan. He is the author of several books, including *The History of Modern Japanese Education* (Rutgers University Press) and *Dr. David Murray: Superintendent of Education in the Empire of Japan, 1873–1879* (Rutgers University Press).

JOSEPH M. HENNING, professor of history at Rochester Institute of Technology, is the author of *Outposts of Civilization: Race, Religion, and the Formative Years of American-Japanese Relations* and the editor of *Interpreting the Mikado's Empire: The Writings of William Elliot Griffis*. Recently, he has published articles in the *U.S.-Japan Women's Journal*, the *Asia-Pacific Journal: Japan Focus*, and the *Journal of American-East Asian Relations*. Henning also served as a Fulbright scholar at Tohoku University (Sendai, Japan).

JAMES M. HOMMES grew up in Japan and has been a full-time history teacher at Trinity Christian School in Pittsburgh, Pennsylvania. He has also taught classes for Geneva College and the University of Pittsburgh, where he received his MA in East Asian Studies and his PhD in History. His dissertation, "Verbeck of Japan: Guido F. Verbeck as Pioneer Missionary, *Oyatoi Gaikokujin*, and Foreign Hero," focused on Verbeck's impact and legacy. He has written several articles, including "Guido F. Verbeck—A 'Living Epistle' in Bakumatsu-Meiji Japan" (*Japanese Religions*).

RYUHEI HOSOYA had a diplomatic career, serving toward the end as executive director of the Director General's Office at UNESCO, and Japan's Ambassador to Madagascar. His research interest in global studies and media theory subsequently led him to academia as professor at the School for Global and Community Studies, University of Fukui, Japan. While in Fukui he headed the Kusakabe-Griffis Foundation. He is the author of *A New Image of The World: Theorizing Globalization*; *The Tabi of Happiness: A Tale of Christmas in Fukui*; and *Questions concerning Humanity and AI: Probing the Mystery of Consciousness and the True Nature of Information.*

A. HAMISH ION received his PhD in Japanese Studies from Sheffield University, United Kingdom, and is emeritus professor of history at Royal Military College of Canada at Kingston, Ontario. He has written extensively on the British and Canadian missionary movements in the pre-1945 Japanese Empire as a significant aspect of the history of Japan's international relations. His publications include *The Cross and the Rising Sun: The Canadian Protestant Missionary Movement in the Japanese Empire, 1872–1931* and *American Missionaries, Christian Oyatoi, and Japan 1859–1873*. He is a co-operating research fellow, Institute of Christian Studies, Meiji Gakuin University, Tokyo.

RUI KOHIYAMA is the president of Ferris University in Yokohama, Japan. She is a scholar of American women's history and the U.S.-Japan relationship. Her book, *Teikoku no fukuin—Lucy Peabody to Amerika no kaigai dendō* [The Gospel of Empire: Lucy Peabody and the American Foreign Mission Enterprise], received the Nakahara Nobuyuki Award for a distinguished book in the field of American Studies. She also wrote *Meiji no "Atarashii Onna": Sasaki Toyoju to musume Nobuko* [The New Women in the Meiji Period: Toyoju Sasaki and Her Daughter Nobuko]. She received a Rockefeller fellowship and a Fulbright scholarship and was a visiting scholar at the University of Illinois, Urbana-Champaign, and the University of California, Berkeley.

KOJI NAKAJIMA is a former visiting professor at Meiji Gakuin University, Tokyo, and currently a visiting scholar at Nagasaki University of Foreign Studies and other universities in Japan. His research focuses on the political and diplomatic history of modern Japan and the history of Japanese Christianity. His publications include *Kindai Nihon no gaikō to senkyōshi* [Diplomacy and Missionaries in Modern Japan] and *Tamuson shokanshū* [The letters of Reverend David Thompson]. He studied at the Department of Political Science of the National University of Milan, Italy, and received a PhD from Tohoku University, Japan.

NORIKO OCHIAI is curator at the Tokyo Metropolitan Edo-Tokyo Museum and a member of the research committee at Ōta-ku Katsu Kaishū Memorial Museum, Tokyo. She has curated numerous special exhibitions at the Edo-Tokyo Museum, including "Katsu Kaishū: 100 Years after His Death" and "Kawamura Kiyoo: A Western-Style Painter of the Meiji Restoration." Her publications include "*Katsu Kaishū nikki* no shiryōronteki kōsatsu: Keiō-Boshinki o chūsin ni" [An examination of the historiography of the *Kaishū Diaries*, with a focus on the Keiō and Boshin eras] and annotations and articles in *Kawamura Kiyoo: Sakuhin to sono jinbutsu* [Kawamura Kiyoo: The person and his works].

YUKAKO OTORI is an associate professor in the Faculty of Letters at Keio University in Yokohama, Japan. She earned her Ph.D. from Harvard University and is the author of "America's Foreign-Born 'Citizens': Disability and the Politics of Child Exclusion" (*Journal of American Ethnic History*). Her Japanese-language article on the invention of unaccompanied alien minors as a legal category won the 2024 Saito Makoto Award from the Japanese Association for American Studies.

FERNANDA PERRONE is the curator of the William Elliot Griffis Collection at Special Collections and University Archives, Rutgers University Libraries. Her recent publications include "Invisible Network: Japanese Students at Rutgers during the Early Meiji Period" (*Kindai Nihon kenkyū*) and "The Rutgers Network in Meiji Japan" (*Rikkyo American Studies*). She also coauthored *The Douglass Century: The Transformation of the Women's College at Rutgers* (Rutgers University Press).

SATOSHI SHIOZAKI is professor in the Faculty of Foreign Languages at Takushoku University in Tokyo, Japan, and served as the dean of the Faculty of Foreign Languages from 2019 to 2024. His research focuses on the history of Japanese students studying in the United States during the Bakumatsu and Meiji Restoration eras. His publications include *Amerika chinichiha no kigen—Meiji no ryūgakusei kōryūtan* [Origins of a "Pro-Japanese Group" in the United States: A story of Japanese students studying in the U.S. in the Meiji era] and *Nichiro sensō—mō hitotsu no tatakai* [The Russo-Japanese War: A story of another battle].

FUJI TAKAGI is emeritus professor of Otsuma Women's University Junior College Division and visiting fellow at the Fukuzawa Memorial Center for Modern Japanese Studies, Keio University, Tokyo. His research focuses on the history of Bakumatsu and the Meiji Restoration eras, and he is the author of several books and articles, including *Yokoi Shōnan to Matsudairia Shungaku* [Yokoi Shōnan and Matsudaira Shungaku] and *Bakumatsu ishinki no Beikoku ryūgaku: Yokoi Saheita no kaigun shūgaku* [Study abroad in America in the Late Tokugawa/Meiji Restoration eras: Yokoi Saheita's naval training]. He was a visiting scholar at Rutgers University from April 2002 to March 2003, conducting research in the William E. Griffis Collection.

NAOTO TSUJI is professor of the Department of Psychology and Education, Faculty of Human Sciences, at Wakō University, Japan. His research areas are the history of education in Japan, including the history of students abroad in the modern era, history of Christianity in Japan, especially on the Christian Schools and missionaries' activities, and thought on education. His publications include *Kindai Nihon kaigai ryūgaku no mokuteki hen'yō—Monbushō ryūgakusei no haken jittai ni tsuite* [The changing purpose of studying abroad in modern Japan: The actual situation of students sent abroad by the Ministry of Education] and *Yuasa Hachirō no ryūgaku keiken: Amerika ni okeru Kirisutokyō kokusaishugi tono deai to sono eikyō* [Yuasa Hachirō's study-abroad experience at the University of Illinois: His encounter with Christian Internationalism and its effects].

JOHN E. VAN SANT is associate professor and graduate program director in the Department of History at the University of Alabama-Birmingham. His teaching and research areas are Japan, East Asia, and World history. His major publications include *Pacific Pioneers: Japanese Journeys to America and Hawaii, 1850–1880*; coeditor, *Far East, Down South: Asians in the American South*; and "Mori Arinori: Japan's Diplomat in Washington D.C." (*Journal of American-East Asian Relations*).

HARUKO WAKABAYASHI is associate teaching professor in the Asian Languages and Cultures Department at Rutgers University, New Brunswick. She is the author of *The Seven Tengu Scrolls: Evil and the Rhetoric of Legitimacy in Medieval Japanese Buddhism*, among other publications on premodern Japan, and "Iwakura Mission and the Network of Japanese Students in the United States" (*Journal of American-East Asian Relations*). She also serves as a board member of the Japan History Council of New York and the Digital Museum of the History of Japanese in New York.

Index

Note: Page numbers followed by *f* indicate figures; page numbers followed by *t* indicate tables.

Available titles in the Ceres:
Rutgers Studies in History series

James M. Carter, *Rockin' in the Ivory Tower: Rock Music on Campus in the Sixties*
Nicholas P. Ciotola and Gary D. Saretzky, *Grant Castner: The Lost Archive*
Thomas Gustafson, *American Anti-Pastoral: Brookside, New Jersey and the Garden State of Philip Roth*
Jordan P. Howell, *Garbage in the Garden State*
Aldo A. Lauria Santiago and Ulla D. Berg, eds., *Latinas/os in New Jersey: Histories, Communities, and Cultures*
Maxine N. Lurie, *Taking Sides in Revolutionary New Jersey: Caught in the Crossfire*
Jean R. Soderlund, *Separate Paths: Lenapes and Colonists in West New Jersey*
Camilla Townsend and Nicky Kay Michael, eds., *On the Turtle's Back: Stories the Lenape Told Their Grandchildren*
Haruko Wakabayashi and Fernanda Perrone, eds., *Rutgers Meets Japan: A Trans-Pacific Network of the Late Nineteenth Century*
Hettie V. Williams, *The Georgia of the North: Black Women and the Civil Rights Movement in New Jersey*